KU-018-069

Acknowledgments

Looking at the final draft of this book I can't help but be surprised and proud of its quality. What many people don't realize is that a project of this magnitude can't be brought about by just one person. Actually, this book is the combined effort of many people, some of whom have done as much work as the author himself, and all of whom have brought their own brand of expertise to the task. So I have many people to thank:

Wendy Katz, for your amazing work. Thanks to your great edits, suggestions, and comments, my chapters look like an intelligent person wrote them!

Eric Dolecki, for doing a magnificent job with the figures and screenshots for this book, turning my scribbled instructions into clear illustrations, thanks a lot!

Robert Firebaugh, for the phenomenal graphics you created to go with the games in this book, and for the very informative chapter on the graphical approach in games.

Mike Grundvig, for developing ElectroServer, miscellaneous server-side scripts, and for writing the appendix on multiuser gaming. Not to mention your great suggestions and guidance for good code structure.

Derek Baird, for your contribution of music and sound effects for the games in this book, and content for the Sound chapter.

Branden Hall, for your wddx_mx.as file, which is a great asset to multi-player gaming.

I am grateful for the support and contributions of the entire Peachpit Press crew and production team, especially Wendy Sharp, Marjorie Baer, Lisa Brazieal, David Van Ness, Elissa Rabellino, and Rebecca Plunkett. I also want to acknowledge Kurt Wolken of Wolken Communica for the cover design and Bentley Wolfe of Macromedia for his sharp-eyed technical verifications.

Support and encouragement of friends and family have enabled me to gain the experience and determination needed to write this book. A big all-around thank you to mom, dad, Grambo, my grandparents, and Janie. Of course I also need to acknowledge the smaller creatures (even though they can't read), Free, Chance, Hayes, and Ross—you furry guys provide a frequent and welcome distraction. And finally, to Kelly, my amazing wife and constant source of inspiration: thank you for being my toughest critic and yet my biggest supporter.

ABOUT THE CONTRIBUTORS

I've already said that a book is not the work of a just one person. In the case of this book, four others helped actually get the material on the pages, and I want to recognize them specifically here.

Derek Baird
www.wireheadmedia.com

Derek Baird is a composer, sound designer, and multimedia developer with a degree in music composition from North Carolina School of the Arts. He's pursued additional studies in film music and music technology at LaGrange College. He is also a professional guitarist who has performed with Grammy-winning acts and played on internationally released albums. Derek currently runs Wireheadmedia.com, an Internet multimedia company that specializes in sound design and high quality music composition.

Derek contributed the "Creating Sound Effects" and "Creating Music Loops" sections of Chapter 12, "The Sound of Games."

Eric Dolecki
www.ericd.net

Eric E. Dolecki is currently a Director of Interactive Technological Innovation, working in Boston, MA. He maintains his own site (www.ericd.net) and contributes regularly within the Flash community. Eric recently won Macromedia Site of the Day for his Flashforward 2002 NYC Event Guide application (which runs via Flash on Pocket PCs, utilizes local XML data storage, and even allows for wireless polling). Eric is co-author of several books, including *Macromedia Flash Super Samurai*, *Flash MX Audio Magic*, and *Flash MX Dynamic Applications*. A winner of numerous interactive awards, and with his work appearing in numerous publications, Eric seeks to help drive Flash in new directions.

Eric created all of the technical illustrations for this book.

Robert Firebaugh
www.electrotank.com
www.vectorkid.com

Robert Firebaugh, with over ten years of illustration and game design experience, is creative director and co-founder of Electrotank, Inc. The games that he has designed have won numerous international awards and have been acknowledged by many publications. In addition to his work with Electrotank, he runs a Web site dedicated to photo-realistic vector artwork created in Flash.

Robert wrote Chapter 11, "Graphics in Games."

Michael Grundvig
www.electrotank.com

Michael Grundvig is a co-founder of Electrotank Inc. He has co-authored and contributed to several books on Flash, presented at an international Flash conference, and moderates on several prominent Flash community Web sites. He is currently employed at Hallmark Cards Inc., in the IT Solutions Center Of Excellence, focusing primarily on Java and Application Architecture development.

Michael contributed Appendix B, "Multiuser Servers."

Contents at a Glance

TABLE OF CONTENTS

PART 1: GETTING STARTED

PART 2: EXAMINING THE NUTS AND BOLTS

Chapter 11: Graphics in Games 273

Chapter 12: The Sound of Games 321

PART 3: THE GAMES

Chapter 16: Pinball   437

Chapter 17: Tic-Tac-Toe: Your First Multiplayer Game   459

Chapter 18: 9-Ball   475

APPENDIXES

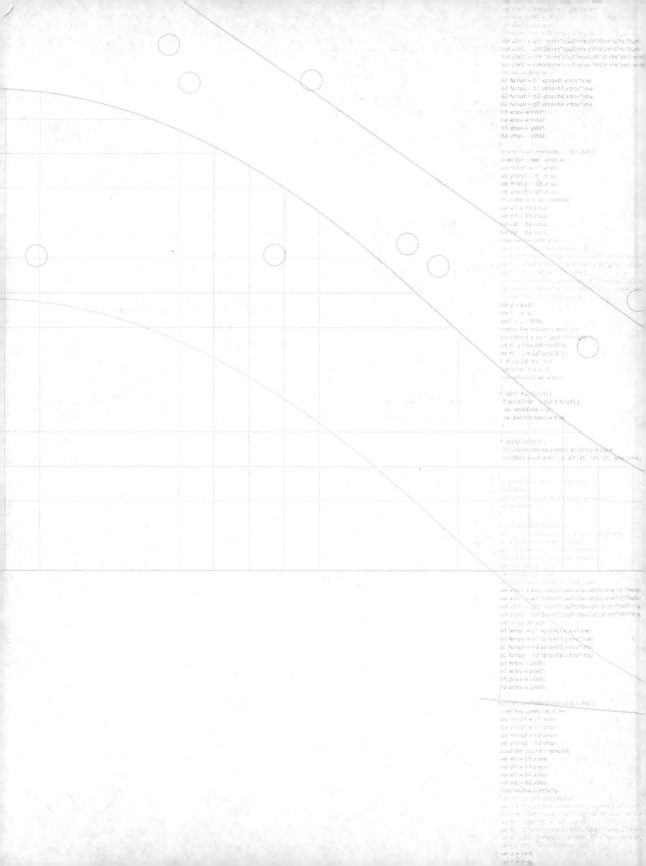

INTRODUCTION

PEOPLE ARE ALWAYS ASKING ME ABOUT GAME DEVELOPMENT—HOW THEY can get into it, what's the best tool for it, etc. I answer questions like this wherever I go. And it got me thinking that if so many people had all these in-depth questions, there must not be a good resource out there....

This book brings you into the world of game development—specifically, game development in Flash, with the powerful ActionScript tool to help you automate, repeat, change, anticipate, and govern the actions of games from a simple word game to a complicated multiplayer game of pool. It is in no way a basic Flash tutorial, and a fair amount of familiarity with Flash is assumed, without which you might have a hard time navigating the terrain.

If you're new to Flash gaming, here you'll acquire the knowledge and techniques to build your own games and a good sense of the overall process and its pitfalls.

If you aren't new to gaming, you'll be able to see what you can do better (or worse) by using Flash, and you'll still come away with the knowledge and techniques necessary to build Flash games.

A book about games wouldn't make any sense without source material—would you rather learn how to create a platform game by hearing about it, or by playing through example files?—and this book is no exception. Each chapter is accompanied by Flash movie files and sometimes other supporting format files to emphasize and describe the point at hand, and allow you to see the function in action.

I welcome your input on this book; you can send me feedback at jobe@electrotank.com. I also encourage you to visit GameBook.net (www.gamebook.net), the Web site for this book, for updates, innovations, and inspiration.

WHY FLASH?

Macromedia Flash MX is many things to many people. In its few years on earth so far, it's been an animation tool, a Web site creation program, an application development program, and now a game development platform. In Part 1 of this book you'll hear more about Flash's strengths and weaknesses in this area, and in the course of this book you'll be able to see some of the many things it can help you achieve.

System Requirements

Windows

200 MHz Intel Pentium processor

Windows 98 SE, Me, NT4, 2000, or XP

64 MB of free available system RAM (128 MB recommended)

85 MB of available disk space

1024 x 768, 16-bit (thousands of colors) color display or better

CD-ROM drive

Macintosh

Mac OS 9.1 and higher, or OS X 10.1 and higher

64 MB of free available system RAM (128 MB recommended)

85 MB of available disk space

1024 x 768, 16-bit (thousands of colors) color display or better

CD-ROM drive

HOW TO USE THIS BOOK

This book introduces you to the world of online gaming, shows where Flash fits into the larger universe of online gaming, shows what it is and isn't good for, and goes into great detail on how to create games using Flash.

Game development isn't all fun and games. It requires a lot of planning, projecting, and imposing logical structures on information. Part 1 introduces you to the general world of gaming, its terminology, and its basic genres. The chapters in Part 2 move through the important concepts that underlie the actual game creation. While not exactly in linear succession, these chapters proceed from the most fundamental of gaming tools (such as trigonometry) to the more complex topics such as collision reactions and the use of artificial intelligence to add complexity and interaction to your games. In the latter portion of Part 2 we introduce chapters on enhancements such as fine-tuning graphics for your games, creating optimal soundtracks, and using high score lists. We end Part 2 with a chapter on understanding (and writing and modifying) an online chat file, without which no online multiplayer game is possible. Wherever you start reading, we'll keep you apprised of what you might need to refer to elsewhere to be sure you are getting the most out of the material.

In Part 3 of the book, armed with the knowledge you've amassed in the several hundred pages leading up to it, you'll work directly with complete games and see exactly what went into them. You'll even see ways you can improve them on your own!

Some of the appendices will guide you through a few complex topics that are intertwined with game design and development but which are, in fact, distinct topics with other applications as well.

We use the following icons to call attention to special sections:

 This indicates a helpful suggestion—advice that will help you get the most out of the subject at hand.

 This means "Pay attention; important stuff here!"

 Indicates that you should open a designated file from the CD to follow along with the text.

 Suggests another idea you might want to try in addition to the main point that's being made.

 This arrow refers you to a related section of the book, where the same topic is discussed in more detail.

This symbol warns you of pitfalls or disadvantages you may encounter in the process being discussed.

The CD-ROM component

The accompanying CD-ROM includes all the example and supporting files necessary to dissect and understand the games discussed in this book. There are also trial versions of ElectroServer and Macromedia Flash MX, as well as 8 additional full and partial games that are not actually dissected in Part 3, but that you can dig into yourself.

PART 1:
GETTING STARTED WITH FLASH GAME DESIGN

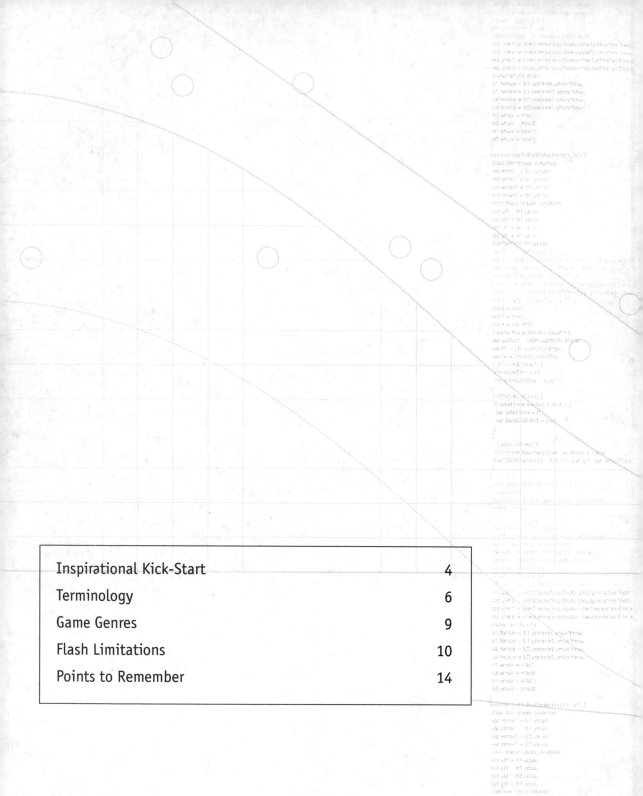

CHAPTER 1

FIRST STEPS

SO YOU WANT TO MAKE FLASH GAMES? WELL, THIS IS A GREAT STARTING place. If you're completely new to game design, the whole idea can seem overwhelming. You may have a great idea for a game, but building an actual game from it is another whole story—setting up for multiple players, 3D motion, and so on. Don't worry—we've all felt that way. And we're here, after all, to demystify the process.

We'll proceed one step at a time. Before you jump in and start making games, I'll introduce you to some general game-world concepts and terminology.

In this chapter, to orient you for your trip into game design, we will discuss the most common Flash game genres, their terminology, and Flash's capabilities as a game-development environment.

INSPIRATIONAL KICK-START

Flash is an incredible authoring tool. With it you can create rich Web pages, advanced applications, and, of course, games. As a Flash game developer, you can create amusements as simple as tic-tac-toe or as complicated as a real-time multiplayer game. Imagine what it would be like to think of an amazing game idea (which you may have already done) and then sit down at your computer and actually build it. With Flash, this

Pictured here are some of the games that you'll know—literally inside and out—when you're done reading this book.

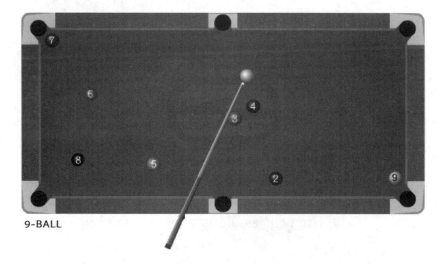

9-BALL

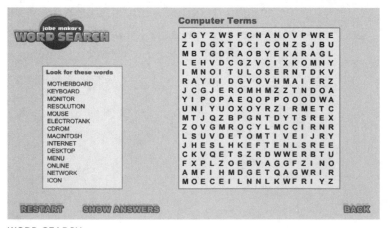

WORD SEARCH

process can be very easy, and you don't need a degree in computer science to do it! You will learn how to tap into the logic you already possess (common sense) and apply that with ActionScript (the programming language used in Flash).

What kinds of games are possible in Flash? Take a look at some of the games that are dissected and explained in detail in the third section of this book. (The source files for these games are provided on the accompanying CD-ROM.) All of the information and techniques needed to make games like these are covered in this book. Soon you will be making your own!

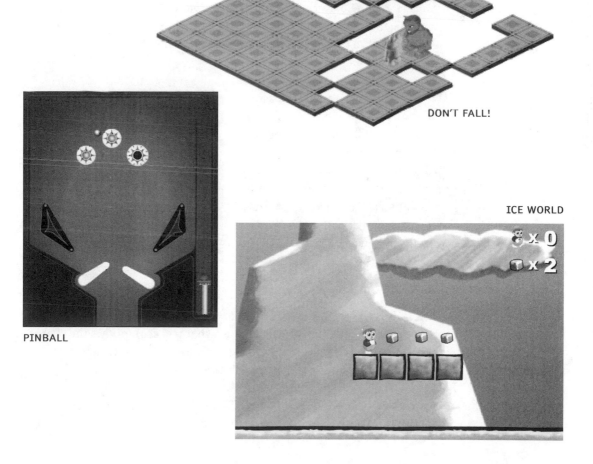

DON'T FALL!

PINBALL

ICE WORLD

TERMINOLOGY

What do you think of when you see the word *isometric? Tile-based? Avatar?* Don't worry, there's no need to run for your dictionary. Entering the world of game development, you'll find that, as with all specialized fields, a lot of descriptive terms are commonly used when talking about games. It is important to understand, or at least have some idea of, what a word means when you run across it in this book. Most of these terms will be described in more detail in later chapters, but here's an overview to get you started.

Game Views

A *game view* is the player's perspective in the game. Is the player seeing everything through a character's eyes, or from above? Each of the possible views has its own name. The game view is sometimes referred to as the *point of view*.

3D—This generic term encompasses almost all possible views of any game that is not two-dimensional. Specific types of popular 3D views have their own terms (listed next). Almost all of the most popular store-bought computer games (such as Unreal Tournament, at right) use a 3D view. While we will not be using a generic 3D engine in this book, we will be using a specific 3D view, *isometric* (see below).

Courtesy of Epic Games, Inc.

Chase—This type of 3D *camera* view is popular in some sports games, like hockey and football. The camera (that is, what you see) follows the character or the action and may even swing around to get the best angle. This game view will not be used at all in this book.

First person—This view is what it would be like to see the environment from the character's point of view. First- person-view games are very popular in shoot-'em-up games like Quake, Half-Life, and Unreal Tournament. We will not use this view in any games in this book.

Isometric—This is one of the most widely used 3D views. You may have seen this view in games such as Diablo (at right) or Electrotank's Mini Golf. It is used frequently because with this view you can get away with graphical tricks that reduce the work of both the programmer and the graphic artist. We will discuss this in detail in Chapter 8, "The Isometric Worldview."

Courtesy of Blizzard Entertainment®

Courtesy of Electrotank, Inc.

Side—This type of view lets you see what is happening from the sidelines. You may have seen this view in games such as Super Mario Brothers or Donkey Kong. Side views are very popular in platform games and are almost always two-dimensional. This view is used in Ice World, shown at left and dissected in Chapter 15.

Third person—This term describes any view that isn't either first person or through another character's eyes. Most of the views listed here, such as isometric, are third-person views.

Top down—The top-down view shows you the game area as seen from above, the way a bird would see it. This view is popular for games like the original Zelda, and for many puzzle games like Minesweeper. At right, of course, is Pac-Man.

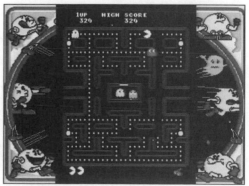

Courtesy of Namco Holding Corp.

General Terms

Here are some commonly used game-development terms whose meanings you should be aware of.

Algorithm—An algorithm is a logical process by which a problem can be solved or a decision made. An algorithm can be represented in a programming language, but it is more abstract than that. For instance, you can create a process to sort a list of names. This process is an algorithm and can be expressed with ActionScript or any other programming language.

Artificial intelligence (AI)—This refers to an algorithm or set of algorithms that can make decisions in a logical way. For example, the AI routine for a bad guy in a game might let him figure out how to find you. Another use of AI is to have a maze or puzzle solved automatically.

Avatar—Sometimes chat rooms are designed to enable people in those rooms to have graphical representations. These are called *avatars,* and the chat is often referred to as an *avatar-chat.*

Collision detection— Also called *hit detection*, collision detection is the act of noting the intersection of two objects. This can be something as simple as determining if the mouse is over a button or as complicated as detecting the overlap of two moving objects.

Collision reaction—This is what happens after a collision has been detected. The term is usually used when talking about physical reactions, such as two billiard balls colliding and moving apart, or a ball bouncing off the ground.

Console—A computer designed for the sole purpose of playing video games. Among the console manufacturers are Nintendo and Sega.

Map—An area that defines the world of the game.

Real-time—Unlike turn-based games, in real-time games you can make a move whenever you like.

Render—To draw an object to the screen. This term is most often used in reference to 3D games: The 3D engine calculates where a projectile should be, and then renders it.

Source code—Also known as *source*, source code is the original work created by a developer. Source code is compiled, or published, into a new file. This compiled file is what users will see, not the source itself. In Flash, the source is a .fla (or FLA) file, and its published version is a .swf (or SWF) file. The .swf file contains only a fraction of the information of in the .fla file. This serves to protect the author's work so that another person cannot take the source. This book's accompanying CD-ROM contains the source for many games.

Turn-based—This refers to a restriction on when you, the game player, can make a move. For instance, chess is a turn-based game; rather than make a move whenever you want, you must wait for your turn. Many multiplayer games are set up this way, as we will see later in the book.

Vector graphics—Notable for their small file sizes and scalability, vector graphics are defined by sets of mathematical points. Flash uses this graphics format to great advantage.

World—The environment of the game.

GAME GENRES

A *game genre* is a type or category of game. As with movies, there are many game genres, and they are often hard to classify. Some games may fit in more than one genre. Here's a list of the most popular genres.

Action—An action game has moving objects and focuses on your timing, reflexes, hand-eye coordination, and quick thinking to achieve a good score. Most games have some action in them but aren't necessarily considered "action games." Space Invaders and Half-Life are good examples of action games.

Adventure—Often confused with RPGs, adventure games let you control a character in an environment while the story is discovered. Unlike what happens in an RPG, your actions do not affect your character's overall abilities. Examples of adventure games range from Super Mario Brothers to the games in the King's Quest series.

Casino—One of the most popular genres to play on the Internet is casino (that is, gambling) games, such as poker and roulette.

Educational—In an educational game, the goal is to educate the player. This game can also be a part of another genre; for instance, you can have an educational puzzle game.

First-person shooter—This style of game lets you see a world through the character's eyes as you run around and try to shoot anything that moves. Typically the action in these games takes precedence over the story.

Puzzle—A puzzle game, also called a *logic game*, challenges your mind more than your reflexes. Many puzzle games are timed or limit the amount of time in which you can make a move. Games like Tetris and Sobokan are good examples of puzzle games. Puzzle games also include some classics like chess and checkers.

Sports—A sports game is an action game with rules that mimic those of a specific sport. For instance, NHL 2002, by Electronic Arts, is an ice hockey sports game.

Role-playing game (RPG)—An RPG is a game in which you, the game player, control a character in its environment. In this environment you encounter other beings and interact with them. Depending on your actions and choices, the character's attributes (such as fighting ability, magical powers, and agility) change, and so may the story. Baldur's Gate is an RPG.

Strategy—This type of game focuses on your resourcefulness and deal-making ability as you try to build and/or run something. In some games, your goal is to successfully build and run a city; in others, what you have to build or run can be anything from an army to a roller coaster.

FLASH LIMITATIONS

Like all software applications, Flash games have limitations. Macromedia has added an amazing number of new features and capabilities to Flash with each release, but it can't do everything (yet). In this section I'll talk about the major advantages and disadvantages of using Flash to develop games, as well as discuss certain types of games that are not easily workable in Flash.

Flash vs. Non-Flash Games

While I'd like to tell you that Flash can outperform all other game-development platforms with its hands tied behind its back, that's just not the case. There are many reasons to choose Flash for game development, and there are many other reasons not to choose Flash. In this section we discuss the major reasons for both.

The pros of using Flash for game development

Not surprisingly, as I've put a lot of time and effort into Flash game development, I'll list the benefits first.

Web deployment—Since Flash files are designed to be viewed in Web pages, Flash is a good choice if you want your game to be available on the Internet.

Small file size—Flash makes use of vector graphics and compressed sound files, so a Flash game's final file size can be exponentially smaller than those of games developed on other platforms.

Plug-in penetration—The plug-in that's required for viewing Flash files in a Web page comes with all major browsers. More than 98 percent of people on the Internet worldwide can view Flash content. The exact penetration for each version of the plug-in is listed on the Macromedia Web site (go to www.macromedia.com/software/player_census).

Server-side integration—Flash games can talk to the server seamlessly. Using Flash's built-in features, you can communicate with server-side applications that make chats, multiplayer games, and high score lists possible.

File sharing between programmer and graphic artists/designers—With Flash, programmers and graphic artists can collaborate using the same files. This is rare in game development.

Ease of use—Perhaps one of the most attractive reasons for choosing Flash is that you can learn the program and start creating games in a very short time. With other languages, it could take years!

The cons of using Flash for game development

As I already mentioned, there are also some strong reasons for not choosing Flash as your development platform. It's important to know them as well, before you get started and encounter unpleasant surprises.

Performance—Macromedia spent thousands of hours making the required Flash plug-in for the Web as small as possible so that the maximum number of people could download it easily. But that required some sacrifices, and the major one was performance. Flash underperforms virtually all other game-development platforms in speed of code execution and graphics rendering. On the other side of the fence, game-development platforms like Macromedia Director and WildTangent perform very well— but have enormous plug-ins. As a result, few people can view such content without being forced to download the plug-in in addition to the game.

Lack of 3D support—Flash doesn't provide native support for real 3D engines or for any sort of texture mapping (the act of applying an image to a 3D polygon).

Lack of operating-system integration—When you run your game as a Projector file, Flash cannot easily talk to the local operating system to do things like browse files on the hard drive. (But this type of integration is possible with the use of third-party software such as Northern Codeworks' SWF Studio, available at http://www.northcode.com.)

Most of the developers who choose Flash as their game-creation tool do so because they want their games to be available to many people easily on the Internet. If the intention is to have the game available offline on CD-ROM, then Flash is still a choice—just not necessarily the best choice.

Infeasible Game Features

It is much easier to talk about things Flash cannot do easily than to discuss everything it *can* do. Here I'll touch on some things that are very difficult to achieve in Flash, or that aren't feasible for another reason. I don't want to say anything is impossible with Flash, because there are so many creative people out there with dozens of tricks to make the seemingly impossible possible.

3D rendering with texture mapping

Many people have created 3D engines with ActionScript. A 3D engine is code that can take 3D coordinates and map them onto your screen. While these engines actually manipulate coordinates in 3D space and then map them correctly back onto a 2D screen, there are three major limitations:

Texture mapping—You cannot map textures (bitmap images) onto an object in Flash. As I have already mentioned, many people make creative attempts to get around program obstacles. This is one of them. Some people have successfully done very simple mapping onto flat surfaces. Nevertheless, this is a limitation. Mapping is not achieved easily and only works in some conditions.

Z-sorting—This refers to the order in which objects appear in front of other objects. In real 3D rendering games, the sorting order is not limited to whole objects, but can actually pierce surfaces of objects (if two things happen to be moving through each other). Flash is limited to sorting at the movie-clip level.

Speed—Three-dimensional engines written in Flash can typically handle only simple shapes, and they retain a frame rate close to the frame rate of your SWF. Complex scenes are often very CPU-intensive, and the frame rate can suffer as a result.

Real-time multiplayer games

Creating this kind of game is certainly possible, but for many reasons it is not easy to accomplish. One of the main factors is the nature of these games. Due to network latency, it would be very difficult, if even possible, to create a real-time multiplayer game like, say, Mortal Kombat. However, some real-time multiplayer games that lack interaction between players, such as a scavenger hunt, might be more feasible. We will discuss this more in Chapter 17, "Tic-Tac-Toe: Your First Multiplayer Game."

Intense real-time calculation

I know this sounds like a vague limitation. But when you're creating a game, it is important (although admittedly difficult) to think ahead and try to guess how intense the calculations are going to be. For instance, a game that has dozens of enemies—who all think for themselves and constantly run around trying to decide what to do next—is an excellent candidate to bog down the computer processor! You'll have to do a lot of testing and experimenting to determine exactly how many of these enemies the computer can handle and still perform well.

This chapter should provide you with a better idea of what types of games exist and which ones are possible in Flash. With this book you'll learn about all the pieces you need to build a game, from graphics to sound, and you'll see how everything was put together in several finished games. By the end of the book you should be well on your way to making your own gaming ideas a reality!

POINTS TO REMEMBER

- Flash is a powerful authoring tool that can help you create games from the simple to the extremely complex.

- Flash's strengths and limitations make it ideal for creating some kinds of games and less than optimal for others.

- ActionScript—the programming language used in Flash—is going to be the main tool through which you bring your games to fruition.

- Familiarizing yourself with game genres and terminology is a good first step toward deciding what sorts, and levels, of games interest you as a developer—and will also show you where you need to brush up!

- For reasons of portability, extensibility, integration, file size, and near-universal access, Flash is a good choice for games you'd like to make available on the Internet.

- Flash is easy enough to learn that you can be up and creating games in a very short time.

- A high cost of the small file sizes and accessibility of Flash games is their slow performance relative to games created on virtually all other game-development platforms.

- Flash is not a true 3D engine.

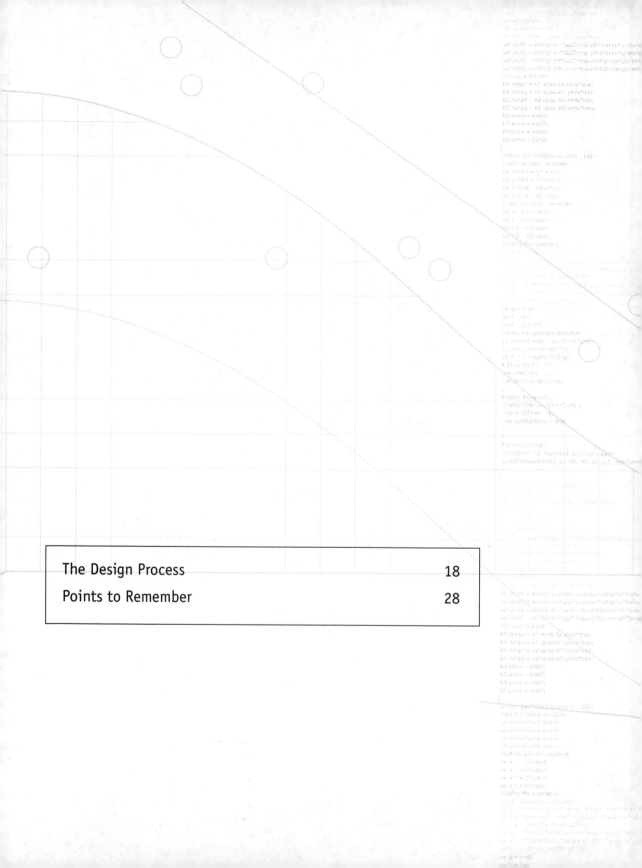

CHAPTER 2

THE PLAN:
FROM IDEA TO DESIGN

IF YOU ARE AT ALL LIKE ME, THEN YOU MAY HAVE AT ONE TIME OPENED up Macromedia Flash and just started making a game. Maybe you had a vague idea of what you wanted the game to do, or maybe you made it up as you went along. This shows that you have a strong creative side and are probably good at developing ideas— but it is not a very good approach to designing a game. With this design-as-you-go approach, you are sure to encounter problems. I have been in this situation before and always ended up wishing that I had planned for certain things in advance.

That's how I came to learn the hard way that you have to have a plan. Yes, tedious as it may seem, that's the big secret. A plan will help you identify possible problems ahead of time and anticipate steps for avoiding or solving them before they ever come up.

In this chapter we'll discuss one game-design process that can help you structure your ideas and build your game intelligently and efficiently. This simple design process will help you plan for every part of the game. (Of course, I don't claim that this is the only way things should be done—there are many equally effective processes out there. This just happens to be the one that works best for me!)

I use the word *design* here to encompass everything about your plan, including your idea, your code, the graphical elements of your game—the whole works.

THE DESIGN PROCESS

All the tasks involved in creating a game can be organized within the steps of the seven-step program I'm about to lay out for you. You'll soon see why: These top-level, quantifiable steps will be relevant to any sort of game. We'll illustrate the steps with the recognizable example of a game of 8-ball (pool). And now, here is the process.

1. *Find an idea.*

2. *Identify your audience, and modify your idea to fit it.*

3. *Decide on the look and feel of your game.*

4. *Identify what you do not know how to accomplish, and find the resources to help you accomplish it.*

5. *Cut back on game features where necessary.*

6. *Build the game.*

7. *Test your game for bugs and usability (quality assurance).*

Looks pretty easy when it's just a list, right? Now let's talk about each of the parts of this process.

Find an Idea

This is probably the most fun step. Before building a game, you've got to come up with a concept. If you're new to game design, it's very important that you start with a simple idea. Starting with a complex game, it's easy to get frustrated or lose hope.

So how do you know if your game idea is complex? That is hard to answer. If your list for step 4 ("Identify what you do not know how to accomplish") is very long, then you may want to start with another game concept. In the beginning you may not know how to accomplish much at all, which is all the more reason to try to find a simple idea.

When you get your idea solidified, map it out step-by-step, as if you were explaining it on an instruction sheet in a commercial game. Make sure that the game has an objective.

The Idea: Multiplayer 8-ball.

The Object: To knock the cue ball into the player's own set of pool balls (solid or striped) to send them into a pocket.

The Rules:

• The game of 8-ball is played on a pool table with six pockets.

• There are 16 balls (numbered 1 through 15, plus the white cue ball). Balls 1 through 8 are each a different solid color. Balls 9 through 15 are each marked with a different-colored stripe.

• This is a two-player, turn-based, multiplayer game.

• Player one uses a cue stick to hit the cue ball into a triangular configuration of the 15 balls.

• Player one chooses either balls 1 through 7 or 9 through 15 for his or her own; the other set goes to the other player. The 8 ball belongs to neither.

If you choose to have an alternate method or rule for dealing with some facet of your game, make sure to spell that out, too. In our example of pool, there's a widespread alternate way to assign stripes or solids—the first player to sink a ball "owns" that style of ball.

- Each player takes turns knocking the cue ball into his or her own pool balls to send them into a pocket. This is typically done one by one.

- When a player has knocked all of his numbered balls into the pockets, he then attempts to knock the 8 ball into a pocket. If the player succeeds, he wins the game.

- If either player knocks the 8 ball into a pocket before he has finished sinking all of his numbered balls, that player loses the game.

- If the cue ball ever goes into a pocket, the player's turn ends.

- If a player hits one of her numbered balls into a pocket without hitting the cue ball into a pocket, then the player's turn continues; otherwise her turn ends.

If 8-ball were your own original game idea, you would probably want to get into much more detail with the game rules. Writing out all the rules of the game gives you something concrete to refer to later, when you're writing the ActionScript. Even if the rules are relatively simple, a quick, linear reference will probably help you organize your ActionScript more easily. And then, of course, with new and more complicated games, it may be difficult to remember every single rule.

RPGs are like the lure of the Sirens

If you are a novice game developer, do not be tempted by the lure of the role-playing game (RPG). A good RPG is a multiplayer game with a complex story; it loads in graphics dynamically, builds screens dynamically, and makes use of pathfinding, enemy AI, and thousands of screens. A game with that kind of complexity—probably the most challenging type of game project you can take on—would typically take you (and the rest of your team) several months to build. Over the last few years I have encountered many people who have brilliant game ideas for massive RPGs. I have seen dozens of people and teams of developers start with an outstanding idea for a Flash RPG, and only one of them that I know of has finished.

Identify Your Audience

Who's going to play? This is one of the most important things to remember when designing a game. If you are designing for a specific purpose, you should use that information to help identify your audience. For many of you, your audience may be just yourself—in which case, lucky you, you can just create any game that strikes your interest! However, if you are designing a game for a client or for another purpose, then there is probably an audience to whom your game should be tailored.

For instance, if you are making a game for a popular sugary breakfast cereal's Web site, then your audience is most likely young kids. A game of 8-ball is unlikely to hold their attention. If your original idea was for a platform game, such as Super Mario Brothers, then you would probably want to modify this idea to use cute characters and to have a simple objective. However, if it turns out that the cereal-eating age group is high school students, then a somewhat more complex theme or objective for the platform game is more likely to keep them interested.

Identifying your audience should not be a difficult task. If you are building a game for a company or client, they should be able to tell you who the intended audience is. If they say, "We would like this game to appeal to all ages," then you are in a tough spot. It's difficult to design a game that will please everyone. In such a case, you are probably better off taking (or looking for a minor new twist on) a tried-and-true idea that has already been shown to appeal to all ages, like checkers. If you are building a game for your own Web site, make sure you have a good idea of the type of visitors you receive or the types of visitors you are trying to attract.

How do you know if your game idea will appeal to a certain audience? This is a difficult question to answer. If your idea is not original or is very similar to some existing games, then it would be in your best interest to use that game as an example. Find out if your target audience is interested in that sort of game. If your idea is unique, you'll have to take the time to develop a simple prototype and try it out on your intended audience to see if the response is what you expected. You can then make modifications and retest. There is no way to accurately predict who will like your game.

Decide on a Look and Feel

You probably know that the term *look and feel* is widely used when describing the creative side of a software application. *Look* refers to the game's overall graphical style, color usage, and animations. *Feel* refers to the usability, as well as the parts of the game that can affect the user on emotional or tactile levels, including story and sounds. But the look itself can contribute to the feel as well.

Deciding on a look and feel for your game should, of course, be related to the intended audience. You don't want to create dark, gothic graphics for a game that will end up on a children's site. Likewise, you probably wouldn't want to have heavy-metal music playing in the background for a game intended to appeal to corporate executives.

If you are unsure of what would be a good look and feel for your game, check out other games targeted to your audience. Note behaviors and operations that you think work particularly well. Studying those games should help you come up with good ideas for your own. (And during the final step, quality assurance, your test audience will make comments on the look and feel of your game, which will help you see how well you hit the mark.)

Identify Your Weaknesses

In this step of the process you look at the rules of your game and list all the gaming concepts, knowledge, and other skills you need in order to complete the game. This is not the place for bluffing! Identify the areas that you know you cannot complete by yourself. With this information you can then find a way to fulfill each of those requirements where your existing knowledge isn't enough. Some of the steps you'll need to take will require research; others may require asking for help.

Let's list the major things needed to create the game of 8-ball.

In **Table 2.1**, the first column contains a list of the requirements for creating a game of multiplayer 8-ball. The second column is where you indicate if you can meet that need. In this table, I have filled in the second column as a typical beginning game designer might. **Table 2.2** contains information on how to satisfy each of these requirements.

TABLE 2.1 ## Knowledge and Assets Checklist

Need	Do I meet this need?
A copy of Macromedia Flash	Yes
Proficiency with ActionScript	Yes
The ability to calculate collision detection	No
The ability to code realistic billiard-ball collision reactions	No
Knowledge of multiuser gaming	No
Access to sounds needed for an 8-ball game, or the ability to create such sounds	Yes
The ability to create all graphical elements needed for the game	No

TABLE 2.2 ## Filling the Knowledge Gaps

Need	Solution/Action
A copy of Macromedia Flash	Install the 30-day trial version of Flash on the CD-ROM that comes with this book, or purchase Flash from www.macromedia.com.
Proficiency with ActionScript	Learn ActionScript. You can buy a Flash book or read the tutorials provided with Flash installation.
The ability to calculate collision detection	Read Chapter 5, "Collision Detection."
The ability to code realistic hilliard-ball collision reactors	Read Chapter 6, "Collision Reactions."
Knowledge of multiuser gaming	Read Appendix B, "Multiuser Servers," and all of the specific game chapters in Part 3 that deal with multiplayer games.
Access to sounds that are needed for an 8-ball game, or the ability to create the sounds	Find someone who can create the sounds for you, or download software such as Syntrillium Software's Cool Edit (www.cooledit.com) to help you record and edit your own sounds. You can find sound effects on the Web at such sites as www.ultimatesoundarchive.com.
The ability to create all graphical elements needed for the game	If you are not skilled at creating graphics, it would be a good idea to find someone to help you. You can find people skilled in graphic design on the boards at Flash Kit (www.flashkit.com).

In this step the main objective is for you to identify all elements of the game that you do not the resources to develop. One of the best things you can do to learn more and get help (other than read this book, of course) is to ask other people for advice on the boards at popular Flash resource sites (see Appendix E).

As a new game programmer, you will probably encounter many things you do not know how to do. It's a good idea, as part of your quest to learn these things, to create several tests of each concept to make sure that you know how they all work. For instance, with the 8-ball game, you might want to start testing collision detection with just two circles. Then, when you understand this level of collision detection, try it with multiple circles. Only when you are confident that you fully understand how to use collision detection with the needed number of spheres should you move on to testing collision reactions.

It's important to understand how these things really work. If you are just copying and pasting code from examples in this book or from another resource without fully understanding the concept, you're going to have trouble later when you're trying to work through any bugs that crop up.

Anything on your list that you will not be able to satisfy, or that you can't find someone to help you with, is subject to being cut from your game. The next step addresses this.

Cut Back

In this step you decide if any features or game rules need to be changed or cut. If you could not meet any one of the requirements in the previous step, then you should consider cutting that feature. Following are some grounds for cutting a feature from your game:

- Not being able to meet all the needs specified in the previous step.

- Realizing (from your basic testing) that this feature would cause the game's performance to suffer.

- A tight deadline will prevent you from finishing the game on time if you try to include all the features.

For example, one of the intended features of this 8-ball game is that it be multiplayer. In order to create a multiplayer game, you need to set up a piece of software on a server that functions as the link between all the players. This is called a *multiuser server* or a *socket server* (as will be explained in Appendix B, "Multiuser Servers"). If you are running your own dedicated server, you can, of course, install whatever you want. But chances are that a regular, commercial ISP will not allow you to install software. So then you are left with the choice either to pay for a more expensive hosting plan (a dedicated server) or to axe this feature of the game. If you cut the multiplayer feature but don't want your audience to have to play alone, then you may have to consider changing another feature. For instance, you might want to develop the game so that two people who are on the same computer can play against each other. Or if you have the time and inclination, you can program an AI computer opponent.

Don't have a dedicated server? Don't worry!

In Appendix B, "Multiuser Servers," we briefly explore options for people who do not have a server with which to host the multiuser software. For example, you may be able to host a simple game from your own home computer!

Another potential problem is the Flash Player application's performance. While Flash is great for developing games easily, one of its greatest limitations is the (lack of) speed at which it executes actions. In other words, it is easy to give Flash too much to do on each frame, hence increasing the amount of time that Flash needs to stay on each frame, which makes the overall frame rate lower. In our 8-ball example, if you don't employ some very tricky or extremely optimized ActionScript, chances are good that the Flash Player will play at a reduced frame rate when calculating collision detection between the 16 balls and each of the six pockets (I know this from personal experience). That is a total of 216 collision-detection checks per frame. While the speed at which these actions execute is dependent on the Flash Player, it is equally dependent on the processor of the computer running the game. If you are using a Pentium 4 computer with a 2-GHz processor and the game barely runs smoothly for you, then you can bet it will not run very smoothly for people with average computers.

So what is the solution? You can spend days or weeks finding ways to optimize the ActionScript for speed—or you can step back, take a deep breath, and cut down on the number of balls your game uses. The pool game called 9-ball uses only ten balls. That means it would only have to calculate 105 collision-detection checks per frame. While calculating this many checks may still be slow on some machines, it is less than half the number of checks for your original game of 8-ball. With some simple ActionScript optimizations you can cut this down even further. For instance, you might only check for pocket collisions when a ball collides with the wall. That would bring the detection down to 45 checks per frame.

The more time and effort you have invested in developing an idea, the more important that idea becomes to you, and so cutting back its features can be difficult. One of the best things about using a design process like this to plan ahead is that you can cut back on some features before spending the time to develop them and getting emotionally attached.

Build the Game

Now that you have an excellent idea of what your final game is supposed to do, you can focus on actually creating it. Strategies for how to build specific games are covered in Part 3 of this book. As there are many types of games, so there are many ways to approach putting them together. In the most generic sense, you will always:

1. *Create or collect all of the game assets, such as graphics and sounds.*

2. *Build all of the major ActionScript functions needed for things like collision detection, collision reaction, and detection of the game rules (like whose turn it is).*

3. *Hook up everything together to form a game ready for testing.*

Quality Assurance

In the quality-assurance (QA) stage of development, you take your working game and test it heavily. (Depending on who you work with and how irreverent you are, you may hear, or make up, more descriptive terms for putting your game through its paces, such as "beating the heck out of it" or "making it cry.") You are looking for bugs and usability issues. Typically during this stage you put your game in front of several people who have not been involved with its development, give them some general direction and requests, and let them have at it. It's amazing the number of bugs that someone unfamiliar with your game can find in a very short time. After your testers are finished playing your game, ask them questions like:

- Were the instructions clear?
- Did the game make sense?
- Was the game fun?
- Did it hold your attention?
- What changes or enhancements would you suggest?
- Did you notice any bugs? If so, what were they?
- Did anything happen that kept you from finishing the game? If so, what was it?
- How were the sounds and music (if any)?

If you don't receive comments on your sound, take that as a good sign! When integrated properly into the game, sound is something most people will not consciously notice. However, if it's done poorly, people will be aware of it and comment on it.

You can treat this process as formally or informally as you like; for example, you can give your testers an official questionnaire. This has the dual benefit of providing them with an easy way to quantify their information, and you with answers to consistent and specific questions. I've created a checklist (QA_checklist.pdf) that you'll find on the CD, in the Chapter02 folder.

Armed with answers to these questions, you can make well-informed decisions about how your game can be improved. You may find that you run through this QA process multiple times until you get the response you want from your testing group.

The primary reason for planning ahead and using a process is to make your work go more smoothly. Without proper planning, you may find yourself having to abandon some of your work (due to unforeseen problems) after investing time in it. Following the process discussed in this chapter, you will be able to take your game idea, break it into logical pieces, identify the possible problems before they occur and solve them, and then assemble the game.

POINTS TO REMEMBER

- If you just sit down and start coding a game, designing as you go, you are sure to encounter problems. You need to have a plan!

- Your plan should include quantifiable, repeatable steps that could apply to any game—not specific steps that pertain only to the one you're working on.

- Make your first game plan a simple one. You have a much better chance of completing it, you'll learn the ropes, and you won't get too frustrated. Avoid role-playing games your first few times out.

- Make sure to find out if the kind of people you *think* will like your game actually will.

- Be realistic about what you know how to accomplish and what you don't up front. Find resources to help you in your deficient areas.

- The more work you put into specific game features up front, the more likely you are to be frustrated if you find you have to jettison them along the way.

- Know where you're going to be able to run a game before you include processor-intensive features that your setup may not be able to support.

- Test, test, test! And don't take the critiques personally. They are all going to help make your game better.

PART 2:
EXAMINING THE NUTS AND BOLTS

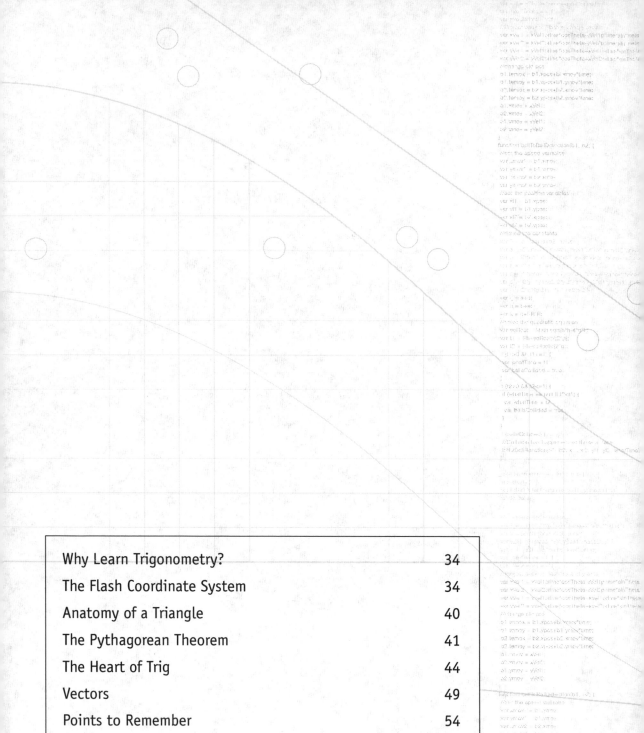

CHAPTER 3

TRIGONOMETRY 101

For those of you who don't remember this from school, trigonometry is the branch of mathematics that deals with the relationships between the sides and angles of triangles. In this chapter we're going to cover the basics of trigonometry, which should handle almost every need you'll have. However, if you would like to learn more about this subject, see Appendix E for book suggestions.

WHY LEARN TRIGONOMETRY?

When programming a game, you'll often need to do things like find the distance between two points or make an object move. (In fact, *very* often!) Here are a few examples:

- Rotating a spaceship or other vehicle

- Properly handling the trajectory of projectiles shot from a rotated weapon

- Calculating a new trajectory after a collision between two objects such as billiard balls or heads

- Determining if a collision between two objects is happening

- Finding the angle of trajectory (given the speed of an object in the x direction and y direction)

You are going to use trigonometry within ActionScripts to complete these (and many other similar) tasks. While you may not need to do so in every single game, the requirement for trigonometry can pop up in any genre. In this chapter I'll discuss the major uses of trigonometry in Flash and how to apply them.

THE FLASH COORDINATE SYSTEM

The coordinate system used in Flash is called the *Cartesian coordinate system*. (This may sound vaguely familiar to you from math classes, and if so, the information here should be a simple review.) Understanding how the Cartesian coordinate system is set up and how to use it is very important for a game developer. Why, exactly? Because in your games you will be creating and moving objects around the screen, using ActionScript to tell an object which coordinates to move to. And to write ActionScript that does this, you've got to have an understanding of the coordinate system. In this section I'll (re)acquaint you with this all-important grid. We'll also discuss how the Flash coordinate system measures angles.

Cartesian Coordinates

The Cartesian coordinate system is grid-based (made up of many equal-sized imaginary squares), with a horizontal axis called the *x-axis* and a vertical axis called the *y-axis*.

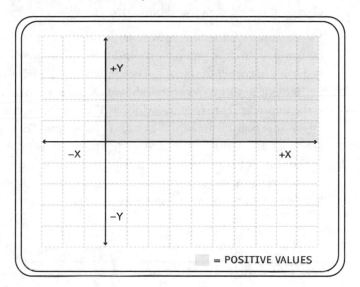

The way we look at this grid in Flash positions the negative side of the *y*-axis higher than the positive side.

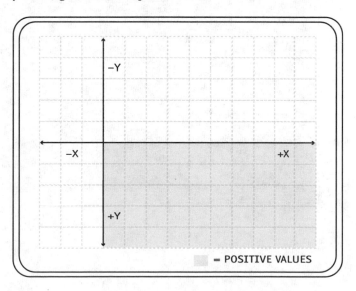

Actually, there is no difference at all between the two coordinate systems you've just seen. What *is* different is how we are observing them. If you stand on your head to view an object, then only the way you are observing it has changed, not the object itself. That is what's happening here. In math class you observed the coordinate system one way; in Flash, you will observe it upside-down and backwards.

Most computer programs use the same orientation of the coordinate system as Flash does. If you have a window open on your computer, you can grab on to a corner to resize it. The contents of the window may resize, or perhaps the amount of content shown changes. But what does *not* change is the upper-left corner of the window. That corner is designated as the *origin*—the point where the *x*-axis and *y*-axis cross. Then all of the contents are contained within the +*x* and +*y* quadrant. If the origin were always, say, in the center of the screen, then as you resized the window the coordinates of every element in your window (images or movie clips) would change. A top-left-origin coordinate system is a great convenience.

ORIGIN —

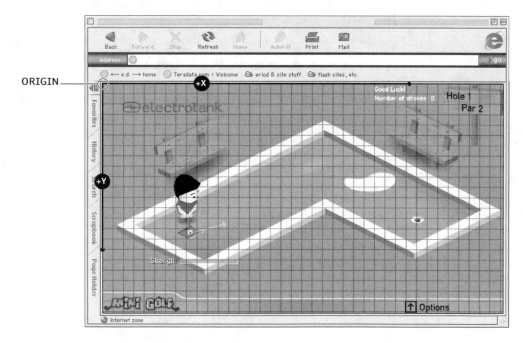

A Cartesian coordinate is a set of two numbers that describe the position of a point. In math, the two numbers in the coordinate are usually grouped in parentheses, like this: (4, 8). The 4 represents a distance along the *x*-axis, and the 8 represents a distance along the *y*-axis.

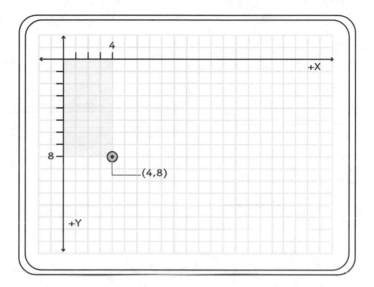

Movie-Clip Coordinate Systems

As you've learned in this section, the origin of Flash's coordinate system is the upper-left corner of the Flash movie. Every individual movie clip also has its own coordinate system (called a *relative coordinate system*). The origin for movie clips is called, in Flash terminology, a *registration point*. At this point in the book, it is just important to know that movie clips contain their own coordinate systems. In later chapters we will make use of these movie-clip coordinate systems.

Angles

Angles are used in two ways in Flash: They are used to rotate objects, and they are used with the trigonometric functions that will be discussed later in this chapter. But before you can use angles to do anything, you need to understand how they are measured in the Flash coordinate system.

Positive angles are measured from the *x*-axis, rotated in a clockwise direction, and with a fixed point at the origin.

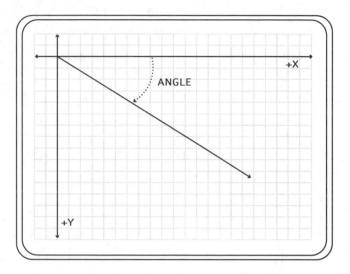

Angles are measured in *degrees* and can have a value of 0° to 360°. The entire coordinate system is made up of four quadrants separated by the axes. Each quadrant covers 90°.

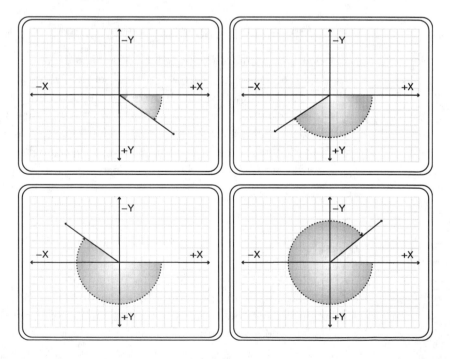

More on Angles

Angle measurements are *repeating*—that is, you can never have an angle greater than 360°. So let's say you have an object that may have actually rotated 720°—two full rotations. That is possible, of course, but its orientation is still 360°. (You determine the end orientation of an angle by subtracting 360 from the total number until it becomes less than or equal to 360.)

Negative angles are also possible. But that description doesn't mean the angle itself is negative, or inverted (that wouldn't make any sense). The negative number merely tells you that the angle was measured counterclockwise from the *x*-axis.

In addition to degrees, there is another common way to measure angles: in *radians*. One full rotation is 2π radians. With degrees, we know that one rotation is 360°, so each quarter rotation is 90°. Likewise, with radians, since a full rotation is 2π, each quarter rotation is $\pi/2$. For those who may not remember, π (*pi*, or Math.PI in ActionScript) is a special number in math, representing the ratio of the circumference of a circle to its diameter. Rounded to two places, it is 3.14. Pi can be accessed in Flash by using Math.PI. For example, here is a way to create a variable that has the value of pi:

```
myPI = Math.PI;
```

So why do you need to know about radians? Because everything you do in Flash with angles—with one exception—needs to be expressed in radians.

Unlike degrees, which are arbitrary, radians form a "natural" unit measurement. The word *natural* here means a unit that (through the use of mathematical theory) has been found convenient and logical. That's probably why mathematicians, physicists, and programmers like radians better, and use them almost exclusively.

The only time you can use degrees directly in Flash is when you're changing the _rotation property of a movie clip. However, human nature and habit being what they are, it is very common (and perfectly all right) to work with degrees in ActionScript, and then convert from degrees to radians just before you need to use the angle. Converting degrees to radians or radians to degrees is easy.

Degrees to Radians	Radians to Degrees
△	△
angle = measured in degrees	angle = measured in radians
newAngle = angle $* \left(\dfrac{\text{Math.PI}}{180} \right)$	newAngle = angle $* \left(\dfrac{180}{\text{Math.PI}} \right)$

ANATOMY OF A TRIANGLE

Trigonometry, as I've said, is based on the relationships of the sides of a triangle to its angles. Before we get into the heart of trigonometry, let's refresh your memory on the basics of triangles and how they fit into the coordinate system.

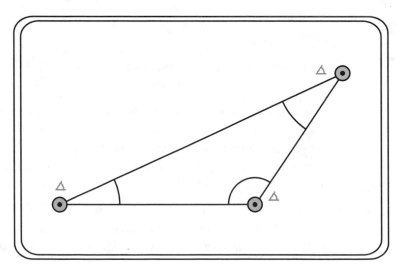

Triangles are made up of three line segments joined in three places. Each of these joints is called a *vertex*. In a triangle there are three angles, one at each vertex. These three angles must always total 180°. As you may remember from geometry class, there are descriptive names associated with certain types of triangles, such as *isosceles, acute, oblique,* and *right*. We are only going to concern ourselves with one of these, the right triangle.

A right triangle is any triangle that has a 90° angle. The right triangle is a very useful tool for us, because two of its sides fit nicely into the Cartesian system we use in Flash—one of them is along the *x*-axis and another is along the *y*-axis. (No other type of triangle can claim this!) Because of this, it is generally easier to gain information about the length of its sides. The side of the triangle that is opposite the 90° angle has a special name, the *hypotenuse*.

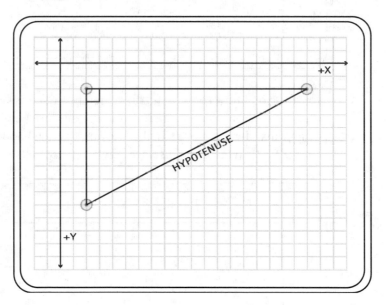

THE PYTHAGOREAN THEOREM

Named after the Greek philosopher Pythagoras, the Pythagorean theorem states a simple but powerful relationship between the sides of a right triangle: *The square of the hypotenuse of a right triangle is equal to the sum of the squares of the remaining two sides.*

So, given a triangle with sides of length *a, b,* and *c* (where *c* is the hypotenuse), the theorem reads $a^2 + b^2 = c^2$.

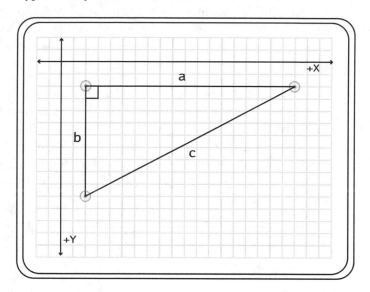

Now that you know (or have finally remembered!) this simple relationship, let's see how you can use it to find the distance between two points. Imagine that there is a black ball at the point ($x1, y1$) and a gray ball at the point ($x2, y2$). What is the distance between these balls?

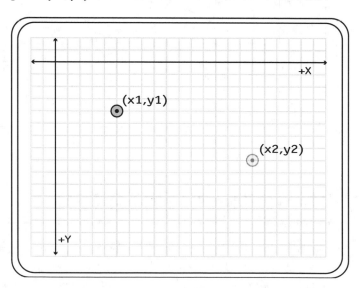

You've probably guessed by now where I'm going with this—you can use the Pythagorean theorem to find the distance between these two points. The only conceptual hurdle in this problem is to realize that there exists an imaginary right triangle whose hypotenuse is the line joining the two balls. But if you've been following along this far, that's probably not too big a hurdle.

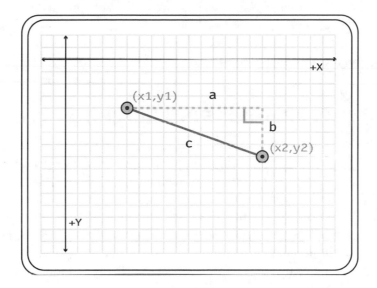

The theorem states that $c^2 = a^2 + b^2$. You'll recall that c is the hypotenuse—that is, the value we're looking for to determine the distance between the two points. So we solve this equation for c to get $c = \sqrt{a^2 + b^2}$. If we write a and b in terms of the information we already know, then we can find the value of c. The side labeled a in the figure above is along the x axis, and its length is $x2-x1$. Likewise, the length of side b is $y2-y1$. Knowing this information, we can write a generic equation that will always give you the distance between any two points:

$$c = \text{distance} = \sqrt{(x2-x1)^2 + (y2-y1)^2}$$

With this mathematical equation you can find the distance between any two points in Flash! This useful little "recipe" will come in handy frequently. For instance, you will use it when detecting most types of collisions in your games. In ActionScript this distance formula would look like this:

```
Distance=Math.sqrt((x2-x1)*(x2-x1) + (y2-y1)*(y2-y1));
```

THE HEART OF TRIG

Is it all coming back to you yet? I hope so, because here's where we get to the real inner workings of trigonometry—where you can see how it's all going to come together. In this section we will cover the *sine, cosine,* and *tangent* functions, as well as *projection*. With knowledge of these operations under your belt, you will be able to understand the programming concepts you'll encounter in the following chapters (especially Chapter 6, "Collision Reactions").

Sine, Cosine, and Tangent

Sine, cosine, and tangent are known as *trigonometric functions*. Although what they mean is very simple, many people have trouble understanding them. This conceptual problem happens because it is easy to think that the trigonometric functions give a result by some esoteric or even mystical process. The truth is that these functions just use various ratios of the triangle side lengths to give results. Look at the triangle in the figure below. Notice that we are using *x* and *y* instead of *a* and *b* to label the side lengths. These are more common side names in programming. Notice the angle in the figure labeled *angle*.

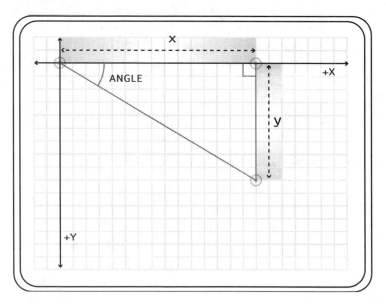

All three of the trigonometric functions are defined by taking ratios of the sides of this triangle. A trigonometric function takes an angle (in Flash it must be measured in radians) and returns a value. For instance, the sine of 45° is .707. To test this for yourself in Flash, here is an ActionScript code snippet you can write:

```
angle=45;
radians=angle*Math.PI/180;
trace(Math.sin(radians));
```

Line 1 in the above code block sets the angle in degrees. Line 2 converts degrees to radians, and line 3 computes the sine and displays the result in the output window.

Table 3.1 lists these "big three" functions, their definitions, which methods of the Math object they correspond to in Flash, and a valid value range that can be returned from these functions.

TABLE 3.1 **Trigonometric Functions in Flash**

Trigonometric Function	Mathematical Definition	Method in Flash (Angle is in radians)	Minimum Result	Maximum Result
Sine	sin(angle)=y/c	Math.sin(angle)	-1	1
Cosine	cos(angle)=x/c	Math.cos(angle)	-1	1
Tangent	tan(angle)=y/x	Math.tan(angle)	Negative infinity	Positive infinity

It wouldn't hurt to commit some simple results of the trigonometric functions to memory. This can help tremendously when debugging a script. Table 3.2 shows some simple values for you to remember, should you choose to.

TABLE 3.2 **Trigonometric Equivalents**

Typical Angles in Degrees	Sine	Cosine	Tangent
0	0	1	0
45	0.707	0.707	1
90	1	0	Infinity
180	0	-1	0

Since you are able to calculate the sine, cosine, and tangent of an angle, it makes sense that there would also be some way to go from a number back to an angle. There is a set of functions for this, called the *inverse trigonometric functions*: *inverse sine*, *inverse cosine*, and *inverse tangent*. Some people use the term *arc* (as in *arcsine*) rather than *inverse*. **Table 3.3** contains a list of the available inverse trigonometric functions.

TABLE 3.3 ## Inverse Trigonometric Functions

Inverse Trigonometric Function	Method in Flash	Description
Inverse sine	`Math.asin(number)`	Returns the angle whose sine is equal to the number
Inverse cosine	`Math.acos(number)`	Returns the angle whose cosine is equal to the number
Inverse tangent	`Math.atan(number)`	Returns the angle whose tangent is equal to the number
Inverse tangent2	`Math.atan2(y, x)`	Returns the angle whose tangent is equal to y/x

The inverse trigonometric functions take a number as an input parameter and return an angle in radians. To convince yourself of how this works, try this example in Flash:

```
input=.707;
trace(Math.asin(input)*180/Math.PI);
```

Line 1 sets a variable called input with a value of .707. Line 2 uses the inverse sine method of the Math object (which returns an angle in radians) and then converts it to degrees. The result is traced in the Output window and should be very close to 45°. (It is not exactly 45° because the true sine of 45° has many more decimal places than .707.)

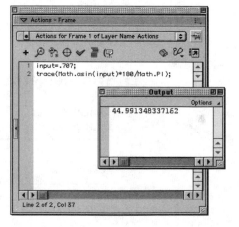

Projection

The word *projection* in the context of trigonometry means to project a quantity (such as distance or velocity) onto the *x*-axis and *y*-axis. Using what you'll learn in this section will help you when building games. For an example of what projection can help you accomplish, open the file shooter.fla in the Chapter03 folder on the CD-ROM. In this file, a ship rotates to point toward your mouse. When you click anywhere on the movie's stage, a projectile fires from the nose of the ship. The velocity of the projectile points toward your mouse (or at least to the place where your mouse was when you clicked it). In order for this movement to be programmed in Flash, the velocity must be projected along the *x*-axis and *y*-axis.

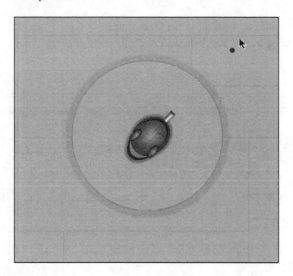

The programmatic movement seen in this example file is not covered until Chapter 4, "Basic Physics."

Imagine a diagonal line of length *len* drawn in Flash at angle *ang*. A piece of this line extends along the *x*-axis and another piece of it along the *y*-axis. If the angle were 0°, then the line would extend only along the *x*-axis. If the angle were 90° then the line would extend only along the *y*-axis. With any other angle, the line extends both in the *x* direction and the *y* direction. (Put another way, no two coordinates on the line have the same *x* or *y* value: A horizontal line always has the same *y* value for all of its coordinates. A vertical line always has the same *x* value for all of its coordinates. A diagonal line never repeats an *x* or *y* coordinate.) If you were to draw a right triangle from this diagonal line, then the two other sides of that triangle would be the pieces that extend along the *x*-axis and *y*-axis.

Finding the length of either (or both) of those pieces by using the values *ang* and *len* is called *projection*. These values are found by using the trigonometric functions that we've already discussed above.

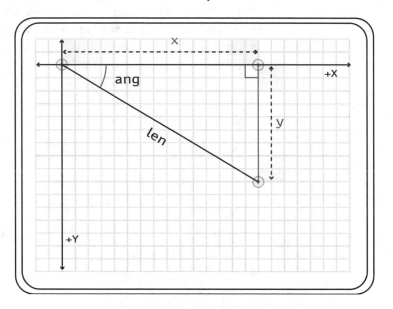

As seen in the previous section:

cos(angle)=*x*/*c*

In the example here, angle is replaced with ang and c with len. So:

cos(ang)=*x*/len

To find the projection of len along the *x*-axis, we solve for *x*:

x=len*cos(ang)

Or with ActionScript:

x=len*Math.cos(ang);

To find the *y* projection we use

sin(ang)=*y*/len

And solve for *y*:

y=len*sin(ang)

Which converts to this in ActionScript:

y=len*Math.sin(ang);

Think of projection like a shadow cast from an object onto the floor or a wall. For the example given in this section, first we would imagine a light source coming from below to cast a shadow on the x-axis. The length of the shadow cast from the line on the x-axis is the same as the projection we would calculate using trigonometry. Next we would imagine a light source coming from far off to the right shining left. The shadow cast on the y-axis is equal to that which we would calculate using trigonometry.

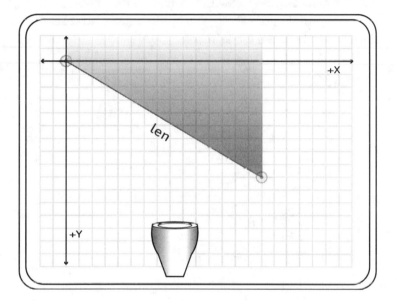

VECTORS

A vector is a mathematical object that has both magnitude (a numeric value) and direction. Velocity is a vector because it has both magnitude and direction. For example, a velocity of 33 kilometers per hour (kph) southeast has a magnitude of 33 and a direction of southeast. Speed is not a vector, and direction is not a vector, but speed and direction together, modifying the same object, form a vector. Here are some other examples of vectors.

- **Displacement** can be a vector when describing the location of one point with respect to another point (whether those points represent two objects, or one object in motion). For example, "New York is 500 miles north of Virginia" or "The ball rolled 3 feet to the left."

- **Force** can be a vector, since the gravitational force that pulls you toward the earth has both a magnitude and a direction.

- **Rotation,** when modified with a direction, is a vector. Think of a clock hand, rotated 90° clockwise.

Graphically, a vector is usually represented as an arrow (in other words, if you had to show a vector in a graph, that's how you'd sketch it). Mathematically, a vector's direction is often specified by an angle. To use the example given above, "33 kph southeast" may alternatively be described as "33 kph at 45 degrees."

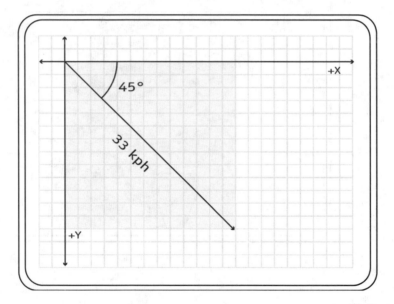

In Flash, vectors are used primarily with physics applications. This is because multiple vectors (of the same type) can be added together to form one resultant vector. Adding vectors is called *superposition*. For example, if a balloon is floating in the air, several forces are being exerted on it simultaneously, such as force from the wind, gravitational force, and a buoyant force (that is, the force that is pushing the balloon up). With three forces acting on one balloon, it might be difficult to figure out what the balloon will do. Will it rise or will it fall? Using superposition, you can add the vectors together to find the resultant vector (and determine the balloon's next move). One vector is much easier to work with than three.

Vectors can be divided up into *x* and *y* components (in this context, the word *components* refers to pieces). This is called *resolving* a vector. You already did this same thing in the "Projection" section. Resolving a vector is nothing more than projecting it along the coordinate system axes. To add vectors together, you must

1. **Resolve all of the vectors into their *x* and *y* components. Those pieces are the remaining two sides of the right triangle.**

2. **Add all of the *x* components together.**

3. **Add all of the *y* components together.**

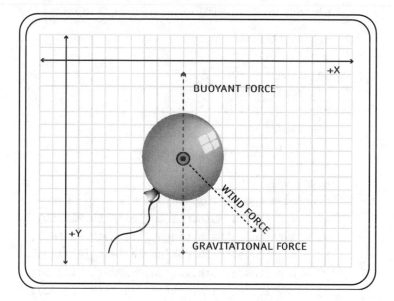

Let's use the example we started above. Imagine a balloon in the air with three forces acting on it:

- A gravitational force with a magnitude of 10 at an angle of 90°

- A buoyant force with a magnitude of 8 at an angle of 270°

- A wind force with a magnitude of 5 at an angle of 45°

To add the vectors together (looking back at our three-step checklist above), the first step is to resolve each vector into its components.

What follows is the balloon example we've been using, written in ActionScript. Nothing will appear on the screen; this is purely a mathematical exercise to introduce you to the role of ActionScript in this process. Later in the book, after I've introduced you to the other concepts necessary to understanding them, we'll delve into many more practical examples.

In the code below, I've used the number *1* appended to the ends of all variables associated with the gravitational force; *2* for the buoyant force; and *3* for the wind force. (The lines that begin with // are comment lines, for information only.) To try this ActionScript yourself, open the Actions panel in Flash and enter the ActionScript below, or open the force_example.fla file from the Chapter03 folder on the CD-ROM.

```
//Gravitational force
angle1 = 90;
magnitude1 = 10;
//Buoyant force
angle2 = 270;
magnitude2 = 8;
//Wind force
angle3 = 45;
magnitude3 = 5;
//Resolve the vectors into their components
x1 = magnitude1*Math.cos(angle1*Math.PI/180);
y1 = magnitude1*Math.sin(angle1*Math.PI/180);
x2 = magnitude2*Math.cos(angle2*Math.PI/180);
y2 = magnitude2*Math.sin(angle2*Math.PI/180);
x3 = magnitude3*Math.cos(angle3*Math.PI/180);
y3 = magnitude3*Math.sin(angle3*Math.PI/180);
```

Notice the `Math.PI/180` factor in each line of ActionScript above. Remember that the trigonometric functions only work with angles measured in radians. This factor converts the angle from degrees to radians.

The next two steps are to add all of the *x* components and *y* components together to form two resultant vectors:

```
//Add the x pieces
x = x1 + x2 + x3;
//Add the y pieces
y = y1 + y2 + y3;
```

You now have the sum of all the forces in the x direction and the sum of all the forces in the y direction. Add these two lines of ActionScript to display the result in the output window:

```
trace("Force in the x direction="+x);
trace("Force in the y direction="+y);
```

When you test the SWF file, you will see that the force in the y direction is 1.53. Since this number is greater than 0, the balloon will be forced to move toward the ground. The force in the x direction is 3.53. This means that the balloon will be forced to move to the right.

Still lost? There is hope!

To many people, math is a dry subject. It is understandable if, when you've finished this chapter, you feel like you have grasped only part of it. Everything will make more sense when you start to see the practical uses of the math you've seen here, and the concepts will become more solidified in your mind. It may make sense for you to reread parts of this chapter when you start to use trigonometry in your games.

With the concepts and techniques in this chapter, you are adding practical skills to your programming toolkit. You will find that these things will come in handy frequently. We will revisit vectors and explore more examples of vector uses in the chapters on physics and collision reactions.

POINTS TO REMEMBER

- Trigonometry is the branch of mathematics that deals with the relationships between the sides and angles of triangles.

- In game programming, trigonometry is used to help determine trajectories, distances, and deflection after a collision, to name a few of its functions.

- Flash uses the grid-based Cartesian coordinate system to identify, place, and move objects.

- By default, the registration point of a Flash movie clip is the upper-left corner of stage or movie.

- The unit of measurement that Flash uses for angles is not degrees, but radians. You can easily convert from one unit of measurement to the other to work in a more familiar manner. The one exception to having to use radians in Flash is when you're changing the `_rotation` property of a movie clip.

- You can use the Pythagorean theorem to find the distance between two points.

- The trigonometric functions sine, cosine, and tangent use various ratios of the triangle side lengths to determine values and, used inversely, to deliver results as angles.

- A vector is a mathematical object that has both magnitude (a numeric value) and direction. For example, velocity is a vector because it has both magnitude and direction. Vectors can be divided up into x and y components to project it along the axes of the coordinate system. This is called *resolving* a vector.

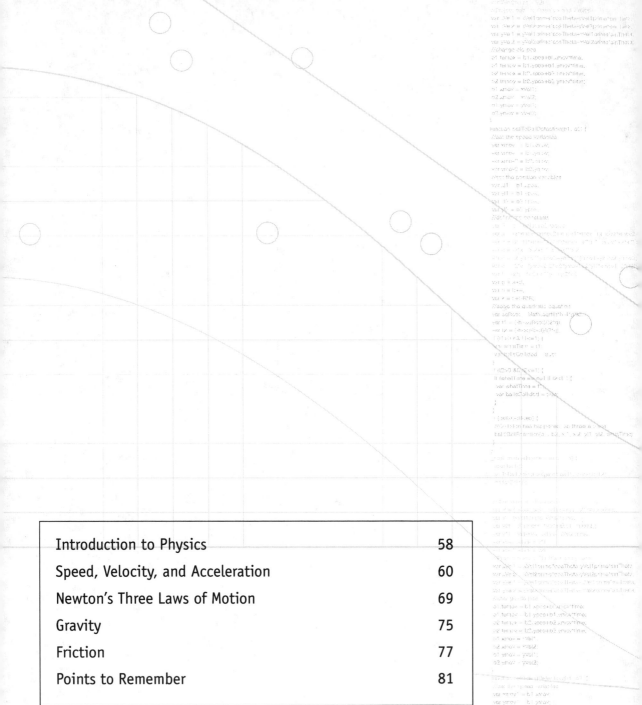

CHAPTER 4

BASIC PHYSICS

HAVE YOU EVER WONDERED HOW TO ADD GRAVITY TO A GAME, OR even just how to make a movie clip move around the screen? Understanding basic physical laws and how to apply them is the key to creating dynamic realism in games. In this chapter you will learn some of the most fundamental physics concepts, such as gravity and friction, and how to apply them in Macromedia Flash using ActionScript.

INTRODUCTION TO PHYSICS

For some reason, there is a common fear or unapproachable feeling about physics. When I was in college and the fact that I was a physics major came up in conversation, I would inevitably get one of three odd looks. The first one implied that I had just sprouted another head; the second made the person appear to have gotten a sour taste in his or her mouth; the third (my favorite) was a consoling glance that said "I am so sorry." I'm not sure what caused this general feeling about physics (hey, my physics-lab buddies and I were really fun guys!), but rest assured that in this chapter we will allay those fears.

Physics is the branch of science that studies and describes the behavior of objects in nature on the most fundamental level. Here are some interactions and occurrences that physics is used to describe:

- An object falling to the ground (remember Isaac Newton and his apple)

- The effect of an electron on a proton

- Electrical current

- The motion of the planets

There are many fields of specialized study within physics, and some areas of physics are very difficult to learn. Fortunately for us, Flash requires us to learn only the basics of the easiest-to-learn type: classical mechanics. Classical mechanics is the one area of physics where it is easy to conceptualize what is happening, or what should happen, in a simple situation. For instance, if you have a ball on a hill, you don't need an advanced degree in science to tell you that the ball will roll down the hill—common sense should suffice. (In other areas of physics, it can be difficult to predict what will happen just by looking at the situation.)

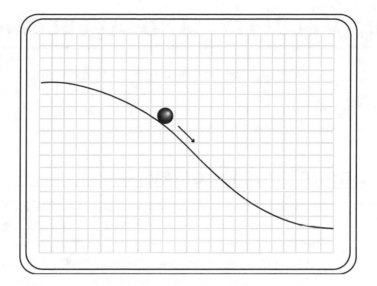

In this chapter we will discuss the basic concepts of speed, velocity, and acceleration; Newton's laws; gravitation; and friction. We will not cover conservation of energy or of momentum until Chapter 6, "Collision Reactions." This is because we are trying to introduce topics and concepts in a somewhat linear fashion. Conservation of energy and momentum are concepts that apply after there has been a collision of objects, and we have not yet reached that point.

One more thing to note before we jump in: I'm going to be making some distinctions between *real* physics and *good-enough* physics. Real physics concerns the motion and reactions that can be described by real physics equations. Everything initially discussed in this chapter is real physics. However, there are situations where the real physics equations may be a little too intense for Flash to calculate frequently. As it turns out, they can be replaced with vastly simplified equations that give good-enough results. We will discuss two of the most commonly used "good-enough" physics substitutes in the "Gravity" and "Friction" sections.

SPEED, VELOCITY, AND ACCELERATION

You may not know the difference between speed and velocity, but you probably have at least some idea of what speed, velocity, and acceleration are. In this section I'll introduce you to these concepts and point out the differences between them.

Speed and Velocity

Velocity is a vector; speed is the magnitude of that vector. In Chapter 3, "Trigonometry 101," we introduced vectors. If you're a linear reader, this concept may be fresh in your mind. But to review, vectors are mathematical objects that contain two pieces of information: a magnitude (also called a *scalar* value) and a direction. For instance, the velocity 30 kilometers per hour (kph) southeast is a vector. Its magnitude (the speed) is 30, and its direction is southeast.

Let's dig a little deeper into the definitions of these important concepts.

Speed: The ratio of distance covered and the time taken to cover this distance. Mathematically, this is written as the equation *speed = distance/time*. For example, if a car travels 30 kilometers in 2 hours, then its speed is 30 kilometers/2 hours = 15 kilometers/hour.

As defined above, speed is distance divided by time. When you read "15 kilometers/hour," you say "15 kilometers per hour."

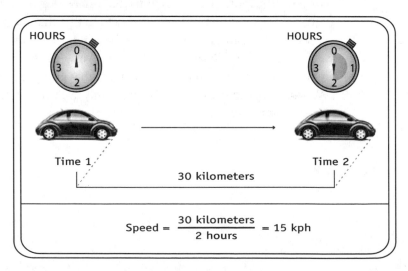

Velocity: A vector formed by combining speed with a direction.

Now let's see how to use this concept of speed and velocity to find the distance traveled in a certain amount of time. If we know the speed at which a car is traveling, how do we know how far it has traveled in, say, 3 hours? Above we said:

```
speed = distance/time
```

By doing simple algebra (multiplying both sides by time), we arrive at this equation:

```
distance = speed*time
```

With this equation we can find how far a car (or any object) traveled if we know its speed and the amount of time it moved. In the same way, if we know how far the car traveled and the speed of the car, then we can calculate the travel time using the final permutation of this equation:

```
time = distance/speed
```

Applying Speed with ActionScript

So now you understand what speed and velocity are. And you understand how if you know any two of the following variables—speed, distance, or time—you can find the remaining value. In many games you are going to need to program movie clips (such as a ball, a car, or a rocket ship) to move. So how do you apply speed to a movie clip? You are about to find out.

We have been talking and thinking about speed as being measured in units of distance/time (distance divided by time). But Flash is not a time-based environment—it is a frame-based environment. To Flash users, one frame can be assumed to be one unit of time. So (as you'll see on your screen if all goes well), it is OK for us to replace every occurrence of a time variable in equations with a variable for frames. For instance, if *distance = speed*time*, then the new form is *distance = speed*frames*. (In other words, speed is no longer 10 miles/hour, it's 10 units/frame.) In Flash we are going to change the definition of speed by replacing time with frames. So let's look at our definition of speed again, this time with our new twist:

Speed: The ratio of distance covered and the frames taken to cover this distance. Mathematically, this is written as the equation *speed = distance/frames*. For example, if a movie clip travels 30 units in two frames, then its speed is 30 units/2 frames = 15 units/frame.

As seen in the new definition above, the unit of distance measurement is not meters but simply units, or pixels. (I prefer to use the word *unit*, because if the Flash movie is scaled to a larger or smaller size, then *unit* is the only word that still applies.) At a scaled size, the pixel dimensions do not change, but the unit dimensions do.

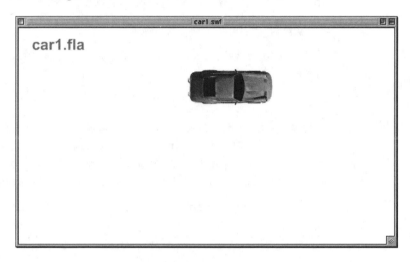

car1.fla

To see a simple application of speed, open up car1.fla in the Chapter04 directory on the CD-ROM. Notice that the frame rate has been set to 24 frames per second (fps) to ensure smooth playback. On the stage you'll see one movie clip with an instance name of Car. There are a few lines of ActionScript on frame 1 of the Actions layer. They read as follows:

```
1   xmov = 3;
2   _root.onEnterFrame = function () {
3       car._x += xmov;
4   }
```

TIP

Throughout the rest of the book, you'll see that I call all *x* direction speeds xmov and all *y* direction speeds ymov, or some variation of these basic names (such as tempxmov or xmov1).

Line 1 sets a variable for the speed called xmov with a value of 3. Line 2 sets up an onEnterFrame clip event. All of the actions listed within an onEnterFrame event are called one time in every frame. Line 3 is where we apply the speed to the object. It takes the current position of the car—car._x—and adds the value of the speed to it. Remember that the speed is units per frame. So a speed of 3 means that we will move the car along the *x*-axis three units in every frame.

Using the Best Frame Rate, 24 fps

When making objects move around the screen using ActionScript, it is appropriate to consider your frame rate. The default frame rate in Flash is 12 fps. The human eye is fooled into thinking that objects are continuously moving when they are really just appearing at different places. Raising the frame rate increases the number of appearances per second, which makes for smoother-looking motion and fools the eye even more. The Flash Player will try hard to meet the frame rate at which you set your SWF. But if the processor speed combined with the intensity of your ActionScript is too much for the computer running the SWF, then the frame rate will drop while the movie is playing. So the key is to find a good frame rate that most computers will run at the intended speed. Through much experimentation and real-world experience, I have found that 24 fps works well for all games.

When you generate a SWF file to test this movie, you will see the car move relatively smoothly. Actually, the car is being redrawn in a new position 24 times per second. In that way, it's a lot like one of those flip books you might have had when you were a kid, with static images giving the illusion of movement. The frame rate is the vehicle (no pun intended) through which we trick the human eye into seeing what appears to be a continuously moving car, although the movement is actually happening in discrete chunks.

ActionScript Review: +=

The operator +=, used in the ActionScript example above, is a shortcut that means "take what is on the left, add what is on the right, and then replace the original value with the result." For instance:

```
x = 2;
x += 3;
```

Now x has a value of 5. Alternatively, the second line could have been written as:

```
x = x + 3;
```

Now, what if you want to make this car move in two directions at once? To see how you'd add a second dimension, *y* speed, open car2.fla. This FLA file has the same setup as the previous example. The only difference you'll find is in the ActionScript used. Open the Actions panel to view the ActionScript on frame 1.

```
1   xmov = 3;
2   ymov = 2;
3   _root.onEnterFrame = function () {
4       car._x += xmov;
5       car._y += ymov;
6   }
```

This differs from the ActionScript in the previous example by two lines of code. Line 2 defines a variable to represent the speed in the *y* direction, and line 5 controls the placement of the car by adding the value of ymov to the car's *y* position. This is done 24 times a second, so the result is what looks like a moving car.

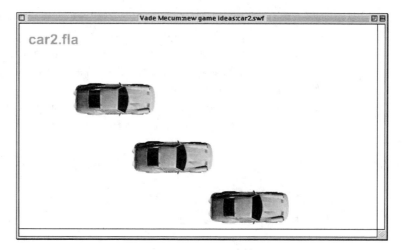

You may have already picked up on a visual problem in this case, though. The car is moving diagonally, but it's facing horizontally. To see how to get the car to face the correct direction, open car3.fla. You will notice that, once more, there are two new lines of code just before the onEnterFrame event. They are:

```
1   angle = Math.atan2(ymov, xmov)*180/Math.PI;
2   car._rotation = angle;
```

In short, line 1 calculates the angle that the car should be rotated, and line 2 rotates the car. Summoning up what we discussed in the last chapter (remember trigonometry?), we know that we can use two sides of a right triangle to find the angle made by the trajectory of the car with the *x*-axis. The key is to think about the horizontal and vertical sides of the triangle as the ones made by `xmov` and `ymov`, respectively.

Before rotation, the car forms an angle of 0° with the *x*-axis. Here we are figuring out how much the car needs to be rotated in order to point in the direction in which it is moving. Knowing the *x* side length (the x speed) and the *y* side length (the y speed), we can find the angle using the inverse tangent `Math.atan2()`. This returns an angle in radians—the angle we'll use to rotate the movie clip. To do this, we must use the `_rotation` property. Simple enough—but just to keep things interesting, the `_rotation` property only accepts angles in degrees! That's what's going on in line 1; we're converting the angle into degrees by multiplying by the conversion factor `180/Math.PI`.

For a slightly more advanced practical example, see shooter.fla in the Chapter04 directory on the CD.

Acceleration

Put quite simply, acceleration occurs whenever the velocity changes. Remember that velocity contains a speed and a direction. So if the speed *or* the direction of something changes, then it has accelerated.

Acceleration, like velocity, is a vector. It has a magnitude and a direction. More specifically, it's a vector with a magnitude that is the ratio of the difference in velocity and the difference in time over which this difference occurred, and the direction in which the acceleration occurred. (If this sounds like three items instead of two, read it again with careful obedience to the commas.)

```
Acceleration = (velocity2 - velocity1)/(time2 - time1)
```

where *velocity2* is the velocity at *time2*, and *velocity1* is the velocity at *time1*. The units of acceleration are measured as distance/time^2.

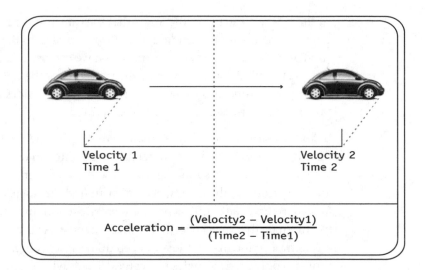

If you know the acceleration of an object and its current velocity, then you can find or project the velocity of that object at any time in the future. Here is the equation to do this:

```
velocity_future = velocity_now + acceleration*time
```

The quantity *time* in the equation above is how far into the future you are looking. Remember that both velocity and acceleration are vectors. In Flash, we have to resolve vectors into their *x* and *y* components before we can use them. After we find the *xspeed, yspeed, xacceleration,* and *yacceleration* (using the techniques used in Chapter 3 and reintroduced earlier in this section), then we can write the following equations:

```
xspeed_future = xspeed_now + xacceleration*time
```

and

```
yspeed_future=yspeed_now + yacceleration*time
```

If you know the current position and velocity of an object, then you can find its position at any time in the future. You can find the future position by using the following equations:

```
xposition_future = xposition_now + xspeed_now*time
→ + 1/2*(xacceleration)*time²
```

and

```
yposition_future = yposition_now + yspeed_now*time
→ + 1/2*(yacceleration)*time²
```

Applying Acceleration with ActionScript

The equations you've just been looking at may seem messy, but their application in Flash is quite easy. Remember that we can replace time with frames in all of our equations. We will always be calculating new values for just one frame later. This is good news for us, because it means we can replace the time with 1 everywhere. Using that trick, we can rewrite the four *x*- and *y*-component equations shown in the previous section.

For future speed:

```
xspeed_future = xspeed_now + xacceleration
```

and

```
yspeed_future = yspeed_now + yacceleration
```

For future position:

```
xposition_future = xposition_now + xspeed_now
⇸ + 1/2*(xacceleration)
```
and

```
yposition_future = yposition_now + yspeed_now
⇸ + 1/2*(yacceleration)
```

As you probably know, you cannot add two quantities that have different units. For instance, 10 meters plus 12 ounces makes … no sense. In the above equations, we appear to be adding quantities that have different units (with apologies to any physicists, mathematicians, and engineers out there). What happened is that we dropped the `frame` variable from the equations. We're getting away with this because we assumed the value of the `frame` variable is always going to be 1 (see the previous paragraph), and since multiplying anything by 1 gives a result of the original value (3*1 = 3), then we just left out that factor. So if you were concerned about the units, you can now rest assured that things are consistent.

After all this theoretical discussion of acceleration, now it's time to apply it within the context of your games. To use acceleration in programming, here is what you should do.

1. *Create a variable to contain the acceleration. For instance,* accel = 2.

2. *Create initial velocity variables for the x and y directions. For instance:*

```
xmov = 0;
ymov = 0;
```

3. *When acceleration should be applied (such as when a certain key is being pressed), modify the speed. For instance:*

```
xmov += accel;
ymov += accel;
```

4. *For every frame, set the new position of the object.*

```
car._x += xmov;
car._y += ymov;
```

Open up car4.fla from the Chapter04 directory on the CD. This is the next evolutionary step in the chain of car examples given earlier in this chapter. Here, the car starts with a slow initial speed and accelerates when the up arrow key is pressed. (As you might expect, when the down arrow key is pressed, the car decelerates.) Here is the ActionScript that accomplishes this.

```
1   xmov = 1;
2   ymov = 1;
3   accel = 2;
4   angle = Math.atan2(ymov, xmov)*180/Math.PI;
5   car._rotation = angle;
6   _root.onEnterFrame =function () {
7       if(Key.isDown(Key.UP)) {
8           xmov += accel;
9           ymov += accel;
10      } else if (Key.isDown(Key.DOWN)) {
11          xmov -= accel;
12          ymov -= accel;
13      }
14      car._x += xmov;
15      car._y += ymov;
16  }
```

Line 3 initializes the acceleration variable. Other than that, the only differences between this example and car3.fla are in lines 7–13. That's where the ActionScript dictates that if the up arrow key is pressed, then the xmov and ymov variables are increased by the value of the accel variable. If the down arrow key is pressed, then the xmov and ymov variables are decreased by the value of the accel variable.

ActionScript Review: Key Object

The Key object lets you get information about the status of the keyboard. You can use this object to find out which key was pressed last, if a certain key is down now, if a certain key is toggled, and more.

The method of the Key object we will use most often for the games in this book is Key.isDown(keyCode), to detect which keys have been pressed by a user. (As you can imagine, capturing "key events" is going to be an important function in controlling games.) For example, Key.isDown(Key.LEFT) returns a Boolean value of true if the left arrow key is pressed, or a value of false if it is not. In a game where I want a character to move to the left every time the user presses the left arrow button, I check for this situation in every frame.

Every key on the keyboard has a corresponding numeric key code that must be passed in to get a result. But some of the keys have premade "verbose" shortcuts that you can also pass in. The ones we will use most frequently are Key.UP, Key.DOWN, Key.LEFT, Key.RIGHT, Key.SPACE, and Key.SHIFT. (For others, see the ActionScript dictionary under the Help menu in Flash, or go to the ActionScript editor and choose Objects > Movie > Key > Constants to see a list.)

NEWTON'S THREE LAWS OF MOTION

A chapter about physics would not be complete without discussing Newton's three laws of motion. Sir Isaac Newton (1642–1727), a brilliant physicist and the father of calculus, developed—among other things—three fundamental laws of motion. Only one of these laws, the second, will we actually apply with ActionScript. However, we will discuss all three, since knowledge of these "basic" facts may help you to solve some programming problems within your games.

Newton's First Law

At some point in your life you may have heard something to the effect of "A body at rest tends to stay at rest; a body in motion tends to stay in motion." While this is not a complete description, it is the gist of Newton's first law of motion. This law is best understood with the concept of *systems*. A system is anything—any entity, whether it contains one or one million objects—you wish to study. For instance, a baseball can be a system. A roomful of people can be a system (as can the room itself, if that's what you're studying). Even an entire planet can be a system.

The astronaut cannot move himself.

For the sake of understanding this law, let's take the example of an astronaut floating with no velocity in space. No matter what he does, he cannot move his *center of gravity* (a point by which you can measure his real position). He can kick his legs and wave his arms, but his velocity is not going to change. There is only one possible way he could move from that position: He'd need to have another system apply a force to him, such as gravity from a planet. With this example in mind, let's take a look at Newton's first law:

The velocity of a system will not change unless it experiences a net external force.

This law does not directly apply to your Flash applications. However, understanding it can help you if you find yourself struggling through conceptual programming problems.

Newton's Second Law

Newton's first law assumes a system that will not change its velocity unless a net external force is applied to it. That begs the question, what is the acceleration (change in velocity) when a net external force *is* applied? Newton's second law answers this question.

The acceleration of an object is inversely proportional to its mass and proportional to the net external force applied.

Mathematically, this is written as follows:

```
net force = mass*acceleration
```

or, as most people see it:

```
F = m*a
```

where *F* is force, *m* is mass, and *a* is acceleration. The net force is the sum of all the force vectors.

This is an immensely handy equation. You can sum all of the forces acting on an object (the net force), and from that sum determine its acceleration. What does this mean for you, and when would you need it? It means that once you have found the acceleration of an object, you can use it with the equations of motion to move the object around on the screen.

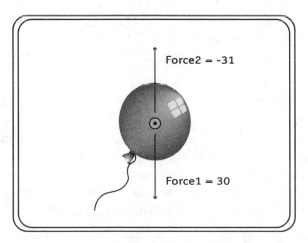

Force2 = -31

Force1 = 30

As an example, open balloon.fla from the Chapter04 directory on the CD. In this file, I've applied two forces to a balloon of mass = 1—a gravitational force of 30 (its weight) and a buoyant force of -31 (the force that makes a helium balloon rise).

Notice that the buoyant force is a negative number. This indicates that the force is pointing in the –*y* direction (also known as "up"). The goal is to code this in such a way that the balloon moves in the correct direction. To move the balloon, we need to know its acceleration. To find its acceleration, we use Newton's second law. The simple process to find the acceleration is as follows:

1. *Sum all of the forces. In this case,* netForce = force1 + force2.

2. *Solve for the acceleration. Since* netForce = mass*accel, *then* accel = netForce/mass.

Let's take a look at the ActionScript for the single movie clip in this file (in the Actions layer):

```
1   ymov = 0;
2   mass = 1;
3   //weight, the downward force
4   force1 = 30;
5   //bouyancy, the upward force
6   force2 = -31;
7   //total force
8   netForce = force1 + force2;
9   //Newton's second law applied to find the acceleration
10  yaccel = netForce/mass;
11  _root.onEnterFrame = function () {
12      ymov += yaccel;
13      balloon._y += ymov;
14  }
```

The first thing you'll notice is that all of the forces are only in the *y* direction. That means we only need to deal with movement in the *y* direction. In line 2, we set the mass variable. (I've just chosen an arbitrary value of 1.) We then define force1 and force2. In line 8, the forces are summed to arrive at a net force. We then apply Newton's second law in line 10. After the acceleration is found in line 10, everything else deals with moving the object and should be familiar from the section on "Speed, Velocity, and Acceleration."

When you test the movie, you can see that since the buoyant force has a greater magnitude than the gravitational force, the balloon floats up.

I hope you can see the power of this law. With it, you can create a complicated situation with an unlimited number of forces acting on an unlimited number of objects. By summing the forces on an object, you can find its acceleration. Even if the situation is complex, the math remains simple—you just keep applying it to the parts until you have solved for all the variables.

Terminal Velocity

In the rising-balloon example we've been using in this section, the balloon accelerates with no upper limit. This means that the balloon will rise faster and faster and will never reach a maximum velocity (except the speed of light, of course). In real life, we know that we are surrounded by atmosphere, and that the atmosphere must have a certain amount of effect on us. As a balloon rises, you know it's going to encounter wind resistance (from the atmosphere), which will oppose (or at least affect) its acceleration. There is no simple equation to calculate the force of the wind resistance, because it depends on several factors. What you should know, though, is that eventually the wind-resistance force will be so large that the sum of all of the forces on the balloon will be 0, and then there will be no further acceleration. At that point, the balloon is traveling upward at its maximum velocity. This is called *terminal velocity*. In games, such as some of those presented later in this book, it's good to set an upper limit to the speed of your objects so they can't move so fast that you can't keep up with them. This upper limit is, of course, subjective, and depends on the game, the object, and the frame rate.

We will add our own terminal velocities just by using simple `if` statements to see if the velocity is too great.

How fast is too fast? An object is moving too fast when game play is no longer fun!

Newton's Third Law

You probably don't think much about physics as you move through your everyday activities, but those activities actually afford lots of examples and physics "problems" to ponder. Here's one: When you sit on a chair, you don't fall through it. Why not? Because while you are exerting a force on the chair (your weight), the chair is also exerting a force on you—in the opposite direction. You may have heard of Newton's third law:

For every action there is an equal and opposite reaction.

Action: You applying a force to a chair by sitting on it. Reaction: The chair exerts a force on you equal to that of your weight but opposite in direction.

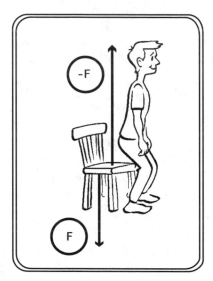

If you're like most people, you are probably now trying to imagine a situation where this does not hold up. But you can't! Try this one on for size: If a baseball is falling toward the earth, the earth is applying a force (its weight) to the baseball. What you may not have realized is that the baseball is applying an equal but opposite force on the earth. The result is that the ball and the earth accelerate toward each other (yes, the ball does move the earth—however small the amount may be).

As with Newton's first law, there is no immediate application of this law in your physics programming. However, if you are trying to code something physical in Flash that is not discussed in this book, then figuring out the logic involved may be easier with the help of this law.

GRAVITY

Gravitational forces are what keep you on the ground and the planets in motion around the sun. Newton postulated that every particle in the universe exerts a force on every other particle in the universe. Massive bodies, such as planets, have an enormous number of particles. All of these particles attract each other, and attract you as well. In this section we're going to discuss two ways to treat gravity mathematically: the "right" way and the "good-enough" way.

Real Gravity

The gravitational force experienced by two objects is calculated by using the equation

```
F = G*(mass1*mass2)/distance²
```

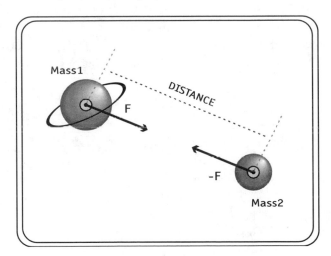

F is the force felt by either object (remember Newton's third law—equal but opposite). The value G is called the *constant of universal gravitation*. For mathematical reasons having to do with absorbing constants into other constants (I hope you'll take my word for this one), we can just assume that G has a value of 1. The value *distance* is the distance between the centers of the two objects.

You are most likely never going to need to apply this realistic treatment of gravity in your games. However, if you would like to see a working example of this in Flash, then take a look at a Flash 5 experiment of mine in realGravity.fla in the Chapter04 directory. There is ActionScript in realGravity.fla that handles collision detection, collision reaction, and gravity.

Good-Enough Gravity

As I mentioned at the beginning of this chapter, there are times when a simplified formula will do for our gaming purposes as well as the complicated, "real" physics I paid a lot of money to learn about in graduate school. We have come to one of those times now. If you've been worrying about having to work through the gravity equations, you'll be happy to hear that there is an easy way to add a gravity effect to your games: Simply come up with a value for gravity—let's say 2—and then add that value to your y velocity in every frame.

To see an example of this, open bounce.fla in the Chapter04 directory on the CD. In this file, I've affected a ball's velocity using faked gravity. I've also added a simple collision-detection trick so that the ball doesn't fall through the floor (we'll talk more about that in Chapters 5 and 6, "Collision Detection" and "Collision Reactions"). Here is the ActionScript:

```
1   ymov = 0;
2   //set gravity
3   gravity = 2;
4   _root.onEnterFrame = function () {
5       ymov += gravity;
6       ball._y += ymov;
7       if (ball._y > 400) {
8           ball._y = 400;
9           ymov *= -1;
10      }
11  }
```

As you can see in line 5, gravity is used to change the ball's velocity in the same way that acceleration was used to do this. In lines 7 through 10 we check to see if the ball is below 400 (which is the height of the floor on the stage in this movie). If so, then it is off the screen, and we set its position back to 400 and reverse the y velocity, ymov. The final result is a ball that bounces in place.

FRICTION

Why do objects slow down? Because they are losing energy. Objects that slow down from the interaction with another object lose energy via heat. This heat is caused by the interaction between the two materials. If this sounds familiar, it probably should—what we're talking about here is simply friction.

Put in more technical terms, a frictional force is one that opposes the direction of motion and is caused by the interaction between two materials. Kinetic energy—the energy associated with the momentum of an object—is lost as heat from the friction, and the object slows down. For instance, when you are driving your car and slam on the brakes (OK, even if you don't actually slam them), the car will use friction to its advantage and slide to a stop. If you then feel the temperature of the tires, you will notice that they are hot. (We'll discuss kinetic energy further in Chapter 6, "Collision Reactions.")

In Flash MX there are two ways to treat friction: the right way and the good-enough way. In this section we'll discuss both.

Real Friction

If you slide a box to the right across the floor, then a frictional force points to the left, opposing the velocity vector. The velocity of the box will approach 0 with a constant deceleration. The equation for sliding friction is:

```
F = u*mass*gravity
```

The quantity *mass*gravity* is the weight of the object. So the greater the object's weight, the greater the friction that will oppose the motion of the sliding object. The *u* factor is known as the *frictional coefficient* (also sometimes called the coefficient of sliding friction).

A *frictional coefficient* is a numerical value between 0 and 1. In real life, this factor is found by experimentation and is different for each surface-object interaction. For instance, a wet ice cube on a rubber floor may have a very low frictional coefficient (.01), whereas a tennis shoe on the same floor may have a higher frictional coefficient (.2). In ActionScript you can simply choose a value for *u* depending on the type of surface you are dealing with.

Using Newton's second law, we can determine the deceleration due to friction:

```
F = mass*accel = u*mass*gravity
```

Canceling out the *mass* on both sides, we get:
```
accel = u*gravity
```

This `accel` variable will be used with the velocity equations we have been working with. Here are the steps you use to apply friction:

1. **Find the acceleration due to friction using the equation accel=u*gravity.**

2. **Apply the `accel` *value to the velocity in every frame (just as we have been doing with acceleration) until the velocity reaches 0.***

Stop applying the variable when the velocity reaches 0. If you don't, the object will actually move in the opposite direction.

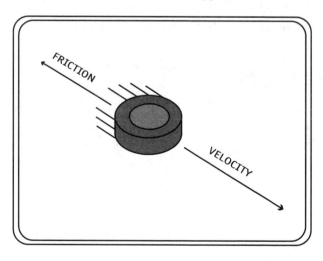

To see this in action, open roll.fla in the Chapter04 directory. In this file we have a ball moving in the *x* direction. It is slowed to a stop by friction. Here is the ActionScript used:

```
1   xmov = 10;
2   gravity = 2;
3   u = .2;
4   accel = u*gravity;
5   _root.onEnterFrame = function() {
6       if (Math.abs(xmov) >= Math.abs(accel)) {
7           if (xmov>0) {
8               xmov -= accel;
9           } else if (xmov<0) {
10              xmov += accel;
11          }
12      } else {
13          xmov = 0;
14      }
15      ball._x += xmov;
16  };
```

In line 1 we give the ball an initial velocity so it has something to slide to a stop from. We then define a gravity variable and the friction constant *u*. In line 4, we use the gravity and the friction constant to find the value of the acceleration due to the friction. The if statements in the onEnterFrame event are there to make sure that we either add or subtract the acceleration correctly (depending on the direction of motion). The if statement also controls what happens to the ball if the velocity is less than the acceleration; if that is true, then in the next frame the ball should be stopped.

Good-Enough Friction

While the method discussed above is the correct way to handle frictional forces, it can be a little confusing and clunky with all those if statements. Here is a faster and easier way to handle friction and achieve a very similar look.

1. *Choose a number between 0 and 1. Let's call this number the decay.*

2. *Multiply the decay by the velocity in every frame.*

That's it!

If the decay is 1, then the velocity never changes. If the decay is 0, then the velocity is 0 after frame 1. If the decay is between 0 and 1, then it will get closer to 0 in every frame. To see an example, open roll2.fla in the Chapter04 directory on the CD. As in the previous example, this movie shows a ball with an initial velocity sliding to a stop … well, sort of. First let's look at the ActionScript:

```
1    xmov = 10;
2    decay = .95;
3    _root.onEnterFrame = function() {
4        xmov *= decay;
5        ball._x += xmov;
6    };
```

As you can see, this is a much simpler way to treat friction (which probably explains why it's also the most commonly used method). The result is a ball that slides from an initial velocity to almost 0 velocity. It is important to note that no matter how many times you multiply a non-zero number by a non-zero number, you will never get zero. This one of the pitfalls of using this method. Later in the book, when we get into some more specific situations with velocity, we will discuss some ways to make the ball stop when a minimum velocity is reached.

To sum up the differences between real friction and good-enough friction, as shown in the examples in the sections above, the correct frictional implementation decreases the velocity linearly—that is, by the same amount in every frame. The good-enough method decreases the velocity by a percentage of the current velocity—a nonlinear decrease. In most circumstances, the difference between these is not going to be worth the amount of coding you'd have to put into the ActionScript to arrive at the "correct" implementation.

This chapter introduced topics that will be used frequently throughout the book, including velocity, acceleration, gravity, and friction. So don't think you've read the last on physics; you will learn more about physics in Chapter 6, "Collision Reactions."

POINTS TO REMEMBER

- Physics is the study of the behavior of objects in nature on the most fundamental level.

- Understanding basic physical laws and how to apply them is the key to creating dynamic realism in games.

- Velocity is a vector formed by combining speed with a direction.

- Acceleration—also a vector—occurs whenever the velocity changes.

- If you know the acceleration of an object and its current velocity, you can find or project the velocity of that object at any time in the future.

- While in the real world we generally think of speed as being measured in units of distance/time, in Flash we think of speed as being measured by frames. So Flash users usually assume one frame to be one unit of time.

- When looking for the balance between creating smooth-appearing motion and not overtaxing the processors of most computers, 24 frames per second seems to offer the best results.

- The amazingly simple trick for applying "good-enough" gravity to your effects is to come up with a value for gravity and add that value to your y velocity in every frame.

- A frictional force is one that opposes the direction of motion and is caused by the interaction between two materials—in other words, it slows something down.

- Kinetic energy—the energy associated with the momentum of an object—is lost as heat from the friction, and the object slows down.

- "Real" frictional implementation decreases the velocity linearly; "good-enough" friction decreases the velocity by a percentage of the current velocity (nonlinearly).

- In most circumstances, the difference between these is not going to be worth the amount of coding you'd have to put into the ActionScript to arrive at the "correct" implementation.

CHAPTER 5

COLLISION DETECTION

WHEN YOU'RE PLAYING A COMPUTERIZED GAME OF PINBALL, OR A platform game like Super Mario Brothers, you probably take it for granted that it has realistic-looking reactions. In pinball, the ball gets hit by the flippers and zooms away; in a platform game, the character lands on a platform or falls to the ground. There is one important thing that has to happen before any of these realistic reactions can take place: There has to be a collision, and the collision must be detected. (OK, that's *two* things.) Once the collision is detected, a reaction can take place—we'll get into that in the next chapter. In this chapter, we'll discuss the ins and outs of collision detection, using both hitTest(),a method of the MovieClip object sometimes useful for this purpose; and math, which is where the real power lies. We will also address the limitations of collision detection in Macromedia Flash and how you can get around them.

WHAT IS A COLLISION?

Before learning how to program collision-detection scripts, it is important to understand what a collision is. I know what it sounds like—something big and crashy. And of course in a lot of cases that's true, but for our purposes, we need to get down to a more basic definition than that. Put simply, a collision happens when two separate shapes share one or more points in space. For instance, imagine two circles touching at their edges, such as two billiard balls resting against each other. These two circles share one point; hence, in physics terms they are *colliding*. Some collisions are simple, such as when the mouse pointer overlaps a movie clip or a button. Other collisions are complicated, such as when a ball bounces off an angled line.

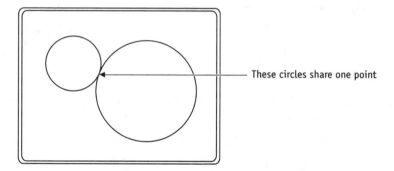

These circles share one point

In this chapter we'll cover several of the most common types of collision detection, including those having to do with intersections or collisions of lines with lines, circles with lines, and rectangles with other rectangles.

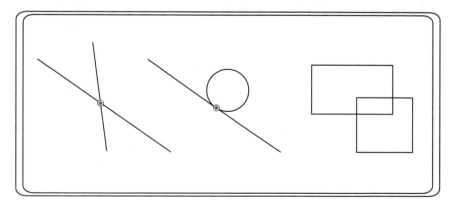

As I mentioned earlier, there are two main types of programmatic collision detection used in Flash: the use of the hitTest() method of the MovieClip object, and the use of math to determine if a collision has occurred.

As you will see from what follows in this chapter, hitTest() has its uses but is vastly inferior to collision-detection scripts that use math. By using math to determine collisions, not only can you determine if a collision is happening, but in some cases you can also tell if a collision is *about* to happen, and at precisely which position this collision will occur. We need this level of precision for some of the more advanced types of games, such as pinball or billiards.

DETECTION USING hitTest()

As you probably know, Flash's MovieClip object contains many methods and properties that assist in working with movie clips. When a movie clip is created, either in the authoring environment or with ActionScript, it inherits all the methods and properties of the MovieClip object. These methods and properties are then available to this new movie-clip instance.

We can use the hitTest() method of the MovieClip object to detect collisions in three simple scenarios. But before we discuss these three types of collisions, I'll introduce you to a new term, *bounding box*. Bounding box refers to the imaginary box that encloses everything in a movie clip. If you have a movie clip with a circle in it, then the bounding box for this movie clip is a square that is exactly big enough to fit the circle, with each side of the box touching the circle. Likewise, if you have an irregular shape or multiple shapes within a movie clip, then the bounding box will be made up of a rectangle that touches the uppermost piece in the movie clip, the leftmost piece in the movie clip, the rightmost piece in the movie clip, and the lowest piece in the movie clip.

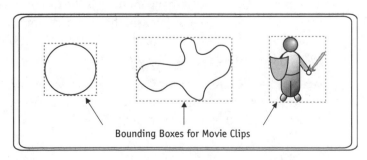

Bounding Boxes for Movie Clips

Now that you have an understanding of the bounding box of a movie clip, we can mention the three types of collision detection that are possible using hitTest().

Movie Clip-Movie Clip Collisions

This type of collision detection determines if the bounding boxes of two movie clips are overlapping. The shapes within the movie clips may or may not be touching, but as long as the two bounding boxes are, then a collision has occurred.

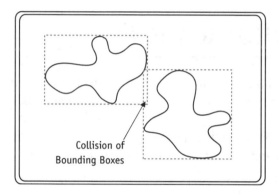

Collision of Bounding Boxes

Now let's delve into the ActionScript involved. Since hitTest() is a method of the MovieClip object, it can be applied only to a movie clip (as opposed to any other kind of object, such as a graphic or a text field). Following is the syntax for using hitTest() to determine if two movie clips are colliding:

```
myMovieClip.hitTest(target_MovieClip)
```

This line of ActionScript starts with the instance name of a movie clip. After the instance name, the hitTest() method is invoked by passing in a parameter. The value of that parameter is the instance name of another movie clip. Translated into English, this line of ActionScript would become a question that would read something like this: "Is the bounding box of myMovieClip colliding with the bounding box of target_MovieClip?"

When this line of ActionScript is executed, Flash gives you an answer to that question. In English you would expect the answer to be "yes" or "no"; in ActionScript, the answer is true (yes) or false (no).

Open movieclip_movieclip.fla in the Chapter05 directory on the CD to see an example. In this FLA file we have two movie clips—shape1 and shape2. This file has been programmed so that shape1 will move to the right, and during every frame it checks to see if there is a collision occurring between shape1 and shape2. If a collision is happening, then we simply execute a trace action to indicate that the collision is happening. Here is the ActionScript used.

The trace action is purely for testing and debugging purposes. If you type *trace("My name is Jobe and I'm a physics major")* in the Flash MX Actions panel and then test the movie, you'll see that message appear in the Output window. Trace actions are only displayed in test-movie mode in the Flash environment, never in a Web page or in the stand-alone SWF file.

```
1   xmov = 3;
2   _root.onEnterFrame = function () {
3       shape1._x += xmov;
4       if (shape1.hitTest(shape2)) {
5           trace("They are colliding!!");
6       }
7   }
```

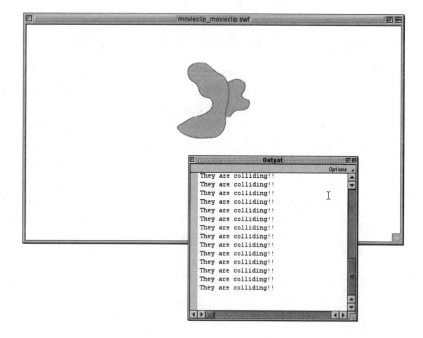

You can see that we start out moving shape1 in the same way we introduced in Chapter 4, "Basic Physics"; first a speed variable, xmov, is set, and then the position is updated in every frame. Where we start introducing new ActionScript is on the fourth line. This is a conditional statement: If the hitTest() method returns a value of true, then the condition is fulfilled and the trace action is executed; otherwise nothing happens.

Here is that same conditional statement converted to words: "If the bounding box of shape1 collides with the bounding box of shape2, then put 'They are colliding!!' in the output window."

For a more practical example, you can check out ball_falling.fla in the Chapter05 directory on the CD. There are two movie clips in this file—ball and floor. Using gravity (as covered in Chapter 4), the ball falls. In every frame, we check for a collision between it and the floor. If hitTest() returns a value of true, then the velocity of the ball is reversed and the ball goes back up. Generate a SWF to test the file. (The quickest way to do this is to press Ctrl-Enter in Windows or Command-Return on the Mac.) Note that if you run the file for 30 seconds or so, the ball gets stuck in the floor. This is due to one of the limitations of hitTest(), which we'll discuss in the "Detection Using Math" section of this chapter.

Movie Clip-Point Collisions

The hitTest() method lets you determine if a point (x, y) is within the bounding box of a movie clip. This can be handy in specific game situations. Usually these are times when the mouse is involved. Simple click-and-destroy–style games make use of this type of collision detection. For example, let's take a balloon game. If the user clicks the mouse when it's positioned over a balloon, then the balloon pops. This is the easiest way to find out if the mouse is over a movie clip without using a button. However, most click-and-destroy games are created with buttons. For that reason, in my opinion, the movie-clip–point method of detection doesn't have many effective uses in games.

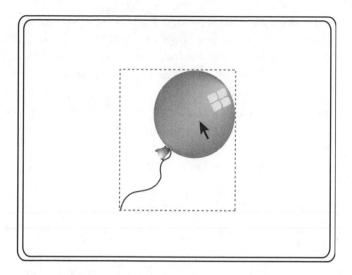

Here is the syntax for using the hitTest() method to determine if a point is colliding with the bounding box of a movie clip:

```
myMovieClip.hitTest(x, y)
```

And here's the English translation: "Does the point with coordinates of x and y fall within the bounding box of myMovieClip?"

As in the previous section, the answer to this question—that is, the result of the line of ActionScript—is going to be true or false.

To see this in action, open the file balloon_pop.fla from the Chapter05 directory on the CD. You'll see a movie clip containing an image of a balloon on the stage. This movie clip has an instance name of balloon. There is ActionScript on frame 1 in the Actions layer that executes when the mouse is clicked. This script then determines if the mouse is over the balloon clip, and if so, then the balloon is "told" to explode. Here is the ActionScript used to accomplish this.

```
1   _root.onMouseDown = function () {
2       mx = _xmouse;
3       my = _ymouse;
4       if (balloon.hitTest(mx, my)) {
5           balloon.play();
6       }
7   }
```

In line 1 of this script we define a function that will be called when the mouse button is pressed down (and not yet released). When this happens, two variables are set—mx and my—to store the *x* and *y* positions of the mouse. Then, in line 4, we use an if statement to determine if the mouse is within the bounding box of the balloon clip. To satisfy this conditional statement, the statement balloon.hitTest(mx, my) must return a result of true, confirming the "collision" of the pointer and the balloon. If the condition is satisfied, then line 5 is executed, and the movie clip called balloon plays a popping animation.

The popping animation was created inside of the balloon movie clip. The first frame of that movie clip shows the balloon in its un-popped state. The frames after that show the balloon popping. The final frame in the animation is blank.

The idea used in balloon_pop.fla can be extended easily to apply to any number of movie clips. To see such an expanded example, open balloon_pop_many.fla from the Chapter05 folder on the CD. In this file, the number of balloons that will be displayed is controlled by a variable. There's a movie clip in the library, again called balloon, whose linkage identifier is also named balloon (see the sidebar "ActionScript Review: attachMovie() and Linkage Identifiers" if this is new to you). With the linkage specified, we can attach the balloon clip to the stage (that is, create new copies of it) as many times as we want. When the mouse button is clicked, we can loop through all of the balloons on the screen using ActionScript, performing a hitTest() on each balloon, to determine if there are any collisions between the mouse and the balloon. Here is the ActionScript used in this example.

```
1   //Number of balloons to be created
2   totalBalloons = 10;
3   //Set the dimensions of the screen so that we can randomly
     → place the balloons
4   screenWidth = 700;
5   screenHeight = 400;
6   //Create and place the balloon instances on the stage
7   for (var i = 0; i<totalBalloons; ++i) {
8       var name = "balloon"+i;
9       _root.attachMovie("balloon", name, i);
10      var x = random(screenWidth);
11      var y = random(screenHeight);
```

```
12      _root[name]._x = x;
13      _root[name]._y = y;
14  }
15  _root.onMouseDown = function() {
16      mx = _xmouse;
17      my = _ymouse;
18      //Loop through all of the balloons looking for collisions
19      for (var i = 0; i<totalBalloons; ++i) {
20          var name = "balloon"+i;
21          if (_root[name].hitTest(mx,my)) {
22              _root[name].play();
23          }
24      }
25  };
```

The second line of code above sets a variable called totalBalloons. The value of this variable determines how many balloons will be created and placed on the stage. Lines 4–14 create and place the balloons on the stage. Lines 19-24 contain an ActionScript loop that checks for a collision with each balloon. The balloons that are created (from lines 4–14) are named sequentially (balloon0, balloon1, balloon2, and so on). In this loop, we dynamically re-create the name of each of these balloons and use these names to reference the movie clips, checking to see if a movie clip of the same name has a hitTest() of true with the position of the mouse. For instance, if the loop is on iteration 12, then the name created is balloon12. Since the value of name is "balloon12" then the action _root[name] is equivalent to writing _root.balloon12. This is how the references to the movie clips are created dynamically in these loops.

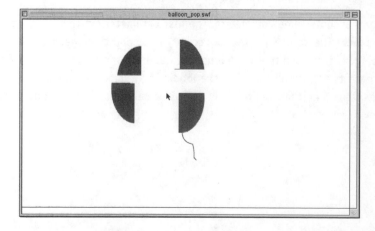

ActionScript Review: attachMovie() and Linkage Identifiers

With ActionScript you can create a new instance on the stage of a movie clip that is in the Flash file's library. Many effects are accomplished this way, such as creating an endless supply of bullets from a gun. In order for ActionScript to pull a movie clip from the library, the clip must be configured to do so. This is very easy. Open the Library panel, find the movie clip you wish to make available, right-click (Windows) or Control-click (Mac) on it, and select Linkage from the contextual menu. In the Linkage Properties dialog box, make sure the box next to Export for ActionScript is checked, and then type in an identifier name. The identifier is how you tell Flash which movie clip you want to attach. To then attach a movie clip, simply use the following action:

```
path.attachMovie(linkage_identifier, new_instance_name, depth)
```

For instance,

```
_root.attachMovie("balloon", "balloon2", 2);
```

ActionScript Review: for Loops

Loops are an immeasurably helpful ActionScript feature. With them you can perform the same actions as many times as you wish. This is particularly useful for doing the same thing to many movie clips. For instance, if you have pictures on the stage named picture1 through picture30 and you want to make them all invisible, you can create a simple for loop to do so:

```
for (var i=1; i<=30; ++i) {
    var name = "picture"+i;
    this[name]._visible = false;
}
```

The for loop accepts three parameters. The first parameter (in this case, var i=1) specifies a starting place. The second parameter (i<=30) is a condition that must be fulfilled to continue looping. If this condition is no longer fulfilled, then the loop ends. The third parameter (++i) increments the variable so that the loop will at some time end. If the loop variable is not incremented, then the condition will always be satisfied, and the loop will never end.

Shape-Point Collisions

With the previous two types of collision detection, we saw that a collision happens with the actual bounding box of a movie clip. There is one other way to use the hitTest() method, and that is to detect a collision between a point and the contents of the movie clip—not just the bounding box. Imagine a movie clip that contains several separate graphics or shapes. Using the hitTest() method, we can tell if a point is colliding with any one of the shapes in this movie clip.

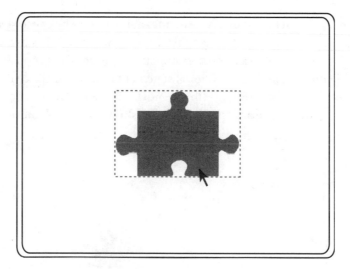

Here is the syntax used to invoke this type of collision detection:

```
myMovieClip.hitTest(x, y, true)
```

You might immediately notice that this is identical to the syntax for the movie-clip–point collision detection, with one change: the addition of the true parameter. When that parameter is set to true, the hitTest() method checks for a collision between the point and the contents of the movie clip. If that parameter does not exist or if it is set to false, then the hitTest() method checks for a collision between the point and the bounding box of the movie clip.

To see an example of this, open puzzle_piece.fla in the Chapter05 directory. On the stage you will see a movie clip with an instance name of piece, containing the shape of a puzzle piece, which happens to be a candid shot of my cat. The ActionScript in this movie simply checks for a collision between the mouse and the shape when the mouse is clicked.

```
1   _root.onMouseDown = function () {
2       mx =_xmouse;
3       my =_ymouse;
4       if (piece.hitTest(mx, my, true)) {
5           trace("Meow!");
6       }
7   }
```

The first line of this code defines a function to be called when the mouse button is pressed. When this function is called, it sets two variables, as in our previous examples, to store the position of the mouse cursor. Then, on line 4, comes a conditional statement that checks to see if the hitTest() of the mouse position with the movie clip called piece is true. If it is true, then a trace action is executed to show you that a collision was detected.

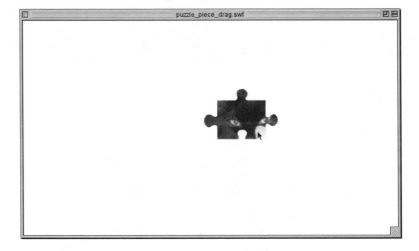

You can see a more practical application of this technique in the file puzzle_piece_drag.fla in the Chapter05 folder on the CD. In that file, the collision detection is coded exactly as it is here; the difference is that instead of giving a trace result when the puzzle piece is clicked, the piece gets dragged until the mouse button is released.

DETECTION USING MATH

As you just saw, using the `hitTest()` method is pretty painless. I've already hinted that creating collision-detection scripts based on math is more difficult than that. So this is probably an appropriate time to tell you what makes this type of collision detection so much better than attempting to use `hitTest()` for all your collision-detection needs. Let's start by listing the limitations of `hitTest()`.

Object-shape restrictions. As you saw earlier in this chapter, the `hitTest()` method only works with the bounding box of a movie clip, or a point and the shape within that movie clip. How would you detect collisions between two pool balls, or between a ball and an angled line? With `hitTest()`, the collision detection for those situations would not be accurate, because it doesn't handle collision detection between the shapes within two movie clips. Using math, we can create collision-detection scripts for many shapes.

Inhibited code-graphics independence. This concept can be tough to grasp. In all of the examples given so far in this book, we have updated the position of a movie clip on the screen by grabbing its current position, adding to it, and then changing the position of that movie clip. It is better practice to keep track of where objects on the screen should be *in code*. For instance, you could have a variable that stores the x position of the ball. When it is time to update the position of the ball with the x velocity, you would add to the variable that stores the x position, and then set the position of the clip on the screen from that variable. This is useful because we can detect a collision before setting the position of the movie clip on the stage. With `hitTest()`, the object must be physically moved on the screen, and then the collision detection is based on the overlap of two graphical elements. We will be using code-graphics independence throughout the rest of the chapter.

Frame-rate dependence. This limitation is related to the one above. Imagine a game of Pong: There is a paddle that's 10 units wide on the left side of the screen. The ball, also 10 units wide, is moving toward the paddle with an x speed of −30 units per frame. It is possible for the ball to be on the right side of the paddle on one frame and to appear on the other side of the paddle on the next frame. With `hitTest()`, no collision would have been detected because the two clips must overlap during a frame (or *within* a frame—for those of you more comfortable thinking of frames in terms of physical space rather than time duration). It is not smart enough to know that the ball went through the paddle. Using math, we can tell if a collision took place in between frames.

Collision was not detected because of the "snapshot" nature of frames.

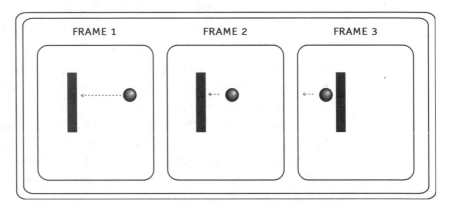

| FRAME 1 | FRAME 2 | FRAME 3 |

To recap, using math for collision detection will allow you to:

• Write scripts that will handle detecting collisions between irregular shapes

• Write frame-independent collision-detection scripts

• Handle all of the collision detection and movement in memory rather than basing it on the placement of the graphics

What follows is a description, with examples, of how to think about and script collision detection between various types of shapes. For some of these we extend the detection script so that it works independently of the frames, and for some we do not.

For some types of collision detection, frame independence doesn't give us any advantages. One such type is line-line collisions; when two lines are intersecting, they are most likely not moving, which means we do not need to use frame-independent collision detection on them. But for some situations, such as circle-line or circle-circle collisions, frame-independent collision detection is a must for fast-paced games, like pool or pinball.

Point-Circle Collision Detection

We begin the examples of mathematical collision detection with one of the simpler types. A good example of where we might use point-circle collision detection is a dart game. The dart's tip is the point, and the target is made up of a series of concentric circles.

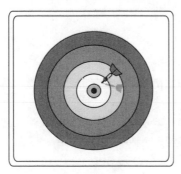

So how do we determine if a point and a circle are colliding? Imagine that you have two movie clips: a circle and a dot (the point). Assume the registration point of the circle movie clip is at the actual center of the circle. Since the point and the circle are movie clips, you can easily find the positions of both. Also, using the distance equation developed in Chapter 3, "Trigonometry 101" (and listed below in ActionScript), we know we can find the distance between the point and the circle. With this information we can write the one condition that determines if a collision is taking place:

If the distance between the point and the center of the circle is less than the radius of the circle, then the point is colliding with the circle.

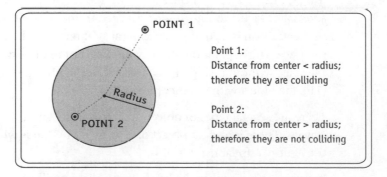

POINT 1

Point 1:
Distance from center < radius;
therefore they are colliding

Point 2:
Distance from center > radius;
therefore they are not colliding

Radius

POINT 2

TIP

Note that the radius of a circle is one-half its width.

To see this in action, open point_circle.fla from the Chapter05 folder on the CD. In this file there are three movie clips—two points and one circle. One of the points is outside the circle and has an instance name of point_clip1, and one of them is inside the circle with an instance name of point_clip2. The circle has an instance name of circle_clip1. The ActionScript in this file was built to determine if a point is colliding with a circle. Here are the first 13 lines.

```
1   //Define point 1
2   point1 = {};
3   point1.x = point_clip1._x;
4   point1.y = point_clip1._y;
5   //Define point 2
6   point2 = {};
7   point2.x = point_clip2._x;
8   point2.y = point_clip2._y;
9   //Define circle 1
10  circle1 = {};
11  circle1.x = circle_clip1._x;
12  circle1.y = circle_clip1._y;
13  circle1.radius = circle_clip1._width/2;
```

What is being done with the ActionScript here is very important, and is similar to what is going to be used for most games and examples given in this book. We create an object for each movie clip. An object (of type object), when first created, is nothing more than an empty storage device. This can be likened to a file cabinet. When you first build (or buy) a file cabinet, it is empty. You then use it to store information about certain things, like your car or house. Unlike a file cabinet, an object object is not a visual or tactile thing—it is data stored in memory. Storing information in this fashion is a good practice because it removes the data from the interface. This separation allows you to add or remove movie clips from the stage without losing the data stored in the object. Later you can reassociate the object with another movie clip.

There are several types of objects in Flash, from MovieClip objects to XML objects. There is also an object of type object. That is what we are using in the ActionScript above.

In future scripts within the book, these objects will contain many other things, such as the properties of the object. For example, in the case of a pool ball, the object would contain the ball's color.

Some programmers choose to use the movie clip itself as the object to store this information. In some cases that would be OK, but in others—for instance, where a movie clip may not always be on the stage—it is not a good idea. Imagine a game in which an enemy character is coming after you. This enemy may leave the screen for more ammo and then come back in 30 seconds or so. In this case it is probably a good idea to remove the movie clip from the stage (for performance reasons) but retain the object that stores the enemy's characteristics so we don't have to start "rebuilding" the enemy from scratch.

In line 2 of the ActionScript above we create a new object, called point1, that we intend to use as a storage container for information about the point_clip1 movie clip. The action point1={} is shorthand for creating a new empty object and giving it a name. (The long-winded way is point1 = new Object(), so you can see why we'd like the shorthand.) In lines 3 and 4 we simply create variables on the object to represent the position of the point_clip1 movie clip. Lines 5–8 create an object for point_clip2 and store information about it in the same way as the point1 object does. Next, an object is created to store the information about the circle_clip1 movie clip. It stores the x and y positions of the movie clip as well as its radius.

The rest of the ActionScript defines the collision-detection function and uses it to test for collisions.

```
1   //Build collision detection function
2   function pointToCircleDetection(point, circle) {
3       var xDiff = circle.x-point.x;
4       var yDiff = circle.y-point.y;
5       var distance = Math.sqrt(xDiff*xDiff+yDiff*yDiff);
6       if (distance<=circle.radius) {
7           trace("Collision detected!!");
8       } else {
9           trace("No collision detected.");
10      }
11  }
12  //Check for a collision between point1 and circle1
13  pointToCircleDetection(point1, circle1);
14  //Check for a collision between point2 and circle2
15  pointToCircleDetection(point2, circle1);
```

First we define a function named `pointToCircleDetection` that accepts two parameters: `point` and `circle`. Both `point` and `circle` are objects passed in when the function is called. To detect a collision, as we spelled out earlier, we have to compare the distance between the point and the circle with the radius of the circle. To make this comparison, we must determine the distance using the Pythagorean theorem (the method shown back in Chapter 3, "Trigonometry 101"). Lines 3–5 show this. In line 6 we compare the distance with the radius of the circle, and if the distance is less than or equal to the radius, we execute a `trace` action to inform us that a collision has been detected. If this condition is not met, then a `trace` action is executed to inform us that no collision has occurred. In lines 13 and 15 we call the detection function while passing in objects whose collision we would like to check. For instance, in line 13 we pass in `point1` and `circle1`. The script will then check for a collision between `point1` and `circle1`. When you generate a SWF movie, you should see two traces in your output window. The first collision detection detected a collision, the second did not.

Circle-Circle Collision Detection

In this section we discuss the logic and scripts needed to determine if two circles are colliding. We will cover this for both frame-dependent and frame-independent situations.

By *frame dependence*, we mean that in every frame we check for a collision, based on where the objects are now (this is like taking snapshots in time). With *frame independence,* in every frame we check to see if a collision has happened at some point between the last frame and the current frame. The frame-dependent collision detection for two circles is a simple extension of the point-circle collision-detection technique. The frame-independent collision detection for two circles involves a lot more logic and math.

Let's look at the easy one first.

Frame Dependent Circle-Circle Detection

Here's our case of frame-dependent circle-circle collision detection:

If the distance between two circles is less than or equal to the sum of their radii, then a collision is occurring.

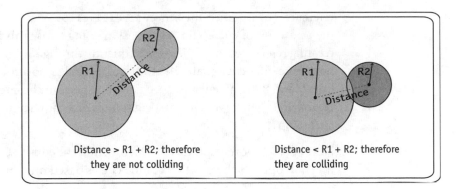

Distance > R1 + R2; therefore they are not colliding

Distance < R1 + R2; therefore they are colliding

To see an example of this in ActionScript, open circle_circle1.fla from the Chapter05 folder on the CD. There are two movie clips on the stage, circle_clip1 and circle_clip2. The ActionScript assigns *x* and *y* speeds to each circle and moves the circles around on the stage. In every frame it checks to see if they are colliding.

As with the point-circle collision detection, we store information about each movie clip in an object. Here is the ActionScript that does this:

```
1   //Define object for the first circle
2   circle1 = {};
3   circle1.clip = circle_clip1;
4   circle1.x = circle1.clip._x;
5   circle1.y = circle1.clip._y;
6   circle1.radius = circle1.clip._width/2;
7   circle1.xmov = 3;
8   circle1.ymov = 1;
9   //Define object for the second circle
10  circle2 = {};
11  circle2.clip = circle_clip2;
12  circle2.x = circle2.clip._x;
13  circle2.y = circle2.clip._y;
14  circle2.radius = circle2.clip._width/2;
15  circle2.xmov = -1;
16  circle2.ymov = 0;
```

First, an object called `circle1` is created to store the information about circle_clip1. In line 3 you may notice something you haven't seen before. We are creating a reference to the movie clip with a name of clip in the object itself. Doing this allows us to point to the movie clip using this new reference. For instance, the action `circle1.clip._x = 100` would move the *x* position of circle_clip1 to 100. (I'm going to use this technique of creating references to movie clips frequently throughout the book.) The next three lines create variables to store the circle's position and radius. In lines 7 and 8, we assign an *x* speed and a *y* speed to the circle. Lines 9–16 do for circle_clip2 what the first eight lines of ActionScript did for circle_clip1.

Next in the ActionScript, we create a function called `moveCircles`. This function updates the positions of the circles based on their speeds.

```
1   function moveCircles() {
2       for (var i=1; i<=2; ++i) {
3           var circle = this["circle"+i];
4           circle.x += circle.xmov;
5           circle.y += circle.ymov;
6           circle.clip._x = circle.x;
7           circle.clip._y = circle.y;
8       }
9   }
```

In this function, there is a `for` loop that loops through and moves each circle. This ActionScript is not unfamiliar (see balloon_pop_many.fla), although this is the first time we have used the movie-clip reference from an object. Remember that we are storing references to circle_clip1 and circle_clip2 as the `clip` variable on both the `circle1` and `circle2` objects, which is where we use them. In lines 6 and 7 you can see that the circles are moved by using the movie-clip reference `clip` that exists on each object.

The function that detects collisions between the circles is called `CircleToCircleDetection`. It is almost exactly the same as the collision-detection script used in the point-circle collision-detection script.

```
1   function CircleToCircleDetection(circle_a, circle_b) {
2       var xDiff = circle_a.x-circle_b.x;
3       var yDiff = circle_a.y-circle_b.y;
4       var distance = Math.sqrt(xDiff*xDiff+yDiff*yDiff);
5       if (distance<=circle_a.radius+circle_b.radius) {
6           trace("Collision detected!!");
7       }
8   }
```

The `CircleToCircleDetection` function accepts two parameters, `circle_a` and `circle_b`. First the ActionScript finds the distance between those two movie clips. Then it reaches a conditional, which checks to see if the distance between the circles is less than or equal to the sum of their radii. If it is, then it executes a `trace` action.

Finally, it creates an `onEnterFrame` event that calls the `moveCircles` function and `CircleToCircleDetection` function in every frame (I'm just mentioning this to wrap up the script; you won't see this event in the code above). Generate a SWF to see it work.

Frame Independent Circle-Circle Detection

OK, that was the easy one! Now it's time to talk about frame-independent circle-circle collision detection. The math in this gets a little tough, so before continuing I would like to recap why it's important for you to slog through this. With all of the collision-detection scripts created so far, Flash checks one time per frame to see if there is a collision right now. You can think of this as being like taking snapshots in time. I am sure you can imagine that if an object is moving fast enough, then in one frame it is on one side of an object, and in the next frame it is on the other side of the object. The collision-detection method we've been using wouldn't be able to detect that kind of collision, since as far as it is concerned, a collision never happened. But with the way I'm about to introduce, we can tell (no matter how fast the object is going) if there was a collision between the previous frame and the current frame. This script has direct application to games like pool, pinball, air hockey, miniature golf, or indeed any game in which two balls (circles) can collide.

Let's discuss the logic needed for frame-independent collision detection. First, it is important to realize that we can still only check for a collision every frame—we can't check in between frames. What we will cover here is how to tell if a collision should have happened in between frames. In Chapter 4, "Basic Physics," we introduced the equations for position and velocity. In Chapter 3, "Trigonometry 101," we introduced how to get the distance between two points. If we know the x and y speeds of each circle (which we do), then we can write equations that specify the x position and y positions of each circle. With these position equations, we can write an equation that determines the distance between the two circles. This leaves us with an equation for the distance between the two circles that is dependent on one variable—time (well, OK, for us it's really frames). If we wanted to, we could stick any time into this equation and find the distance that the circles would be apart at that time. Likewise, we could insert a distance, and then solve for the time during which the two circles would be this distance apart. It is the latter example that we are interested in now. The same main condition must be met for the two circles to be colliding: The distance between the two circles must be less than or equal to the sum of their radii. So this is what we do:

1. *Write equations for the x and y positions of both circles. These equations are based on the x and y speeds.*

2. *Use the equations for the x and y positions of both circles to write an equation for the distance between the two circles.*

3. *In the distance equation, use the sum of their radii for the distance, and solve for the time (which is frames).*

4. *Do this for every frame. If the time is less than or equal to 1, then the collision happened between the last frame and the current frame.*

Let's look at this in math form before touching the ActionScript.

1. For circle 1:

```
x1 = xl1+xmov1*t
y1 = yl1+ymov1*t
```

For circle 2:

```
x2 = xl2+xmov2*t
y2 = yl2+ymov2*t
```

The variables xl1, yl1, xl2, and yl2 represent the position of the circle at the end of the previous frame (since we have not yet updated this frame). The variable l stands for "last," as in "last frame." The variable t represents the time starting from the end of the previous frame.

2. The distance between the two circles:

```
distance = √(x2-x1)² + (y2-y1)²
```

3. Set the distance as the sum of the radii, and solve for time:

```
distance = radius1+radius2 = √(x2-x1)² + (y2-y1)².
```

Solving for the time is very difficult. We must insert the equations for x1, y1, x2, and y2. We then square both sides of the equation (to get rid of the square root sign). What we are left with is a quadratic equation. Quadratic equations have two solutions, which means that when we solve for the time, we will get two answers. Conceptually we can see why in this case we will get two separate times. Imagine two circles moving toward each other. At one time they will be touching on an edge. As time goes on, they will move through each other, but just as they are about to separate, they will be touching exactly at one point again. The two times found by solving the quadratic equation give the two times that a collision can occur. When we have our two answers, we look at the lower of the two times and discard the other one.

By defining these constants,

```
R = radius1+radius2
a = -2*xmov1*xmov2+xmov1²+xmov2²
b = -2*xl1*xmov2-2*xl2*xmov1+2*xl1*xmov1+2*xl2*xmov2
c = -2*xl1*xl2+xl1²+xl2²
d = -2*ymov1*ymov2+ymov1²+ymov2²
e = -2*yl1*ymov2-2*yl2*ymov1+2*yl1*ymov1+2*yl2*ymov2
f = -2*yl1*yl2+yl1²+yl2²
g = a+d
h = b+e
k = c+f-R²
```

we can write the vastly simplified quadratic equation as

$$g*t^2+h*t+k = 0$$

Using the quadratic formula to solve for the time, we arrive at

$$t1 = \frac{-h+\sqrt{h^2-4*g*k}}{2*g} \quad \text{and} \quad t2 = \frac{-h-\sqrt{h^2-4*g*k}}{2*g}$$

4. This calculation is performed for every frame. If either of the times is less than or equal to 1, then a collision happened between the previous frame and the current frame. This works for any possible velocity; there is no limit.

If you are interested in seeing this math worked out more rigorously, check out circ_circ_frame_independent.pdf in the Chapter05 directory on the CD. It shows this worked out manually.

Solving Quadratic Equations

Any equation in which the variable has an exponent of 2 (and no other terms with a higher exponent) is a *quadratic equation*. For instance, $a*t^2+b*t+c = 0$ is a quadratic equation. All quadratic equations have two solutions; this means there are two values for the variable for which the equation is valid. The simplest example is $x^2 = 4$. This is a quadratic equation with the two solutions 2 and -2. There is a formula called the *quadratic formula* that is used to find the two solutions. Using $a*t^2+b*t+c = 0$ as an example, here are the solutions for *t*:

$$t = \frac{-b+\sqrt{b^2-4*a*c}}{2*a} \text{ and } t = \frac{-b-\sqrt{b^2-4*a*c}}{2*a}$$

In the circle-circle example given in this section, the quadratic equation was manipulated until it could be written in standard quadratic-equation form. From there it is easy to solve.

Now let's look at an example of this in ActionScript. Open circle_circle2.fla from the Chapter05 folder on the CD. There are two movie clips on the stage, ball1 and ball2. At its most fundamental level, the ActionScript used here performs all of the following tasks:

1. It defines an object for each movie clip to store information about that movie clip.

2. It defines a function that updates the position of the movie clips in memory (not on the stage).

3. It defines a function that checks for collisions between any two balls (circles).

4. It defines a function that physically places the balls on the screen.

5. It creates an `onEnterFrame` event to call all of these functions in every frame.

Here is the ActionScript that defines the objects:

```
1   game = {};
2   game.numBalls = 2;
3   for (var i=1; i<=game.numBalls; ++i) {
4       var name = "ball"+i;
```

```
5      game[name] = {};
6      game[name].clip = _root[name];
7      game[name].xpos = game[name].clip._x;
8      game[name].ypos = game[name].clip._y;
9      game[name].radius = game[name].clip._width/2;
10     game[name].xmov = 0;
11     game[name].ymov = 0;
12 }
13 game.ball1.xmov = 1;
14 game.ball1.ymov = 2;
15 game.ball2.ymov = 1;
```

First we create an object called game. This object will store all of the other objects we create. The only reason for having this *container* object, game, is to keep from polluting the timeline with unneeded data. We can keep track of everything we need to about the balls in the game object. In the second line we set a variable on the game object that stores the number of balls we have chosen to use.

Next, we loop for each ball, create an object for it, and store information about that ball in its object. Notice that we are giving the balls no starting speeds. In lines 13–15 we assign starting velocities to the balls.

Then comes the following ActionScript:

```
1  function moveBalls() {
2      for (var i=1; i<=game.numBalls; ++i) {
3          var ob = game["ball"+i];
4          ob.tempx = ob.xpos+ob.xmov;
5          ob.tempy = ob.ypos+ob.ymov;
6      }
7  }
```

This function loops through the list of balls (in this case, just two) and updates their temporary positions in memory to their current positions plus their speed. We do not yet update the position of the actual movie clip on the stage. I encourage you to get into this habit of creating a temporary position of the movie clip in memory, because when we start dealing with collision reactions, we will update the temporary position of the movie clip (due to multiple collisions or forces) possibly several times before we actually place the movie clip on the stage.

Let's analyze an example. Imagine that you are coding a game in which a ball bounces off a wall. This ball may be moving very fast. Now imagine that on one frame the ball is not colliding with the wall, and on the next frame you detect that half of the ball is colliding with the wall. When this happens, you do not want to update that ball's position on the stage to show this. Rather, it is a good idea to update its position in memory to reflect where the ball *should* be and then render the ball on the screen. So, if it is detected that the ball is colliding with the wall (no matter how deep into the wall the ball is), then we should update the ball's position in memory so that the ball is just barely touching the wall. At the end of the frame, we render the ball on the screen, and it looks as if it is just barely touching the wall (which is what we want). In real life, a ball would not move past the wall boundary.

Next we create a function to render the balls onto the stage.

```
1   function renderBalls() {
2       for (var i=1; i<=game.numBalls; ++i) {
3           var ob = game["ball"+i];
4           ob.xpos = ob.tempx;
5           ob.ypos = ob.tempy;
6           ob.clip._x = ob.xpos;
7           ob.clip._y = ob.ypos;
8       }
9   }
```

This function simply sets the physical position of each movie clip using the value of the *x* and *y* position variables on the object, which are xpos and ypos.

Now (drum roll, please) we come to the function that handles the collision detection itself. It's a fairly large function, but it follows exactly what we discussed about the logic for determining the collisions.

```
1   function ballToBallDetection(b1, b2) {
2       //set the speed variables
3       var xmov1 = b1.xmov;
4       var ymov1 = b1.ymov;
5       var xmov2 = b2.xmov;
6       var ymov2 = b2.ymov;
7       //set the position variables
8       var xl1 = b1.xpos;
```

```
9      var yl1 = b1.ypos;
10     var xl2 = b2.xpos;
11     var yl2 = b2.ypos;
12     //define the constants
13     var R = b1.radius+b2.radius;
14     var a = -2*xmov1*xmov2+xmov1*xmov1+xmov2*xmov2;
15     var b = -2*xl1*xmov2-2*xl2*xmov1+2*xl1*xmov1+2*xl2*xmov2;
16     var c = -2*xl1*xl2+xl1*xl1+xl2*xl2;
17     var d = -2*ymov1*ymov2+ymov1*ymov1+ymov2*ymov2;
18     var e = -2*yl1*ymov2-2*yl2*ymov1+2*yl1*ymov1+2*yl2*ymov2;
19     var f = -2*yl1*yl2+yl1*yl1+yl2*yl2;
20     var g = a+d;
21     var h = b+e;
22     var k = c+f-R*R;
23     //solve the quadratic equation
24     var sqRoot = Math.sqrt(h*h-4*g*k);
25     var t1 = (-h+sqRoot)/(2*g);
26     var t2 = (-h-sqRoot)/(2*g);
27     if (t1>0 && t1<=1) {
28         var whatTime = t1;
29         var ballsCollided = true;
30     }
31     if (t2>0 && t2<=1) {
32         if (whatTime == null || t2<t1) {
33             var whatTime = t2;
34             var ballsCollided = true;
35         }
36     }
37     if (ballsCollided) {
38         //Collision has happened, so throw a trace
39         trace("Ouch!");
40     }
41 }
```

First we give the function a name, `ballToBallDetection`, and set two parameters, b1 and b2. When this function is called, the two objects will be passed in and represented by b1 and b2. In lines 2–11 we define the speed and position variables needed. Next, we define all of the constants in terms of the speed and position variables. The variable names match what we discussed earlier in this section.

With lines 24–26 we solve the quadratic equation. In line 24 we set a variable called sqRoot whose value is equal to the square-root term in our solution to the quadratic equation (remember that there are two solutions, both of which contain the same square-root term). We set this as a variable so that it can be reused for both solutions (lines 25 and 26). At this point, we have two times at which the balls will collide. What follows in the ActionScript (lines 27–36) is logic to determine if the time was in the past, the present, or the future. If the time is in the past or the present, then it is less than or equal to 1, and a collision has occurred. If the time is in the future (greater than 1), no collision has occurred. If a collision has occurred, then we store the time at which this collision happened (using the whatTime variable). We will use this information in Chapter 6, "Collision Reactions." Also, when a collision is detected, a variable called ballsCollided is set to true. When ballsCollided is true, a final if statement executes a trace action to let you know that a collision was detected.

Generate a SWF to see this work.

With this collision-detection script, you can determine when in the future a collision may happen. When you solve the quadratic equation for time1 and time2, it tells you any time in the future when the balls will intersect, even if it is a million frames into the future.

Looking more than one frame into the future is something I have not yet found a need for, but should a use come for it, we'll know how to do it!

Line-Line Collision Detection

In this section we will discuss the equations for lines and for line segments, and how to tell when lines are intersecting. I have never encountered a situation in which I needed a collision-detection script for two moving lines, so we will just cover detection for two stationary lines.

It may not be immediately obvious to you how—or where—this type of collision detection might come in handy. As an active member of many Flash user boards on the Internet, I frequently see the question of how to tell if two lines are intersecting. The most important application of this that we will see is in circle-line collision detection. One step in the process of detecting the collision of a circle and a line is to test to see if two lines are intersecting.

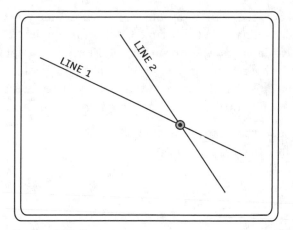

The Equation of a Line

Time once again to think back to your high school math class. You may remember this equation:

y = m*x+b

where *m* is the slope of the line, and *b* is the *y* intercept (the spot where the line intersects the *y*-axis). This is the equation for a straight line. The slope, *m,* is defined as the *rise* over the *run* of the line. For instance, if the line is at a 45° angle, then the rise of the line equals the run, so the slope is 1. If you have a line that is closer to horizontal, then its rise is less than the run, and therefore the slope is small—far less than 1. If the line is exactly horizontal, then the rise is 0, and therefore the slope is also 0.

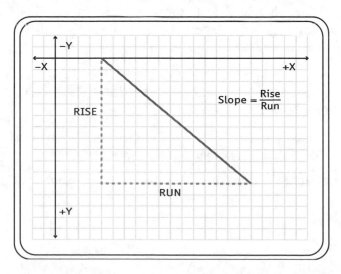

If you know the slope and y intercept of a line, then you can draw that line. Open draw_line.fla in the Chapter05 directory on the CD. You'll notice that there are no movie clips in this file. The ActionScript it contains builds an object that represents the properties of a line (its slope and y intercept) and then draws the line using two functions. Here are the first few lines of ActionScript in this file, which are used to build the object.

```
1   _root.createEmptyMovieClip("clip", 1);
2   clip.lineStyle(0, 0x000000, 100);
3   line1 = {};
4   line1.m = 1;
5   line1.b = 100;
```

In the first line we simply create an empty movie clip on the stage. The line that will be drawn using this ActionScript will be drawn in this movie clip.

It is a good programming practice to create a movie clip to hold lines drawn with Flash's dynamic drawing tools. Why? Because this procedure makes cleanup easier—you can just remove the movie clip when needed. For instance, if you create a drawing application (in which dynamically creating lines is a common occurrence), then you will most likely want a "clear screen" function. It is much easier to remove one movie clip that contains all of the drawn lines than to remove many individual lines. Also, if all the lines had been drawn on the main timeline, then the cleanup would be all the more difficult.

In line 2 we specify a line style for the movie clip. Before anything can be drawn in the movie clip, we have to inform Flash of how we would like it drawn. This method tells the movie clip that we want the line to be a hairline (which is a thickness of 0), the color to be black (which has a hex value of 0x000000), and the alpha value to be 100.

If you are interested in learning more about Flash MX's new drawing Application Programming Interface (API), check out the ActionScript Dictionary from the Help menu in Flash.

Lines 3–5 create an object called line1 that holds the variables m (for the slope of the line) and b (for the y intercept).

Next, we write two functions that work together to draw the line.

```
1   function findY(line, x) {
2       var y = line.m*x+line.b;
3       return y;
4   }
5   function drawLine(line) {
6       //Choose an x
7       var x = 300;
8       //Find the y
9       var y = findY(line, x);
10      //Move the pen
11      clip.moveTo(x, y);
12      //Choose another x
13      var x = 0;
14      //Find the y
15      var y = findY(line, x);
16      //Draw line
17      clip.lineTo(x, y);
18  }
19  drawLine(line1);
```

The function findY() was created to calculate the y position from the line object passed in and the x position (using the equation for the line $y = m*x+b$). After that, starting on line 5, we use the drawLine() function. You need two points to draw a line, of course, and so this function chooses two x positions, finds the appropriate y positions from those, and draws a line between this pair of points. On line 11 you see the moveTo() method. This method is used to move the starting position of the Flash "pen" to the coordinates passed in. (The Flash pen, sometimes called the virtual pen, is a place that you cannot see, with the coordinates (0,0), where Flash will start drawing if you were to call the drawing methods. The moveTo() method only moves the position of the pen—it draws no lines. There is a method called lineTo(), found in line 17, that handles drawing the line. It draws a line from the current pen position to the coordinates passed in. The final line is what calls the function. This function call passes in a line1 object reference to the drawLine() function. The drawLine() function then uses this reference to access information on the object.

It is important to note that all lines are infinite in length, although in this case we are showing only a portion of the line in question. A portion of a line is called a *line segment*.

Intersecting Lines

All lines that are not parallel to each other intersect at some point, and any two lines that have the same slope are parallel. So, to tell if two lines intersect, you simply compare their slopes. If the slopes are not equal, then they *do* intersect somewhere in space. In this section, we're going to learn how to find out at what coordinates any two lines intersect.

Slope 1 ≠ Slope 2; therefore they intersect at some point

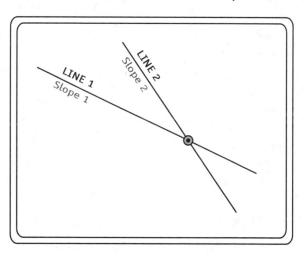

First, let's look for the point of intersection. Say we have two lines whose equations are

`y = m1*x+b1`

and

`y = m2*x+b2`

At the point where these two lines intersect, the *y* value (in the equations above) is the same, and the *x* (in the equations above) is the same. With this knowledge, we set the two equations equal and write:

`m1*x+b1 = m2*x+b2`

and we solve for *x* to get:

`x = (b2-b1)/(m1-m2)`

This is the *x* position at which the lines intersect. To find the *y* position, simply stick this *x* value back into either of the two line equations (I've chosen the first):

```
y = m1*x+b1
```

Open lines_intersecting.fla from the Chapter05 folder on the CD to see this in action. This file uses the same functions as we did in the previous example. Also, since we are now dealing with two lines, we have created a second `line` object. There is an instance of a movie clip on the stage called `dot` that, when calculated, will be moved to the point of intersection. Here is the function that calculates the intersection.

```
1  function findIntersection(line_a, line_b) {
2      var x = (line_b.b-line_a.b)/(line_a.m-line_b.m);
3      var y = line_a.m*x+line_a.b;
4      dot._x = x;
5      dot._y = y;
6  }
```

This function accepts two parameters, `line_a` and `line_b`, which are references to `line` objects. It then uses the equation we derived above to find the *x* position of the intersection. Once this *x* position is found, it is plugged into the equation for the line represented by the `line_a` object to find the *y* position. Then the dot movie clip is placed on the stage using these two values. When you test the movie, you will see that the dot appears over the intersection of the two lines.

Determining If Two Line Segments Are Intersecting

This is an easy extension of what we have already accomplished in this section. The technique we just introduced allows us to determine if two lines are intersecting. To do this, we find the coordinates of the intersection between these lines as if they were not segments, and then check to see if this point falls within the boundaries of each segment. It may not be obvious when something like this would be useful. Without thinking very hard, I can only come up with one common use, but it's a big one. It occurs when detecting a frame-independent collision between a circle and a line. This is covered in detail in the next section.

Lines intersect, but the segments do not; therefore there is no collision

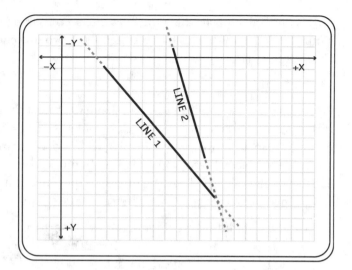

Lines intersect, and so do the segments; therefore a collision is occurring

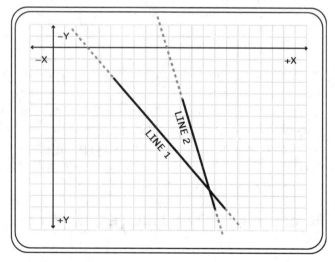

Open line_segments_intersecting.fla in the Chapter05 directory. After defining the objects that represent the lines in this file, we add two variables, x1 and x2, that are the boundaries of the line segment. I modified the drawLine() function from the same function in the previous example file to take the x1 and x2 boundaries of each line and to find the y1 and y2 boundaries from them. Here is the modified drawLine() function.

```
1    function drawLine(line) {
2        //Choose an x
3        var x = line.x1;
```

```
4      //Find the y
5      var y = findY(line, x);
6      line.y1 = y;
7      //Move the pen
8      clip.moveTo(x, y);
9      //Choose another x
10     var x = line.x2;
11     //Find the y
12     var y = findY(line, x);
13     line.y2 = y;
14     //Draw line
15     clip.lineTo(x, y);
16   }
```

In this function we move the pen to one boundary and then draw a line to the other boundary. The result is a visual representation of the line segment. After this function is called, the line object contains the x and y coordinates for both of the line-segment boundaries. Before this function is called, the line object only contains the x1 and x2 line boundaries. The y1 and y2 boundaries are calculated in this function, on lines 5 and 12, and then stored on the line object in lines 6 and 13.

The findIntersection() function also has a major addition for our current purposes—it now checks the point of intersection to see if it is within the segment boundaries on both lines. Here is the function:

```
1    function findIntersection(line_a, line_b) {
2        var x = (line_b.b-line_a.b)/(line_a.m-line_b.m);
3        var y = line_a.m*x+line_a.b;
4        dot._x = x;
5        dot._y = y;
6        if ((x>=line_a.x1 && x<=line_a.x2)
      → || (x<=line_a.x1 && x>=line_a.x2)
      → || (y>=line_a.y1 && y<=line_a.y2)
      → || (y<=line_a.y1 && y>=line_a.y2)) {
7            var segment_a = true;
8        }
9        if ((x>=line_b.x1 && x<=line_b.x2)
      → || (x<=line_b.x1 && x>=line_b.x2)
      → || (y>=line_b.y1 && y<=line_b.y2)
      → || (y<=line_b.y1 && y>=line_b.y2)) {
```

```
10          var segment_b = true;
11      }
12      if (segment_a && segment_b) {
13          trace("The lines are intersecting!!");
14      }
15  }
```

The first five lines of this function are identical to the `findIntersection()` function in the previous example. What follows in the remainder of the function are conditional statements that check to see if the intersection point is within the boundaries of the segments. Lines 6–8 check to see if the point is between the *x* boundaries or between the *y* boundaries of `line_a`. If it is, then the point lies on the segment. Lines 9–11 do the same thing as 6–8, but for `line_b`. If the point lies within the boundaries of both segments, then a `trace` action is executed, letting you know that an intersection has been encountered.

You might have expected to see a section on point-line collision detection before circle-line collision detection. I didn't include that technique for two reasons. First, in my experience, point-line collision detection is not very useful. Second, unless you are doing frame-independent collision detections, it's almost impossible that a point-line collision will ever be detected.

If you are really interested in point-line collisions, pay special attention to the final scripts developed in the next section. Using them, you'll be able to set the radius of a circle to 0, and thereby detect point-line collisions (a circle of radius 0 is a point).

Circle-Line Collision Detection

In this section we discuss frame-independent circle-line collision detection. This operation has direct application to any game that involves a ball bouncing off (or rolling down) a banked wall or hill—games like pinball and miniature golf.

We begin by discussing the logic needed to detect a collision between a circle and a line. We are assuming that the line is stationary and the circle is moving. We are also assuming that a collision is not yet taking place when detection begins (so if the ball is colliding with the line when the script starts, then the script will fail). In the previous section we developed a way to determine where two lines intersect. We will use that here as well. A ball in motion builds an imaginary line as it moves (its trajectory). We determine where this line of trajectory and the main line intersect. Once this is found, we use trigonometry to figure out the precise spot at which the circle collides with the line. Then we find the point of collision on the line (where the circle touches the line). Finally, we look at the current position of the circle and figure out how long it will take for the circle to reach the collision point. If this result is less than or equal to one frame, then a collision has occurred.

To recap, this is the process of frame-independent circle-line collision detection more concisely:

1. *Determine the intersection point between the path of the circle and the line.*

2. *Use trigonometry to find the coordinates of the circle when it initially collides with the line.*

3. *Find the coordinates of the point of collision on the line itself.*

4. *Calculate the number of frames it takes for the circle to move from its current position to this collision position. If this number is less than or equal to 1, then a collision has occurred.*

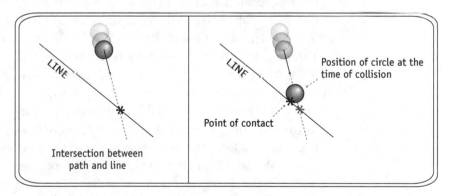

You have already seen how to accomplish what is in steps 1 and 4, in the sections above. So before dissecting an example FLA file, let's look at how to accomplish what is in steps 2 and 3.

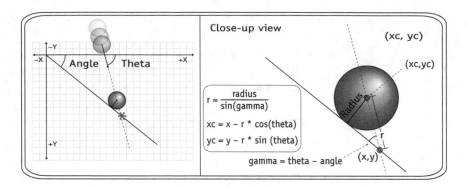

The results of step 1 show us where the path of the circle intersects the line. This intersection point is where the center of the circle would touch the line if it were to make it this far along the path. (After we add collision reactions in the next chapter, the circle will not make it this far; it will have reacted and rebounded when its edge touched the line.) As you can see, this is not the point at which a collision first occurs. If you were to take the circle and slide it backward along its path until only one point intersected with the line, then you would have found the collision point. We can find this point using trigonometry. A right triangle is formed by the radius of the circle; the segment of the circle's path between the line-line intersection and the collision point; and the piece of the line that is between these two intersections.

The angle gamma in the image above is the difference between the angle of the path of the ball and the angle of the line. Our goal in this step is to find the position of the circle when it first touches the line. Remember, we're going to find this position by using some trigonometry. Be sure to look at the image above to help you understand the relationships between the values we're using. The length of the path segment, r, is equivalent to *radius/sin(gamma)*. We find this relationship by inspecting the right triangle and using the projection information discussed in Chapter 3, "Trigonometry 101." This relationship tells us the length of that line segment. With that information, we can use trigonometry again to find the position of the circle. The x position of the circle at first collision is the x position of the line intersection of the path and line minus *r*cos(theta)*. And the y position of the circle at the first collision is the y position of the line intersection of the path and line minus *r*sin(theta)*. (Theta is the angle that the path of the ball makes with the x-axis.)

In step 3, we are looking for the actual point where the circle touches the line—the point of contact. In the previous step we found the point where the circle is when it touches the line, but not actually the point on the circle that touches the line. To find this point, we must imagine a line drawn from the center of the circle through the point of contact. This is a line perpendicular to the line with which we are colliding. We then find the intersection between these two lines. This point is what we are looking for. We can compare this point with the boundaries of the line segment to determine if the collision happened.

There is only one thing we have not discussed in how to create the perpendicular line—the equation for that line. We know the equation for the main line (it is stored in the line object), and we know that this new line is perpendicular to the main line. A line perpendicular to another line has a slope that is the negative inverse of it. So if the main line has a slope of 3, then all lines perpendicular to it have a slope of $-\frac{1}{3}$.

All perpendicular lines to this have a slope of $-\frac{1}{3}$

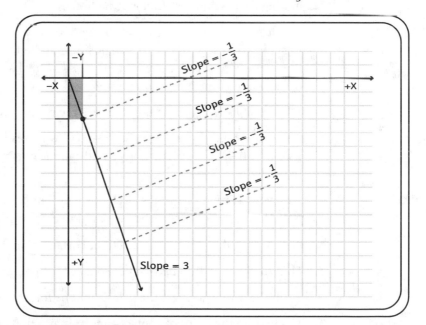

Wow—there are a lot of steps to this, but the result is something cool: frame-independent collision detection! Let's look at an example. Open circle_line.fla from the Chapter05 folder on the CD. There are two movie clips on the stage. One of them has an instance name of ball1 and will be the movie clip that represents a circle. The other movie clip does not have (or need) an instance name. It is there so that we can use `attachMovie()` to create new instances of it. It will contain a line that will be drawn using ActionScript. There is a lot of ActionScript in this file, more than 100 lines. We are going to focus on describing the ActionScript in the `getFrame()` function. But first, here is an overview of all the ActionScript for this example of circle-line collision detection.

- An object called `ball` is created to hold information about ball1.

- A function is created to make it easy to create lines on the stage. An object is created for each line to store information about that line.

- A function called `getTempPositions()` is created. This function is not yet necessary for what we're going to do with this file. However, when you later add gravity and collision reactions, this function will be more useful. Its duty is to create a temporary position in memory of all moving objects. It was built to handle updating positions due to gravitational, wind, or other external forces.

- A function called `render()` takes the temporary position of each moving object and sets that as the real position. It then physically places the movie clips on the screen. In this file we only have one moving object, so the function is quite simple and short.

- A function called `getFrames()` handles the collision detection.

- A function called `bankCollisionDetect()` was created to loop through all the lines on the screen and call the `getFrames()` function for each line.

- An `onEnterFrame` event calls `getTempPositions()`, `bankCollisionDetect()`, and `render()` in every frame.

Now let's look at the `getFrame()` function. This function does several things:

1. Finds the intersection between the path of the ball and the line.

2. Finds the position where the ball should be for initial contact.

3. Determines the point of contact and compares that with the boundaries of the line segment.

4. Calculates the number of frames it will take for the ball to reach the collision point.

Steps 3 and 4 are not dependent on each other, and in this function they swap places. Here is the ActionScript for step 1.

```
1    function getFrames(tempLine, point) {
2        //Step 1
3        var slope2 = point.ymov/point.xmov;
4        if (slope2 == Number.POSITIVE_INFINITY) {
5            var slope2 = 1000000;
6        } else if (slope2 == Number.NEGATIVE_INFINITY) {
7            var slope2 = -1000000;
8        }
9        //The y intercept of the ball trajectory
10       var b2 = point.y-slope2*point.x;
11       //intersection point
12       var x = (b2-tempLine.b)/(tempLine.slope-slope2);
13       var y = tempLine.slope*x+tempLine.b;
```

In this step we search for the intersection between the path of the ball and the line. The slope of the path of the ball is its *rise* over its *run*. Notice lines 4–8. If the ball has no speed in the *x* direction (xmov=0), then the slope is either infinity or –infinity. But since our calculations break down at infinity and –infinity (and nowhere else), we add some simple conditional logic that sets the slope to either 1,000,000 or –1,000,000 if infinity or –infinity, respectively, was detected. (We use 1,000,000 because it is a high enough number that our collision detection will be accurate, but not high enough to make the calculations fail.) Lines 9–13 should look familiar by now—they are what determine the intersection between the two lines.

Now we move on to the ActionScript for step 2.

```
1        //Step 2
2        //The angle that the ball is moving
3        var theta = Math.atan2(point.ymov, point.xmov);
4        //The difference between the angle of the line and
         → of the ball trajectory
5        var gamma = theta-tempLine.angle;
6        //modify x and y
7        var sinGamma = Math.sin(gamma);
8        var r = point.radius/sinGamma;
```

```
9      //The ball's position at point of contact
10     var x = x-r*Math.cos(theta);
11     var y = y-r*Math.sin(theta);
```

In this step we want to find out where the ball should be (its *x* and *y* positions) when it first collides with the line. We do this by using the trigonometry described earlier. The variable names are the same as described before and match the figure. Lines 10 and 11 give us what we're looking for.

We perform step 4 next, before step 3. Here is the ActionScript for this step.

```
1      //Step 4
2      var dis = Math.sqrt((x-point.x)*(x-point.x)
       ⇥ +(y-point.y)*(y-point.y));
3      var vel = Math.sqrt(point.xmov*point.xmov
       ⇥ +point.ymov*point.ymov);
4      var frames = dis/vel
```

This step is refreshingly short. Here we calculate the number of frames it will take the ball to get from its current position to the point at which it is colliding with the line. Thinking back to the chapter on basic physics, we remember that *distance = velocity*frames*. If we solve this equation for frames, we get *frames = distance/velocity*. So if we find the distance between the current position and the collision point, and the velocity along that line, then we can find the number of frames it takes to get there! In line 2 we employ the Pythagorean theorem yet again to obtain the distance. In line 3 we use that same theorem one more time, to find the velocity along the path. Finally, in line 4, we get the number of frames by taking the ratio of distance and velocity.

To see a more detailed representation of how the time (frames) can be found, see line_ball_time_calculation.pdf in the Chapter05 directory.

In step 4 we check the physical point of contact to see if it is within the boundaries of the line segment.

```
1      //Step 3
2      //now check to see if point of contact is on the line
       ⇥ segment
3      var slope2a = -1/tempLine.slope;
4      var b2a = y-slope2a*x;
5      //point of contact
6      var xa = (tempLine.b-b2a)/(slope2a-tempLine.slope);
```

```
7     var ya = slope2a*xa+b2a;
8     if ((xa>tempLine.x1 && xa<tempLine.x2)
      → || (xa<tempLine.x1 && xa>tempLine.x2)
      → || ((ya>tempLine.y1 && ya<tempLine.y2)
      → || (ya<tempLine.y1 && ya>tempLine.y2))) {
9         //within segment boundaries
10    } else {
11        //not within segment boundaries
12        //set frame1 high
13        var frames = 1000;
14    }
15    return frames;
```

To find the coordinates of the point of contact, we imagine a line drawn through the center of the circle and the point of contact. The goal is to find the slope and y intercept of this line (which means we know everything about it) and then, with that information, to see where this line intersects with the main line. This intersection is the point of contact. We know the slope of the main line, and we know that all lines perpendicular to it have a slope that is the negative inverse of its own. Line 3 shows how we find the slope of the imaginary line. Remembering that the equation for a line is $y = m*x+b$ and remembering that we have the coordinates for one point on that line (the center of the circle), we can plug in the x, y, and m (slope) values to find b (the y intercept). Line 4 shows this. Now we have all the information we need about both lines, so we can find the intersection between them. Lines 6 and 7 obtain the coordinates of the line intersection using the technique we have used a few times now. This code block ends with a conditional statement that compares this point (the intersection) with the boundaries of the line segment. If the point falls within the boundaries, then nothing happens. If this point (which is the intersection between the two lines) does not fall within the segment boundaries, then a collision did not happen and so frames is set to 1000 (something high). If the frames variable value is less than or equal to 1 and the point of contact was within the boundaries of the line segment, then the collision is valid. The last line of code above returns the frames variable as the result of the function. The function that called the getFrames() function, bankCollisionDetect(), has the frames returned to it and can then check to see if the frames are less than or equal to 1.

We will see this again in the next chapter, *Collision Reactions*. You are on your way to creating a game with advanced techniques!

Point-Rectangle Collision Detection

After what you have seen in this chapter so far, what remains is very simple to understand and apply. (We will not be including frame-independent collision-detection scripts in this or the next section.)

Since this is not frame-independent collision detection, point-rectangle collision detection is like taking snapshots in time. And if the point is going fast enough, it can move through the rectangle without a collision being detected.

The logic for detecting a collision between a point and a rectangle is simple. The position of the point is compared with the position of each wall of the rectangle. If the point's *x* position is greater than the *x* position of the left wall and less than the *x* position of the rectangle's right wall, and the point's *y* position is greater than the *y* position of the top wall (remember that the *y*-axis is inverted in Flash) and less than the *y* position of the bottom wall, then a collision is occurring.

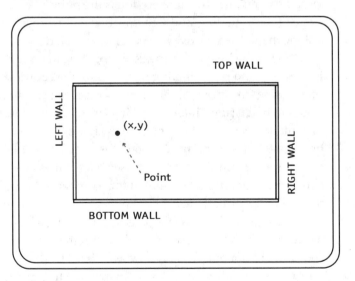

Open point_rectangle.fla to see an example. There are two movie clips on the stage, point_clip1 and rectangle_clip1. The ActionScript creates an object to store the information for the point and for the rectangle. Then, in every frame, the point is moved, and a check is performed to detect collisions. Here is the ActionScript used to create the objects.

```
1   //Create an object to store information about point_clip1
2   point1 = {};
3   point1.clip = point_clip1;
4   point1.x = point1.clip._x;
5   point1.y = point1.clip._y;
6   point1.xmov = 3;
7   point1.ymov = 1;
8   //Create an object to store information about rectangle_clip1
9   rectangle1 = {};
10  rectangle1.clip = rectangle_clip1;
11  rectangle1.x = rectangle1.clip._x;
12  rectangle1.y = rectangle1.clip._y;
13  rectangle1.width = rectangle1.clip._width;
14  rectangle1.height = rectangle1.clip._height;
```

You have seen this many times by now. We create an object for each movie clip on the stage to store information about that movie clip. Notice that for the rectangle we are storing its position (its registration point is at the upper-left corner) as well as its width and height. Next in the ActionScript are two functions, one for creating a temporary position of the point in memory and the other to position the movie clip on the stage. We will not list these functions here, since they are identical to what we have seen several times already. Here is pointRectangleDetection(), the function that detects collisions between the point and the rectangle.

```
1   function pointRectangleDetection(point, rectangle) {
2       //position of the point
3       var x = point.x;
4       var y = point.y;
5       //left and right walls
6       var x1 = rectangle.x;
7       var x2 = x1+rectangle.width;
8       //top and bottom walls
9       var y1 = rectangle.y;
10      var y2 = y1+rectangle.height;
11      //check to see if the point is within all of the walls
12      if (x>x1 && x<x2 && y>y1 && y<y2) {
13          trace("Collision Detected!!");
14      }
15  }
```

This function accepts two parameters, `point` and `rectangle`, which are references to two objects. First, two variables are created that represent the position of the point. Then in lines 6–10, the x and y positions of the walls are assigned to variables. Finally, in line 12, a conditional is started that checks to see if the x position of the point is greater than the left wall but less than the right wall, and that the y position of the point is greater than the top wall and less than the bottom wall. If this condition is met, then a collision is occurring, and a `trace` action is executed. Finally (although this is not shown above), an `onEnterFrame` event calls `getTempPositions()`, `pointRectangleDetection()`, and `render()` in every frame.

Rectangle-Rectangle Collision Detection

Like point-rectangle collision detection, collision detection between two rectangles is easy to perform. `Rectangle_a` is colliding with `rectangle_b` if all of the following are true:

1. The x position of the right wall of `rectangle_a` is greater than the x position of the left wall of `rectangle_b`.

2. The x position of the left wall of `rectangle_a` is less than the x position of the right wall of `rectangle_b`.

3. The y position of the bottom wall of `rectangle_a` is greater than the y position of the top wall of `rectangle_b`.

4. The y position of the top wall of `rectangle_a` is less than the y position of the bottom wall of `rectangle_b`.

They are colliding!

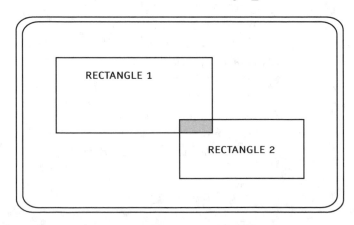

RECTANGLE 1

RECTANGLE 2

To see an example, open rectangle_rectangle.fla from the Chapter05 directory on the CD. The ActionScript in this file is very similar to the previous example, so we will only discuss the function that handles collision detection, RectangleRectangleDetection(). Here is the ActionScript:

```
1   function RectangleRectangleDetection(rectangle_a,
      rectangle_b) {
2       //left and right walls
3       var x_a1 = rectangle_a.x;
4       var x_a2 = x_a1+rectangle_a.width;
5       //top and bottom walls
6       var y_a1 = rectangle_a.y;
7       var y_a2 = y_a1+rectangle_a.height;
8       //left and right walls
9       var x_b1 = rectangle_b.x;
10      var x_b2 = x_b1+rectangle_b.width;
11      //top and bottom walls
12      var y_b1 = rectangle_b.y;
13      var y_b2 = y_b1+rectangle_b.height;
14      //check to see if the point is within all of the walls
15      if ((x_a2>x_b1 && x_a1<x_b2) && (y_a2>y_b1 && y_a1<y_b2))
16      {
17          trace("Collision Detected!!");
18      }
19  }
```

This function accepts two parameters, rectangle_a and rectangle_b, which are references to objects. In lines 2–14, we set variables to store the positions of the left, right, top, and bottom walls of both rectangles. Then, in line 15, an if statement uses the logic we mentioned above to determine if a collision is taking place. It compares the positions of the walls in rectangle_a with the positions of the walls in rectangle_b. If the condition is met, then the rectangles are colliding and a trace action is executed.

COLLISION DETECTION WITH ADVANCED SHAPES

In this chapter we have developed frame-independent collision-detection logic and scripts for circle-line collisions (or point-line collisions, if you set the radius to 0). This is much more powerful than you might realize. With this knowledge, you can create simple or complicated shapes without any extra-fancy math. For instance, think of an octagon. Ordinarily you might not know how to detect a collision between a circle and an octagon. Well, why not put eight lines together and run a detection script for each of those lines? Suddenly, circle-octagon collision detection is a very easy thing! The shape in question doesn't have to be regular, either; you can create a star shape, a triangle, or even the shape of a house; the detection works because each line is treated separately.

Many shapes can be created with line segments. Collision detection is performed on each line segment separately.

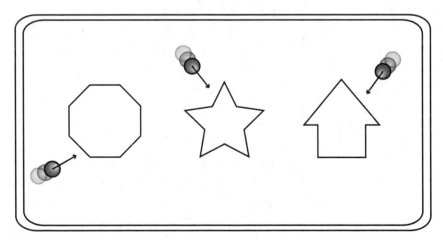

There is one problem you may encounter: multiple collisions at once. Imagine a rectangle shape and a ball colliding with the corner. It is likely that your script will detect two separate collisions. This is fine if you just want to know if a collision took place, but if you want to use a collision *reaction* (covered in the next chapter), then which line should the circle react to? The answer is simple: Keep track of the `frames` variable for each collision. The lowest one is the collision that occurred first. You can then make the circle react to the appropriate collision.

If you are interested in developing your own collision-detection scripts for shapes not covered here (for instance, point-ellipse collisions), follow this simple formula:

1. *List the conditions that must be met for a collision to take place.*

2. *Figure out how to determine if each condition is met.*

You may have to pick up a book on geometry or trigonometry if you are looking for the equations that define more complicated objects such as ellipses or toroids (doughnut shapes). See Appendix E for book suggestions.

Collision detection is a fundamental requirement for most games, however simple they may be. With what you've learned in this chapter, you can detect collisions between almost any two objects. Combine all this knowledge with what you'll gain in the next chapter, and you will soon be creating advanced games like pinball and billiards!

POINTS TO REMEMBER

- A collision occurs when two separate shapes share one or more points in space.

- In Flash you can use two main types of programmatic collision detection: `hitTest()` and math.

- Using math is considered the superior method of collision detection because in addition to confirming detections in the present, you may also be able to use it to determine the future time and location of a collision.

- Limitations of `hitTest()` include its limited abilities with complex shapes, its close relationship to specific graphics or movie clips, and its dependence on frame rates.

- Code-graphics independence is a liberating method of working with movie clips. It uses objects to store information about each movie clip. Storing information in an object—separate from its actual interface element—is a good practice because it allows you to add or remove movie clips from the stage without losing the data.

- You can use the Linkage feature to enable ActionScript to create an unlimited number of new instances of any kind of symbol (not just movie clips) in the Flash file's library.

- Loops are an immeasurably helpful tool to use with ActionScript, especially when your work involves performing identical tasks on a number of elements such as movie clips.

- Using math for collision detection also allows you to work with irregular shapes, write frame-independent collision-detection scripts, and handle all of the code in memory, rather than basing it on the placement of the graphics.

- The frame-independent collision-detection logic (and scripts) that you've learned here can be applied to the creation of any other simple or complicated shapes by breaking them down into lines.

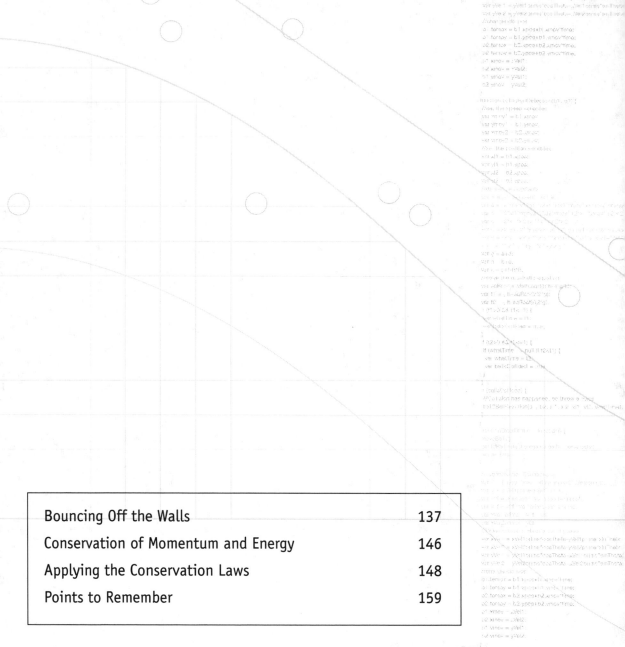

CHAPTER 6

COLLISION REACTIONS

THIS IS THE CHAPTER IN WHICH THINGS REALLY START TO COME TOGETHER. You will be applying many ideas you learned from previous chapters. In Chapter 4, "Basic Physics," you learned the concepts and equations needed to move movie clips around the screen. With the added concepts of gravity and friction you were able to add even more realism to a programmed system. In Chapter 5, "Collision Detection," you learned how to detect collisions between many types of objects—some moving, some not. The logical next step is to learn the physics and equations involved in making objects (movie clips) react to a collision in a physically realistic way. In this chapter we will look at several useful examples of collision reactions. For a few of them, we'll also learn about (and apply) the laws of conservation of momentum and energy. By the end of this chapter you will be able to program billiard-ball collisions, a box or a ball bouncing off a floor or wall, and even a ball bouncing off an angled line! Suddenly games like pinball, pool, and air hockey won't seem quite as mysterious.

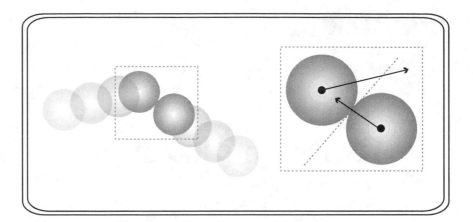

I've divided the collision types we'll cover in this chapter into four loosely connected categories:

- **Object-wall collision reactions.** This type of reaction should occur when an object like a circle or a rectangle collides with a wall or a floor.

- **Circle-line collision reactions.** This type of reaction occurs when a circle collides with an angled line (for example, in pinball physics).

- **Rectangle-rectangle collision reactions.** This type of reaction occurs when two rectangular objects collide straight on (no rotation).

- **Circle-circle collision reactions.** This type of reaction occurs when two circles (for example, billiard balls) collide at any angle.

We are sticking to these collision reactions for several reasons. The main reason is that most other collision detections do not need a physical reaction. For instance, a point collision with a balloon will most likely result in an animation of a balloon popping, not a programmed reaction. The intersection between two lines is usually used to determine something bigger, like the collision between a ball and a line, so we do not attempt to program any reaction for two lines intersecting.

Another reason why we're only covering a few types of collision detection and reactions is that it's often a good idea to assume that simpler shapes are being used. If your game involves throwing a baseball at a watermelon, then instead of developing specified circle-ellipse collision-detection techniques, it would be faster to assume that the watermelon is a circle (or even a rectangle). The collision detection will be good enough, and the script will run faster than if you were detecting a more complicated shape. This corner-cutting technique is used in almost every major computer game on the market. For instance, in Tomb Raider, the main character is assumed to be a cylinder, rather than a person with complicated proportions. (Betcha didn't know that, did you?) This geometric approximation makes the collision detection much easier without sacrificing much.

BOUNCING OFF THE WALLS

A wall is any object that cannot move as a result of a collision, but that can be collided with. For instance, if you throw a tennis ball at a wall, the wall does not move, but it certainly gets hit! By this definition, even the paddles in a simple game of Pong are considered walls. In that case, they are walls that can move, but their movement is not the result of a collision. In this section we'll look at collisions with walls, and collisions with lines of any angle, which are often used as walls. (Later in this chapter we'll work with the less stationary objects.)

Object-Wall Reactions

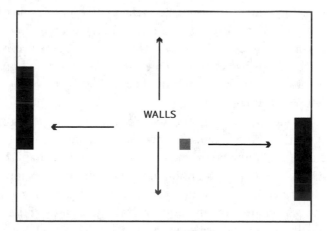

WALLS

An object-wall collision (affectionately called *ball-wall*) is the easiest type of collision to program a reaction for. Think of the tennis-ball example again. When the tennis ball bounces off the wall, it rebounds at the same speed at which it struck the wall. (Since this is an elastic collision—more on that later—there's no energy lost in the collision, and therefore no loss in speed.) This is good news for us, because it means that when we detect a collision with a wall, we can just reverse the object's speed. Note that we would only reverse the speed component that is perpendicular to the wall, as shown in the image below.

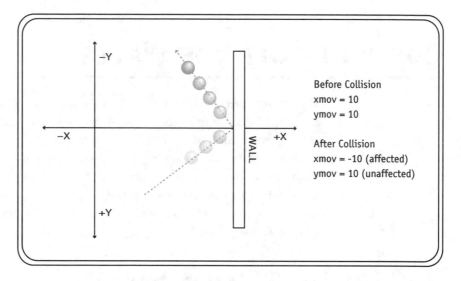

Let's look at a practical example of this. Open pong1.fla in the Chapter06 directory. This is an unfinished version of a very simple game, Pong. In Pong, a ball moves across the screen, and it is up to you to keep it from leaving the screen on your side (the left). There are two paddles on the screen that move vertically. One paddle is on the left boundary of the game area, and the other is on the right boundary of the game area. The left paddle is controlled by the user (that's you), and the right paddle is controlled by the computer using a simple AI script (discussed in Chapter 9, "Artificial Intelligence"). There is an instance of a ball movie clip on the stage (within the board movie clip); it's a square shape, but it's still called a ball. The registration point for this movie clip is its top-left boundary. There is collision detection between the ball and the paddles, and between the ball and the top and bottom of the game area. If the ball collides with a paddle, then its *x* speed is reversed. If the ball collides with the top or bottom of the game area, then its *y* speed is reversed.

We are not going to discuss most of the ActionScript in this file. Rather, we are going to focus on the areas where collision reactions are used. If you have read through the previous chapters on collision detection and physics, then you are familiar with just about all of the ActionScript in this file. What may be new to you are two things:

1. The `game.gameAI()` method (which will be discussed in Chapter 9).

2. The manner in which the methods were created. All of the methods were created on the game object itself, rather than in the timeline. This is not a necessity, but it brings us a little bit closer to coding in an object-oriented way.

A function that belongs to an object is called a *method*. This is just a terminology shift; there is really no substantive difference between the two. Like many people whose first programming language is ActionScript, I often use the terminology incorrectly. I sometimes say "method" when I mean "function," or the other way around. Wasn't it Shakespeare who said, "That which we call a function by any other name would still process data"?

In this particular file, collision reaction is implemented in every place where a collision-detection script sits. We check for collisions in the methods `game.checkForWalls()` and `game.checkPaddleCollisions()`. Here is the ActionScript for the `game.checkForWalls()` method:

```
1   game.checkForWalls = function() {
2       if (this.ball.tempy<0) {
3           //hit top wall
4           this.ball.tempy = 0;
5           this.ball.ymov *= -1;
6       } else if (this.ball.tempy+this.ball.radius>this.height) {
7           //this bottom wall
8           this.ball.tempy = this.height-this.ball.radius;
9           this.ball.ymov *= -1;
10      }
11  };
```

If you remember from the previous chapters, we usually create a temporary position in memory describing where an object will be, `tempx` and `tempy`. We use this temporary position to check for collisions. The upper boundary of the game board is 0; the lower boundary is `game.height`. In line 2 of the ActionScript above, we check to see if `ball.tempy` is less than 0. If it is, then a collision is occurring with the top wall, and the `if` statement is entered. Line 4 sets `ball.tempy = 0,` which positions the ball right up against the top wall. This is a necessary step. Due to the frame-based nature of Flash MX, `ball.tempy` could be substantially less than 0, and if we did not set it right up against the boundary and we only reversed the speed when a collision occurred, then it would look as if the ball went into the wall rather than bouncing off the wall. In line 5 we finally perform the very simple collision reaction: We reverse the *y* speed of the ball.

The `else if` piece of the conditional statement, in line 6, checks to see if the *y* position of the ball's bottom edge is greater than the *y* position of the game's lower boundary. (The bottommost part of the ball is its *y* position plus its height.) You may recall that the value for the *y* position of the game's bottom boundary was set earlier in the frame as game.height. Since the checkForWalls() method belongs to the game object, then we can access this property by using this.height, which we do in line 6. If this condition is satisfied, then we know the ball is colliding with the bottom wall, and we enter this piece of the if statement (lines 7–9). In line 8 we set the position of the ball so that it sits right up against the bottom wall. We do this for the same reason as we did it for the top wall—so the ball doesn't look as if it has gone through the wall. In line 9 we reverse the ball's *y* speed; this is our collision reaction.

Now let's look at the game.checkPaddleCollisions() method:

```
1   game.checkPaddleCollisions = function() {
2       if (this.ball.tempx
        <this.leftPaddle.x+this.leftPaddle.width
        && this.ball.tempx+this.ball.radius
        >this.leftPaddle.x
        && this.ball.tempy+this.ball.radius
        >this.leftPaddle.y && this.ball.tempy
        <this.leftPaddle.y+this.leftPaddle.height) {
3           //left paddle collision detection
4           this.ball.tempx = this.leftPaddle.x
            +this.leftPaddle.width;
5           this.ball.xmov *= -1;
6       }
7       if (this.ball.tempx
        <this.rightPaddle.x+this.rightPaddle.width
        && this.ball.tempx+this.ball.radius
        >this.rightPaddle.x
        && this.ball.tempy+this.ball.radius
        >this.rightPaddle.y && this.ball.tempy
        <this.rightPaddle.y+this.rightPaddle.height) {
8           //right paddle collision detection
9           this.ball.tempx = this.rightPaddle.x
            -this.ball.radius;
10          this.ball.xmov *= -1;
11      }
12  };
```

In this ActionScript, the if statements look complicated, but the concept here is one that you have already used in the Collision Detection chapter, when we talked about rectangle-rectangle collision detection. They are each simply checking for a collision between two rectangles—the ball and a paddle. We saw how to perform rectangle-rectangle collision detections in the previous chapter. Here, we check for the following conditions:

• The left side of the ball has a smaller x than the right side of the paddle.

• The right side of the ball has a greater x than the left side of the paddle.

• The top side of the ball has a smaller y than the bottom side of the paddle.

• The bottom side of the ball has a greater y than the top side of the paddle.

If all four of the above conditions are met, then a collision has occurred between the ball and the paddle. This check is done in exactly the same way in lines 2 and 7: once for the left paddle and once for the right paddle. If the condition in line 2 is met, then the ball is colliding with the paddle, and lines 4 and 5 are executed. Line 5 positions the ball so that it is just barely touching the paddle on the right side. Line 5 reverses the ball's x speed. Likewise, if the condition in line 7 is met, then the ball is placed so that it is just barely touching the paddle on the right, and its speed is reversed.

Keep in mind that we are not using frame-independent collision detection here. This means that if you were to take this young game and try to make it into a full-grown game in which the ball gets steadily faster, then you might encounter the typical "snapshot" collision-detection problems. So if the ball is moving fast enough, it may move straight through a paddle. You can, if you choose, use the ball-line collision-detection scripts developed in the previous chapter for each wall of the paddles. This would give you frame-independent Pong.

Now let's look at another example: a ball falling under gravity and bouncing off a floor. Open ball_floor.fla in the Chapter06 directory. On the stage you see the movie-clip instances ball_clip and floor_clip. The ActionScript in this file creates an object called ball to store information about ball_clip, sets a temporary position for the ball, checks for a collision with the floor, and renders the ball. If the script detects a collision between the ball and the floor, then the ball is set to be touching the floor, and its speed is reversed. There is one added feature involved in this process that has not yet been introduced: *decay*. In this example, a variable called decay is set with a value of .6. Here is the ActionScript for the collision-detection function.

```
1    function ballFloorDetection() {
2        if (ball.tempy+ball.radius>floorY) {
3            ball.tempy = floorY-ball.radius;
4            ball.ymov *= -1*decay;
5        }
6    }
```

If a collision is happening, then the ball's speed is reversed and multiplied by the variable decay. Decay is a way to have the ball bounce less high on each successive bounce; it lowers the magnitude of the speed by a percentage each time a collision happens. All decay values are between 0 and 1. For instance, in this file we are using a decay of .6 (set at the top of the frame, not shown here). That means each successive bounce will rebound with only 60 percent of the speed with which it collided in the first place.

The possible values for decay are all positive numbers (including zero), but the realistic range is between 0 and 1. If decay is set to 0, then the ball will stick to the ground. If decay is set to 1, then the ball will bounce to the same height forever. If the decay is set to a value greater than 1, the ball will bounce higher on each successive bounce (which is no longer a decay). When you generate a SWF from this file, you'll see that the ball will bounce a few times and then stop. This mimics the behavior of a regular old basketball. The goal of this chapter is to show you how to program realistic reactions. Adding a decay factor is one easy way to add realism to your floor or wall collision reactions.

Circle-Line Reactions

Circle-line, or ball-line, reactions occur when a ball collides with a line at any angle (such as the angled walls in a game of pinball). There are three steps to finding the resultant *x* and *y* velocities of a ball after a collision with a line:

1. ***Project the x and y velocities onto the line of action (for example, the line, or the bank, if you're still thinking pinball).***

When two objects collide, the momentum affected is the component that lies along the *line of action*—the imaginary line that runs perpendicular to the tangent line that goes through the point of collision.

2. *Reverse the velocity that lies along the line of action. This is done because the only piece of the velocity affected by the collision is the one that lies along the line of action. The velocity that lies along the "real" line (the one that the ball collides with) is unaffected by the collision.*

3. *Project the velocities that are along the line and the line of action back onto the x and y axes. This gives us the final result we were looking for: the x and y velocities after the collision.*

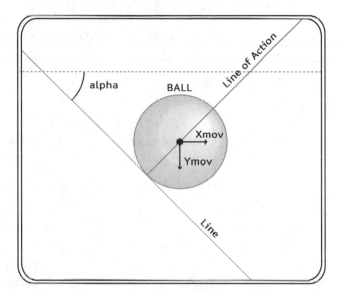

Project xmov and ymov onto line of action and the line.

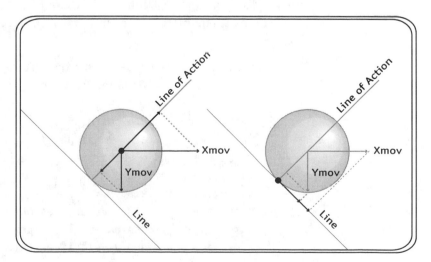

Now that you've seen the quick overview of how to find those velocities, we'll jump in and go through it step by step. Let's call the *x* velocity of the ball *vxi* (*v* for "velocity," *x* for "*x* direction," *i* for "initial") and the *y* velocity of the ball *vyi*. The projection of *vxi* and *vyi* onto the line of action is *vyip* (*p* stands for "prime"):

```
vyip = vyi*cos(alpha)-vxi*sin(alpha)
```

The projection of *vxi* and *vyi* onto the line itself is *vxip*.

```
vxip = vxi*cos(alpha)+vyi*sin(alpha)
```

Now that step 1 is complete, we move on to step 2 and reverse *vyip* (remember that *f* stands for "final").

```
vyfp = -vyip
vxfp = vxip
```

Notice that the final velocity along the line *(vxfp)* is unchanged. Now we move on to step 3 to project *vyfp* and *vxfp* back to the *x* and *y* axes to arrive at the final velocities, *vxf* and *vyf*.

```
vxf = vxfp*cos(alpha)-vyfp*sin(alpha)
vyf = vyfp*cos(alpha)+vxfp*sin(alpha)
```

These two values, *vxf* and *vyf*, are the *x* and *y* velocities of the ball at the moment after the collision. Using this in ActionScript is not difficult. Let's take a look at an example. Open the file ball_line.fla in the Chapter06 directory. The ActionScript in this file is very similar to that in the ball_line.fla file you saw in Chapter 5, "Collision Detection." The main addition to the ActionScript in this file is the function ballLineReaction(). Here is that function:

```
1    function ballLineReaction(tempLine, point, x, y) {
2        var lineDecay = tempLine.lineDecay;
3        var alpha = tempLine.angle;
4        var cosAlpha = math.cos(alpha);
5        var sinAlpha = math.sin(alpha);
6        //get the x and y velocities of the ball
7        var vyi = point.ymov;
8        var vxi = point.xmov;
9        //project the x and y velocities onto the line of action
10       var vyip = vyi*cosAlpha-vxi*sinAlpha;
11       //project the x and y velocities onto the line
```

```
12      var vxip = vxi*cosAlpha+vyi*sinAlpha;
13      //reverse the velocity along the line of action
14      var vyfp = -vyip*lineDecay;
15      var vxfp = vxip;
16      //translate back to Flash's x and y axes
17      var vyf = vyfp*cosAlpha+vxfp*sinAlpha;
18      var vxf = vxfp*cosAlpha-vyfp*sinAlpha;
19      //set the velocities of the ball based from the results
20      point.xmov = vxf;
21      point.ymov = vyf;
22      point.tempx = point.x+point.xmov;
23      point.tempy = point.y+point.ymov;
24  }
```

This function is called from the getFrames() function when a collision has been detected. A reference to the line object is passed in as tempLine, and a reference to the object that represents the ball is passed in as point. The x and y positions of the ball at the point of contact are also passed into this function. Line 2 sets a variable called lineDecay. This is a value between 0 and 1 that reduces the rebound velocity. (The concept of decay was introduced earlier in this chapter. If decay has a value of 1, then there is no decay.) Next we set variables to store the cosine and sine of the line angle (lines 4 and 5). We store these values because they are needed more than once throughout the ActionScript, and as you've already seen, it is quicker for Flash to reuse the variables than to calculate the sine and cosine repeatedly. To match variable names with what we worked out in this section, we set two variables, vyi and vxi, from the y and x velocities of the ball (lines 7 and 8). In line 10 we project vyi and vxi onto the line of action, and in line 12 we project vxi and vyi onto the line. We then reverse the velocity along the line of action, vyip, and multiply it by lineDecay. The act of reversing this velocity is the reaction to the collision. Next, in lines 17 and 18, we project back onto the x and y axes. In lines 20 and 21 we update xmov and ymov on the ball object with the new velocities. Finally, we update tempx and tempy on the ball object (lines 22 and 23).

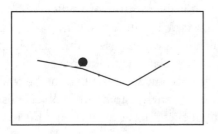

Generate a SWF from this file to see it in action. You will note that three lines are created. The ball falls under gravity onto a line and bounces around a bit. Eventually the ball comes to a rest in a small dip.

CONSERVATION OF MOMENTUM AND ENERGY

In this section we're going to discuss two physical laws that give us some mathematical relationships that help determine the resultant velocities of two collided objects. But before discussing the *laws* of conservation of momentum and conservation of energy, we of course need to introduce the *concepts* of momentum and energy.

Review: What Are Momentum and Energy?

Momentum is a quantity associated with all objects and characterized by an object's mass and velocity. Momentum is a vector whose direction is given by the velocity. Mathematically, this is momentum:

```
momentum = mass*velocity
```

Usually the variable for momentum is the letter p. Here is an example of how you would use ActionScript to calculate the momentum of something moving in the x direction:

```
p = mass*xmov
```

Momentum is not too difficult to conceptualize. Imagine a 100-pound man and a 200-pound man running at the same velocity. Common sense tells you that the 200 pound man has more momentum. But now you can prove that with the equation above. The 200-pound man has twice the momentum.

Energy is a little bit more difficult to explain, even though we are all familiar with it in various everyday forms. It is the measure of a system's ability to do work. Energy is classified into two main categories: *kinetic energy* and *potential energy*. Kinetic energy (which is all we will use in this chapter and indeed the whole book) is the energy associated with the movement of an object. Potential energy is the energy stored in an object that can be converted to kinetic energy. This includes the energy stored in an object raised off the ground (gravitational potential energy), electrical energy, nuclear energy, and chemical energy.

Kinetic energy is dependent on an object's mass and speed. Mathematically, here is the kinetic energy of an object:

kinetic energy = $(\frac{1}{2})$*mass*speed^2

Kinetic energy is usually represented by *E, KE,* or *T* (don't ask me why). We will use *KE* or *ke* to represent kinetic energy. Here is an example of how the above equation would be written in ActionScript:

ke = $(\frac{1}{2})$*mass*speed*speed

The Conservation Laws

Now that we've introduced momentum and energy, it is time to spell out the simple laws of conservation of momentum and conservation of energy. Basically, these laws, or rules, state that the quantities of momentum or of energy will not actually change in the course of a collision. (In other words, in this case the word *conserve* simply means "doesn't change.") Let's start with momentum. The momentum of an object (or system) is conserved if the total force on it is 0. As an example, consider two billiard balls moving toward each other. Ball1 has the momentum p1_initial, and ball2 has the momentum p2_initial. If we sum these two momentums, then we get the total momentum before the collision, P_initial. After the balls collide and rebound, each has a new momentum—p1_final and p2_final. If we sum these two momentums, we get P_final. According to the conservation law for momentum, the total momentum after the collision is the same as the total momentum before the collision (if there is no net external force acting on the system, such as wind). If this condition is met, then *P_initial = P_final.*

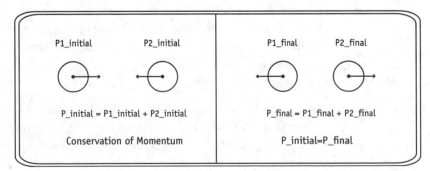

It is important to note that we are talking about *elastic* collisions here. In elastic collision, both kinetic energy and momentum are conserved. We aren't going to get into inelastic collisions, in which only momentum is conserved (for example, rain sticking to a ball in the air, hence changing the mass of the object).

The billiard-ball example given above describes the most common and likely use you'll have for applying this conservation law: the collision and rebound of two objects. This law applies to other types of events as well, events involving individual objects dividing into pieces (for example, a stage separating from its base rocket ship, or a plate breaking). We aren't going to cover those here, because they are not commonly used in Flash games.

Like momentum, energy is conserved when the final energy is equal to the initial energy. There is a more complicated definition for the energy-conservation law, but it includes some concepts that take a lot of explanation. It should be assumed that in all of the cases we deal with in this book, the total energy at the instant before a collision is the same as the energy at the instant after the collision. Let's use the same billiard-ball example to spell this out. The sum of the kinetic energy of each ball before the collision—ke1_initial and ke2_initial—is KE_initial. The sum of the kinetic energy of each ball after the collision—ke1_final and ke2_final—is KE_final. The law of the conservation of energy tells us that the final kinetic energy is the same as the initial energy, so *KE_initial = KE_final*.

APPLYING THE CONSERVATION LAWS

In this section we'll apply these two conservation laws to help us find the motion of objects after a collision.

The derivation of the equations here is also shown worked out on paper in collision_reaction.pdf in the Chapter06 directory on the CD-ROM.

You may be wondering why we have introduced these conservation laws. The reason is that we're going to apply them to help us find the motion of objects after a collision—we are looking for structures and relationships that will enable us to determine the new velocities of objects after they collide. In this section we'll derive the equations that can tell us the new velocities of two collided objects. We will then apply these equations in two cases: two rectangles colliding and two billiard balls colliding.

Let's assume that two objects, object1 and object2, are moving toward each other. Object1 is of mass *m1* and velocity *v1i*, and object2 is of mass *m2* and velocity *v2i*. The two objects collide elastically. We want to learn the new velocities of each object after the collision.

In the equations below, i signifies "initial" and f signifies "final."

Before the collision

Momentum of the objects:

```
p1i = m1*v1i
p2i = m2*v2i
Pi = p1i+p2i
```

Kinetic energy of the objects:

```
ke1i = (1/2)*m1*v1i²
ke2i = (1/2)*m2*v2i²
KEi = ke1i+ke2i
```

After the collision

```
p1f = m1*v1f
p2f = m2*v2f
Pf = p1f+p2f
```

Kinetic energy of the objects:

```
ke1f = (1/2)*m1*v1f²
ke2f = (1/2)*m2*v2f²
KEf = ke1f+ke2f
```

Apply the law of the conservation of momentum

```
Pi = Pf = P
m1*v1i+m2*v2i = m1*v1f+m2*v2f
KEi = Kef
(1/2)*m1*v1i²+(1/2)*m2*v2i² = (1/2)*m1*v1f²+(1/2)*m2*v2f²
```

Rearranging and combining the two equations above, we get the following:

```
v1i-v2i = v2f-v1f
V = v1i-v2i
```

So,

```
v1f = v2f-V
```

Using the above equation with the equation for *P*, we get the final results:

```
v2f = (P+V*m1)/(m1+m2)
v1f = v2f-v1i+v2i
```

If you are interested in seeing more of the in-between steps in the above derivation, you can check out collision_reaction.pdf in the Chapter06 directory. To use this information, all we need to do is calculate the values for *P* and *V*, and then use the last two equations. In the next section, we'll look at an example of how we might use this in Flash.

Rectangle-Rectangle Reactions

Open rectangle_rectangle.fla in the Chapter06 directory. You may notice that this is the same file we used in Chapter 5, "Collision Detection"— with a few modifications and additions. During the object definitions at the beginning of the ActionScript, we add `rectangle1.mass = 1` and `rectangle2.mass = 1`. In conservation-of-momentum situations (for example, collisions), the mass of any one specific object is not important. What is important is the *relative* masses—how the masses compare. Here, as you can see, both objects have a mass of 1. If we set the mass of both objects to 1,000,000, the result would be the same. If the mass of `rectangle1` is 5 and the mass of `rectangle2` is 1, then `rectangle1` is five times as massive as `rectangle2`. This would produce the same results as if `rectangle1` had a mass of 50 and `rectangle2` had a mass of 10 (in both cases, the mass ratio is 5 to 1).

Another change to this file is that instead of executing a `trace` action when a collision is detected, we execute a function called `reaction()`. This function calculates the new velocities of the objects after they have collided.

```
1   function reaction (a, b) {
2       var m1 = a.mass
3       var m2 = b.mass
4       var v1i = a.xmov
5       var v2i = b.xmov
6       var V = v1i-v2i
7       var P = m1*v1i+m2*v2i
8       //the new x speed of b
9       var v2f = (P+m1*V)/(m1+m2)
10      //the new x speed of a
11      var v1f = v2f-v1i+v2i
12      //take the new speeds and put them in the objects
13      a.xmov = v1f
14      b.xmov = v2f
```

```
15     //update the tempx positions with the new speeds
16     a.tempx = a.x+a.xmov
17     b.tempx = b.x+b.xmov
18  }
```

The parameters a and b are references to the rectangle objects. They are passed into this function when it is called. Lines 2 and 3 set the mass variables. Lines 4 and 5 set the initial speed variables. The next two lines set the quantities V and P. Lines 9 and 11 solve for the new speed of each object. We then take these new speeds and update the xmov variable in each of the objects (lines 13 and 14). And since we are updating the xmov variables, we also need to update the tempx variables (lines 16 and 17).

To see an example of this in Flash (not in a game) with multiple rectangles of different masses, check out railroad.fla in the Chapter06 directory. This file was created with Flash 5, so don't be surprised if the ActionScript looks a little different from what you would expect with Flash MX.

Generate a SWF to test this file. You will see that when the two objects collide, they rebound realistically. You can change the mass values of each of the rectangles to convince yourself that the physical realism holds up.

from railroad.fla

Circle-Circle (Billiard-Ball) Reactions

The steps involved in showing the realistic reaction from colliding billiard balls are more complicated than those for a reaction of two rectangles. The conservation equations we developed do not change at all; the trick is to figure out what is conserved. Remember, when two objects collide, the momentum affected is the component that lies along the line of action. For instance, in the rectangle collision discussed above, the line of action is the imaginary line between the two centers of the rectangles, which is along the x-axis. Therefore, the momentum affected lies along the x-axis. If these two rectangles were also moving in the y direction, then their y velocities would be unaffected when colliding. When two balls are colliding, their line of action is drawn between the two centers. The amount of momentum that lies along this line is what is affected in the collision.

So we must use trigonometry to find the velocity of each ball that lies along this line. Finding the amount of one vector that lies along another line is called *projection*, and it was covered extensively in Chapter 3, "Trigonometry 101." Here we project the *x* and *y* velocities of each ball onto the line of action. The velocity components that lie along the line of action are what are affected by the collision. We can then use the conservation equations to find the new velocities. With the new velocities, we can project backward to get the new velocities along the *x* and *y* axes.

If this sounds confusing, that's only because it *is* confusing! If you just want to use the result, then skip ahead a few pages to where we dissect the FLA file. If you are interested in understanding how we arrive at the ActionScript, then stay right here. (And if you want to see this worked out on paper, then open up billiard_ball_reactions.pdf from the CD.)

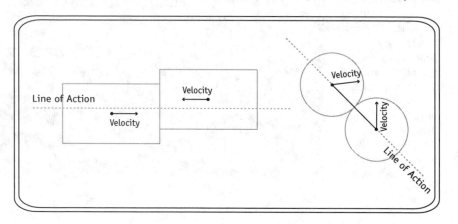

We have two billiard balls, ball1 of *x* velocity *xvel1* and *y* velocity *yvel1*, and ball2 of *x* velocity *xvel2* and *y* velocity *yvel2*. Our goal is to project the *x* and *y* velocities onto the line of action. We can then apply the conservation equations to these velocities.

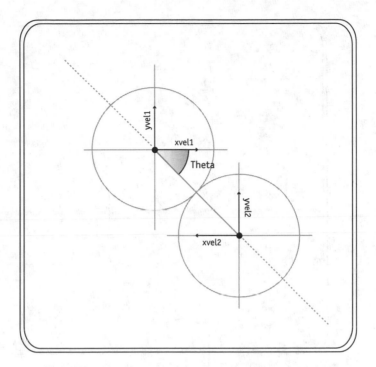

The velocity along the line of action from the projection of ball1's x and y velocities we call *xvel1prime,* and it is calculated as follows:

xvel1prime = xvel1*cos(theta)+yvel1*sin(theta)

This equation is made up of the projection of the x and y velocities of ball1 using the angle theta, which is the angle that the line of collision makes with the x-axis. The component of the velocity of ball1 that is perpendicular to the line of action (which is unaffected by the collision) is

yvel1prime = yvel1*cos(theta)-xvel1*sin(theta)

You'll see that this equation is also a combination of the projection of the x and y velocities of ball1. The component of the ball2 velocity that lies along the line of action we call *xvel2prime:*

xvel2prime = xvel2*cos(theta)+yvel2*sin(theta)

The component of the velocity of ball2 that is perpendicular to the line of action (which is unaffected by the collision) is

yvel2prime = yvel2*cos(theta)-xvel2*sin(theta)

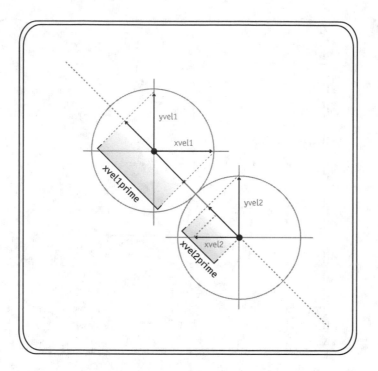

Using the conservation equations developed earlier in this section, we use the mass of each ball, along with *xvel1prime* and *xvel2prime,* to find the new "rebounded" velocities of each ball along the line of action. They are *v1f* and *v2f* (as above, *f* indicates "final").

Using *v1f* and *v2f* and *yvel1prime* and *yvel2prime,* we can find the new velocities along Flash's *x* and *y* axes. This requires us to project back out from the line of action to the axes using the angle theta. Here are the new velocities of each ball.

$xvel1 = v1f * \cos(theta) - yvel1prime * \sin(theta)$
$yvel1 = yvel1prime * \cos(theta) + v1f * \sin(theta)$
$xvel2 = v2f * \cos(theta) - yvel2prime * \sin(theta)$
$yvel2 = yvel2prime * \cos(theta) + v2f * \sin(theta)$

And here's a boiled-down recap of the process we've just completed:

1. ***Project the x and y velocities of each ball onto the line of action.
    This is necessary because at the time of collision the only velocities
    (momentums) affected are those that lie along the line of action.***

2. *Apply the conservation equations to these projected velocities to find the new velocities after the collision.*

3. *Using the new velocities along the line of action and the velocities perpendicular to the line of action, project everything back onto Flash's x and y axes. This will provide the final new velocities after a collision has occurred.*

Now let's see this in ActionScript. Open billiard_ball.fla in the Chapter06 directory. The ActionScript in this file is almost identical to that of circle_circle2.fla in Chapter 5, "Collision Detection." The differences in the ActionScript are as follows:

1. We add a mass variable to the ball objects during the object definitions at the beginning of the ActionScript. For the ball1 object we set the mass to 1 with the action game.ball1.mass = 1, and for the ball2 object we set the mass to 1 with the similar statement game.ball2.mass = 1.

2. In the ballToBallDetection() function, we no longer execute a trace action when a collision is detected. Instead, we call a function called ball2BallReaction(). When it's called, we pass the ball2BallReaction() function the following information:

   b1, b2, xl1, xl2, yl1, yl2, whatTime

   If you remember, b1 and b2 are references to the ball objects, xl1 and yl1 are the starting positions of ball1, xl2 and yl2 are the starting positions of ball2, and whatTime is the number of frames since the last frame that it takes for the collision to occur (this number is between 0 and 1).

3. We add a function called ball2BallReaction(). This function calculates what the new velocities of each ball should be after the collision.

Here is the ball2BallReaction() function:

```
1   function ball2BallReaction(b1, b2, x1, x2, y1, y2, time) {
2       //get the masses
3       var mass1 = b1.mass;
4       var mass2 = b2.mass;
5       // -----set initial velocity variables
6       var xVel1 = b1.xmov;
7       var xVel2 = b2.xmov;
```

```
8      var yVel1 = b1.ymov;
9      var yVel2 = b2.ymov;
10     var run = (x1-x2);
11     var rise = (y1-y2);
12     var Theta = Math.atan2(rise, run);
13     var cosTheta = math.cos(Theta);
14     var sinTheta = math.sin(Theta);
15     //Find the velocities along the line of action
16     var xVel1prime = xVel1*cosTheta+yVel1*sinTheta;
17     var xVel2prime = xVel2*cosTheta+yVel2*sinTheta;
18     //Find the velocities perpendicular to the line of action
19     var yVel1prime = yVel1*cosTheta-xVel1*sinTheta;
20     var yVel2prime = yVel2*cosTheta-xVel2*sinTheta;
21     // Conservation Equations
22     var P = (mass1*xVel1prime+mass2*xVel2prime);
23     var V = (xVel1prime-xVel2prime);
24     var v2f = (P+mass1*V)/(mass1+mass2);
25     var v1f = v2f-xVel1prime+xVel2prime;
26     var xVel1prime = v1f;
27     var xVel2prime = v2f;
28     //Project back to Flash's x and y axes
29     var xVel1 = xVel1prime*cosTheta-yVel1prime*sinTheta;
30     var xVel2 = xVel2prime*cosTheta-yVel2prime*sinTheta;
31     var yVel1 = yVel1prime*cosTheta+xVel1prime*sinTheta;
32     var yVel2 = yVel2prime*cosTheta+xVel2prime*sinTheta;
33     //change old pos
34     b1.tempx = b1.xpos+b1.xmov*time;
35     b1.tempy = b1.ypos+b1.ymov*time;
36     b2.tempx = b2.xpos+b2.xmov*time;
37     b2.tempy = b2.ypos+b2.ymov*time;
38     b1.xmov = xVel1;
39     b2.xmov = xVel2;
40     b1.ymov = yVel1;
41     b2.ymov = yVel2;
42   }
```

Lines 2–9 in this ActionScript handle initializing all of the variables we
need from the ball objects. References to the two colliding ball objects are
passed into this function as b1 and b1. The variables being initialized are
the *x* and *y* velocities of each ball and their masses. We need to know the

angle of the line of action, so we calculate it in lines 10–12; in lines 10 and 11 we calculate the rise and run of the line of action, and then in line 12 we calculate the angle using atan2. Since we will be using the sine and cosine of theta several times, in lines 13 and 14 we set variables to hold those values so that they don't need to be calculated repeatedly. In lines 16 and 17 the velocity of each ball is projected onto the line of action. These are the velocities affected during the collision. Next, we calculate the velocities perpendicular to the line of action. They are only included to help us project back onto the Flash axes. In lines 21–27 the conservation equations are applied. The results of this (lines 26 and 27) are the new velocities along the line of action after the collision. Now that we have the new velocity along the line of action, we can translate back to Flash's x and y axes. We do this in lines 29–32. These are the new velocities of each ball, and need to be stored on each ball. But first we set the temporary position of the ball to be exactly where the balls should have been when they first collided (lines 34–37). Now we change the velocity on the ball objects in lines 38–41.

Generate a SWF to test this file. You will see that when the two balls collide, they react in a realistic way. Close the SWF and change the mass of one of the balls to something bigger, like 10 or 20. Then test the file again, and you will see that the conservation equations are working properly. You have just learned the hardest part of making a game of pool!

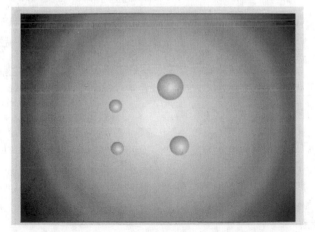

If you would like to look at another implementation of this, see realGravity.fla in the Chapter06 directory. This file was created with Flash 5 quite some time ago, so the ActionScript may look slightly different from what is presented here (but it still works perfectly well, of course). The file has collision detection and reactions of four massive spheres. Each sphere attracts all of the other spheres gravitationally. The result is four spheres slowly moving toward one another. When they collide, they bounce off each other.

Ever-Evolving ActionScript

I have written and rewritten collision detection and collision reaction scripts many times. And the more experienced I become as a programmer, the more and better ways I see to program these events. Everything that I have shown you so far has worked very well for me. But I will inevitably encounter a situation—maybe even before finishing this book—where one of the collision detection or reaction techniques that I have written does not do what it should. It may work great in most situations, but then one particular case crops up which I didn't take into account, and where my script won't work.

What I am saying is that these scripts are a great starting place. And for the games used in this book they work very well. But as Flash grows as a programming platform, and as the demand for complicated or original games gets larger, we will be forced to further refine these techniques— techniques with which we currently see, and have, no problems. We may even have to scrap them for newer and better ways. If these issues of Flash growth and development interest you, then you should try to actively keep up by reading related topics on Flash resource sites. In addition, future revisions of this book will undoubtedly contain additions to these scripts, and some may even be completely rewritten.

In this chapter we covered the major types of collision reactions, including rectangle-rectangle reactions, billiard-ball reactions, and ball-line reactions. With this knowledge you will be able to add a new level of realism to your games. You will see the collision reactions you learned in this chapter applied to at least two of the games, 9-ball and Pinball, in Part 3 of this book.

POINTS TO REMEMBER

- In designing an object, it is often better to use a shape that is simpler than, though similar to, the particular final shape you had in mind. This will allow for easier, faster collision detection, which might be worth the trade-off of a specific complex shape.

- Creating methods on the game object itself, rather than in the timeline, is a good programming practice that helps keep the process flexible and not tied to graphics on the screen.

- The variable decay allows you to control the slowdown of an object by lowering the magnitude of its speed by a percentage each time a collision with a wall or floor occurs. This allows a bouncing ball in Flash to act more like a ball would in real life; it eventually stops bouncing.

- Momentum is a vector which is stated mathematically as momentum = mass*velocity. The momentum of an object (or system) is conserved if the total external force on it is 0.

- Energy is the measure of a system's ability to do work. Kinetic energy is associated with the movement of an object. Potential energy is stored in an object, and can be converted to kinetic energy (a ball sitting on the roof of a house has potential energy that is converted to kinetic energy when it falls). Energy is conserved when the final energy in a collision is equal to the initial energy.

- The quantities of momentum or of energy do not change in the course of a collision in a closed system (that is, one with no net external forces). Think of hitting a cue ball dead-on into another ball and seeing the cue ball sit perfectly still while the other moves away.

- Elastic collisions are those in which *both* kinetic energy and momentum are conserved.

- When two objects collide, the momentum that is affected is the component that lies along the line of action.

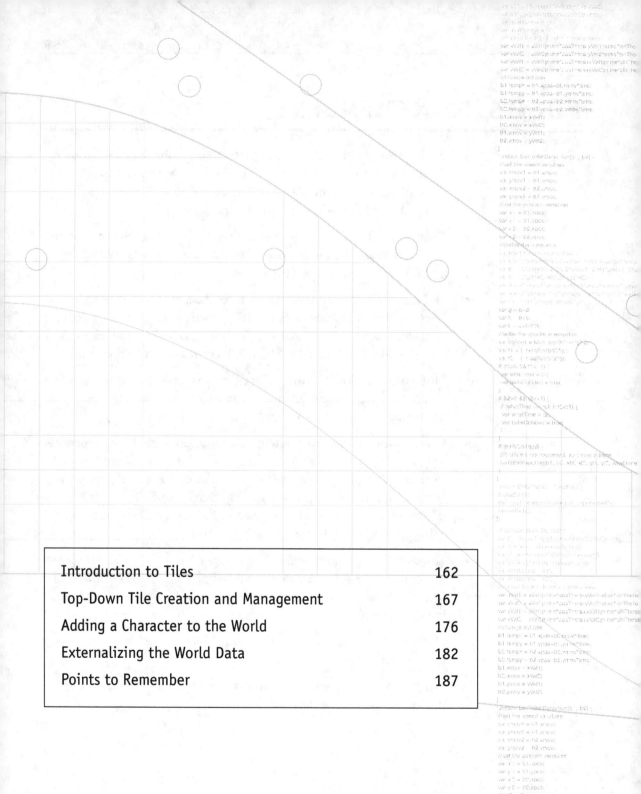

CHAPTER 7

TILE-BASED WORLDS

YOU HAVE PROBABLY NOTICED THAT MANY GAMES IN A TOP-DOWN OR three-dimensional view tend to have a large map (an area that defines the world of the game). It would be a tremendous amount of work for a graphic artist to create every scene in the game without being able to reuse any visual assets. Luckily for the graphic artists (and, as we will see, for the programmers as well), the concept of *tile-based worlds* can make game creation much easier. In a tile-based world, we can reuse all graphical assets and also assemble worlds with code.

From Diablo to Pac-Man, tile-based worlds (TBWs) are used to make game creation a more efficient process, and to lighten CPU load. In this chapter you will learn about this and other advantages of using a TBW. We will close by looking at a simple example of how the tile-based world of a game like Pac-Man would be created. This is a must-read chapter for anyone who is serious about becoming a game programmer.

INTRODUCTION TO TILES

Pac-Man and Diablo are two popular examples of tile-based worlds.

Courtesy of Namco Holding Corp.

Courtesy of Blizzard Entertainment®

A *tile*—also known as a *cell*—is a rectangular (usually square) area of a map. A tile can be any size, but is often set up to be approximately the size of the character you are using, or at least the size of the part of the character that touches the ground, such as feet or wheels. The map is completely made up of tiles. You probably won't be surprised to hear that in Macromedia Flash, a tile is a movie clip. Imagine a top-down view of a ten-by-ten grid of square tiles in Flash. Each tile can have as many frames as you wish. Frame 1 might contain a patch of grass. If the entire ten-by-ten grid were showing frame 1, then the world would look like a big patch of grass, since you wouldn't see a difference between one tile and the next. You might have other frames in this tile—for instance, one for a bush or a rock. In this way, you can create your game environment by "tiling" the tile movie clips (just like you would tile your kitchen) and then sending each tile to a specific frame. Perhaps frame 2 is of a patch of grass, frame 5 is a sidewalk, and frame 6 is water. Using these three frames, you can create a TBW that looks like a grassy park with a pond and a walkway meandering through it. And of course you can add many more types of tiles to produce more-complicated designs. By creating a grid like this—using tiles that have multiple frames—you are creating a TBW!

In the Chapter07 directory on the CD, you'll find a game called Shark Attack! (shark_attack.swf) that we at Electrotank created for a client. This game is a very good example of a TBW. Use the arrow keys to move the character around in this isometric world.

In Shark Attack!, the fish needs to avoid the shark, overcome obstacles, get the key, and unlock the door.

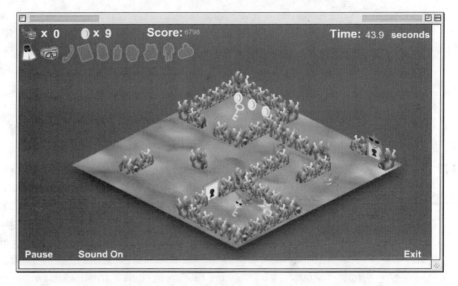

The tiles in the world of this game have numerous frames.

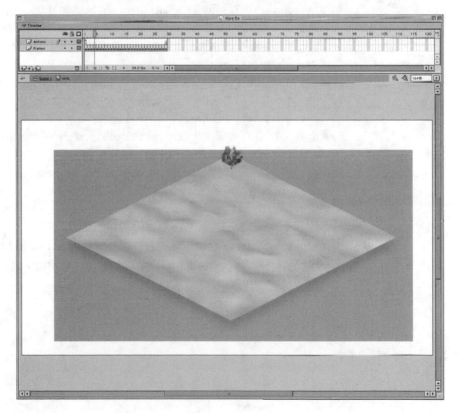

This simple technique is very powerful. You can create a whole city using tiles for grass, road, sidewalks, bushes, walls, and so on. This allows you to reuse your graphical assets efficiently and conveniently. In the case of puzzle games that use TBWs, such as Pac-Man and Minesweeper, the complexity of the tiles is low. They usually just have a few different items that they need to show, such as a dot to be collected, or a maze wall. These games profit from the use of TBWs mostly because TBWs reduce the amount of processing that occurs by using a simple math trick. This trick is explained in the next section.

One of the most convenient programmatic benefits of using TBWs is their ability to easily store information about certain areas of the map. To take advantage of this, I use a two-dimensional array in which each element represents a tile in the world. An object is stored in each element, and then information about the tile that it represents is stored in this object. For instance, if a tile were of a rock, then information might be stored in the object to say there was a rock in this spot and that the character could not move through it. Or if the tile were sand, then information might be stored to specify that the character should be slowed to half its regular speed when passing through this cell. In a game like Pac-Man, in which there might be a 15-by-15 grid, there would be a two-dimensional array with an object that represented each tile. That's 225 (15 times 15) objects. Each object would contain information saying if it was a wall, if it was empty, or if it contained a dot to be collected. How this information is stored (in this case, the two-dimensional array) is called a *data structure*. A common alternative to the two-dimensional–array data structure is to store and name the objects logically. In the Pac-Man example, the 225 objects would be created and given logical names, each based on the cell it represented. So, for instance, the name of the object representing the cell in the third column and eleventh row would look something like `cell3_11`. This is the way we store data in the example game we're working with in this chapter.

ActionScript Review:
Arrays and Two-Dimensional Arrays

An array is a type of object that can store multiple pieces of data. Each piece of data is called an *element*. For instance, names = ["Jobe", "Kelly", "Wendy"] is a line of ActionScript that creates an array called name that contains three elements. The length of this array is 3, and it is considered a one-dimensional array. Each element has a number called an *index* associated with its position, starting with 0. So in our example, "Jobe" has an index of 0 and "Wendy" has an index of 2. To retrieve the contents of an index in an array, you must use the index like this: myName = names[0]. That line of ActionScript would create a variable called myName with a value of "Jobe."

Each element in an array can store any data type, including objects, strings, and other arrays. If you store another array as an element in the array, then you are creating a *two-dimensional array*. For instance, names - [["Jobe", "Kelly"],["Free", "Chance"]] is a two-dimensional array. The main array contains two elements, each of which stores another array with two elements. You access an element of the main array the same way as above—by using the index. You then access an element of the array that is being stored in that element by the same syntax. So to access the name "Free" from this two-dimensional array, I use this syntax, names[1][0]. That points to the array that has an index of 1 (which is the second array) and then points to the first element of that array. With all of this in mind, if we had a 20-by-20 TBW that had all of its objects stored in a two-dimensional array called cells, then we could access the object that represents the cell in the 17th column and 9th row by using the syntax cells[17][9].

Another very useful feature of TBWs is their ability to store the information needed to build the world in an external file or a database. Using a standardized protocol like XML, you can easily store such information. This is great news, because it means you can create a game and load in an unlimited number of levels! Usually you'll need a *level editor*—an application you build, and that assists you in creating a level. You usually "program" the level editor to output information in savable form, such as an XML document (which is just text) you can store in a file or a database. That file can be loaded into the game, and Flash will interpret it and use the information in it to dynamically build the level. In the final section of this chapter we'll look at a simple example of a level editor. The example mentioned earlier, Shark Attack!, loads its levels from external XML files. You can see them in the same directory. They are level1.xml, level2.xml, and level3.xml. You can open and view them with a normal text editor like NotePad or SimpleText.

Board games like chess and checkers are not usually considered tile-based worlds, but they can be treated as such. You can use the same two-dimensional–array data structure to store information about the tiles, such as the tile color, or which piece is sitting in the tile.

If you are really itching to see how all this looks and works in an actual game, just hang on. In the third section of this book we'll see this information applied in the tile-based game called Don't Fall!

TOP-DOWN TILE CREATION AND MANAGEMENT

In Chapter 8, "The Isometric Worldview," we'll continue our discussion about TBWs as we explore their role in isometric-view games.

Most TBWs in Flash are going to be in either top-down view or 3D isometric view, like Shark Attack! The way you store and manipulate the tile data is exactly the same for both of those views, but the way you display the tiles on the screen is not. In this chapter we look at how to create the tiles in the top-down view and how to store information about those tiles. In the last part of this section, we'll introduce a very powerful but simple math trick that can greatly reduce the processing needed to use a TBW.

Creating the Grid and Storing Information

To build the grid of tiles on the screen, you must use *nested loops*—loops within loops. If you wanted to build just one straight line of ten tiles, you would only need to use one loop. In each iteration of that loop (remember that in this example there would be ten iterations per outer loop) you would use attachMovie() to create an instance of a movie clip, and then you would place it in the correct spot on the stage. Since a grid has several of these types of lines right under each other, we loop the loop to create the entire grid. Remember that we have one loop to create a row of tiles, so then we run this loop one time for each row we want to add.

Think of the inner loop as a day and the outer loop as a week. The inner loop loops through 24 hours in a day, but it does this from start to finish for each day (the outer loop). So over the course of one week, there would be 7*24 iterations.

We have an outer loop set to loop, say, ten times. For each loop there is an inner loop that adds the movie-clip tiles to the row. Here is sample ActionScript that would handle just adding one line of ten movie clips to the stage.

```
1   for (var i=1; i<=10; ++i) {
2       //code to add and place the movie clip
3   }
```

That would add one horizontal line of ten movie clips. To make this a grid, we need to start this loop one time for each row that we want to add. So we add an outer loop.

```
1   for (var j=1; j<=10; ++j) {
2       for (var i=1; i<=10; ++i) {
3           //code to add and place the movie clip
4       }
5   }
```

What happens is this:

- The outer loop starts at j=1 (which is row 1). While j=1, the inner loop runs from i=1 to i=10 placing movie clips. Row 1 is now complete.

- The outer loop moves to j=2 (which is row 2). While j=2, the inner loop runs from i=1 to i=10 placing movie clips. Row 2 is now complete.

- And so on, eight more times.

Open grid.fla in the Chapter07 directory on the CD to see an example. You will see two movie clips on the stage. One of them has an instance name of grid, and the other has no instance name but has a library name of tile. This movie clip also has a linkage identifier of tile so that we can create instances of it on the stage using ActionScript. In addition, the tile clip has eight frames, each with a different tile. The grid movie clip was placed there so that we can attach the movie clips to it. Building the grid in a movie clip is cleaner than attaching dozens of movie clips to the main timeline. This is the first in a string of example files we'll look at in this chapter, each one building on the previous. By the end of the chapter you'll have a very simple Pac-Man–like start to a game. The ActionScript in this file does three things:

1. Creates an object called game that we use to store information about the grid.

2. Creates a function called buildGrid() that builds the grid on the stage and builds the data structure that we use to store information about each tile.

3. Executes the buildGrid() function.

Here is the ActionScript used to create the game object.

```
1   game = {};
2   game.columns = 10;
3   game.rows = 10;
4   game.spacing = 30;
5   game.depth = 1000;
6   game.path = _root.grid;
7   game.numberOfTypes = 8;
```

Line 1 creates the game object, and all of the following lines add information to that object. Lines 2 and 3 define the dimensions of the grid; line 4 defines the spacing (the number of units between the registration points of the tiles). The next line sets a variable to the object called depth. This value will be incremented and used to assign a depth to each newly created movie clip. As we have seen in the previous chapters, we are starting to make it a habit to store references to movie clips in an object. That makes our code more object-oriented. So in line 6, you can see that a reference to the grid movie clip is created. Whenever we want to do anything with the grid, we don't have to type _root.grid—we type *game.path*. The reference game.path will be interpreted as _root.grid since that is the reference we pointed it to in line 6 above. If at some point during the game-design process we had to change the name or location of the grid movie clip, then all we would have to do to update the code would be to change the game.path reference to point to the new grid location. If we did not use this game.path reference, then changing the name or path to grid would be a large undertaking, because we'd have to update a lot of code. The final line of ActionScript above sets a variable called numberOfTypes on the game object. This variable stores the number of tile types there are in this game definition. Since we have eight frames in the tile clip, each a different tile, then we give numberOfTypes a value of 8.

Next, a function called buildGrid() is defined.

```
1   function buildGrid() {
2       for (var j=1; j<=game.rows; ++j) {
3           for (var i=1; i<=game.columns; ++i) {
4               var name = "cell"+i+"_"+j;
5               var x = (i-1)*game.spacing;
6               var y = (j-1)*game.spacing;
7               var type = 1;
```

```
8          game.path.attachMovie("cell", name, ++game.depth);
9          game.path[name]._x = x;
10         game.path[name]._y = y;
11         game[name] = {x:i, y:j, name:name, type:type,
        → clip:game.path[name]};
12      }
13    }
14  }
```

This function uses nested loops, as described earlier in this section. The outer loop loops through the number of rows. In each iteration of the outer loop, the inner loop loops through for each column. Each tile (which we call a *cell* here) is named uniquely by using the row and column of the cell as part of that cell's name. For instance, if the cell belongs to column 8 and row 6, the name would be cell8_6. In lines 5 and 6, the intended position of the new movie clip is calculated. Then a variable called type is created with a value of 1. This refers to the frame that the tile will display. In this example we start each tile on frame 1. Next, the movie clip is created and positioned. In line 11 we do something really important—we create an object to store information about the cell that was just created, such as its type, its name, and a reference to the movie clip it represents.

The final line of ActionScript in this file (not shown) is buildGrid(). It calls the function that we just dissected to create the grid.

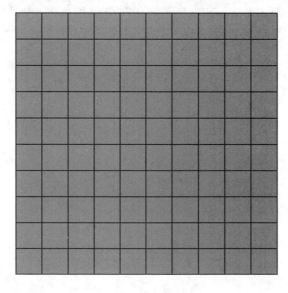

Precision Detection

Now it's time to introduce the trick I mentioned: a simple but powerful maneuver that lightens the processor load in TBWs tremendously. Imagine this: If the game of Pac-Man were written in Flash, how would you detect if the Pac-Man character was colliding with a dot to be collected (or eaten, or whatever it is that Pac-Man does with it)? First of all, in Pac-Man everything moves fairly slowly, and precision isn't important, so hitTest() would not be a bad choice. Many early game programmers (including myself at one time) have guessed that you'd need to loop through the entire board, constantly performing hitTest(), to see if Pac-Man has collided with any dots. That is not a very efficient process. Luckily there is a trick that allows us to easily know which cell Pac-Man is in, and therefore only check for a collision in that cell. And of course, one collision detection is a lot less CPU-intensive than 100 collision detections. Let's see how to determine which cell Pac-Man is in.

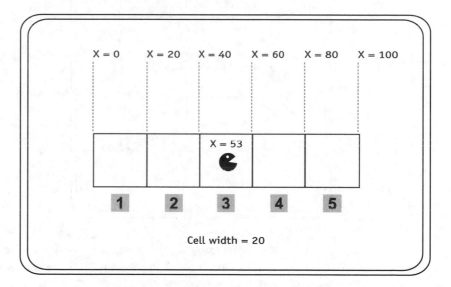

First, let's look at only one direction, horizontal. In the figure above, you can see that there are five cells, each with a width of 20. Pac-Man's *x* position is 53. Which cell is he in?

```
1   spacing = 20;
2   x = 53;
3   cell_column = Math.ceil(x/spacing);
```

In line 1, we set a variable called `spacing`. That is the width of each cell. Line 2 creates a variable called *x* that stores the position of Pac-Man. In line 3 we employ the simple math trick by dividing the position by the spacing. We then round that number up to the nearest integer. With this trick we can easily find which cell Pac-Man is in! This works in the same way for a vertical situation.

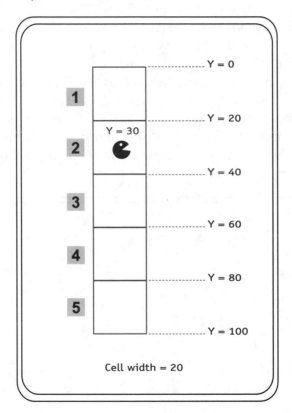

Like the horizontal example, this one also contains five cells, each with a width of 20. The *y* position of Pac-Man is 30. Here is how you find the number of the cell he's in:

```
1   spacing = 20;
2   y = 30;
3   cell_row = Math.ceil(y/spacing);
```

By putting both of these together, we can locate Pac-Man's position in the grid. We find the row and the column he's in, and that specifies the cell in the grid.

```
1  spacing = 20;
2  x = 53;
3  y = 30;
4  cell_column = Math.ceil(x/spacing);
5  cell_row = Math.ceil(y/spacing);
```

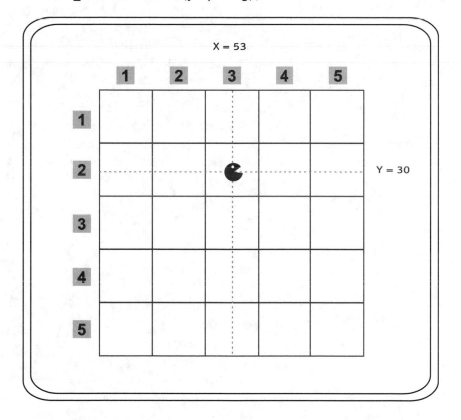

Now that we know which cell Pac-Man is in, we can perform a hitTest() between the Pac-Man movie clip and a dot in that tile. Perhaps you can now understand why this is such a powerful trick. If you are making a game in which the character is walking around, and a few tiles contain water, then when your character is in one of those cells, you can make him swim, or drown, or just slow down a little bit. What typically happens is the following:

1. *You detect which cell the character is in.*

2. *You look up the object that represents that cell.*

3. *You look at the type of cell that your character is in. If it is a cell of fire, then your character might get hurt. If it is a cell with a secret key, then your character can pick it up and gain points.*

Now let's look at a simple example of this trick. Open grid_click.fla in the Chapter07 directory. This file is a modified version of grid.fla. With the added ActionScript in this file, you click a cell and its type changes. If you click one cell enough times, it arrives back at its original cell type. I've used the trick I just introduced to determine which cell was clicked when the mouse button was pressed. Here is the added ActionScript:

```
1   function gameClicked(mx, my) {
2       var x = Math.ceil(mx/game.spacing);
3       var y = math.ceil(my/game.spacing);
4       var cell = "cell"+x+"_"+y;
5       var ob = game[cell];
6       if (ob.type<game.numberOfTypes) {
7           ++ob.type;
8       } else {
9           ob.type = 1;
10      }
11      ob.clip.tile.gotoAndStop(ob.type);
12  }
13  _root.onMouseDown = function() {
14      var mx = _xmouse;
15      var my = _ymouse;
16      if (game.path.hitTest(mx, my)) {
17          gameClicked(game.path._xmouse, game.path._ymouse);
18      }
19  };
```

Look at lines 13–19 first, the onMouseDown event. When the mouse button is pressed, the coordinates of the mouse are saved. If these coordinates are over the grid movie clip (referenced by game.path), we call the gameClicked() function above, passing the coordinates of the mouse into gameClicked(). In lines 2 and 3 we use the trick described in this section to determine the cell that was clicked. In the following line we construct the name of the object that contains information about this cell, and then in line 5 we create a reference to that object called ob. Lines 6–10 check to see if ob.type is less than 8, and if it is, we increment it; otherwise we set it back to 1. Finally, on line 11, we change the frame where the movie clip is to match that of the tile type.

Create a SWF from this file and test it out. Click the cells to change the cell types. Types 2–8 are walls. You can easily create unique configurations of the board.

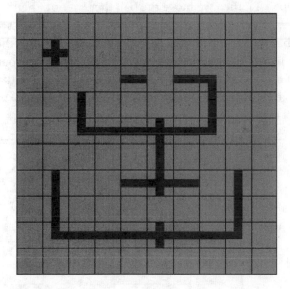

In the next section we will go over how to add a character to this TBW.

A character can be anything from a ball to a human. In most games, a character is something the game player can relate to, usually some living being. In the example given in the next section, the character is a ball.

Adding a Character to the World

In this section we're going to add a character to the simple world we have just created. Our character is nothing more than a ball. The goal is to be able to move the ball around the grid using the arrow keys. If a cell has a type of greater than 1, it is a wall, and we will not let the ball enter this cell.

When an arrow key is pressed, we look ahead to see where the edge of the ball would be if we were to move it there. If the edge is in an acceptable cell (type = 1), then we move the ball there; if not, then we disregard the key press. More specifically, if the right arrow key is pressed, then we look at the ball's current position, plus the ball's speed, plus the ball's radius to form a number that represents the far right edge of the ball if it were to be moved one quantity (or unit) of speed to the right. We then check to see in which cell that far-right point is. If it is in a cell of type = 1, then we move the ball there.

Looking ahead: where is he going to go?

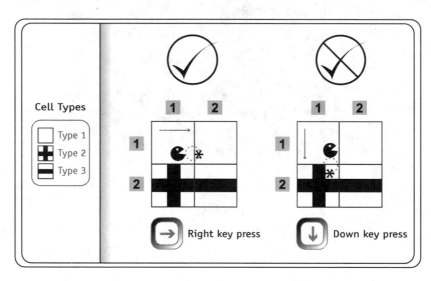

To see this in action, open character_in_grid.fla in the Chapter07 directory. You will see a new movie clip inside the grid movie clip. It is the character and has an instance name of `ball`. The ActionScript has three additions:

1. A function called `initializeBall()` that creates an object to hold the information about the character (which is a ball). This function also creates a few new variables on the `game` object.

2. A function called moveBall(). When this function is called, it moves the ball to a new position if that new position is valid.

3. An onEnterFrame event. This checks for key presses in every frame. If one of the arrow keys is pressed, then the moveBall() function is called.

Here is the initializeBall() function:

```
1   function initializeBall() {
2       game.speed = 3;
3       game.path.ball.swapDepths(10000);
4       game.ball = {startx:1, starty:1, clip:game.path.ball};
5       var x = (game.ball.startx-1)*game.spacing+game.spacing/2;
6       var y = (game.ball.starty-1)*game.spacing+game.spacing/2;
7       game.ball.clip._x = x;
8       game.ball.clip._y = y;
9       game.ball.x = x;
10      game.ball.y = y;
11      game.ball.radius = game.ball.clip._width/2;
12  }
```

The purpose of this function is to initialize all objects and variables needed to hold information about the ball. Line 2 above sets a variable called speed to the game object. This represents the speed at which the ball can move. If a key press is detected on any frame, then the ball will be moved that amount. The next line moves the ball movie clip to a high depth. This is done so that we can see it over the tiles that were attached to the stage. If we do not send the ball to a higher depth than the tiles, then it will be hidden behind the tiles. In line 4 an object called ball is defined on the game object. This object is used to store information about the ball, such as the starting position of the ball and a reference to the movie clip it represents. You'll notice that we set the variables startx and starty both to 1. This is because we are going to start the ball in the first tile. The next two lines use the startx and starty position to calculate the place on the stage where the ball needs to be placed. We add game.spacing/2 to both positions so that the ball will be centered in the tile rather than on its registration point. In lines 9–11 we store the x and y positions of the ball and its radius on the ball object.

Next, let's look at the onEnterFrame event. We'll save the moveBall() function for last.

```
1   _root.onEnterFrame = function() {
2       if (Key.isDown(Key.RIGHT)) {
3           moveBall("right");
4       } else if (Key.isDown(Key.LEFT)) {
5           moveBall("left");
6       }
7       if (Key.isDown(Key.UP)) {
8           moveBall("up");
9       } else if (Key.isDown(Key.DOWN)) {
10          moveBall("down");
11      }
12  };
```

There are two conditional chunks of code in here. One checks to see if either the right or left arrow key is pressed; the other checks to see if either the up or down arrow is pressed. If the right or left arrow key is detected as being pressed, then the moveBall() function is called, and the name of the pressed key is passed in as a string. Likewise, if the up or down arrow key has been detected as being pressed, then the moveBall() function is called, and the pressed key is passed in as a string.

Now let's look at the moveBall() function. It is not complicated, but it is fairly long. This is because we repeat the same sorts of actions for each arrow key (four times).

```
1   function moveBall(dir) {
2       ob = game.ball;
3       if (dir == "right") {
4           var tempx = ob.x+ob.radius+game.speed;
5           var tempy = ob.y;
6           var cellx = Math.ceil(tempx/game.spacing);
7           var celly = Math.ceil(tempy/game.spacing);
8           var tempCell = game["cell"+cellx+"_"+celly];
9           if (tempCell.type != 1) {
10              return;
11          } else {
12              ob.x += game.speed;
13              ob.clip._x = ob.x;
14          }
```

```
15      } else if (dir == "left") {
16          var tempx = ob.x-ob.radius-game.speed;
17          var tempy = ob.y;
18          var cellx = Math.ceil(tempx/game.spacing);
19          var celly = Math.ceil(tempy/game.spacing);
20          var tempCell = game["cell"+cellx+"_"+celly];
21          if (tempCell.type != 1) {
22              return;
23          } else {
24              ob.x -= game.speed;
25              ob.clip._x = ob.x;
26          }
27      } else if (dir == "up") {
28          var tempx = ob.x;
29          var tempy = ob.y-ob.radius-game.speed;
30          var cellx = Math.ceil(tempx/game.spacing);
31          var celly - Math.ceil(tempy/game.spacing);
32          var tempCell = game["cell"+cellx+"_"+celly];
33          if (tempCell.type != 1) {
34              return;
35          } else {
36              ob.y -= game.speed;
37              ob.clip._y = ob.y;
38          }
39      } else if (dir == "down") {
40          var tempx = ob.x;
41          var tempy = ob.y+ob.radius+game.speed;
42          var cellx = Math.ceil(tempx/game.spacing);
43          var celly = Math.ceil(tempy/game.spacing);
44          var tempCell = game["cell"+cellx+"_"+celly];
45          if (tempCell.type != 1) {
46              return;
47          } else {
48              ob.y += game.speed;
49              ob.clip._y = ob.y;
50          }
51      }
52  }
```

This function accepts a parameter called `dir`. It represents the string that is passed in, telling the function which key was pressed. In line 2 of the function, we set a reference to the `game.ball` object called `ob`. Setting a temporary reference is not absolutely necessary, but it does make the typing a little shorter and actually speeds up the ActionScript a little bit. Next we have an `if` statement that checks to see if `dir` is `"right"`, `"left"`, `"up"`, or `"down"`. Very similar actions are repeated for each of the four pieces of this conditional statement. First let's look at lines 3–14, the `"right"` conditional. The first action in this chunk of code, line 4, sets a variable called `tempx` that represents the ball's right edge. Since the user is trying to move the ball to the right, we check to see if the ball's right edge would still be in a valid cell if we moved it in that direction. To do this, we use our math trick to determine the cell using the variables `tempx` and `tempy`. We then check the object that represents the cell the ball would be over. If the `type` variable on that object is 1, then it is a valid move. If it is not valid (line 9), then we return out of the function (line 10). If it is a valid type, then we update the ball's position (lines 11–14).

The next three parts of this big conditional statement do the same thing as the first part, except in how they calculate the ball's edge and update the ball's position. The edge of the ball we are interested in depends on the direction of movement. If the down key was pressed, then we are interested in the lowest edge of the ball. If the left key was pressed, then we are interested in the leftmost edge of the ball. Finally—all together now—if the up key was pressed, then we are interested in the topmost edge of the ball.

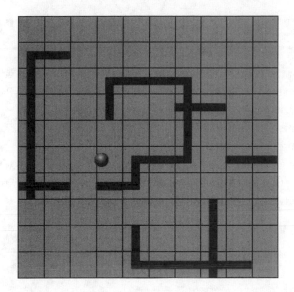

Generate a SWF from this file. You can then use your arrow keys to move the ball around. Click the grid to add some walls. Move the ball around and notice how it will not enter a cell that has a wall. Notice that all walls are treated in the same way; it doesn't matter what the wall looks like or how much of the cell the wall occupies. Using creatively drawn walls or smaller cell sizes, this is not as apparent.

One other thing to note is that this is just one way to treat cells in a TBW. More-advanced games have real collision detection within a cell. In that case, the ball could enter a cell that has a wall, but then collision detection checks would kick in to make sure the ball did not move through the wall itself.

EXTERNALIZING THE WORLD DATA

One of the best features of TBWs is the ease with which you can store the data that represents a world. For instance, for a game of Pac-Man (without the ghosts) you can easily create a text document to store the type of each cell. This text document is usually XML formatted. At a later date this information can be loaded into your game and the world can be built. In this section we'll look at a simple example of how to do this. (We're going to assume that you have some knowledge of XML and how to work with extracting data from XML objects in Flash.)

Here is the XML structure we will use to store the world data:

```
<map>
    <row>
        <cell type="1" />
        <cell type="3" />
    </row>
    <row>
        <cell type="2" />
        <cell type="1" />
    </row>
</map>
```

The XML listed above only describes a two-by-two grid. We're going to create an XML file that describes a ten-by-ten grid. So there will be ten <row> nodes, and ten <cell> nodes in each <row> node. In the XML above, the first <row> node represents the first row of cells in a grid. The two <cell> nodes in the <row> node represent the two cells in that row in a grid. The type attribute in the <cell> node represents the frame that that cell should show.

Open game.fla from the CD. Take a look at the tile movie clip in the library. It's got a simple new addition—a movie clip with an instance name of dot on frame 1. As the ball moves over the dots, they disappear, much as they do in Pac-Man. There are three frame labels in this movie, Start, Create Game, and Play Game. The Start frame gives you two choices,

Create Game or Play Game. If you click the Create Game button, then you are taken to the Create Game frame. On this frame you can configure a level and then click to have the XML for this level generated. If you choose Play Game, you are taken to the Play Game frame. On this frame the data for the level is loaded from an XML file and the level is created. You can then move the ball around on this level, collecting dots.

Let's look at the Create Game label first. This is a very simple level editor. On this frame you can click each cell individually to change its type. Once you are happy with the configuration of the board, you can click the Generate XML button, and an XML document representing this map will be generated and then shown in the Output window. The Generate XML button calls a function called generateXML(). Here is the ActionScript in this function:

```
1  function generateXML() {
2      var xml = "<map>";
3      for (var j=1; j<=game.rows; ++j) {
4          xml += "<row>";
5          for (var i=1; i<=game.columns; ++i) {
6              var name = "cell"+i+"_"+j;
7              var type = game[name].type;
8              var temp = "<cell type=\""+type+"\" />";
9              xml += temp;
10          }
11          xml += "</row>";
12      }
13      xml += "</map>";
14      trace(xml);
15  }
```

This function creates an XML document like the one shown earlier in this section, except that it has ten <row> nodes, and ten <cell> nodes per <row> node. First, a local variable called xml is defined with "<map>" as its value. Then we loop through the entire board. At the beginning of every outer loop, we append "<row>" to the xml variable. For each iteration of the inner loop, we create a <cell> node with a "type" attribute that stores the value of the current cell's type. This node is then appended to the xml variable. At the end of each outer loop, we append "</row>" to the xml variable, closing the current <row> node. After all the loops, we close the root node by appending "</map>" to the xml variable. Finally, we trace the xml variable so that its contents are shown in the Output window.

Generate a SWF file from this, and test the XML generation. Once you have created a level you're happy with, copy the contents from the Output window and save it to a file called game.xml in your current working directory. Now how will this file of yours get used? You're about to find out. Next we're going to discuss the Play Game frame; that's where this file will be loaded, and your level will be created from it.

Close the SWF file and look at the FLA file again. Move to the Play Game frame. This frame loads the game.xml file, interprets it, and builds the level. Once the level is built, the character can move around the level collecting dots. There are a few ActionScript additions to this frame that you have not yet seen. There is a simple collision-detection function that checks for ball-dot collisions, and there is the code that loads and interprets the XML. Here is the code that loads the XML and defines the event handler for the onLoad event:

```
1   board = new XML();
2   board.onLoad = buildGrid;
3   board.load("game.xml");
```

An XML document must be loaded into an XML object, so first we're going to create an XML object called board. Also, so that we will know when the file is finished loading, in line 2 we set an event handler for the onLoad event for the board XML object. When the file is finished loading, the function buildGrid() is called. In line 3 we load a file into the XML object, passing in the path to the file.

The buildGrid() function is changed substantially from the one you've gotten used to seeing in our previous examples. Here it interprets the XML and builds the level from it.

```
1   function buildGrid() {
2       board = board.firstChild;
3       var tempArray = [];
4       tempArray = board.childNodes;
5       for (var j=1; j<=game.rows; ++j) {
6           var tempArray2 = [];
7           tempArray2 = tempArray[j-1].childNodes;
8           for (var i=1; i<=game.columns; ++i) {
9               var name = "cell"+i+"_"+j;
10              var x = (i-1)*game.spacing;
11              var y = (j-1)*game.spacing;
```

```
12              var type = tempArray2[i-1].attributes.type;
13              game.path.attachMovie("cell", name, ++game.depth);
14              game.path[name]._x = x;
15              game.path[name]._y = y;
16              game[name] = {x:i, y:j, name:name, type:type,
                → clip:game.path[name],
                → dot:game.path[name].tile.dot};
17              game[name].clip.tile.gotoAndStop(type);
18          }
19      }
20      initializeBall();
21  }
```

Line 2 of this function sets the contents of the XML object to that of its first
child node. The next two lines create an array of the child nodes of the
<map> node. That means that every element in this array contains a <row>
node. Lines 6 and 7 create an array that contains the child nodes of the jth
<row> node from the tempArray array. The child nodes of a <row> node are
the <cell> nodes. In line 12 we set a local variable called type that stores
the number extracted from the type node of the ith <cell> node in the
tempArray2 array.

There is one more addition to the ActionScript on this frame—the
detectDot() function. A reference to a cell movie clip is passed into this
function, and a hitTest() is performed between ball and dot. If the
hitTest() method returns a value of true, then a collision occurred, and
dot has its visibility set to false.

```
1   function detectDot(tempCell) {
2       if (game.ball.clip.hitTest(tempCell.dot)) {
3           tempCell.dot._visible = false;
4       }
5   }
```

This function is called from the moveBall() function. You may remember
that in the moveBall() function there are four chunks of code, one for
each arrow key. If the place where you attempt to move the ball is valid,
then the detectDot() function is called.

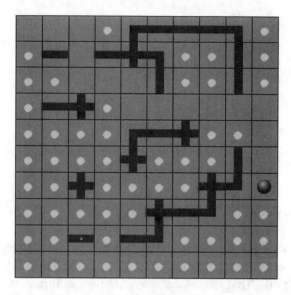

Generate a SWF from this file. When you click the Play Game button, you'll notice that your XML file has been loaded and interpreted. You can now move the ball around the map and collect dots! This is a very simple example of a TBW with an editor.

In this chapter you have learned what makes up a tile-based world. You have also seen the main benefits of using TBWs—reuse of graphical assets and some programming advantages. With the knowledge gained in this chapter, you will be able to build more-complicated tile-based worlds. In the third section of this book you will see more TBW examples.

POINTS TO REMEMBER

- Tiles (also called *cells*) allow the reuse of most visual assets you create for a game, and can be the building blocks for the appearance of many games.

- Tiles help you assemble an entire game world using code.

- Using a simple math trick only possible with TBWs, you can greatly reduce the processing power needed to run your game.

- A tile is a movie clip.

- The data structure used with tile-based worlds (one object for each tile) makes storing information about each tile very easy.

- You can easily store the information needed to build a TBW in an external file or database. This information, which usually represents a level in a game, can later be loaded in, and the world or level constructed.

- Nested loops are used to build a grid of tiles for your game.

- A trick to pinpoint the location of a character allows you to then perform collision detection only between the character and the objects in that cell, which reduces the code intensity because you are not checking for collisions with every object on the screen, only the ones in that cell.

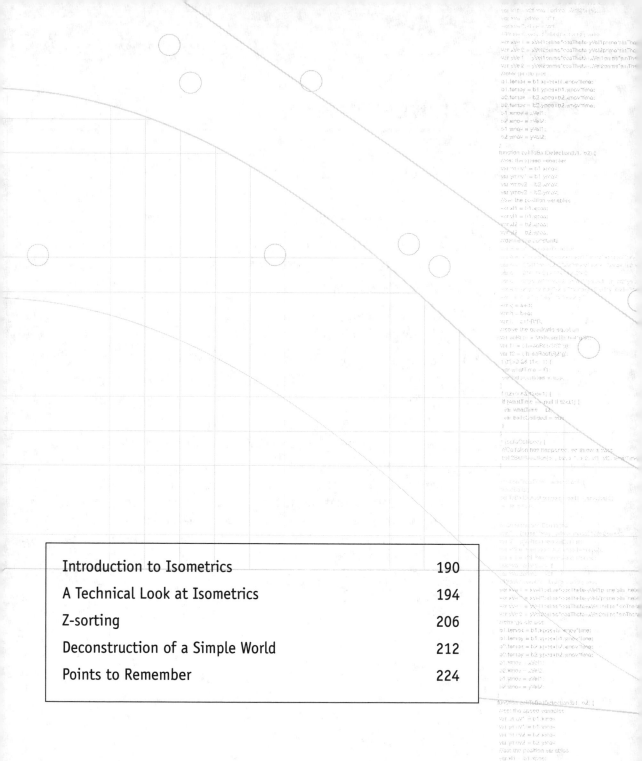

CHAPTER 8

THE ISOMETRIC WORLDVIEW

AN *ISOMETRIC* VIEW IS A SPECIFIC THREE-DIMENSIONAL (3D) VIEW. IN 3D, as you have undoubtedly seen in some non-Flash games, the camera (the viewpoint of your computer screen) can move anywhere and rotate anywhere. There is a specific position of this camera that gives an isometric view. This view is popular in many games, including Diablo II, and has been shown to be very effective when used properly in Flash. In this chapter we will discuss why this view is popular and how to treat it mathematically. We'll also provide real examples of how to use it. To get the most out of this chapter, you should have read, or be familiar with the concepts learned in, Chapter 7, "Tile-Based Worlds."

INTRODUCTION TO ISOMETRICS

Sometimes explaining and understanding a concept is easier with comparisons. With this in mind we will briefly discuss 3D in games in general and then specifically talk about isometrics.

It is rare today to find professionally created games for sale that are not 3D. Even games that are typically only two-dimensional, such as card games, often have some sort of 3D element. As mentioned in Chapter 1, "First Steps," 3D can be applied to a game in many ways. Games like Unreal Tournament use a real 3D engine. A 3D engine can rotate objects and display them correctly onscreen, changing the camera's viewpoint at any time, and uses very detailed z-sorting. *Z-sorting* is the concept and act of placing one object on top of another to give the appearance of it being in front. (In Flash, the objects we'll work with will be movie clips.) The sequence in which we arrange the objects is called the *stacking order*. Each object in the stack is at a specific depth—assigned by a relative numeric value—also known as a z-index. Z-sorting can be applied to several different types of situations including a 3D world (as in this chapter) or the open windows of your operating system.

Courtesy of Epic Games, Inc.

For instance, your keyboard is in front of your monitor, so it has a higher z-sorting number—the closer to the game player, the higher the number.) One of the most powerful things about advanced 3D engines, such as the one written for a game like Unreal Tournament, is that they can map bitmaps to shapes. (For instance, the bitmap of a human face can be mapped onto the shape of a head, which is a polygon. When this shape rotates in the 3D world, it appears to be a human head.) With this type of 3D engine, all shapes are rendered (created) onscreen mathematically. There are usually some premade bitmaps, like the human face mentioned above, but for the most part all of the objects are created and moved on the fly. This type of engine is very processor-intensive, and because of the real-time creation of objects, it can limit the game's level of detail.

Early on in the online game world, developers discovered that a 3D world was great for many types of games but that changing camera views wasn't always important. With this in mind, some games were developed with only one camera view—an isometric view (the angles of which will be discussed in the next section).

At this point, before we talk more about the isometric view, it is important to note the concept of *perspective*. Imagine that you are standing on a long, straight road. As you look down this road, its two sides appear to converge

far off in the distance. As we all know, the sides of the road do not actually converge way off in the distance. If you were to travel to the end of the road, then you would see that it is just as wide at the end as it is at the beginning. This visual illusion is called perspective. Without perspective, the road would appear to stay the same width, and in fact it would probably be impossible to get a feeling for how long the road is. Perspective helps to give us an idea of an object's dimensions.

The well-known game
Diablo II is a good
example of a game with
an isometric viewpoint.

Courtesy of Blizzard Entertainment®

Games that use an isometric view do not use perspective. Why is this so important? Imagine creating a first-person-view 3D game in Flash. As a car drives by your character, the perspective of the car is constantly changing. New parts of the car are revealed as the car moves by, and eventually it vanishes. As the character with the first-person-view walks down the street, the perspective of every object on the screen is constantly changing. To create a game like that, you would need a true 3D engine. Yes, very limited versions of this can be created in Flash (with highly advanced tricks), but for the most part it should not be considered a realistic possibility—not as of this writing, anyway. With an isometric view there is no perspective. This means we can create many different angles of objects, and then place those objects on the screen. For instance, with an isometric view you can create a tree and place it anywhere in the world without having to worry about its size or perspective, since those attributes are never going to change. This is good news for first-time as well as seasoned Flash developers, because it means we can create 3D games without a 3D engine.

A road in an isometric world never converges. But the amazing thing is, it looks great!

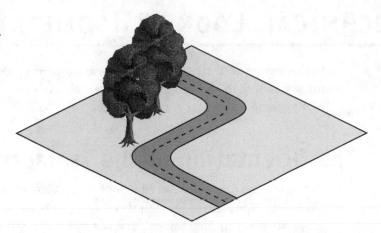

There is some controversy over what constitutes a 3D engine. In this chapter I give you equations and functions to handle placing and moving objects in a 3D world and then mapping that onto a 2D screen. To some people this is a 3D engine; to others (usually hard-core programmers) a 3D engine has to be able to handle real-time graphics rendering as well.

Let's recap the main points introduced here:

- An isometric view is a specific camera angle in a 3D world (mathematical specifics are in the next section).

- In an isometric world you don't use perspective. The implication of this is that you can create reusable objects rather than having to render them in real time.

- An isometric view is much less processor-intensive than other 3D views, which makes it more workable in Flash.

Next we will discuss the math, geometry, and trigonometry used to create this view and to display it on a 2D screen (that is, projecting from a 3D to a 2D plane).

TIP

I don't mean to discourage anyone reading this chapter from attempting more of a "real" 3D approach in games. With Flash's drawing API and with cool tricks (which you can find on the Web or develop yourself), you can accomplish some amazing things. In fact, I have been working on something of my own—a car-racing game—that wasn't finished in time for this book. If you are interested in seeing this game, it will probably be on my Web site, Electrotank (www.electrotank.com), sometime in spring 2003.

A TECHNICAL LOOK AT ISOMETRICS

In this section we'll take a different look at isometrics. We'll discuss everything you need to know in order to place objects in an isometric world and to map them back to the computer screen.

The Orientation of the Isometric World

Before moving forward, we need to look at the Flash coordinate system in a new way. Up to this point in the book we have been seeing the coordinate system as two-dimensional; that is, having an *x*-axis and a *y*-axis. Flash does not have a *z*-axis, but if it did, the positive end would extend out past the back of the computer screen.

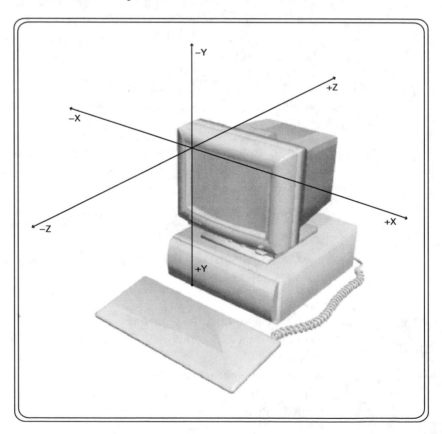

The isometric world we will be dealing with can be conceptualized (and then treated mathematically) as a second 3D coordinate system sitting inside this Flash coordinate system. Let's call this second system "the isometric system" and the first "the Flash system." The Flash system is stationary; it cannot move since it is bound to your computer monitor. The isometric system is only isometric when it is oriented in a specific way within the Flash system. Please note that the isometric system does not change when its orientation changes. The only thing that makes it isometric is how it is seen from the Flash system.

Before it is rotated, the new coordinate system is aligned with Flash's coordinate system.

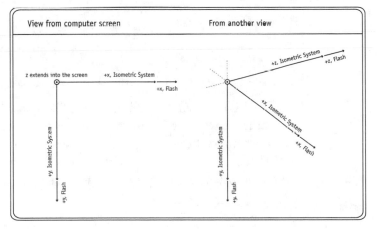

Now let's assume that the isometric system is completely aligned with the Flash system. In this case, there is no difference between the Flash system and the isometric system; in fact, it is not yet isometric. What has to happen to this second system to make it appear isometric, as seen from the Flash system?

- It must be rotated 30° around its *x*-axis.

  The *x*-axis is treated like an axle, so it stays still while the coordinate system rotates. Before the rotation, all three axes lie along all three of Flash's axes. After the rotation, the isometric system's *x*-axis still lies along Flash's *x*-axis, but the other axes are no longer aligned.

Rotated 30° around the
x-axis

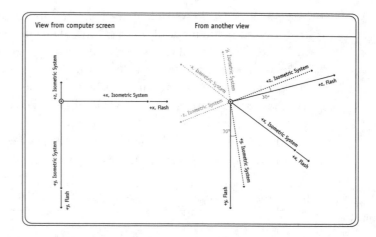

- It must then be rotated 45° around its own *y*-axis.

  During this rotation, the *y*-axis is treated like an axle, so it stays stationary while the rest of the isometric system is rotated around it. When this rotation has been completed, all three of the isometric axes are in different positions from their starting places, and it appears to be an isometric system as seen from the Flash system.

Rotated around isometric
system's y-axis 45°

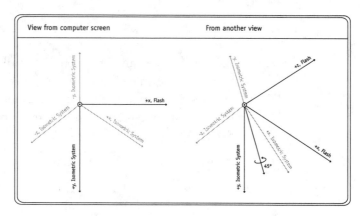

Final product: the isometric
view as seen from the Flash
coordinate system (your
monitor).

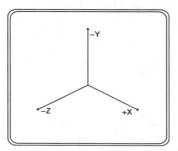

Take a look at the demo.swf file in the Chapter08 directory on the CD. This file was created to help you visualize how these two rotations take place. It shows a straight-on orientation in the Flash system (before it is isometric) and then rotates the cube in two steps. When it is finished animating, the cube is seen in an isometric view.

Cube in an isometric world

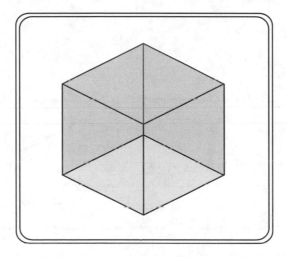

Why is this view called *isometric*? If you look at the cube in the figure above, you will notice that only three faces are exposed. The area of each of these three faces is the same. The prefix *iso* means "the same," and *metric* signifies "measurement."

Placing an Object in the Isometric World

Throughout this book we have been advocating using code to describe visual elements—their position, speed, and other properties—and to store this information (as opposed to storing information in the movie clips themselves). If the position of something needs to be updated on the stage, then we do so at the end of the frame after all needed calculations are done. We take the position that we have calculated in memory and then assign that value to the _x and _y properties of the movie clip. This technique will be used in this chapter as well: We will discuss the position coordinates in the isometric system and in the Flash system, and how to move between them.

Before continuing, I want to mention some restrictions we will be observing. First, look at the image below.

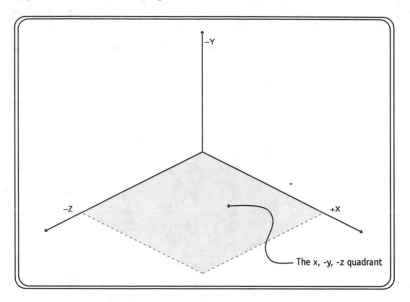

We are going to restrict where we place objects to the quadrant of the isometric world formed by the *x*- and −*z*-axes. Specifically, if we extend this quadrant upward in the −*y* direction, we form an *octant* (a quadrant infinite in size, extended in an orthogonal, or perpendicular, direction). This octant is shown in the image below.

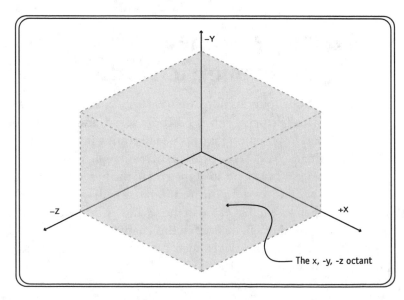

The reason we restrict object placement to this octant has to do with z-sorting. (As a reminder, z-sorting refers to changing the depth of movie clips to make them appear to be at the correct distance from the screen.) For instance, as a character walks around a tree, you want the character to appear behind the tree at some points but in front of it at others. The issue of finding a good way to handle z-sorting has plagued Flash developers for a long time. With this octant restriction, we can use a technique I developed for z-sorting that makes it lightning-fast. We'll talk about this in the next section. To recap, the reason why we restrict object placement to this octant is so that we can use a specific and fast z-sorting technique. If someone comes up with something better, please let me know!

When working with 3D worlds, the coding architecture we've been using throughout this book (mentioned in the first paragraph of this section) is no longer just good practice, it's a necessity. We will now store three coordinates that represent each visual element—x, y, and z—in an object. These are the coordinates of anything in the isometric world. For instance, a character might have the coordinates (100, 10, -50) in the isometric world. In order to display this character on the screen, we have to figure out what the x and y positions of the movie clip on the screen need to be so that it looks as if the character is sitting at those isometric coordinates. So the next logical step is to find this linkage between the isometric system and the Flash system.

We know that the isometric system is related to the Flash system by the two rotations (30° and 45°) discussed in the previous section. Using our knowledge of trigonometry, we can map (project) any point from the isometric system into the Flash system. This is done in two steps, one for each rotation. To map from the isometric system to the Flash system we start with the points in the isometric system and then apply the two rotations to the coordinates. This actually maps the coordinates from the isometric system to an in-between system (after the first rotation) and then from the in-between system into the Flash system. During the first rotation, the y-coordinate is unchanged (because the y-axis is the fixed axis around which the system rotates); during the second rotation the x-coordinate remains unchanged. Here is the math to back it up. We start with the coordinates of a point *(xpp, ypp, zpp)*. The *pp* is a mathematical convention; when an x-coordinate is changed to a new system, it is usually called *xp* (or *x'*). This is read as "x prime." When it is changed two times (as we do in this case), it is called *xpp* (or *x''*). This is read as "x double prime." So we start out with *(xpp, ypp, zpp)*, and after the first rotation we'll have *(xp, yp, zp)*. After the second rotation we'll have *(x, y, z)*. So let's begin.

We start in the isometric system with points *(xpp, ypp, zpp)*. To map this to the Flash system we must move through two angles. We treat them one at a time. First we will map the coordinates to the intermediate system by rotating them around the *y*-axis 45° to arrive at three new coordinates *(xp, yp, zp)*:

```
xp = xpp*cos(45) + zpp*sin(alpha)
yp = ypp
zp = zpp*cos(45) - xpp*sin(alpha)
```

Notice that *yp* is equivalent to *ypp*. This is because the system was rotated around the *y*-axis, so the *y*-coordinate was not changed. Next we rotate the coordinates *(xp, yp, zp)* around the *x*-axis 30° to arrive in the Flash coordinate system *(x, y, z)*:

```
x = xp
y = yp*cos(30) - zp*sin(30)
z = zp*cos(30) + yp*sin(30)
```

We now have the coordinates of where *(xpp, ypp, zpp)* should appear in the Flash system. You may have noticed that while we end up with *(x, y, z)*, we still don't really have a *z*-axis in Flash. As mentioned earlier, we can think of a *z*-axis that moves into the computer screen. This conceptualization helps when trying to do things like mapping from 3D to Flash's system. Movie clips have _x and _y properties, but no _z property. So when the above math is changed into ActionScript, we can forget about the final *z*-coordinate. If we were not using an isometric view, we would most likely want to have real-time perspective changes. In that case, you would want this *z*-coordinate to hang around, because you would use it to calculate perspective. In our isometric case, though, we don't need it.

Let's see a working example of how to position an object, given its coordinates in the isometric system. Open position.fla in the Chapter08 directory. There are three layers in this file: Assets, Actions, and Object Definitions. The Assets layer contains all of the movie clips and buttons. At the top left of the stage you see three dynamic text fields. They are there to show you the current coordinates of the ball in the isometric system. On the right side of the stage there are two text fields that show you the *x*- and *y*-coordinates of the ball in Flash's system. In the middle there is a movie clip with an instance name of floor. Floor contains a graphic of a square floor in an isometric world. Also contained in that movie clip are a movie clip with an instance name of ball and a movie clip with an instance name of shadow. The shadow clip will move around with the ball to help give you a better idea of where the ball is. As the ball changes *y* positions, the shadow does not; this helps the player visualize the object's location. (A visual cue—or clue—in a 3D world would be that the ball changed size according to its location; a correlative cue in the isometric world is the location of the object's shadow to help you understand the behavior of the object itself.) On the bottom-right side of the stage are two buttons with which you can control the ball's *y* position in the isometric world.

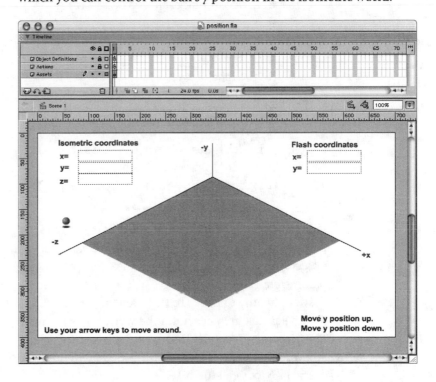

Use your four arrow keys to move the ball around. You can change the ball's *y* position by using the buttons on the bottom-right side of the screen. Notice that your ball will not move through the floor—we imposed the octant restriction.

Now let's look at the ActionScript involved in all of this. I have written an object called isometricAS, which is contained on the layer called Object Definitions. This object contains three very helpful methods for working with isometrics. We will talk about two of these methods (mapToScreen() and mapToIsoWorld()) very soon, and will save the third (calculateDepth()) for the next section.

The ActionScript in the Actions layer makes use of what was defined in the Object Definitions layer and handles things like capturing key events and placing the ball and shadow on the screen.

Let's look at the actions in the Object Definitions layer. First we see this:

```
1   isometricAS = function (maxx, maxz) {
2       this.maxx = maxx;
3       this.maxz = maxz;
4       this.theta = 30;
5       this.alpha = 45;
6       this.theta *= Math.PI/180;
7       this.alpha *= Math.PI/180;
8       this.sinTheta = Math.sin(this.theta);
9       this.cosTheta = Math.cos(this.theta);
10      this.sinAlpha = Math.sin(this.alpha);
11      this.cosAlpha = Math.cos(this.alpha);
12  };
```

First we create the object itself, called isometricAS. By creating it as a function object, we are setting it up so that we can later create instances of this object by invoking the constructor new isometricAS(). There are two parameters, maxx and maxz. We will discuss these in the next section since they apply only to the calculateDepth() method. In lines 4 and 5 we set the angles that are needed for the world to be isometric—30° and 45°. Then in the next several lines we calculate the sine and cosine of these angles and store the values. (This way we will not have to calculate them every time we need them.)

Next, we create this method on the isometricAS object:

```
1   isometricAS.prototype.mapToScreen = function(xpp, ypp, zpp) {
2       var yp = ypp;
3       var xp = xpp*this.cosAlpha+zpp*this.sinAlpha;
4       var zp = zpp*this.cosAlpha-xpp*this.sinAlpha;
```

```
5      var x = xp;
6      var y = yp*this.cosTheta-zp*this.sinTheta;
7      //var z = zp*this.cosTheta+yp*this.sinTheta;
8      return [x, y];
9   };
```

This method takes the coordinates of a point in the isometric system and maps its *x*- and *y*-coordinates in the Flash system. It does so by the same math steps that we went over earlier in this section.

Notice that line 7 is commented out. Earlier in this section when we talked about the math, I mentioned that we wouldn't need the *z*-coordinate when we were in the Flash system. I kept that line of ActionScript in there just in case you want it. If you ever decide to display a non-isometric view in which you'll need to apply perspective changes, then you will need this coordinate.

In line 8 we return the values *x* and *y* (which are the positions as they appear in the Flash system) as an array.

The final method of the `isometricAS` object that we will discuss in this section does something we have not yet discussed:

```
1   isometricAS.prototype.mapToIsoWorld = function(screenX,
    → screenY) {
2     var z = (screenX/this.cosAlpha-screenY/
      → (this.sinAlpha*this.sinTheta))*
      → (1/(this.cosAlpha/this.sinAlpha+
      → this.sinAlpha/this.cosAlpha));
3       var x = (1/this.cosAlpha)*(screenX-z*this.sinAlpha);
4       return [x, z];
5   };
```

This function maps the coordinates *(x, y)* from the Flash system into the isometric system. Since we have only the *x*- and *y*-coordinates from the Flash system, we cannot map that to an *(x, y, z)* position in the isometric system; we can only map it to two coordinates. This method is useful when we want to capture the user's mouse position and then find out where that would be in the isometric world.

If you have ever played Electrotank's Mini Golf game, then you have seen this used; as you move the mouse around the character, the character rotates to follow. Then, when you click, the character hits the ball. In order to calculate what angle the mouse made with the character, we map the mouse coordinates to the isometric world. The angle as it appears on the screen is not the angle that is truly in the isometric world.

We're not going to use this method in this section, but we will show a direct application of it in the final section in this chapter. I am not going to show the math involved in deriving the above equations, as it got pretty hairy, but I will tell you that I used the equations in the mapToScreen() method and worked backward.

Select the frame in the Actions layer, and open the Actions panel. Let's look at the first three lines of the ActionScript:

```
1   iso = new isometricAS();
2   ball = {x:0, y:0, z:0, clip:floor.ball,
    → shadowClip:floor.shadow};
3   speed = 5;
```

In line 1 we create an instance of the isometricAS object. In the next line we create an object called ball, which will be used to store all of the information about the ball movie clip that we will be moving around in the isometric world. We initialize this object at position (0, 0, 0) and give it references to the ball movie clip and the shadow movie clip. In line 3 we set the speed. This simply specifies how much to move the ball every time an arrow key is pressed.

Next, we create a function called captureKeys():

```
1   function captureKeys() {
2       if (Key.isDown(Key.RIGHT)) {
3           ball.x += speed;
4       } else if (Key.isDown(Key.LEFT)) {
5           ball.x -= speed;
6       }
7       if (Key.isDown(Key.UP)) {
8           ball.z += speed;
9       } else if (Key.isDown(Key.DOWN)) {
10          ball.z -= speed;
11      }
12  }
```

When this function is called, it checks to see which arrow keys are currently pressed down. If any are, then it changes the ball's position in either the x or z direction in the isometric system by the amount of speed.

Here is the function that is called to place the ball and the shadow on the screen:

```
1   function placeBall() {
2       var temp = iso.mapToScreen(ball.x, ball.y, ball.z);
3       ball.clip._x = temp[0];
4       ball.clip._y = temp[1];
5       var temp = iso.mapToScreen(ball.x, 0, ball.z);
6       ball.shadowClip._x = temp[0];
7       ball.shadowClip._y = temp[1];
8   }
```

In line 2 we call the mapToScreen() method of the isometricAS object, passing in the ball's coordinates. The result is stored as an array called temp. We then use the values of this array to position the ball on the screen (lines 3 and 4). In line 5 we do almost the same thing as we did in line 2 except that we pass in 0 as the value of the y position. We then use this array to place the shadow movie clip on the screen. We passed in the value of 0 for the y position because the shadow should always be on the ground, which has a y position of 0. But the x and z positions of the shadow should always be the same as the ball's. This adds a very simple and helpful effect to an object that's moving around in a 3D environment. To mention Electrotank's Mini Golf again, you can see how useful something like this is in that game. It is especially evident when the ball flies off a ramp. You can see the shadow move down the ramp as the ball goes through the air.

Now we come to a function called changeY(). As you can guess, this function changes the ball's y position. It is called when either of the two buttons at the bottom-right side of the screen is clicked.

```
1   function changeY(num) {
2       ball.y += num;
3       if (ball.y>0) {
4           ball.y = 0;
5       }
6   }
```

When this function is called, the ball's y position is increased by the amount of the parameter passed in. If the y position is ever below the floor, then we set it equal to the floor. This is so the ball cannot go through the floor.

Finally, we arrive at the onEnterFrame event:

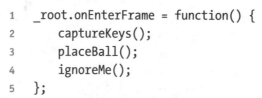

```
1   _root.onEnterFrame = function() {
2       captureKeys();
3       placeBall();
4       ignoreMe();
5   };
```

Check out the bonus file position_with_gravity.fla in the Chapter08 folder on the CD. It's similar to position.fla; the main difference is that this one has gravity so that the ball can bounce around in the isometric world.

This event calls captureKeys() and placeBall() in every frame. Ignore the ignoreMe() function—it is just there to help display the coordinates on the screen for you to see when testing the file.

That's everything! You are now on your way to building an isometric world. It's best to make your isometric world a tile-based world. You will see an example of this in the final section of this chapter.

Z-SORTING

We've come across the concept of z-sorting a few times already in this chapter, and now we can finally discuss it in detail. Once again, z-sorting is the term used to describe the creation of the stacking order of movie clips. If two movie clips are overlapping, of course they can't both be on top. The one on top is said to have a *higher depth*. You are probably familiar with the concept of depth in Flash, but let's review a little bit and go over a few things you may not know about depths in Flash.

Each timeline in a Flash movie can have up to 16,384 depths, and each depth can hold only one movie clip. When you manually place movie clips in a timeline, they are assigned a depth starting at -16,383. Each additional movie clip manually placed in the timeline has a depth higher than the previous one, with numbers moving closer to 0. When you use ActionScript to create instances of movie clips, you assign them a depth. It is recommended by Macromedia (and is common practice) to assign positive depths to movie clips created with ActionScript. Depth 1 does

Don't Go Too Deep!

Be careful how high a depth you use; if it is too high, then you can no longer easily remove the movie clip using removeMovieClip(). The highest depth to which you can assign a movie clip without losing the ability to use removeMovieClip() is 1,048,575. The depth 1,048,576 is too high. However, if your movie clip is above 1,048,575, you can use swapDepths() to bring that movie clip back down below this critical number and then use removeMovieClip().

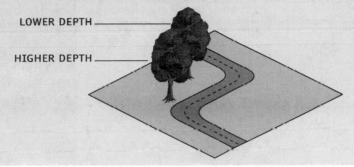

LOWER DEPTH

HIGHER DEPTH

not have to be filled before depth 2. This means that you can, for instance, use attachMovie() and assign the new movie clip a depth of 2,000,000.

The goal of z-sorting in our isometric world is to assign each movie clip to a specific depth so that the objects in the world appear to be stacked correctly. With z-sorting we can make it so that a character can walk around an object like a tree. The tree's depth remains constant, while the character's depth changes as it moves.

Isometric worlds in Flash are usually also tile-based worlds. All of the files presented in this chapter from now on use tiles to create the world. In addition to all the advantages of tile-based worlds that were introduced in Chapter 7, "Tile-Based Worlds," we can add z-sorting. Z-sorting in a tile-based world is much easier to handle than it is in a non-tile-based world. What we do is assign a depth to each tile, with a gap of something like 5 between depths. So one tile might have a depth of 100, and the next tile might have a depth of 105. Then as the character moves onto the first tile, we give it a depth of 101, and when the character moves onto the next tile, we give it a depth of 106. Next, we'll discuss how to assign the depth to each tile.

As you know, in order to create a grid of tiles, you must use nested loops. One way to assign depth is to base it on where you are in the loop. But that's a limited technique that we won't use here. Instead, we use an equation that will give us a unique depth for each cell. This equation works for any *y* position. So if you decide to create a complicated isometric world in which there are multiple levels (such as the inside of a two-story house), then this equation will still work perfectly, giving you the correct depths to use.

First we establish a boundary of the largest *x* tile number we expect to use. If it is a 10-by-10 tile-based world, then this boundary is 10. In the following mathematical exercise we use the letters *a* and *b* to represent the maximum number of tiles that can be found in the *x* and *z* directions.

```
a = 10
b = 10
```

Then, assuming we are trying to find the depth of the tile specified by (*x, y, z*), we can write the following:

```
floor = a*(b - 1) + x
depth = a*(z - 1) + x + floor*y
```

In order for these equations to give a valid final result (depth), *x, y,* and *z* must all be positive values. So when we write this with ActionScript, we make use of the `Math.abs()` method of the `Math` object in Flash to ensure that the values are positive. Since we are assigning values based on the tiles themselves, we can use integers for *x* and *z*. For instance, the cell 3_5 would have an *x* of 3 and a *z* of 5. Since we are only dealing with one level (flat ground), the value of *y* remains 0.

Each tile contains its depth.

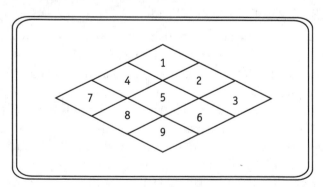

To see this in action, open depth.fla from the Chapter08 folder on the CD. In this file is a 10-by-10 grid of tiles created in the isometric world. When each tile is created, we assign a depth to it using the calculateDepth() method. There are three layers in the main timeline: Object Definitions, Actions, and Assets. The Assets layer contains one movie clip called floor. This movie clip contains the tile movie clip and the ball movie clip. The Actions layer contains a lot of ActionScript needed to create the tiles, change some of the tiles to display objects, and move the ball movie clip. The Object Definitions layer contains the same ActionScript as it did in the position.fla example file in the previous section. We did not discuss the calculateDepth() method at that time. Let's look at it now:

```
1    isometricAS.prototype.calculateDepth = function(x, y, z) {
2        var leeway = 5;
3        var x = Math.abs(x)*leeway;
4        var y = Math.abs(y);
5        var z = Math.abs(z)*leeway;
6        var a = this.maxx;
7        var b = this.maxz;
8        var floor = a*(b-1)+x;
9        var depth = a*(z-1)+x+floor*y;
10       return depth;
11   };
```

This method contains the math equations we discussed earlier, translated into ActionScript. In line 2 we create a variable called leeway. We multiply this number by both *x* and *z* when they are passed in. This enables us to separate the depth of each tile by at least the value of leeway (5). So one tile may have a depth of 250 and the next one would have a depth of 255. If leeway had a value of 1, then each depth would be 1 more than the previous. Notice the use of Math.abs() in lines 3–5. This ensures that the values of *x*, *y*, and *z* are positive. In lines 8 and 9 we calculate the depth and then return it in line 10.

Now let's look at the function that creates the tiles, buildFloor():

```
1    function buildFloor(path) {
2        path.tile._visible = false;
3        world.tiles = [];
4        var y = 0;
5        for (var j = 1; j<=10; ++j) {
6            for (var i = 1; i<=10; ++i) {
```

```
7          if (j == 1) {
8              world.tiles[i] = [];
9          }
10         var depth = iso.calculateDepth(i, y, j);
11         var name = "cell"+i+"_"+j;
12         path.attachMovie("tile", name, depth);
13         var clip = path[name];
14         world.tiles[i][j] = {x:i, y:y, z:j, depth:depth,
               → clip:clip};
15         var x = (i-1)*world.cellWidth;
16         var z = -(j-1)*world.cellWidth;
17         temp = iso.mapToScreen(x, y, z);
18         clip._x = temp[0];
19         clip._y = temp[1];
20      }
21    }
22 }
```

There is an object in the timeline called world (which we'll see in the "Deconstruction of a Simple World" section later on) that was created to store information about this isometric world. In line 3 above we create an array on the world object called tiles. This is a two-dimensional array, and each element of the array is an object that represents a tile. In line 4 we set the variable *y* equal to 0. This is the level on which the tiles will be created. Look at line 10. This is where we find the depth of the current tile that is being added to the screen. We do this by passing in the *x* tile number, the *z* tile number, and the *y* level (0). In line 12 we add the tile using attachMovie(), and assign it a depth from the variable we created in line 10 called depth.

Next let's take a look at the function used to place the ball on the screen:

```
1 function placeBall() {
2      ball.x = ball.x;
3      ball.y = ball.y;
4      ball.z = ball.z;
5      var temp = iso.mapToScreen(ball.x, ball.y, ball.z);
6      ball.clip._x = temp[0];
7      ball.clip._y = temp[1];
8      var cellx = Math.ceil(ball.x/world.cellWidth);
9      var cellz = Math.ceil(Math.abs(ball.z)/world.cellWidth);
```

```
10      var depth = iso.calculateDepth(cellx, 0, cellz);
11      var depth = depth+1;
12      ball.clip.swapDepths(depth);
13  }
```

Take a look at lines 8–12. In lines 8 and 9 we find the tile that the ball is currently on top of by using the trick learned in the "Precision Detection" section of Chapter 7 (a method for determining where the character is located, so that we then had to perform collision detection only in that cell). We then determine the tile's depth in line 10 by invoking the calculateDepth() method of the isometricAS object. Next, in line 11, we increase the value of the depth by 1. This is so that the ball will appear on top of the current tile. (If we didn't do this, we'd be setting the depth of the ball to the same depth as the tile, which would destroy the instance of that tile.) Finally, in line 12 we set the ball's depth using swapDepths().

That isn't all of the ActionScript in this file. We don't explain all of the ActionScript because you have seen the techniques used in the rest of this file before. In the next section we will discuss some more of the Action-Script, as well as add some more to this file.

Generate a SWF from this file to see z-sorting in action. Two plants will appear on the screen, along with a grassy tile-based ground and a sidewalk. The ball will appear at the edge of the floor. You can then use the arrow keys to move the ball around. Watch the ball move around the plants and the blocks sticking up through the floor; it appears in front of or behind the plant and the blocks as appropriate. You may notice that nothing is stopping you from moving the ball directly onto a cell that has an object, so the z-sorting can look a little bit odd if you move through an object. In the next section we add a character who can walk around in this world. We also add some collision detection to make sure the character doesn't move onto a tile that contains an object.

DECONSTRUCTION OF A SIMPLE WORLD

You have now seen the geometry and trigonometry needed to understand the isometric system's orientation with respect to the Flash system and how to handle z-sorting in an isometric world. With these concepts under your belt, it's an appropriate time to start thinking about more fun stuff, like the isometric world itself. In this section we deconstruct a file that contains a character, and see how the character interacts with its surroundings.

Open iso_world.swf from the Chapter08 directory on the CD. You'll quickly see that this file looks almost the same as the depth.fla file we used in the previous section. The only cosmetic difference is that instead of moving a ball, you'll be moving a character. In this movie you can click anywhere on the tiles and the character will start walking toward the point where you clicked. You'll see that a tile can be either grassy or concrete, and can contain either no objects or a plant or block. The character cannot walk through an object and so will stop walking when the next step would bring a collision.

Now open iso_world.fla in the same directory. Here you'll see that not only does the file look similar, but the majority of the ActionScript is the same, too. Before talking about the ActionScript, let's take a look at the character movie clip itself. Open the library and double-click the character library item.

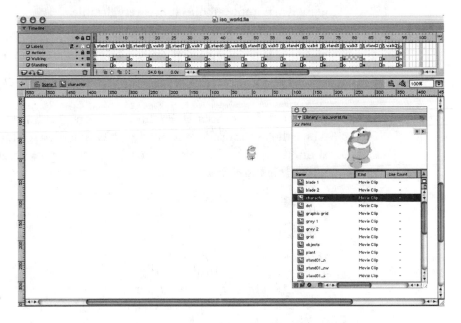

Notice that there are 16 frame labels in this timeline. The artist who created this character created eight different angles of it. For each of the eight angles there is a standing pose and a walking animation (called a *walk cycle*). The standing pose for the first angle is in the frame labeled stand1, and the corresponding walk cycle is in walk1. In the SWF, when you click somewhere on the tiles, the angle your mouse makes with the character (in the isometric world, not in the Flash system) is calculated. From this angle the script determines which of the eight character angles to display. We then move to the walk cycle for that angle. When the character stops walking, we move to the stand frame for that angle.

Now double-click the tiles library item. This is the movie clip that is attached to the screen several times to create the floor. There are two movie clips within this timeline, called innerTile and objects. The innerTile movie clip contains two frame labels, Grass and Concrete.

The objects movie clip contains two frame labels, Block and Plant. The Plant label has an isometric view of a plant, and the Block label has an isometric view of a thick tile that protrudes from the floor. With this simple setup we can easily create many types of tiles. For instance, we can show a plant but change the floor of that tile to show concrete instead of grass. This simple architecture is very flexible.

Now move back to the main timeline. Select the frame in the Actions layer, and open the Actions panel. We are going to go through the majority of the ActionScript in this frame, much of which was not discussed in the previous section.

First, let's look at the buildWorld() function. This function is called to initialize the world itself. It creates the objects needed to store information about the world, and calls functions to do things like creating the tiles and initializing the character.

```
1   function buildWorld(maxx, maxz) {
2       world = new Object();
3       world.maxx = maxx;
4       world.maxz = maxz;
5       world.cellWidth = 29;
6       world.width = maxx*world.cellWidth;
7       world.length = -maxz*world.cellWidth;
8       world.path = this.floor;
9       var path = world.path;
10      buildFloor(path);
11      buildCharacter(path);
12  }
```

In line 2 we create an object called world that is used to store information about the world. It stores the array that represents the tiles (created with the buildFloor() function), properties of the world dimensions (maxx and maxz), and the object that represents the character. This object will be discussed soon, when we cover the buildCharacter() function. Also stored on this object is the tile's width in the isometric world.

How Wide Is Your Tile?

You might wonder how you can find out the width of a square tile in an isometric world. Easy—you just use the Properties inspector to find the tile's width in the Flash system, and then divide this number by the square root of 2 (approximately 1.414). The result is the width of this tile in the isometric world. Alternatively, if you are the one creating the tile, then you can do this trick:

1. Draw a square in Flash (say, 100 by 100).
2. Rotate the square by 45°.
3. Scale down this square's height by 50 percent.

What you are left with is precisely what that square looks like in an isometric world. And you know what its width is in the Flash world because you created it (100, in this case).

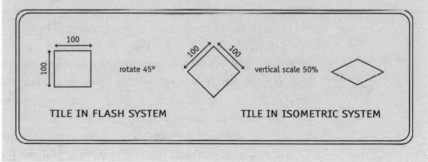

What you are left with is precisely what that square looks like in an isometric world. And you know what its width is in the Flash world because you created it (100, in this case).

Now let's look at the buildCharacter() function (which is called in line 11 of the ActionScript on the previous page):

```
1   function buildCharacter(path) {
2       world.char = new Object();
3       world.char.tempx = 10;
4       world.char.tempy = 0;
5       world.char.tempz = -10;
6       world.char.speed = 4;
7       world.char.feeler = 10;
8       world.char.width = 10;
```

```
9      world.char.xmov = 0;
10     world.char.zmov = 0;
11     world.char.moving = false;
12     world.char.clip = path.character;
13     positionCharacter();
14  }
```

This function initializes the object that represents the character. This object is called char and is on the world object. In lines 3–5 we set the temporary position of the character to give it a starting place. Through the course of the other functions that are called, this temporary position becomes the character's current position (that is, tempx, tempy, and tempz become x, y, z). In line 6 we create a variable called speed. When you click a tile, the character will attempt to walk there. The speed at which the character walks is determined by the value of the speed variable.

Next, we set an oddly named variable called feeler. This one requires a little explanation. In our previous file examples (and in this file as well), the object being moved around is represented by one point. We all know that a character in real life is three-dimensional and hence characterized by more than one point. If we use just one point to determine where the character is going, then when the character is on the edge of a tile bordering an object such as a block, some of the character is already on the block's tile. This is because the point that represents the character is still on the previous tile, but some of the graphic elements are overlapping the block. This presents a visual problem, but there is no actual programming problem. Everything still works, but it just may not look as good as you would like. There is more than one way to handle, or eliminate, this visual issue. The most proper way is to treat the character as if it were a cylinder or a cube (as we mentioned in Chapter 6, "Collision Reactions"). We're going to take an even simpler approach—we'll use something called *feelers*. Imagine an insect walking around. Before the majority of the insect's body moves onto a new surface, its feelers first inspect that surface. In our case, we extend the feelers a distance of 10 pixels along the direction in which the character is walking. If the feelers find an object in a cell not yet (but almost) reached, the character stops moving. This works amazingly well in this file. The feelers are nothing you can see; they are just code. You will see this technique used in the detectObjects() and worldClicked() functions.

In line 11 we set a variable called moving. This will always have a value of true or false. If true, then the character is moving.

In line 13 the function positionCharacter() is called. This function handles placing the character on the screen. It is called here but will also be called during every frame in an onEnterFrame event:

```
1  function positionCharacter() {
2      world.char.x = world.char.tempx;
3      world.char.y = world.char.tempy;
4      world.char.z = world.char.tempz;
5      var temp = iso.mapToScreen(world.char.x, world.char.y,
       → world.char.z);
6      world.char.clip._x = temp[0];
7      world.char.clip._y = temp[1];
8  }
```

In lines 2–4 we set the character's x, y, and z positions based on its current temporary positions in memory. We then use this placement to determine the character's x and y placement on the screen using the mapToScreen() method of the isometricAS object. Finally, we place the character on the screen.

The next logical step would be to discuss the function used to move the character from one point to another. But during this movement, collision detection occurs, using the feelers to see if the character is about to enter a tile that contains an object. So before we talk about how to move the character, let's talk about the functions that create the objects on the screen and change the types of tiles that are displayed.

```
1   function makeObject(x, z, object) {
2       world.tiles[x][z].isObject = true;
3       world.tiles[x][z].clip.objects.gotoAndStop(object);
4   }
5   function changeGroundTile(x, z, object) {
6       world.tiles[x][z].clip.innerTile.gotoAndStop(object);
7   }
8   function changeManyGroundTiles(x, xnum, z, znum, object) {
9       for (var i = 0; i<xnum; ++i) {
10          for (var j = 0; j<znum; ++j) {
11              world.tiles[x+i][z+j].clip.innerTile.gotoAndStop
                → (object);
12          }
13      }
14  }
```

These three functions are fairly self-explanatory. The first one, makeObject(), adds an object (either a plant or a block) to a tile. It then also sets the property isObject to true in the tiles array. We use the isObject property with the feelers when detecting a collision (more on this later). The next function, changeGroundTile(), simply changes the type of tile displayed. You can change a tile from grass to concrete or the other way around. The function changeManyGroundTiles() does the same thing as changeGroundTile() except that it applies to many tiles at once. You specify the starting x and z positions and then how far to extend in each direction.

Now that we've got that collision-detection discussion taken care of, we can move on to the "next logical step" I mentioned above—moving the character itself. When you click the mouse button, the well-named worldClicked() function is called. This function maps your mouse pointer's x and y positions onto the x, -z plane in the isometric world. It then takes these values and compares them with the world's boundaries. If the mouse was clicked within the world's boundaries and the character was not already moving, then many things happen. Let's look at those things.

```
1   function worldClicked(xm, ym) {
2       var temp = iso.mapToIsoWorld(xm, ym);
3       var xm = temp[0];
4       var zm = temp[1];
5       if (!world.char.moving && xm>=0 && xm<=world.width
        → && zm>=world.length && zm<=0) {
6           var x = world.char.x;
7           var z = world.char.z;
8           world.char.startx = x;
9           world.char.startz = z;
10          world.char.endx = xm;
11          world.char.endz = zm;
12          var angleSpan = 360/8;
13          var angle = Math.atan2(zm-z, xm-x);
14          var realAngle = angle*180/Math.PI;
15          realAngle += angleSpan/2;
16          if (realAngle<0) {
17              realAngle += 360;
18          }
```

```
19        var frame = Math.ceil(realAngle/angleSpan);
20        world.char.clip.gotoAndStop("walk"+frame);
21        world.char.frame = frame;
22        world.char.moving = true;
23        var cosAngle = Math.cos(angle);
24        var sinAngle = Math.sin(angle);
25        world.char.xmov = world.char.speed*cosAngle;
26        world.char.zmov = world.char.speed*sinAngle;
27        world.char.feelerx = world.char.feeler*cosAngle;
28        world.char.feelerz = world.char.feeler*sinAngle;
29    }
30 }
```

The condition in line 5 checks to see if the clicked area is within the boundaries of the world and if the character is not already moving. If the condition is satisfied, then it is OK to proceed and to prepare the character for movement. What does this preparation involve? For the character to be able to move, we have to determine the angle at which to move, the angled frame (1 of 8) to have the character display, and the speed in each direction for the character to walk. In lines 8 and 9 we store the character's starting position. (This starting position is used later to determine if the character has reached the destination.) In the next two lines we store the character's end position. Then, in line 12, we create a variable called angleSpan that stores the amount of degrees for each of the eight possible angles that the character can show. We will then use this value (along with the angle made with the mouse and the character found in line 14) to determine which of the eight frames to display in line 19. When using Math.atan2() to determine an angle, we'll sometimes get negative angles. Negative angles are perfectly valid, but I prefer to work with positive angles. Since angles are cyclic (that is, 350 is the same as -10), we can just add 360 to any negative angle to get its positive representation. This switch is performed in line 16. As mentioned above, line 19 calculates which character frame number to display in the character movie clip. We apply this in line 20 and store the value in line 21. We then set the property moving to true on the char object. Next we store the values of the sine and cosine of the angle, since they are used more than once (lines 23 and 24). We then use trigonometry to calculate the speed at which to move the character (lines 25 and 26), in the same way as we have done many times throughout this book. And finally, we set the feelerx and feelerz values. These are the values we will add to the temporary positions when checking for collisions.

Next we have the moveCharacter() function. This function is called in every frame.

```
1   function moveCharacter() {
2       if (world.char.moving) {
3           world.char.tempx = world.char.x+world.char.xmov;
4           world.char.tempz = world.char.z+world.char.zmov;
5           world.char.tempy = world.char.y+world.char.ymov;
6           var sx = world.char.startx;
7           var sz = world.char.startz;
8           var ex = world.char.endx;
9           var ez = world.char.endz;
10          var tempx = world.char.tempx;
11          var tempz = world.char.tempz;
12          if ((ex-sx)/Math.abs(ex-sx)
            → != (ex-tempx)/Math.abs(ex-tempx)
            → || (ez-sz)/Math.abs(ez-sz)
            → != (ez-tempz)/Math.abs(ez-tempz)) {
13              world.char.moving = false;
14              world.char.xmov = 0;
15              world.char.zmov = 0;
16              world.char.tempx = ex;
17              world.char.tempz = ez;
18              world.char.clip.gotoAndStop
                → ("stand"+world.char.frame);
19          }
20      }
21  }
```

The first task of this function is to check to see if the character is moving. If so (that is, moving has the property of true), then we move on. Lines 3–5 set the temporary position of the character based on its current position and its speed in each direction. Then we create references to its starting and ending positions so that the already-long if statement in line 12 looks a little more reasonable. The condition we are looking for in line 12 is pretty simple, even though it looks complicated. We are trying to determine if the character has reached its destination. If it has, then the sign (+ or -) of the difference between A) its current position and the destination and B) the starting position and the destination will be different (in either the *x* or *z* direction).

Let's take an example of the character moving only in the *x* direction. The starting position is 10, and the end position is 100. The sign of the difference between the ending position and the starting position is + (positive). You find this by dividing the difference by the absolute value of the difference:

```
(endx-startx)/Math.abs(endx-startx)
```

We compare this value with the value of the sign of the difference between the end position and the current position. So if the current position is 30, then `(100-30)/Math.abs(100-30)` is positive. Since this is the same as the sign from the starting and ending positions, the character has not yet reached the destination (whew!).

At some point the character's current position will be greater than the destination—say, 105. The value of `(100-105)/Math.abs(100-105)` is negative. Since this value no longer matches the positive value found with the starting and ending positions, we know the character has reached the destination. We perform this check for both the *x* and *z* directions. Once one of these two conditions is met, the character needs to stop walking.

In line 13 we set the moving property to `false` and then the velocities to 0. In lines 16 and 17 we set the character's temporary position to be the destination. Then, in line 18, we change the frame the character is displaying to the standing frame.

The last function we need to look at is `detectObjects()`. This function is called in every frame to determine if the character is about to step on a frame that contains an object (like a plant or a block).

```
1    function detectObjects() {
2        //Extend a little in the direction of motion
3        var x = world.char.tempx+world.char.feelerx;
4        var z = Math.abs(world.char.tempz+world.char.feelerz);
5        var x_tile = Math.ceil(x/world.cellWidth);
6        var z_tile = Math.ceil(z/world.cellWidth);
7        if (world.tiles[x_tile][z_tile].isObject != true) {
8            var x = world.char.tempx;
9            var z = Math.abs(world.char.tempz);
10           var x_tile = Math.ceil(x/world.cellWidth);
11           var z_tile = Math.ceil(z/world.cellWidth);
12           var depth = world.tiles[x_tile][z_tile].depth+1;
13           world.char.clip.swapDepths(depth);
14       } else {
```

```
15        world.char.tempx = world.char.x;
16        world.char.tempz = world.char.z;
17        world.char.xmov = 0;
18        world.char.ymov = 0;
19        world.char.moving = false;
20        var frame = world.char.frame;
21        world.char.clip.gotoAndStop("stand"+frame);
22     }
23  }
```

In lines 3–6 we add the feelerx and feelerz values to the temporary *x* and *z* values to determine which tile the feeler is touching. Then, in line 7, a conditional statement checks to see if there is an object in the tile that feelers are in. If there is, then we skip to the else leg of the ActionScript, which stops the character from walking, using the same code we used in the moveCharacter() function. If there is no object in that tile, then we enter the first leg of the if statement. We determine the depth of the tile that the character is currently on, and then add 1 to that depth. Then we move the character to that depth using swapDepths().

We have now discussed all of the functions used in this file. Let's look at when these functions are called. Here are the last 17 lines of ActionScript in this frame:

```
1   maxx = 10;
2   maxz = 10;
3   iso = new isometricAS(maxx, maxz);
4   buildWorld(maxx, maxz);
5   _root.onEnterFrame = function() {
6       moveCharacter();
7       detectObjects();
8       positionCharacter();
9   };
10  makeObject(2, 8, "plant");
11  makeObject(5, 4, "plant");
12  makeObject(6, 9, "block");
13  makeObject(5, 9, "block");
14  makeObject(5, 8, "block");
15  changeManyGroundTiles(2, 5, 3, 1, "concrete");
16  changeManyGroundTiles(6, 1, 3, 5, "concrete");
17  changeManyGroundTiles(6, 5, 8, 1, "concrete");
```

In lines 1 and 2 we set the number of tiles that are to be used in the world in both the *x* and *z* directions. We then create an instance of the isometricAS object, passing in these *x* and *z* boundaries. They are used by the isometricAS object when calculating depth. Next, in line 4, we call the buildWorld() function, passing in the *x* and *z* boundaries. The buildWorld() function stores this information on the world object and in turn calls the buildFloor() function, which uses these values. Next we set up an onEnterFrame event. This calls the functions moveCharacter(), detectObjects(), and positionCharacter() in every frame. The final eight lines of ActionScript place the objects on the screen and create the concrete tiles.

Generate a SWF from this file. Click different tiles around the world. Notice how the depth of the character changes as the character moves around a plant or a block.

With this basic introduction to isometric worlds, you should be able to start making some very interesting and fun environments that can be used for games or for chats.

POINTS TO REMEMBER

- An isometric world is the easiest type of 3D world to create in Flash.

- There is no perspective change in an isometric world.

- One of the best features of an isometric world is that you can reuse graphical assets at any place in the world, as is, because there is no perspective change.

- An isometric system is created by rotating a system that is currently aligned with the Flash system by 30° around the x-axis and then by 45° around the new y-axis.

- Because of the useful (and fast) depth-calculation equation we use, we are able to restrict positioning to the x, $-y$, $-z$ octant.

- Making an isometric system using tiles (that is, a tile-based world) is the most efficient and best way to create an isometric world. It makes collision detection and z-sorting much easier.

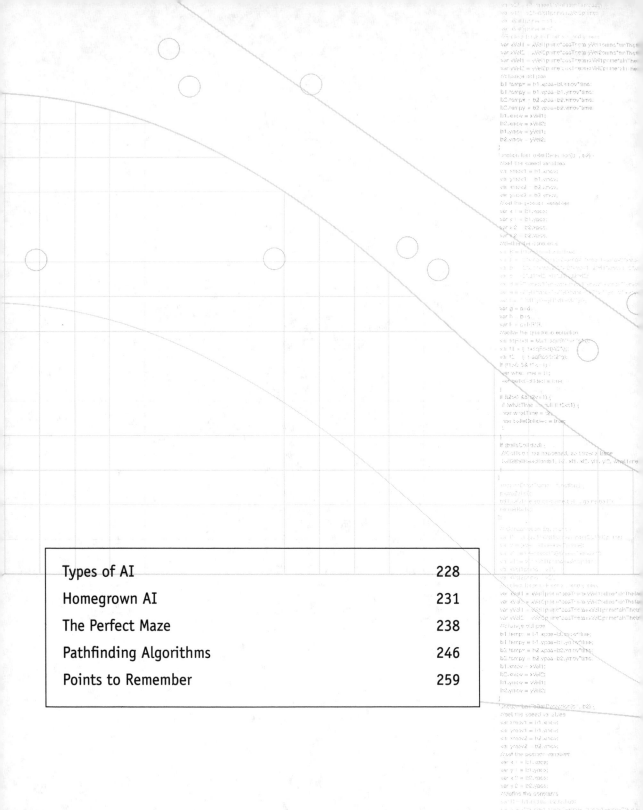

CHAPTER 9

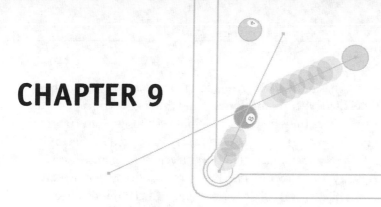

ARTIFICIAL INTELLIGENCE

ARTIFICIAL INTELLIGENCE (AI) IS A MACHINE'S ABILITY TO PERFORM TASKS that we think require intelligence. For example, if in real life a cop were trying to capture someone on foot, then he would try to take all possible shortcuts. The shortcuts would depend on where he was, where he wanted to go, and his own knowledge of the area involved. In a computer game, a character can be programmed with similar behavior. That is one application of AI.

The concept of AI has been around for a long time. Noted philosophers in the 1800s debated whether machines could think. The concept of AI was thrust a little more into the public eye in the 1980s with the upsurge of arcade games. But what really got people very interested in this topic was the famed chess match that pitted IBM's Deep Blue against chess Grandmaster Garry Kasparov in 1997. Kasparov lost the six-game match, and (as they say) history was made. Since then, artificial intelligence has rooted itself even further into games much more complicated than chess. You have probably seen some pretty amazing AIs used in real-time strategy games.

Getting back to reality (meaning Flash, of course!), you probably know that as smart as you think this program is, Flash simply doesn't have the power to support an ActionScript-written, Deep Blue level of intelligence. But it can write a good enough script to help you produce the kind of AI you'd need to help make most of your games interesting and fun. Certainly there are some games in which no AI is needed, such as multi-player checkers (because your opponent has a brain!). But for many games, even ones as simple as Pong or a basic platform game, an AI of some sort is a requirement to keep the game player engaged. In this chapter we introduce the topic of AI in Flash, mention the major flavors of AI seen in games, and give example implementations.

TYPES OF AI

You now probably have a pretty good idea of what AI is. So let's focus for a while on what you can *do* with it. More specifically, we will talk about the role(s) of AI in gaming. Here are some of the major uses of AI in games today.

Pathfinding. This is one of the biggest topics for game developers, especially those who are new to AI. *Pathfinding* is the act of finding a path between one point and another. In a game like Diablo (or in our example iso_world.fla file from the last chapter), you click to walk to a location. If there is an object in your way, then you walk around it. In most advanced games of this sort, the entire path that you will walk is calculated at the moment you click (rather than as you walk).

Pathfinding also works for your enemies. Using various pathfinding techniques, an evil critter may be programmed to scamper around objects and toward you.

Although there are many types of pathfinding algorithms, the one that is considered by all authorities to be the best is A* (pronounced "A Star"). This algorithm will be covered in the last section of this chapter.

Level generation. Some games rely on random but intelligent level creation at runtime. For instance, if you play a certain game twice, the level architecture (walls and rooms) may be the same from one game to the next, but the enemy placement and secret items may be in new positions. Alternatively, the entire level may be completely new from one game to the next, as is the maze in this chapter. This type of level generation is driven by an AI. Sometimes the AI may be a popular algorithm known to many developers; at other times it may have been created from scratch for a particular game.

Enemy behavior. Using pathfinding, an enemy may know how to find you, but what does he do when he gets to you? He may hit you with a sword; he may change his mind and run away, or maybe he just wants to chat. In addition to the pathfinding AI, there is a separate AI that controls enemy-behavior options. This can be one of the most complicated components to program in enormous games created for worldwide distribution (or so I've heard). However, an AI of this sort for an RPG in Flash could be much simpler, as the rest of the game would probably be much simpler (as compared with one from the big boys).

Neural networks. A *neural network* is an AI that can learn. It gives results based on internal numeric parameters that are adjusted in real time. The result is a machine that can behave differently in different situations. This concept has only recently begun being used in games. Imagine some sort of strategy war game—you versus the AI, each armed with planes, tanks, ships, and soldiers. If you repeatedly use your planes to attack the enemy, then the AI will learn from this. It will think, "Hey, I need to take measures to prevent more plane attacks. I've got it! I'll send my tanks in to blow up his planes." This makes for a very "human" AI. A pattern is identified and deemed bad, and then measures are taken to disrupt it. Neural networks are also largely used in e-learning applications. For example, an AI in a software application that instructs you in touch typing might be programmed to chastise you if you type naughty words, or to suggest you take a break when it detects that you are pounding on all the keys at once.

You Win Some, You Lose Some

It is very important to note that, to be used well in a game, an AI should offer a certain difficulty range. For instance, if you were playing against Deep Blue in a game of chess, you would be sure to lose. A game is only fun if you have a chance at victory. A game is also only fun if you know that there is a chance that you *won't* win—that way, if you do win, you have a sense of accomplishment. So there should be a balance. Create an AI that is perfect—as perfect as you can, anyway. You can always find ways to dumb it down or mix it up, but it's hard to introduce ways of making it smarter once you've written it. For instance, if you've created an AI that never loses a game of checkers, then you could do something as simple as making every other move of the computer be chosen randomly rather than intelligently. This would make the AI less effective but the game more fun. Exactly how much should you dumb down the AI? That can only be determined by testing the game with game players.

Turn-based games. An AI can be written to play turn-based games such as checkers and chess. There are many different levels of AI for these types of games. The main two are ones that look at the board now and just decide what the next best move is; and ones that form strategies, have a sense of history, and look ahead. You can find a lot of AI algorithms (not many in ActionScript) on the Internet for games like chess, checkers, Connect Four, and Scrabble.

Custom logic. Any of the types of AI I've already mentioned can make use of custom logic. I list this as a separate category to include the miscellaneous AI uses that don't belong in the other categories. You can use AI to control just about anything in a game, from behavior to colors to volume to repercussions to speed to difficulty. As a basic example, in the Chapter09 directory you'll find a simple game of Pong with an AI. The opponent paddle is intelligent enough to follow the ball. Or you can create an AI to determine when a certain event should happen in a game. For instance, if you think the user is performing too well in a car-racing game (and if you like being cruel to your game players), you might initialize a thunderstorm to make the game a little more difficult.

In the rest of this chapter we'll look at custom AI, AI used to generate a random but perfect maze, and A* pathfinding.

HOMEGROWN AI

In this section we'll talk about creating your own AI, as opposed to using AI algorithms found elsewhere. The information presented here does not even scratch the surface of learning how to create *any* AI—that's another subject for a much longer, more technical book. Here the information covers a specific AI.

To introduce you to the kind of script we're going to discuss, from the Chapter09 directory on the CD open shark_attack.swf, which should look familiar from Chapter 7, "Tile-Based Worlds." Shark Attack! is an isometric tile-based-world game, with some AI enemies, that I created for a company called Simply Scuba. You are the red fish. The goal is to collect the key and go to the door. Collect coins and objects as you go, for more points. Watch out for the sharks, though; they are the enemies. Double-click the SWF file to open it. Play a few levels (there are only four included) and notice the behavior of the sharks. They are controlled with a fairly simple but effective AI. In this section you will learn how an AI very similar to this was created.

Rules for Controlling Characters

By this point in your odyssey through this book, you are ready to complete this game on your own!

Open run_away.fla in the Chapter09 directory. This file contains the enemy AI for an unfinished game called Grave Robber. Here, we will look at how enemies (also called "baddies") behave. The baddies are zombies, and the good guy (well, as good as a thief can be) is human—he is controlled by you. You walk around trying to rob graves, and every time you do, the zombies try to "get" you. There are walls that you cannot pass through. In this file, there is no collision detection between the hero and the baddies, since we are only illustrating behavior. Warning: This file (and in fact every example file we use in this chapter) uses tiles, so if you haven't yet familiarized yourself with tile-based worlds, then you might want to take the time to do so (see Chapter 7). We will only discuss the ActionScript used in the AI for this file, not the world creation or how we handle wall collisions.

Use Test Movie to take a look at this world. Move around and try to notice the behavior of the enemy zombies. The AI used here is very similar to the AI used in the Shark Attack! game.

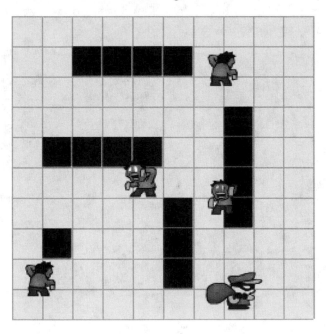

There is a script within the code that instantaneously changes the direction of the enemy's motion. To be concise, I'll call the running of this script an "update." Now let's look at the rules that the zombies follow in this update to produce their behavior: homing in on the thief.

- The characters' movement is restricted to horizontal only or vertical only at any given time.

- The update script checks the hero's location relative to the enemy's, and stores the information as follows:

  Horizontal motion
  −1 if the hero is to the left of the enemy
  0 if the hero is in the same column
  1 if the hero is to the right of the enemy

  Vertical motion
  −1 if the hero is above
  0 if the hero is in the same row
  1 if the hero is below

- If the horizontal and vertical values are both 0, then the enemy is in the same tile as the hero, and the update does not change the path of motion.

- If either horizontal or vertical is 0, then the script changes the direction of motion to have the hero move along the other. For instance, if the horizontal value is −1 and the vertical value is 0, then the script knows that the hero is in the same row to the left, and it makes the enemy move left.

- If both the horizontal and vertical values are non-zero, then the script randomly chooses one of the two directions and makes the baddy move that way. For instance, if the vertical value is −1 and the horizontal value is 1,then the AI knows the hero is somewhere to the top right of the enemy. It then randomly chooses either vertical or horizontal and moves toward the hero in that direction.

- The update script contains a randomization condition (in the form of an `if` statement). At random times the script will choose a completely random direction to move, no matter what the state of the board is. This is the AI's "dumb-down" feature. The frequency of this random "imperfection" makes the AI behave unpredictably.

So now we know the logic that is performed when the update script is executed. But *when* is it executed? Here are the conditions for which the update script can be executed:

- When the enemy bumps into a wall or any immovable object.

- When `maxtime` number of frames has passed since the last update. The value of `maxtime` is different for each enemy.

Drawbacks and Solutions

Before we look at the actual ActionScript for bringing this AI to life, I want to mention the drawbacks of this AI. You may notice that the enemies usually stay pretty close to walls. With this behavior, if you had a fairly empty world, then the enemies would tend to stay along the outer edge of the world. This AI works best with worlds that have many walls—environments that are almost mazelike. If you mostly like this AI but want to make it more intelligent than the wall-hugging behavior implies, you can do that without too much trouble. Here are some ways you can smarten it up:

- Program the update to make the character move toward the center of a tile to continue motion rather than hugging up against a wall. This is more of an aesthetic enhancement, but it also gives the appearance of greater intelligence.

- When a character collides with a wall, give higher priority to turning another direction rather than moving into the wall again. With the current AI you can slam into the wall a few times before moving away. This is not all that noticeable because the collisions happen so fast, but it does happen.

- Add diagonal motion.

Enemy ActionScript

OK, now it's finally time to look at the ActionScript used in this AI. This function, `baddyAI()`, is called in every frame. It loops through an array of enemies and determines if it is time for an update. If it is, then it performs the update.

```
1  function baddyAI() {
2      for (var i = 0; i<game.baddies.length; ++i) {
```

```
3      var ob = game.baddies[i];
4      ++ob.time;
5      var cell_x = Math.ceil(ob.x/game.cellWidth);
6      var cell_y = Math.ceil(ob.x/game.cellWidth);
7      var cell_over = game.tiles[cell_x][cell_y];
8      var cell_x_temp =
       → Math.ceil(ob.tempx/game.cellWidth);
9      var cell_y_temp =
       → Math.ceil(ob.tempy/game.cellWidth);
10     var cell_over_temp =
       → game.tiles[cell_x_temp][cell_y_temp];
11     if (!cell_over_temp.empty
       → || ob.time == ob.maxtime) {
12        ob.time = 0;
13        ob.maxtime = 30+random(30);
14        ob.tempx = ob.x;
15        ob.tempy = ob.y;
16        var tempDir = ob.dir;
17        var xmov = 0;
18        var ymov = 0;
19        var speed = Math.abs(ob.speed);
20        var xsign = (game.char.x-ob.x)/
          → Math.abs((game.char.x-ob.x));
21        var ysign = (game.char.y-ob.y)/
          → Math.abs((game.char.y-ob.y));
22        if (random(10) == 0) {
23           var xsign = -1*xsign;
24           var ysign = -1*ysign;
25        }
26        if (xsign == ysign || xsign == -ysign) {
27           var ran = random(2);
28           if (ran == 0) {
29              var xsign = 0;
30           } else {
31              var ysign = 0;
32           }
33        }
34        if (xsign != 0) {
35           var ymov = 0;
```

```
36              var xmov = xsign*speed;
37              if (xmov>0) {
38                  var dir = "right";
39              } else {
40                  var dir = "left";
41              }
42          } else if (ysign != 0) {
43              var xmov = 0;
44              var ymov = ysign*speed;
45              if (ymov>0) {
46                  var dir = "down";
47              } else {
48                  var dir = "up";
49              }
50          }
51          ob.dir = dir;
52          ob.clip.gotoAndStop(dir);
53          ob.xmov = xmov;
54          ob.ymov = ymov;
55      }
56  }
57 }
```

This is a pretty long function, but don't panic—there is a lot of reappearing information. That is mostly because of the several if statements and because everything we do for the *x* direction we also do for the *y* direction. As with many of the files created in this book, here we have an object called game that stores information about the game. There is an array called baddies stored in game that contains one object for each enemy ("baddy") in the game. This function loops through the baddies array and checks out each baddy object to determine if it is time to run an update. Line 3 sets a temporary reference called ob to the current enemy that we are inspecting in the baddies array. In the next line we increment the time variable in ob. Remember that one of the conditions to determine if it is time for an update is if maxtime is the same as time. We will perform this check further down (line 11). In lines 5 and 6 we determine which cell the enemy is currently over, and in lines 8 and 9 we determine which cell the enemy would be over at the end of the frame. The cell that the enemy would be over at the end of the frame is given a temporary reference called cell_over_temp. In line 11 we check two conditions to determine if it is time for an update. First, if cell_over_temp is not empty (that is, if it contains an object), then we perform an update. Second, if the time variable is the same as the maxtime variable on the enemy object, then we also do an update.

Let's look at the update (starting in line 12). First we set time back to 0 so that the counter will start over. Next we semi-randomly set a new maxtime value. There is nothing special about the numbers chosen for this randomization. You can change them and get different behaviors of the enemies. If you are interested in repurposing this AI and want some control over its difficulty level, this is one line of code you might want to play around with. In the next two lines we set the enemy's position to where it was at the beginning of the frame (lines 14 and 15). Then we store the current direction of the enemy as tempDir. This is a string value that is "left", "right", "up", or "down". We then set the values of the x and y velocities to 0 so that we can reassign them from scratch (lines 17 and 18). In lines 20 and 21 we determine the sign for the x and y directions, specifying where the hero is with respect to this enemy. Remember, these can have values of −1, 0, or 1.

In lines 22–24 we insert the random dumbing-down process mentioned earlier in this section. This will cause the script to reverse the direction of an enemy approximately one out of every ten times it runs.

In line 26 we determine whether the enemy is in the same row or column as the hero. If he is not, then we randomly choose either the x direction or the y direction to move in. The direction we do *not* want to move in we set to 0. So, when xsign is set to 0, we will move toward the hero in the y direction. Next, in lines 34–39 we perform similar tasks for either the x or the y direction, depending on which is non-zero. For the direction that is non-zero we set the speed in that direction and also set the temporary variable dir to store the string value of the direction of motion. This is then used in line 52 to display a certain frame in the enemy movie clip so that the zombie appears to be walking in the correct direction. In lines 53 and 54 we store the newly established x and y velocities on the enemy object.

That's all of it! As far as AIs go, this one is elementary, but for simple games it is good enough.

Are you interested in creating games along the lines of Pac-Man? The AI used here would probably work great for characters and figures like the ghosts in that game.

THE PERFECT MAZE

You are probably very familiar with mazes—surprisingly fun puzzles that can keep you interested for a long time. In this section we talk about the AI involved in creating random but perfect mazes. But first you should know what a perfect maze is, as opposed to an imperfect one. A perfect maze is one in which exactly one path exists between every two cells. In a perfect maze, you can choose any two cells and there will always exist a path between the two—but only one. In a perfect maze, a looped path is not possible, and there are no closed-off areas.

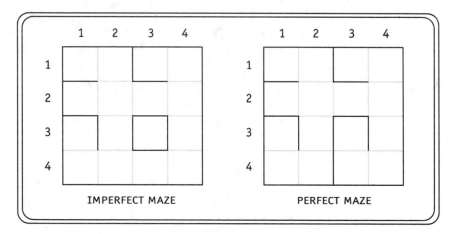

IMPERFECT MAZE   PERFECT MAZE

In the figure above, you can see both perfect and imperfect mazes. The imperfect one has both a closed-off cell and multiple paths between some cells. The perfect maze has no closed-off areas, and only one path exists between any two cells. Here is a larger, more interesting perfect maze.

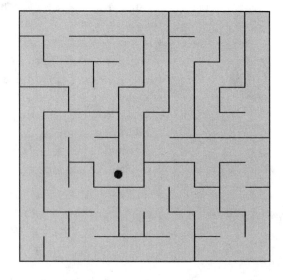

Rules for the Perfect Maze

This is a pretty simple application that makes use of two-dimensional arrays to store information about each tile. The maze is tile-based, and each tile has four walls. Now let's look at the rules for creating a perfect maze.

1. *Choose how many rows and columns you want in the maze. You have **rows*columns** number of cells in this maze. All the walls of these cells are currently up. Create a variable called* `cellsVisited` *with a value of 0.*

2. *Create an array called* `visitedList`. *When a cell is visited, it will be added to this array.*

3. *Choose a random starting cell. Make this the current cell. Increment* `cellsVisited`.

4. *If the value of* `cellsVisited` *is equal to the number of cells, your maze is finished. Otherwise move on to step 5.*

5. *Create an array called* `neighbors`. *Look at each of the immediate neighbors of this cell. We will call them* "east", "west", "north", *and* "south". *Add any neighbor that has never been visited to the* `neighbors` *array. If any of the neighbors have at one time been visited, then they are not added to this array.*

6. *Randomly choose a neighbor from the* `neighbors` *array. If the* `neighbors` *array is empty (indicating that all of the neighbors have been visited), then move on to step 9. Otherwise, continue to step 7.*

7. *Move to this randomly selected neighbor, knocking down the wall between the current cell and this neighbor cell.*

8. *Make this neighbor cell the current cell, and add it to the* `visitedList` *array. Return to step 5.*

9. *Move to the previous cell in the* `visited` *array, deleting the cell you are currently in from the* `visitedList` *array. Return to step 5.*

The images below show an example of how a 3X3 maze would be created.

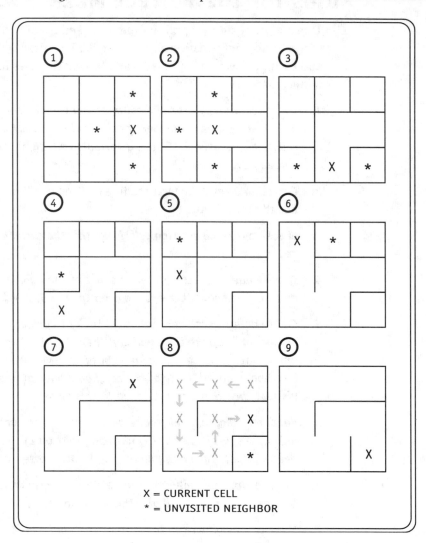

X = CURRENT CELL
* = UNVISITED NEIGHBOR

Using ActionScript to Create the Perfect Maze

Now that you have a good understanding of the algorithm, let's take a look at how it can be written in ActionScript. If you truly understand this algorithm (which you can probably do without too much trouble), and if you have a firm grasp of ActionScript, you should be able to write the ActionScript for this algorithm on your own. But just in case you don't want to try, we have done it for you.

Open maze.fla in the Chapter09 directory. Using the Test Movie command, take a look at the SWF. If you initialize the SWF several times, you will see that the maze is different each time—always perfect and always unique. Also, notice that there is a dot in the top-left cell. You can move this dot through the maze using the arrow keys on your keyboard.

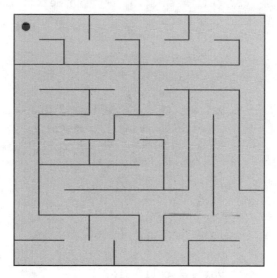

In maze.fla there are three layers: Object Definition, Implementation, and Assets. The Object Definition layer contains the algorithm that creates the maze in memory. The Implementation layer contains the ActionScript needed to create a visual representation of the maze that we created in memory. The Assets layer contains the movie clips needed to display the maze.

We are most concerned with the ActionScript in the Object Definition layer, since that contains the AI algorithm for maze creation. There are 75 lines of code in this frame, all for one long function.

```
1   maze = {};
2   maze.createMaze = function(horizontal, vertical) {
3       this.rows = horizontal;
4       this.columns = vertical;
5       this.totalCells = this.rows*this.columns;
6       this.startRow = random(this.rows)+1;
7       this.startColumn = random(this.columns)+1;
8       this.cellsVisited = 0;
9       this.currentCell = "cell"+this.startRow+"_"
        → +this.startColumn;
10      this[this.currentCell] = {name:this.currentCell,
        → x:this.startRow, y:this.startColumn, exists:true};
11      this.visitList = [];
12      this.visitList.push(this[currentCell]);
13      while (this.cellsVisited<this.totalCells) {
14          var cell = this[this.currentCell];
15          var neighbors = [];
16          if (cell.x-1>0) {
17              //west cell
18              var x = cell.x-1;
19              var y = cell.y;
20              var westCell = "cell"+x+"_"+y;
21              if (!this[westCell].exists) {
22                  neighbors.push([westCell, "west",
                    → "east", x, y]);
23              }
24          }
25          if (cell.y-1>0) {
26              //north cell
27              var x = cell.x;
28              var y = cell.y-1;
29              var northCell = "cell"+x+"_"+y;
30              if (!this[northCell].exists) {
31                  neighbors.push([northCell, "north",
                    → "south", x, y]);
32              }
33          }
```

```
34        if (cell.x+1<=this.rows) {
35            //east cell
36            var x = cell.x+1;
37            var y = cell.y;
38            var eastCell = "cell"+x+"_"+y;
39            if (!this[eastCell].exists) {
40                neighbors.push([eastCell, "east",
                 → "west", x, y]);
41            }
42        }
43        if (cell.y+1<=this.columns) {
44            //south cell
45            var x = cell.x;
46            var y = cell.y+1;
47            var southCell = "cell"+x+"_"+y;
48            if (!this[southCell].exists) {
49                neighbors.push([southCell, "south",
                 → "north", x, y]);
50            }
51        }
52        //randomly choose a neighbor
53        if (neighbors.length>0) {
54            var nextCell = random(neighbors.length);
55            //knock down wall
56            cell[neighbors[nextCell][1]] = true;
57            //retrieve the name of the new cell
58            var newName = neighbors[nextCell][0];
59            this[newName] = {};
60            var newCell = this[newName];
61            newCell.exists = true;
62            newCell.x = neighbors[nextCell][3];
63            newCell.y = neighbors[nextCell][4];
64            newCell.name = this.currentCell;
65            //knock down the wall
66            newCell[ncighbors[nextCell][2]] = true;
67            this.currentCell = newName;
68            this.visitList.push(this.currentCell);
69            ++this.cellsVisited;
```

```
70              } else {
71                  //step back to the last cell
72                  this.currentCell = this.visitList.pop();
73              }
74          }
75  };
```

We begin by creating an object called maze. Next, we add a method to this object, called createMaze(), which accepts two parameters that specify the number of columns and the number of rows to be calculated for the maze. They are stored as columns and rows. The total number of cells in this maze is calculated by multiplying rows by columns. This value is stored as totalCells. We then randomly select a cell to start from and store this as currentCell (lines 7–9). In line 10 we create an object that represents this starting cell, and give it four properties: name, x, y, and exists. The exists property gives us an easy way to check to see if a cell has been visited. If exists is true, then the cell has been visited. Next, we create an array called visitedList and insert the object that represents the current cell into it. We have now given the AI a starting place. One cell exists; it is in the visited array. Now we can perform a while loop until the cellsVisited variable is equivalent to totalCells (line 13). When cellsVisited is equivalent to totalCells, then the maze has been completed.

In line 14 we create a reference to the object that represents the current cell. Lines 15–51 perform step 5 from above: The neighbors array is created. Then we check to the west, north, east, and south of the current cell for cells that have not yet been visited. If we find one, then we add it to the neighbors array. When it is added to the neighbors array, we store string names of the wall in each cell that would be knocked down if we chose to visit this cell. For instance, for the neighbor to the east we store the string values "east" and "west". That means if we choose to visit this cell, then we will knock down the east wall in the current cell and the west wall in the neighbor cell. Visually, these are the same wall, but in code each cell keeps track of its own walls.

In line 53 we start step 6. If the neighbors array is not empty, then we randomly choose a neighbor (line 54); otherwise, we step back in the visitedList array (lines 70–73). Once a random neighbor is chosen, we perform steps 7 and 8 from above, and must also do the following:

1. Create an object for that neighbor cell.

2. Knock down the walls between the current cell and the neighbor cell.

3. Increment the `cellsVisited` variable.

4. Set the neighbor cell as the current cell.

This is all done in lines 54–69. As mentioned above, if there were no elements in the `neighbors` array, then we move on to lines 70–73, where we step back to the previous cell.

I hope you'll agree that while this script was long, it wasn't all that complicated, right?

Visual Implementation of the Perfect Maze

We are not going to dissect the ActionScript found in the Implementation layer. However, I will briefly describe what it does. First, it calls the `maze.createMaze()` method. When that has finished, the `maze` object contains many other objects that are named in this fashion: `cell1_1`, `cell1_2`, `cell1_3`, and so on. This naming scheme is the same as in all of the tile-based worlds you have seen or will see in this book. The ActionScript then performs a nested loop to add all of the tiles to the stage. During each iteration, the ActionScript looks up the corresponding cell object in the `maze` object and looks at its `east` and `south` properties. If `east` is not `true` then the east wall should be visible and is made visible. If `south` is not `true`, the south wall should be visible and is made visible. The script only cares about the east and south walls of each cell because we can build the maze with only those pieces of information. The east wall of `cell1_1` is the same as the west wall of `cell2_1`, so we only need to display this wall one time. Likewise, the south wall of `cell1_1` is the same as the north wall of `cell1_2`.

The rest of the ActionScript in that frame handles the movie clip that the user moves through the maze.

PATHFINDING ALGORITHMS

As we've mentioned before, a pathfinding algorithm is one that finds any path between two points. Usually these two points are the centers of two different tiles in a tile-based world. (In fact, I can't think of an implementation of pathfinding that is not in a tile-based world.) To help get you started learning about pathfinding algorithms, here are a few of the most popular types. (Note: These algorithms perform the pathfinding all at once in memory and then give a complete path—usually in the form of an array—as the final result.)

- One that starts at the first tile and randomly walks from tile to tile (in memory) until the goal is reached.

- One that starts at both the starting tile and the goal tile and walks randomly until the paths intersect.

- One that moves in the direction of the goal from a particular starting point until it hits an obstacle. It then moves along the obstacle until it can get around it. This pathfinding trick—used by many real-life robots—is called *tracing*.

Each of these types of pathfinding algorithms has its benefits and weaknesses. Some are superfast to compute but can yield very long or odd-looking paths. Some give nice-looking paths under certain conditions, such as in an environment with no concave obstacles like closets. As always, you have to weigh the pros and cons and choose your trade-offs.

The best-known pathfinding algorithm is A*. Provided that you fulfill some conditions (that we will discuss in a while), A* is guaranteed to return the shortest possible path between two points. Like the other pathfinding algorithms, however, A* also has a drawback: It is slow. The A* algorithm is one of the most (if not *the* most) CPU-intensive pathfinding algorithms. Still, regardless of its speed, A* is used more than any other pathfinding algorithm in games. When you play games like Diablo, and you click in an area on the screen, the character walks to that position. If there is an obstacle in the way, the character walks around the obstacle. In any game you play that has pathfinding ability like this, the game is probably using A*. In this section we're going to introduce you to that algorithm and walk you through it.

The A* pathfinding algorithm finds the way from point A to point B.

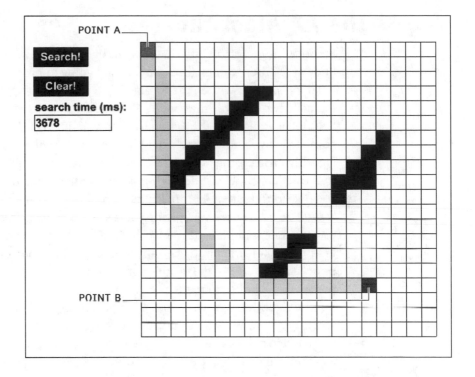

In the image above you can see a basic implementation of the A* pathfinding algorithm. What you see is a 20-by-20 grid. The white cells are empty cells. The black cells contain walls. The gray cell at the top left (point A) is the starting position of a character; the dark gray cell at the bottom right (point B) is the ending position of that character. The light gray path that connects the two is the path created by the A* pathfinding algorithm.

Every Flavor A*

Video games are a multibillion-dollar industry. So as you can imagine, a lot of money has been spent in trying to find better and faster pathfinding algorithms. To that end, there are many variations of A*. These variations usually result from optimizations and modifications to the A* algorithm. In this section we don't offer any optimizations or major modifications to the A* algorithm; we present it in its basic form.

The A* Algorithm

Before we continue on into that specific algorithm, however, you need to know a few more things about how we are going to proceed, and with what tools. I have written the A* algorithm in ActionScript and have included two example files on the CD that use that ActionScript—but I will not be explaining the ActionScript to you line by line; instead, I'm going to tell you how to use what I have created. I will discuss in detail the algorithm itself using *pseudo-code,* and then make some general references to the ActionScript. Pseudo-code is a representation of an algorithm in a codelike form (sort of like an outline of a chapter). It mentions what you should do in code without giving you a specific syntax. This means that pseudo-code is not language-specific; Java programmers, ActionScript programmers, C++ programmers—any kind of programmer—can read and understand it. One of the beauties of pseudo-code is that it tends to be pretty short. For instance, the pseudo-code used here is just over 30 lines, but the algorithm written in ActionScript is nearly 170. In pseudo-code you might have a line that informs the reader to delete an element from an array, but in real code you would have to loop through the array to find the element and then delete it, which would take several lines of code.

I learned the A* algorithm from pseudo-code found on gamasutra.com (see Appendix E for pathfinding links). My pseudo-code of the A* algorithm bears a resemblance to the one that I found on Gamasutra (www.gamasutra.com), but is not the same. If two people sit down and write plot summaries for *Star Wars: Episode II,* the summaries will probably both have the same content, but it will be described differently. That is the same thing here: They're two different descriptions of the same algorithm.

Branching Out with Pathfinding

Although primarily used for pathfinding, the A* algorithm is actually much more general than that. You can use it to find the solutions to many types of problems. My understanding of A* as applied to pathfinding is pretty solid, but my general understanding of A* regarding other applications is, well, nonexistent. If you are interested in using A* for tasks other than pathfinding, you can probably find any number of resource sites on the Internet to help you with that.

Basic A* terminology and functionality

As with many math-based concepts, the A* pathfinding algorithm uses a handful of terms you have to be familiar with in order to proceed. These terms describe the states, actions, and results that go along with this process:

- A *node* is the representation of the current state of the system. In pathfinding, the current state is simply the tile that we are currently inspecting. So as far as we are concerned, a node is a tile.

- The act of *expanding* a node means that (in code) you visit each of the node's neighbors.

- A *heuristic*, in A*, is an educated guess, based on a chosen unit of measurement, that yields a number. (That is pretty vague, right? We will talk more about heuristics soon.)

- The *cost* is a numeric amount that we assign to the act of moving from one node to another.

- The *score* is made of the sum of the cost and heuristic of every node you visited along the path to the current node.

With these terms in place, let's see how they apply to the algorithm, and more generally, how A* works. As you now know, A* finds the shortest path between two points. But what measurement are we using? Time? Distance? Number of steps? While A* can be used to search according to pretty much any measurement, we choose to use distance. Other measurements might be time (to find the path that takes the shortest time to walk) or the number of tanks of gas used (to find the path that uses the smallest amount of gas in a car). To the cost of moving between one tile and its vertical or horizontal neighbor we will assign a value of 1 (1 foot, 1 mile, 1 tile—it doesn't matter). The cost of moving between one tile and a neighboring diagonal tile is 1.41. The number 1.41 is the distance between the centers of two neighboring diagonal tiles.

The heuristic is the best guess of how far the center of the current tile (that you are inspecting during the search) is from the destination tile. You can make this guess fairly easily using simple logic. When visited, each node is assigned a score of f:

$$f = g + h$$

The value h is the heuristic—the best guess of the distance between that tile and the goal. The value g is the sum of the scores of every node visited along the path to the current node. This may be best understood with an analogy. Let's say you are planning a trip from New York to Paris. You are on a tight budget, so you want to find the path that will cost the least. You can think of New York, London, Lisbon, Brussels, Madrid, and Paris as nodes. In the course of your research, you calculate the cost from New York to London and store that. But you also calculate the costs of traveling from Lisbon to New York, London to Paris, and so on. In the end, if you apply other rules (not yet discussed) with A*, you find the best path (for cost). Let's assume that this path turns out to be New York–Madrid–London–Paris. In New York (as in all nodes), $f = g + h$. Remember that g is the sum of all the fs of the previous nodes. Since New York is the starting node, there are no parents, so $g = 0$ in New York. For Madrid, $f = g + h$ also (as in all nodes). In this case, g is not 0 because Madrid was visited from another node. The g value is made up of the f from New York. So g is the running total of cost up to the current node. If you were actually on this trip, then g would be the amount of money spent up to your current position.

At this point it is appropriate to mention one of the most amazing features of A*—the way it handles terrain. Above, I said that the cost of going from one tile to the next is either 1 or 1.41. That is true if all tiles are of equal size, but that statement does not always have to be true. Let's say some of the tiles are made up of water. Chances are, you probably don't want to send your character through the water unless it is absolutely necessary. So you then assign a cost of, let's say, 10 to any node transition (moving from one node to another) that involves water. This will not guarantee that the path does not go through the water, but it will give extreme preference to paths that don't. If the water is a stream going completely through the map and there is no bridge, then A* will certainly end up giving you a path through the water. However, if there is a bridge, and it is close enough, then A* will give you a path that includes the bridge. Alternatively, if your character is half man and half fish, then he may prefer water. In this case, you may give land a lower cost than water. With all this in mind, I should probably modify my initial statement that A* always finds the shortest path. Now that you know more, I can further specify that A* will always find the path with the lowest score. In many cases (such as those of maps in which there is no terrain change, like the implementations used later in this section), the path with the lowest score also happens to be the shortest path.

A* spelled out, almost in English

Now let's look at the algorithm itself in pseudo-code.

```
1    AStar.Search
2        create open array
3        create closed array
4        s.g = 0
5        s.h = findHeuristic( s.x, s.y )
6        s.f = s.g + s.h
7        s.parent = null
8        push s into open array
9        set keepSearching to true
10       while keepSearching
11           pop node n from open
12           if n is the goal node
13               build path from start to finish
14               set keepSearching to false
15           for each neighbor m of n
16               newg = n.g + cost( n, newx, newy )
17               if m has not been visited
18                   m.g = n.f
19                   m.h = findHeuristic( newx, newy )
20                   m.f = m.g + m.h
21                   m.parent = n
22                   add it to the open array
23                   sort the open array
24               else
25                   if newg < m.g
26                       m.parent = n
27                       m.g = newg
28                       m.f = m.g + m.h
29                       sort the open array
30                       if m is in closed
31                           remove it from closed
32           push n into the closed array
33           if search time > max time
34               set keepSearching to false
35       return path
```

This algorithm makes use of two lists (which are arrays in Flash), open and closed. The open array contains the nodes that have at one time been visited. The closed array contains all nodes that have been expanded (that is, all of its neighbors have been visited). We use the open array as a *priority queue*. We use the open array not only to store nodes, but also to store nodes in a certain order. We keep the array sorted from lowest score (f) to highest score. Every time we add a node to the open array or change the value of g in a node in the open array, we must re-sort the array so that the nodes are in order from lowest to highest score.

In lines 2 and 3 above we create the empty open and closed arrays. In pathfinding we need a starting place and a destination, so that comes next. S is an object that represents the starting node. We set s.g to 0, since the starting node has no parents, so the cost (g) to get to it is 0 (line 4). Next, we find the heuristic h for the start node. (Remember that the heuristic is the estimated cost from the current node to the goal.) We then store the value of f, which is the sum of s.g and s.h, on the starting node (line 6). Since s has no parents, we set s.parent to null. Next, we push the s node into the open array (line 8). The s node is now the first and only node in the open array.

In line 9 we set the variable keepSearching to true. While it remains true, we will keep performing the A* search. When we have determined that we have found a path, that no path exists, or that we have been searching for too long, we will set keepSearching to false.

In line 11 we take a node from the priority queue. We then check to see if this node is the goal. If it is, we have reached the goal; then we stop searching and build the path (lines 12–14). If it is not the goal, we expand the node. Expanding the node means that we visit each of the node's neighbors. In line 16 we find the g of the neighbor node, m, that we are currently looking at. We then check to see if this node has ever been visited. If it has not yet been visited, then we enter the portion of the algorithm in lines 18–23. We set the value of g on m; it is the f from its parent, n. Next we calculate and store the heuristic and f on m. Finally, we set the parent property to be that of the previous node, n. If this node has been visited before and now has a lower g, then we enter the portion of the algorithm in lines 25–31.

At this point I want to mention something more about *g*. When a node is first visited, it is assigned a *g* based on the path taken to get to that node (as we have already discussed). But it is possible, and likely, that that node will be visited again during the search through another possible path. If the *g* from this new path is lower than the *g* from the previously stored path, then we replace the old *g* with the new *g* (line 27). In line 26 we set the parent property of *m* to be the node that we are coming from. The parent property is what we use at the end of the search to construct the final path. We can move from the goal node all the way back to the starting position by following the parent properties. Next, we recalculate the *f* and then have to re-sort the open array. We re-sort the open array because we have just updated one of the nodes with a lower *f*, so this node may now take priority over another.

I have to be honest with you—I'm not quite sure what lines 30 and 31 are for! It was in the pseudo-code from which I learned the A* algorithm, and I have included it in my ActionScript implementation. But it is a part of the algorithm that has never been visited during any of the example searches I have constructed (I put a trace action in that part of the code so that I would be informed if it was ever entered). Throughout my dozens and dozens of tests I have never experienced a use for this. The algorithm, written in ActionScript, to the best of my knowledge works exactly as it should, and always returns the path with the lowest score. However, I have kept that part of the algorithm around even though it seems to be unnecessary, just in case I someday realize when it *would* be needed. If you are an A* whiz, then let me know your thoughts!

After all of the neighbors of *n* are visited, we move on to line 32. In this line we push *n* onto the closed array because it has been completely expanded We then check the time to make sure that we haven't been searching for too long. If we have been searching too long, then we set keepSearching to false. Otherwise, we move on to the next node in the queue (line 11). If keepSearching is false, we stop searching and build the path.

You have now been formally introduced to A*! Don't feel bad if you are having trouble understanding the algorithm; it is not the easiest thing in the world to grasp. It took me several articles on the Internet before I felt like I fully understood basic A*.

Implementing A*

You have seen the A* algorithm and should have at least a basic understanding of how it works. I have written the A* algorithm in ActionScript on an object called astar. Let's take a look at how it's implemented.

Open astar.fla in the Chapter09 directory on the CD. Look at the actions on the A* layer. The astar object contains another object, called nodes. The nodes object contains information about certain tiles. For instance, the nodes object might contain an object called cell8_2 that contains information saying that the tile contains a wall. If a tile contains a wall, then no path can go through it.

In this implementation of A* there is no built-in support for different types of terrain, though it wouldn't be hard to add (see the next subsection for more on that). In this implementation a tile either is available to be walked on or is not. There is no other distinction between tiles.

To use the astar object to perform a path search, you must do the following:

1. **Paste the** astar **code in your movie.**

2. **Define starting x and y tiles for the search. Here's a sample syntax:**

   ```
   astar.s.x = 5;
   astar.s.y = 8;
   ```

3. **Define a destination x and y. This destination is contained in the goal node (g); you can use this syntax:**

   ```
   astar.g.x = 10;
   astar.g.y = 13;
   ```

4. **Define all forbidden tiles in this way:**

   ```
   astar.nodes["node"+x+"_"+y] = astar.solidOb;
   ```

5. **Then perform the search and capture the returned array like this:**

   ```
   path = astar.search();
   ```

   Path is a two-dimensional array that describes the complete path from the starting node to the goal node. Each element in the array contains another array with two elements. The first element in each of the two element arrays contains the *x* position of a tile along the found path. The second element in each of these two element arrays contains the *y* position of a tile along the path. For instance, the first tile on which to step has an *x* of path[0][0] and *y* of path[0][1]. The second tile on which to step has an *x* of path[1][0] and *y* of path[1][1].

Tweaking the Numbers for Realism

The astar object includes a property called preventClipping. If this value is false, then the search will truly return the shortest path. In this case, a character can walk across from one tile to another diagonally, and half of the character will appear on the two neighboring tiles as it moves from one tile to the next. If neighbors contain no obstacles, then this is what we would want to happen. However, if a neighbor contains an obstacle, then the character will appear to partially walk through the corner of that obstacle. Luckily there is a way around this unrealistic behavior. By default, the preventClipping property has a value of true. When true, the algorithm will not return a diagonal move from one tile to another if one of the neighbors contains an obstacle. This gives a path that is more realistic, but not necessarily the shortest path. However, it is the shortest path that looks good.

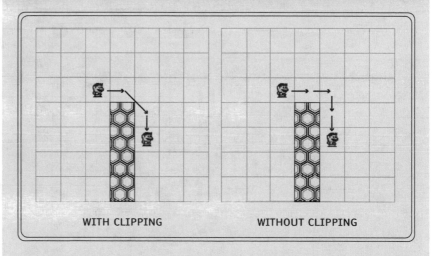

WITH CLIPPING   WITHOUT CLIPPING

In this A* implementation I have modified the cost() function to return very large values for diagonal moves that would normally clip. The result is that with preventClipping set as true, the path moves more naturally around the object, without any clipping. Diagonal moves are still made—just not when clipping would occur. If you prefer the pure A* path, then set preventClipping to false.

If no path is found, then the path is returned as null. If the search takes too long, then it is aborted and the path is returned as null. There is a variable called maxSearchTime on the astar object. By default, this variable is set to 5000 (5 seconds), but of course you can change it to suit yourself.

Using Test Movie, take a look at the SWF of astar.fla. You will see a 20-by-20 grid of tiles. Click any tile to add a starting point, and then click any other tile to add a goal. Then click every tile you want to make into a wall. Finally, click the Search button. You will see a path appear on the screen. To search for another path, click the Clear button and start over.

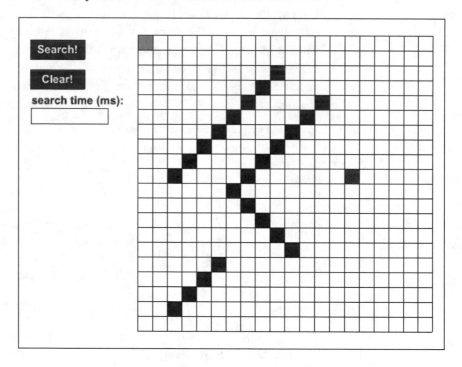

To see a more interesting application of A*, open iso_ai_astar.fla in the Chapter09 directory and generate a SWF using Test Movie. You should recognize this scene from Chapter 8, "The Isometric Worldview." Click anywhere on the map. Notice that the character immediately walks to the destination, moving around the objects. This is just a simple example of the kind of situation where we'd benefit from using A*, but as you can imagine, it's going to work really well for any kind of game that resembles this kind of world.

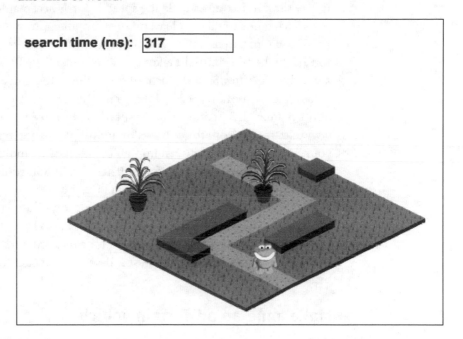

search time (ms): 317

Variations on A*

You've now seen and experienced my version of the A* algorithm. For games that are similar to the isometric example shown in the previous section, my implementation is probably good enough for what you're doing. However, if you are going to be using maps that are larger than about 20 by 20 tiles (which is likely), you will quickly realize that my A* version is just not fast enough. Or you may want to take advantage of the multiterrain features of A* that I haven't included in my version. For a faster A* or one that handles multiple terrains, you'll have to modify my A* version, build your own, or use one that someone else has created. In the next two sections I briefly discuss both speed and multiterrain support.

Not fast enough for you?

As you may have noticed in astar.fla, the speed at which the path is found is very slow. In iso_ai_astar.fla the speed is *barely* acceptable. In that file the search tends to take (at least on my computer) from 80 milliseconds (ms) to 400 ms. In astar.fla a simple search with no walls going from the top-left to the bottom-right takes 3 to 4 seconds! When building this A* algorithm in ActionScript, I focused on getting it to work and making it easy to use—not on speed. However, in the coming months I will probably optimize this ActionScript for speed (so feel free to check up on www.electrotank.com to see how I'm doing). If you are in a rush to get your hands on a blazingly fast implementation of A* in ActionScript, take a look in the astar_optimized folder. There you'll find some very fast A* files created by Casper Schuirink. What takes my A* 3 or 4 seconds, Casper's can do in 150 ms to 200 ms, and most typical searches are under 100 ms. As with all highly optimized files, they also have their disadvantages. One major con, in this case, is that the files are not necessarily easy to port over to your own applications. Ease of use is sacrificed for speed, so be cautious.

Make mine an all-terrain vehicle

In the previous section I mentioned that you can modify my A* implementation to handle other terrains. You can do this in the cost() function. The cost() function is passed information on the parent node and the current node. With this information, A* calculates a cost. If you want to add different types of terrain, such as sand, water, or oil, then you would set a property of your choice (for example, terrain = "water") on the node that represents that tile. Then when the cost is calculated, you check to see what type of terrain the tile has, and then calculate a cost from that. Good luck!

POINTS TO REMEMBER

- Pathfinding is the act of finding a path between one point and another.

- Pathfinding and controlling enemy behaviors are the main areas in which you'll probably use AI.

- AI can be used to generate random maps.

- Using a special algorithm, you can generate a random perfect maze.

- A* (pronounced "A star") is the best pathfinding algorithm known. It is guaranteed to find the path of the lowest score, should any path exist, between two points.

- Although it's the best pathfinding algorithm, A* is also very CPU-intensive and slow.

- A* can handle multiple types of terrains and find the best path through these terrains to the goal.

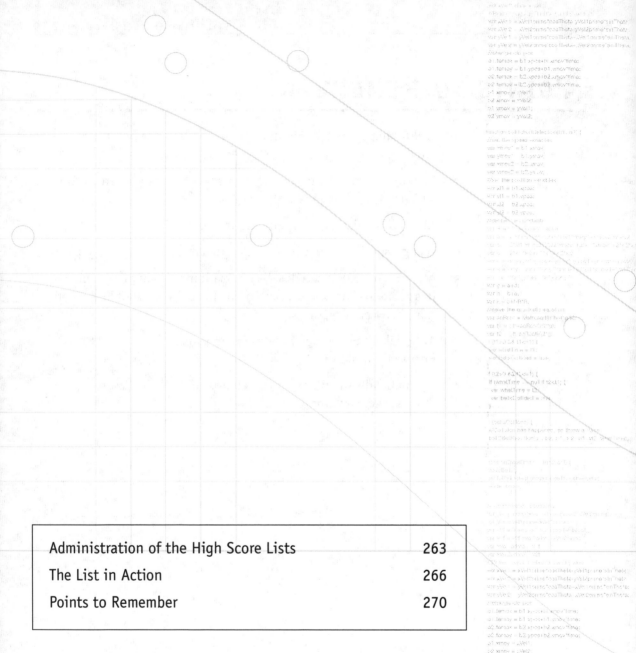

CHAPTER 10

USING A HIGH SCORE LIST

A *HIGH SCORE LIST*—ALSO CALLED A *LEADER BOARD*—DISPLAYS A LIST of the best scores for a game. The term "high score list" is somewhat of a misnomer, because the list actually displays the best scores, which are not always the highest scores. A good example is golf, in which the lowest score is the best score.

In this chapter you will learn how to add a high score list to a game, as well as how to configure and administer it. We provide you with all of the files you need to get a high score list working in a game. However, you will need a Windows server to use it successfully. Your Flash game saves your score by contacting a server-side script and sending it information (which, in this case, it stores in the database). Our high score list uses ASP pages as the server-side scripts and a Microsoft Access database to store the information. And—in case I haven't made this point clear already—ASP pages need a Windows server to be interpreted correctly.

Encryption

As you may know, I co-own a popular Flash game site called Electrotank. More than 2 million people play our games every month. When you run a site with that many people playing your games, you are bound to get some people who will try to figure out a way to cheat the high score list. Using some unethical tools, they can look at the ActionScript in the game and find the URL to which the game points when submitting a high score. From this information they can easily create something that will submit fake scores to the score list. The score list, of course, doesn't know the difference between the faked scores and the real scores. This leads to a really annoying problem: cheaters. If there is a way for people to cheat, they will eventually find it. This is not as rare as you may think it is. (For example, the score lists got tampered with on another [Flash 4] game site I used to own as well.) Since this problem isn't going away, you just need to take a few extra steps to make cheating more difficult.

With the files included for this book, we've increased the high score list security a little bit: We have enabled *encryption*. It is definitely not foolproof—in all likelihood this system will get hacked, too—but it will make the hackers' job much harder, so it will be hacked by a smaller number of people. We encrypt everything in Flash before sending it to the server. When the server receives the information, it then decrypts it and uses it. Good encryption algorithms require a key to encrypt or decrypt. We have an encryption function and pass in a key, which can be any string we choose, such as "thisIsTheKey," and the string that we want encrypted. The function returns encrypted information, which is unique to the key, and you can then send that to the server. In order to decrypt the information, the server needs the same key you used to encrypt it in the first place.

You may be thinking, "That sounds like pretty tight security; why can it still be hacked?" Well, we are storing both the encryption algorithm and the key in the game file. That is a security issue, but there isn't much we can do about that. After you understand everything in this chapter, you can take these files and try to increase the security yourself a little more. One thing you can do is load in the key from a separate file, and maybe even load in the encryption function through another SWF file. This is still not hack-proof, but every step you take is one more that a hacker will also have to go through. You want to make it not worth the hacker's while.

ADMINISTRATION OF THE HIGH SCORE LISTS

The name of the administration tool we use for the high score lists is UberScore Administrator. This tool gives you a lot of control over the lists. It allows you to perform the following administrative duties:

- Create an unlimited number of high score lists.

- Give each list a name and configure certain properties differently for each.

- Set one list to consider lower scores to be better, and another list to have higher scores be better.

- Limit the number of scores displayed.

- Set a score list to accept only one score from a person, or to accept many. (If you set it to accept just one, then it will accept another only if it is better than that user's current score.)

- Delete a user.

- Edit the information about a high score list (sort order, number of scores, name of list).

In order for a person to be able to submit a score, that person must be a registered player. We will show you how to register (or create) a player later.

Assuming that you have a Windows server up and properly running, take the entire hs directory that's in the Chapter10 directory on the CD and upload it to your Windows server. Remember the URL of this directory—we'll call it the "score URL."

Go to the score URL in your Web browser. You should see these two links: Administer Users and Administer Scoreboards. Click the Administer Users link. At this point you have not created any users, but you will see a couple of "test" users I created so that you can learn what the Administrator looks like with real data. When there are user names in the system, you will see letters at the top that are links that correspond to the first letters of those names. For instance, if the user "Frank" is in the system, then you will see the letter *F* at the top. You can click the *F* to view all of the users whose names start with *F*. You can delete a user, if you wish, by clicking the Delete link next to the user's name. That's about all you need to know about administering users.

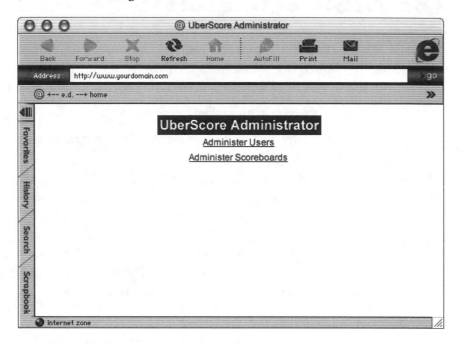

Click the Back to UberScore Administrator link. From there, click Administer Scoreboards to enter the Board Administrator area. A scoreboard is the same thing as a high score list. You have not created any yet, so you probably won't see any in a list on this page. However, if I left one in the database from testing, feel free to delete it; in any case, you'll see in this area that you can edit, clear, or delete any existing scoreboard. You can create a new scoreboard by clicking the Create New Board link. You are presented with five configurable fields:

Board Name. I recommend using the name of your game here.

Return Count. The number you insert here is the maximum number of scores that will be returned in the high score list. A number between about 50 and 100 is typical.

Multiple Scores Per User. This is a drop-down list that lets you choose Yes or No. If you choose Yes, then any person can have an unlimited number of scores in the list. If you choose No, then a person can have only one score at a time.

Only Insert If Better. This field also lets you choose either Yes or No. If Yes, then a person's score will be inserted only if it is better than a score he or she already has in the list. This works in conjunction with the Multiple Scores Per User field. If a user has opted to have multiple scores, then of course it doesn't matter if the score is better or worse. If the user can have only one score, and Insert Only If Better is set to Yes, then the user's score can be replaced by a better score, but not a worse score. If Insert Only If Better is set to No and Multiple Scores Per User is set to Yes, then every time the user gets a score, it will replace the current score, even if it is worse.

Sort Order. The choices here are Ascending and Descending. If you choose Descending, that means a higher score is better, so the scores will be listed from highest to lowest. If you choose Ascending, then a lower score is better, and the scores will be sorted from lowest to highest.

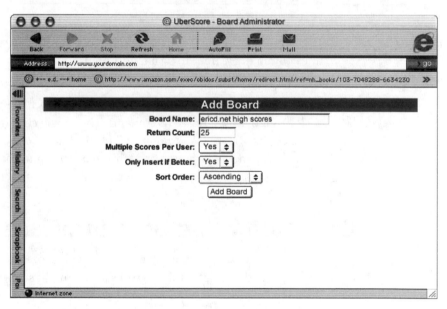

As you have seen, with this administration tool you can view or delete users, as well as manage the scoreboards. What you cannot do with this tool is create (or register) users, log in, or submit scores. Those are done directly from the game, and we'll talk about them in the next section.

THE LIST IN ACTION

You now know how to create and manage scoreboards using the UberScore Administrator. Create a new scoreboard and then continue with this section. Remember the BoardID number, because you'll need it below. In this section you will learn how to use the High Score List movie clip that's on the CD. We are going to discuss only a few portions of the ActionScript provided, as the rest of it is fairly straightforward and not within the scope of this book.

Open highscore.fla in the Chapter10 directory on the CD. You will see two layers in the main timeline: Actions and Assets. The Actions layer contains only one line of code:

```
_global.score = random(400);
```

This sets a variable to the *global space* (that means it is available in all timelines within this game) to be a random number between 0 and 400. You will see why soon.

The Assets layer contains a movie clip that appears to be blank. Double-click this movie clip to see its contents. The movie clip, which has a library name of High Score List, contains all of the ActionScript needed for a player to log in, create a user, and submit a score, and for the game itself to load and display the score list. First we'll look at its actions.

Configuring the User-Interface Frames

There are nine labeled frames here in the High Score List movie clip, corresponding to the nine possible screens a user might see when attempting to submit a score.

Login or Register. On this frame the user is given a choice to log in or to register. If Login is selected, then the user is taken to the Login frame. If Register is chosen, the user is taken to the Register frame. A user must be logged in to submit a score, and must be registered in order to log in.

Login. On this frame the user can log in by entering a user name and password and then clicking Submit. When Submit is clicked, the information is encrypted and sent to the server, and the user is taken to the Waiting frame.

```
                         Registration


             Username:   UberUser

             Password:   *****

                Email:   you@domain.com


             Submit




  Skip to Score List
```

The server then decrypts the information and determines if the information is valid. A response is received from the server. If the information is invalid, the user is taken to the Login Failed frame. If the information is valid, the user's userID is extracted from the XML returned from the server, and the user is taken to the Display frame.

Register. The user can register a new account on this frame. There are three fields on this frame: Username, Password, and Email. When the user clicks Submit, the information is sent to the server and the user is taken to the Waiting frame. If the information is acceptable, then the user is taken to the Display frame. If the information is not acceptable, the user is taken to the Register Failed frame and a message is displayed, informing the player that (for instance) the user name already exists or the email address is invalid. This message is sent from the server.

Waiting. This frame appears whenever information has been sent to the server and the user is waiting for a reply.

Login Failed. This frame appears when a log-in attempt did not succeed. The user is given the choice to try logging in again.

Register Failed. This frame appears when a registration attempt is unsuccessful. A text field on the screen displays a message from the server explaining what was wrong with the registration. Typically, the problem is that the user name has already been taken.

Display. A text field on this screen displays a message telling the player what user name is currently being used and the score that will be submitted. The user can then choose to submit the score with this user name or to log in with a different name. The user will see this frame after she logs in successfully, registers, or submits another score.

Inserted. This frame simply informs the user that his score has been inserted into the database.

List. On this frame you can see the high score list. When the frame is visited, the high score list is loaded. After a few seconds you will see the list appear.

On all of these frames except List you can skip directly to the high score list by clicking the button on the bottom left.

Configuring the ActionScript

Two of the layers in this movie clip contain actions. The Encryption layer contains the function that encrypts and decrypts information. The Actions layer contains the ActionScript needed to do everything else. The bulk of the ActionScript is used to create or parse XML.

Let's look at the first few lines of ActionScript in the Actions layer:

```
1    theKey = "ThisIsTheKey";
2    URL = "http://myDomain.com/hs/hs.asp";
3    scoreBoardID = 4;
4    score = _global.score;
5    username = _global.username;
6    userid = _global.userid;
```

The first line contains a variable called theKey. This is the key used for encryption and decryption. It is very important to remember that this key must exactly match the key in the ASP file. The files on the CD-ROM are already matched up. If you change the key in one place, remember to change it in the other place! In line 2 there is a variable called URL, which contains the path to the hs directory with `hs.asp` added to the end. This URL is the path to the server-side script that will handle everything we do from Flash. Next you see `scoreBoardID`. This must contain the BoardID of the scoreboard to which you want scores submitted. (You can find the BoardID from the UberScore Administrator.) In line 4 we set a variable called `score` from the `_global.score` (which we set from the main timeline). We assume that the `_global.score` exists before you reach this frame. When your game is over and you are about to send the user to the frame that contains this movie clip, the script first sets `_global.score` to the user's current score. The next two lines set `username` and `userid` based on those same variables in `_global` space. The first time during a game when the user arrives at this frame, both of these variables will have a value of `null`. This is because the game doesn't yet know who the user is. However, after the user logs in, then `_global.username` and `_global.userid` will have values. Then, if the user tries to submit another score at a later time during the same session, she will not have to log in again since the game remembers her information.

Now look at the actions at the bottom of this frame:

```
1    if (_global.username == null) {
2        this.gotoAndStop("Login or Register");
3    } else {
4        this.gotoAndStop("Display");
5    }
```

If the user name does not yet exist, then we give the user a choice to log in or to register. If the name does exist, then the user has already logged in and we send him to the Display frame.

TIP

If you would rather display the high score list in a different way, then start by modifying the `displayList()` function.

The rest of the ActionScript used is fairly straightforward. Several XML objects are used to send and receive data from the server. Also, you should be able to easily customize the look of all the frames used here. I purposefully used a simple design on each frame so that it would be easy to customize.

POINTS TO REMEMBER

- You need a Windows server to run the server-side scripts.

- With UberScore Administrator you have control over many attributes of a high score list, including the number of scores returned, the sort order, and whether a user can submit multiple scores.

- The encryption key in a server-side script must match the encryption key in the Flash High Score List movie clip. If the keys do not match, neither Flash nor the server-side script will correctly interpret the information.

- Set the user's score to global space like this:

```
_global.score = currentScore
```

This must be done before the High Score List movie clip is reached.

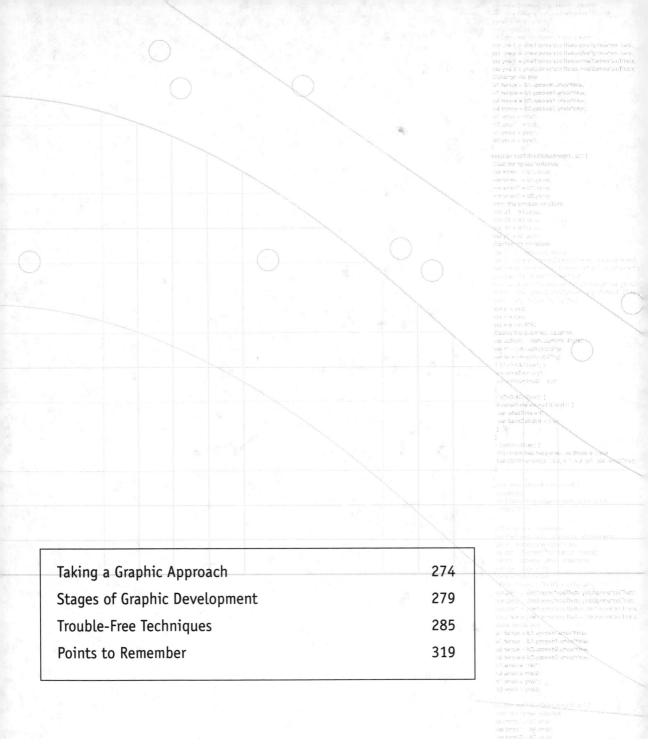

CHAPTER 11

GRAPHICS IN GAMES

THE FIRST THING A USER IS GOING TO EXPERIENCE AND REACT TO IN YOUR game is not how it sounds or how it scores or even what it does, but how it *looks*. So you want to make a good first impression. The graphic environment and quality of your game will usually set the tone for the entire game, whether or not you're going for a professional-looking setup. And how you approach the development of your graphics will dictate how successfully you achieve the desired appearance. Just as with the approach we recommend for the entire game-design process, you want to stick with a plan for developing your graphics so that you won't have to make, or change, your decisions midway through.

The optimal way to approach the task of developing your graphics is to take a bird's-eye view of everything you must accomplish with your graphics. In this chapter we cover the three main phases of the graphics-development process, and show you how to optimize your creation time and stay organized along the way. The last part of this chapter covers actual graphics techniques, and we reveal tricks of the trade that will help you work faster and more efficiently.

TAKING A GRAPHIC APPROACH

Before you dive into your visual tasks, there are a few important topics to think about: What types of graphics will be most appropriate for your game? What kinds of tools will you need to create your graphics and animations, and how can you best use them? Once you are finished with your graphics, who is going to actually put them in the game? If you're not doing the programming yourself, have you established the right communications and processes to make this go as smoothly as possible?

If that burst of questions scared you a little, don't worry. We all have to ask them over again for every project. And here we're going to help you learn how to answer them.

If you're working with a production team—possibly even if you're working by yourself!—it might be helpful to use a checklist. Having one will help everyone keep track of what needs to get done, and when, and what has already been completed. A checklist is best broken down into major sections (such as still graphics and animations), with a brief description for each item. The tasks will vary with your work, of course, but as you read through this chapter, you'll pick up ideas for what you might include.

To see a copy of the checklist we used for the Word Search game in Part 3 of this book, open the asset_checklist.pdf file in the Chapter11 directory on the CD.

Different Types of Graphics

The main decision you need to make in choosing a graphic format is whether to use raster or vector images. A *raster* is a two-dimensional, rectangular, pixel-based grid. Raster graphics—obviously also pixel-based— can be created with programs like Adobe Photoshop, Procreate Painter, and Microsoft Paint (to name a few). Some of the common raster file formats are GIF, JPEG, PNG, and BMP. A *vector* is, for our purposes, a mathematical formula that describes shapes that make up an image. Vector graphics can be created with programs like (again, to name only a few) Macromedia Flash, Macromedia Freehand, Corel Draw, and Adobe Illustrator. Common vector formats include EPS and SWF.

A raster image for a game background, created in Photoshop.

A vector version of the same game background, drawn in Flash.

When using raster graphics in your game, the JPEG file format is the most commonly recommended. In most cases, a JPEG will give you a small file size and is not processor intensive. One drawback of this format is that it does not support alpha channels (the Flash feature that allows your image to be transparent). Sadly, raster formats that support alpha channels can produce very large files and are not optimal for Flash gaming use. If you have to have an alpha channel, I would suggest using the GIF format. GIFs support one level of 0% alpha and, if compressed, could give acceptable results. BMP (short for *bitmap*) is not a strong format for game purposes, and BMP files should be imported into Flash only if absolutely necessary or for tracing purposes.

The optimal way to create vector graphics for your games is to make them directly in Flash (more on that below, in the "Identify Your Tools" section).

Of course you need to look at the different formats in light of the visual style you want for your game. Choose the format that seems best, and test out the different flavors of that format to make sure it fits the bill—not just visually but also technically. For instance, if your graphics look great but slow the game down 50 percent, that format may not be worth it.

In terms of visual effect, in most cases vector graphics are easier to work with, not only because Flash is a vector graphic program but because of their scalability and support of alpha channels. Raster graphics tend to be somewhat more troublesome. One reason is that they are less flexible (once you scale them, you'll start to see their pixels). Another is that, if you use the JPEG format to keep their size down, you have no alpha channel support. Without that, if you actually want to see through something, you'd have to "cut a hole" in the image.

Identify Your Tools

Equally important to your design process is that you have the right tools for the job. Just as you would do when compiling a shopping list for a home project, think of all the tasks involved and make sure you have the tools and materials you need. Will you be able to create the graphics and animations with nothing more than Macromedia Flash? Are there other programs that can make your job easier? Do you need anything besides software? Your list might include one or more of the following:

Scanner—A must if you're going to do any sketching-out of your game ideas and characters (and I'm going to recommend strongly that you do). The device should scan at least 300 dots per inch (dpi), and can work in either black and white or color.

Graphics tablet—Whether you plan to trace your scanned artwork or to work from scratch, a graphics (or drawing) tablet and stylus are going to save you a lot of time, and increase your precision as well.

Vector drawing program—There are many vector drawing programs out there; the most serious and popular were mentioned in the section above. It is just a matter of identifying the best one for you—every artist has his or her preference. Many artists use other vector drawing programs to draw their vector artwork, and some draw right in Flash. In my own experience, it's always been a time-saver to create art in Flash. Importing your art from another vector drawing program tends to mean you've got to optimize the art for gaming use. By creating your vector graphics directly in Flash, you can draw your graphic once and have it be optimized for your game. (If you want any reassurance about Flash's drawing abilities, check out Vectorkid [www.vectorkid.com]. All his vector art was created in Flash 4 and higher.)

Raster drawing program—Some art styles (such as photo-realism or a sketchy crayon look) cannot be rendered in any vector drawing program and are best achieved in a raster drawing program. (Even if you could create them in Flash, you would end up with graphics that would be very processor intensive and would really slow down your game.) But use raster art wisely, because even it can slow you down.

3D program—You don't necessarily need a specific 3D program, but it could really help if you have to create lots of views or frames of an animated character, or when you need to shoot all of your graphics at specific angles. Learning how to use a 3D program isn't easy, though, and could take up a lot of your time; if you are busy and can afford to, you might consider contracting out to someone else to render your 3D images. (We also discussed 3D imaging in Chapter 8, "The Isometric Worldview.")

Graphic Preparation

Before jumping right in and creating your graphics, you should identify how the ActionScript programmer would like the graphics prepped for implementation, if you're not going to do the programming yourself. Most of the time, the ActionScripter will provide Flash files with placeholder artwork, and it is the artist's job to replace those graphics with the final versions. Communication is very important if you wish to have a fluid transition from graphic creation to implementation.

The library in Flash is key to keeping your assets organized. If you use a lot of movie clips or other symbols, it's a good idea to break your library down into categories, such as User Interface Elements, Characters, Items, Special Effects, and Background Elements. To divide your library, just make new folders by clicking the New Folder icon at the bottom of the Library panel.

Of course every artist has his or her own preferred workflow, and I wouldn't ever say that one was better than another. But if you're looking for a starting point, here's my basic approach to graphics preparation. First I analyze the project's asset checklist, explore the Flash files I've been given, and identify all the placeholders to make sure I understand where I'm supposed to place my graphics and animations. (Placeholders are usually simple, solid-color rectangular fills, although basic text can also be used as a placeholder.) You'll mostly see these placeholders within movie clips, which can be accessed from the Flash file's library. The more movie clips you have, the more helpful it will be to give them specific and descriptive names. For instance, in the Character category you might see my movie clips named like this: Badguy01_leftright, Badguy01_up, Badguy01_down, Badguy02_leftright, Badguy02_up, Badguy02_down, Mainchar_leftright, Mainchar_up, Mainchar_down, and so on. The library stores items in alphabetical order, so your character movie clips will be easy to access.

This rectangular object is a placeholder for a graphic of a piece of fruit in the game Fruit Smash (which you can find in the OtherGames directory on the CD).

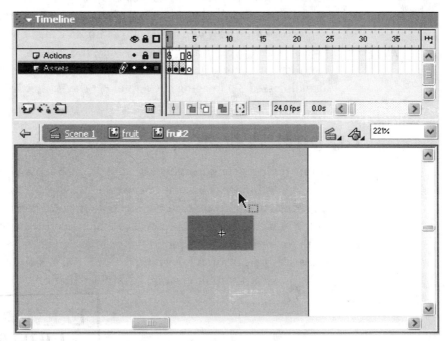

STAGES OF GRAPHIC DEVELOPMENT

It's fun to just sit down at the computer and start drawing—more fun than thinking hard about the visual details of an entire game and determining what is necessary to achieve them. Yet when you're producing professional artwork and animations, that's what you have to do. Dividing the graphic-development process into three distinct stages will help keep you focused and organized, and help you in working with team members and strict client deadlines, saving you time and headaches.

Stage 1: Brainstorm

For this phase, all you need is a plain old pencil and paper. Sketch out all your different ideas for any graphical parts of your game. For instance, let's say you have been thinking about several ways to design a main character in your game. Get all those ideas down on paper. Make sure to think about the various ways the character may appear in the game, such as running, jumping, carrying a book, or hitting a ball.

Initial sketches for the main character of Ice World (see Chapter 15, "Ice World: A Platform Game").

Character sketches may be the most fun of the lot, but don't stop there. Continue with everything else that will appear in the game: backgrounds, objects, obstacles, user-interface layout, and navigation elements. These are all very important aspects of your game.

For example, for our platform game I designed a main character whose left-to-right movements the user will control, and who has to collect items. Notice in the sketches above that I have fleshed out a couple of different ways I could go with the character. Because this game is geared toward a young audience, I have worked to create a character that is child-friendly and by its appearance encourages children to want to move it around a lot. Once they get started, they'll see that they can make the character jump, collect items, and kill bad guys.

Now is also a good time to start fleshing out your game's general color scheme, and thinking about its look and feel. What colors best represent your game's topic or theme? Because our platform game will be marketed to a younger audience, we will be using a lot of pastel colors; against the pastels we've used a bright baby blue, navy blue, and yellow in the main character, which I think stands out really well and is very appropriate for this game. As for a look and feel, we are going for soft and warm, with cartoonlike characters.

 Open the file ice_world.swf in the Chapter15 directory to see the colors we've been working with for this game.

Brainstorming can be a hard process, but remember—these sketches are not for the world to see. They're just a way to help you with your ideas, and ideas aren't wrong.

Stage 2: Focus

Once you've got your ideas on paper, think back to your main vision of the game, and what you wanted the game's focus to be. Look at the sketches you created for your main character. Keep the sketches you feel best fit your game vision. For example, in the sketches I drew, all the characters seem pretty cool to me, but you'll notice that I decided to keep character design B. Why? Because B fits best with our vision of the game, being more of a rectangle shape, and because it has the look and feel we want. This is the stage where you have to make the hardest choices; it's painful to have to jettison good ideas just because they aren't the best fit. We talked some about this in Chapter 2, "The Plan: From Idea to Design"; it's always best if you can focus in quickly on the "right" ideas so you don't have to invest too much time in the others. But even then, don't throw them away; you never know when they'll be right for another project.

A.

B.

Once you've chosen a design and a look and feel that are at least in the direction you want, you can flesh out that design by adding detail to your sketches until you think you've produced a close-to-final version.

Stage 3: Produce

As you may notice, in each phase we produce more detailed work. This is exactly what you want to do: start with all of your initial brainstorming ideas, and end up with what you think will work the best—even if you have to let go of some of your pet designs in the process. Once you know the direction in which you want to go with your main character, and know how you want to approach his creation on a technical level, it's time to start drawing the character in your computer. Of course, to do this you've got to scan your sketch. Contrary to popular belief, you don't have to save your scans as TIFFs. And for our purposes that's just as well, since other, smaller formats will serve our needs. I recommend saving the image as an uncompressed BMP file if you're just using it to trace in Flash, or as a JPEG if you plan to use it as actual art in the game. Either is fine, just as long as it isn't compressed. Import your scanned sketch into Flash, place it on a blank layer, and lock the layer. Create another blank layer and make sure it's above the layer that contains your sketch. This way you can draw on that top layer without disturbing your original sketch.

In general, it's easiest and fastest to trace your sketch using the line tool. This gives you the smallest amount of vector points. Notice how I've traced my character's body, starting off with a line and manipulating that line to match the curve I wish to make. Creating and connecting more of these curves gives me the shape I want, and a highly optimized file as well. (It's highly optimized because the line tool applies a minimal number of points necessary to trace the shape.) Once the shape is rendered, color it in, using colors you picked out in the Focus stage.

When you have a final drawing of your character, you've got to animate it. But it's important to remember that the more frames we create for this character, the bigger our file will be, so it's a good idea to reuse as many frames as possible. In our example game, the character is required to walk left and right. (He must also jump, duck, and die.) Because the left walking animation is a mirror reflection of the right walking animation, we can get away with drawing just a single walking animation. That's easy enough.

The fully rendered main character from the Ice World game, transformed in Flash from a sketch.

But for the jumping animation, we might want our character to look blurred as he jumps. Unfortunately, we can't achieve that effect in Flash; we must look to a raster graphic for that. In other words, to create this animation we have to integrate vector graphics with raster graphics. I use Photoshop to draw my raster graphics. First, I export the vector drawing of the character as a BMP file. (On a Mac, export your drawing as a JPEG.) Then I open it in Photoshop and apply one or more blur effects. Because these raster graphics will be used directly in the game, I export the graphic out of Photoshop as a compressed JPEG, which gives the graphic the best possible combination of good looks and small file size.

When you import any JPEG back into Flash, it imports as a rectangle, so you must break it apart (choose Modify > Break Apart) and trim away the white areas.

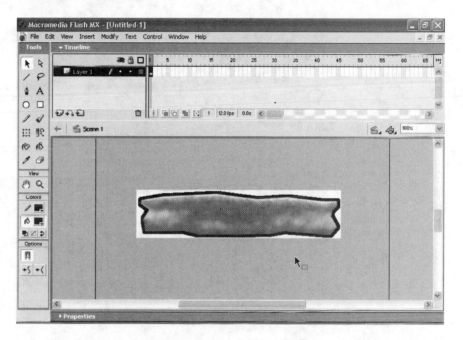

After you have broken down the graphic, use the line tool to draw an outline around the part you want to keep. Make the stroke color red, or some other color that will stand out, as these outlines are going to serve as temporary guidelines to help you in your task.

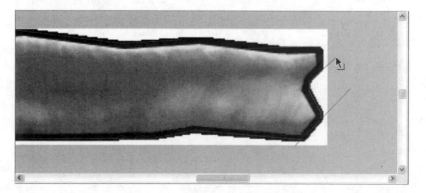

This outline allows you to select the part of the graphic you want to keep and the part of the graphic you want to get rid of. With your arrow tool, select the part of the graphic you want to discard, and press Delete to remove it.

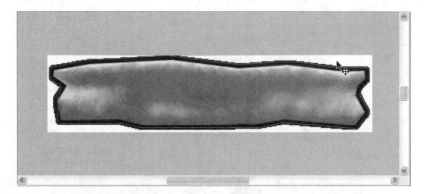

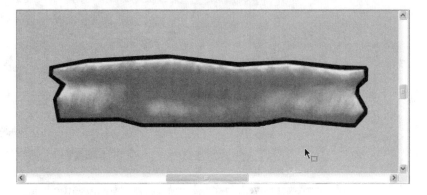

If you did not trim closely enough the first time, you can use the arrow tool to fine-tune the outline.

TROUBLE-FREE TECHNIQUES

Anyone who works on a computer knows that things take longer to do than we think they should. Creating graphics is no exception—in fact, it could be one of the worst offenders, because graphics programs are so full of features that you can't help but keep trying more effects.

What we all really want is to create all the effects we want—quickly. This section covers several techniques I have learned that help me create more professional-looking artwork in less time. Most of them are simple, eye-catching effects we'll create entirely in Flash. Whenever it's possible to do this, it saves you the time and trouble of managing transfers between programs. Even more important, it keeps your vector-art file sizes small, which of course improves the streaming of your game. Every byte helps!

Light and Shadow

Lighting is a key element of your gaming graphics. In this exercise I will show you how using lighting skillfully in your game can spice up your graphics and help them look more realistic and professional. I'm using as an example a flat drawing of an apple that I drew for the game Fruit Smash (which you can find in the OtherGames directory on the CD), but you can apply it to any graphic element in your game.

1. Start with a character or object that is not lighted yet.

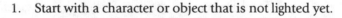

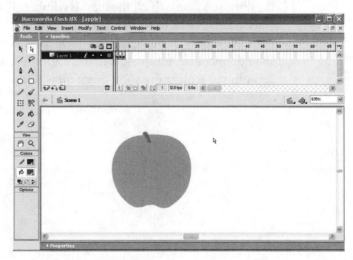

2. Think about where you want your main light source to come from.
    Most of the time you can visualize this. But you may also find it help-
    ful (especially the first few times) to sketch it out on paper to see how
    the object might look. I save a lot of time by sketching out ideas first,
    since drawing them digitally in Flash can take some time.

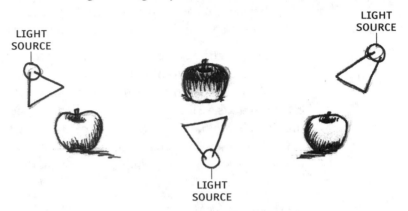

    Once you've chosen the direction for your light source, be consistent
    in applying it to all of the other objects in your game. For instance, if
    you were to take each of the apples in the image above and use them
    in one graphic with the light sources coming from different angles,
    they would seem not to be in the same environment, and would be
    unbelievable or strange and distracting.

3. Draw the main highlight on the object. For the apple example, I am
    going to make a radial gradient from yellow to green and position it in
    the direction from which the light is coming. The yellow and green I
    choose are specific to this particular apple, with the lighter color (in
    this case, yellow) representing the more concentrated light source; you
    should, of course, pick colors that are appropriate to your object. We
    are going to replace the solid-green fill with the new radial gradient.

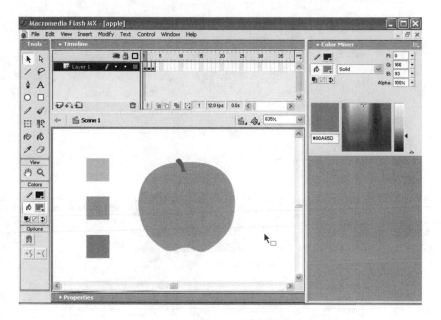

4. When you've chosen the two new colors, add them to the Color Swatches panel. Open the Color Mixer and create a radial gradient with the two colors you just added to Color Swatches, and apply the radial gradient to the object.

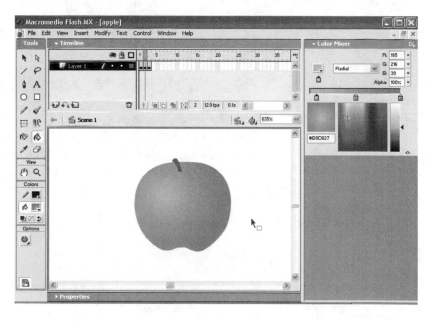

When a light shines down on an object, it not only makes that object brighter, it also creates a shadow cast from that object. In our example, the apple doesn't touch the ground, so the shadow is only on the apple, making the apple darker on the opposite side of the light gradient. This shadow will consist of two alpha levels of a dark green. Because it is transparent, you can put it on a higher layer or group it floating on top of the main gradient.

5. Create a new layer, and use the pen tool to draw the shape of your shadow.

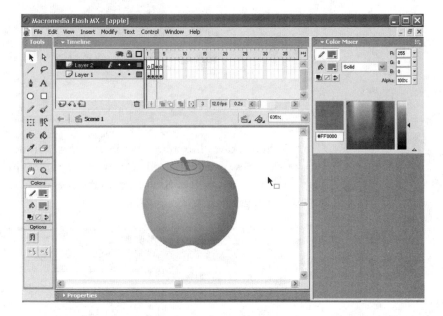

6. In the Color Mixer, create a fill color of #016D3D, at 50% alpha, and add it to the Color Swatches panel. Change the alpha to 30% and add it to your Color Swatches panel as well. With the paint bucket tool, select the 50% alpha #016D3D color swatch and apply it to the center outline, to get a darker effect.

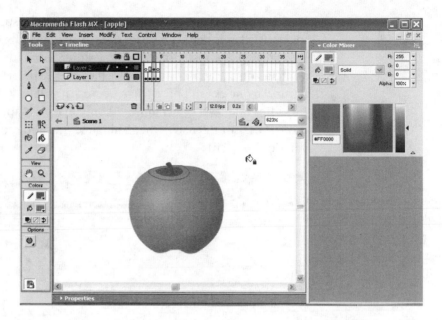

7.   Select the 30% alpha #016D3D color swatch and apply it to the outer outline. Use the arrow tool to select the red outline and delete it.

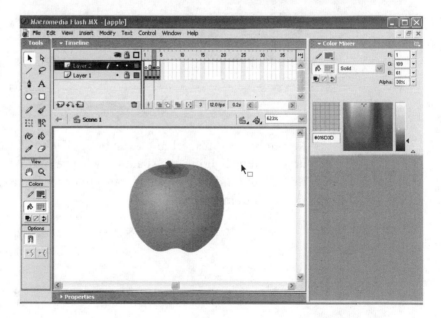

For the greatest optimization of vector graphics, be sure to draw only as much detail as is appropriate for the size at which the object is going to be displayed. For instance, notice that I didn't draw any spots or little scratches on the apple. Most apples have these characteristics, but this particular one doesn't need them because it will be viewed at a small size. Including that level of detail would only make my apple file larger and more processor intensive when animated. In short, don't put detail where you don't need it!

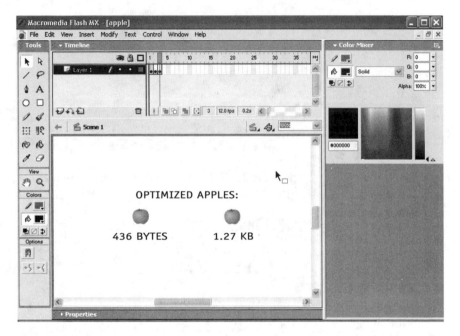

Remember that this technique can be applied to almost everything you draw. Adding lighting and shadows will give your work a more professional look, and it's a finishing touch that will make your gaming graphics stand out from the rest.

Adding Depth

Adding the illusion of depth to the graphics in your games is a good way to make objects appear more real and engaging, and to encourage the user to pay attention to certain objects at certain times. In short, depth can make your gaming world a more captivating environment and a more exciting experience.

BACKGROUND

MAIN CHARACTER

FOREGROUND
GRAPHICS

BAD CHARACTER

To give the illusion of depth to any of your gaming graphics, you mainly manipulate the attributes of color, focus, or speed. We'll examine each of these areas here, and I'll use the example of the platform game Ice World (see Chapter 15, "Ice World: A Platform Game"). In every game, of course, the user controls or manipulates the main character. In some games, the user also has control over other environment variables, such as platforms, bad guys, items to collect, and background elements. By working with depth, you will be able to show dramatic changes in characters and environments, where you can attract the user's attention to whatever elements you choose.

Color

Color (and color changes) can make your most important game elements pop out. Typically, the main character, bad guys, and collectable items are the main focus of a game, and therefore the ones you want to design to receive the most attention.

Though it's not so apparent here in black and white, the game characters and elements with which the user interacts most are the most brightly colored.

Choose bright, bold colors and lots of contrast to make your main characters stand out. To have the characters pop even more, you can apply a black outline to them. This provides great contrast between the characters and the environment elements.

If the main characters are the ones you want to bring forward, it stands to reason you'd want to downplay your background elements, such as platforms and ledges. I use more muted colors for these elements. It's also a good idea to remove their outline paths to help them blend into the environment.

You can divide up the background elements among layers to create an illusion of depth. In our example, I've limited myself to two layers, because multiple layers can be very processor intensive. To visually separate the two, I used the visual convention of making the elements darker the further they are in the background. If you have already drawn your background in Photoshop, you can darken it easily by simply adjusting the brightness. If you want to make this adjustment in Flash, you can convert your background into a symbol and add a Tint effect (from the Color drop-down menu in the Properties panel). Tint it with a darkish color that works for your design. Make sure the percentage of the tint is between 10 and 90 so that you can really see the effect—outside of that range the effects are not very apparent.

Focus and blur

Focus is a very important feature in your world; it's a fairly easy way to help you add great depth to the environment and to call attention to central elements. You can add or remove focus from your elements by applying a blur effect. This is best done in a raster program. Although the effect can be achieved to a certain level in Flash, blurred vector graphics are often too processor intensive to use in your game. For optimum performance, it's best to blur only background elements so that you can get away with using raster blurs, and keep Flash from having to do any blurring at all.

Where you may run into some difficulty with raster-image integration is in the area of performance. JPEGs are the most optimal raster format to import in terms of size, so we have to deal with their limitations in other areas. Specifically, JPEGs don't support an alpha channel (so, no transparency), and they come in with a rectangular outline or bounding box, unless you trim them in Flash, as we discussed earlier in this chapter. If you wanted to blur a main character, you'd need the transparency of an alpha channel to help blend it in. Unfortunately, transparency and alpha channels are only supported in formats that are larger in size and therefore not great options for use in Flash. However, of those larger formats, PNG is the most manageable and therefore most useful (as opposed to TIFF, which supports great-looking alpha channels but is not recommended for import into Flash).

Speed

The property of speed comes into play when the user interacts with the game and sets off a chain of reactions that cause the elements of the game world to animate. The illusion of speed is created in the ActionScript, which is written to make the graphics move, and move at the right speed. To give you a simple example from our platform game, open the ice_world.swf file in the Chapter15 directory. Notice that as the main character walks forward, the elements further in the background appear to move more slowly than the elements closer to the user.

The Quest for Realism

Making your game look more realistic can be a challenge when you're working within Flash's drawing limitations. You can draw realistic-looking graphics in Flash as vector art, but in most cases that would actually be too processor-intensive for Flash to handle. The most common way to create realistic graphics is by working with a raster program like Photoshop, and then importing them into Flash as JPEGs. But beware: Even with the compression abilities of JPEGs, if you use too many raster files, your game file size could get out of hand. So, predictably, you have to make trade-offs. I usually recommend using a combination of both formats, weighted toward one or the other format type depending on the look you are going for. For example, let's say you're creating graphics for an isometric world. You could make all your background and environment graphics in raster format, and your characters in vector format. The fact that background and environment graphics are mostly static and rectangular will probably work in your favor; given that when raster graphics are imported into Flash they are rectangular, that's a lot less trimming you may have to do. As for the characters, because they are mostly small and, once animated, will need quite a few frames, you'll need to fill in less detail and will also benefit from the vector graphic's small file size.

Drop Shadows

You can create a basic drop shadow from a couple of gradient shapes. For our example, we will apply the drop shadow to a floating menu, but you can apply this basic concept to your own user interfaces and also to more complex shapes.

If you use Flash's quick keys, this exercise goes very quickly. Here we're assuming that you have your keyboard shortcuts set to default.

1. Using the rectangle tool (R) with a bevel of 10 pixels, create a rectangle in the middle of the stage. To set your bevel, before you draw the rectangle click the Round Rectangle Radius button, located in the Options section of the Tools panel, and enter a value for the Corner Radius setting in the text dialog box that pops up.

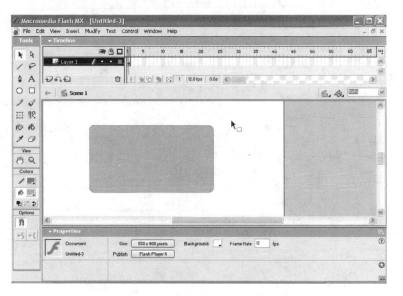

2. With the arrow tool (V), select the stroke of one edge of the rectangle and scale it by 200% (Ctrl-Alt-S in Windows or Command-Option-S on the Macintosh). While the line is still selected, and with Snap to Objects selected in the View menu, move the line to connect with the place where the line and the corner curve meet.

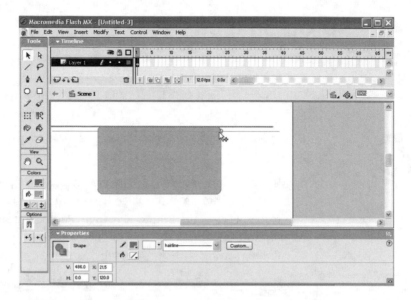

3. While the line is still selected, copy it (Ctrl-C in Windows or Command-C on the Mac), paste it in place (Ctrl-Shift-V in Windows or Command-Shift-V on the Mac), and move it outside the rectangle, creating the start of a border around the rectangle.

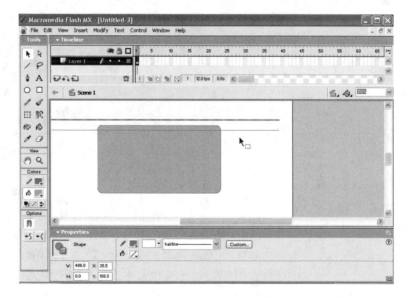

4. Repeat steps 1–3 for the strokes on the other edges.

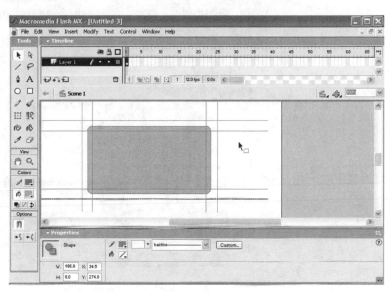

5. Create your drop-shadow gradients.

    Make a linear gradient from #000000 100% alpha to #000000 0% alpha, and add it to the Color Swatches panel. Then make a radial gradient from #000000 100% alpha to #000000 0% alpha. Place the #000000 100% alpha color for both linear and radial gradients in the middle of the gradient spectrum, and add it to the Color Swatches panel.

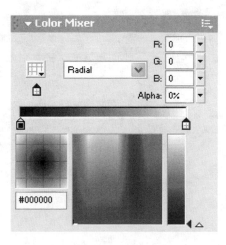

6. Grab the paint bucket tool (K), select the linear gradient you just made, and apply the gradient to the long top area.

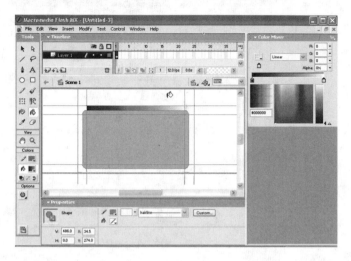

7. Select the fill transform tool (F), and use the transformation knobs to edit the gradient so that it fades from 0% alpha at the top to 100% alpha at the bottom.

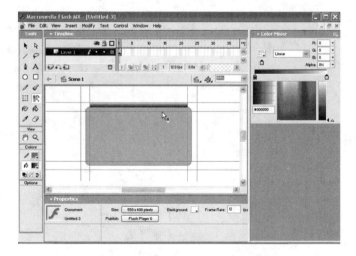

8. Repeat steps 6 and 7 for the bottom, left, and right sides.

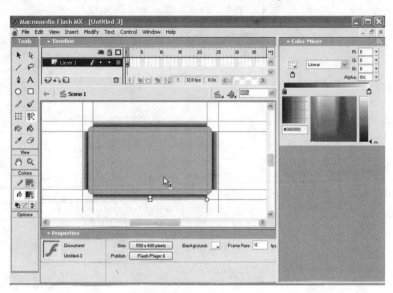

9. Grab the paint bucket tool (K) again, select the radial gradient that you made, and apply it to all the corner sections.

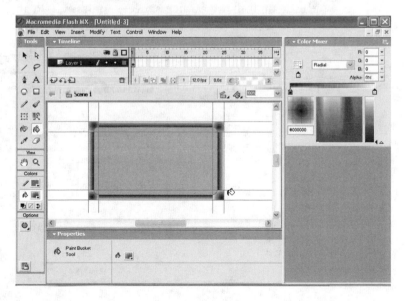

10. Select the fill transform tool (F), and edit your radial gradients so that the center of the gradient intersects with the hairline strokes.

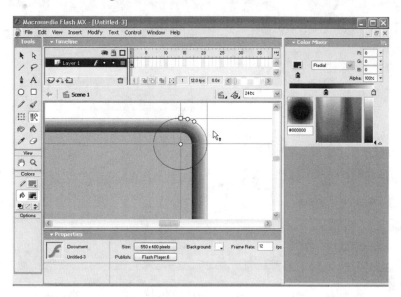

11. Still using the fill transform tool, move the scale and stretch handles until all the gradients meet seamlessly. (Go ahead and delete the lines; you will be able to see your gradients much more easily.)

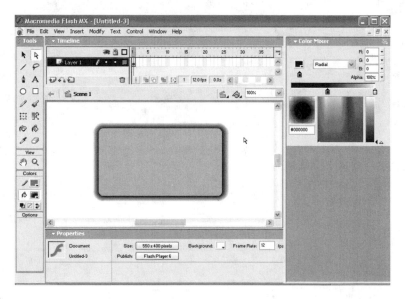

You should be able to apply this technique to just about anything. Try modifying the colors and the alpha percentage to get different looks.

The same drop-shadow technique, applied to a user-interface item.

User-Interface Lighting

Giving your user interface some highlights with gradient fills can be simple and effective, although it may take a bit of practice. This type of lighting effect is great for relatively large objects, because such objects have room to display the fine gradations of color in a gradient. (On smaller objects viewed at 100%, sometimes the gradients look a little odd, since they don't have room to display properly.) To show you how to use this technique, we will walk through adding a gradient highlight to our existing rectangle that has the drop shadow.

1. Open the existing rectangle (if it isn't open already), grab the ink bottle tool (S), and apply a red hairline stroke to the outside of the rectangle.

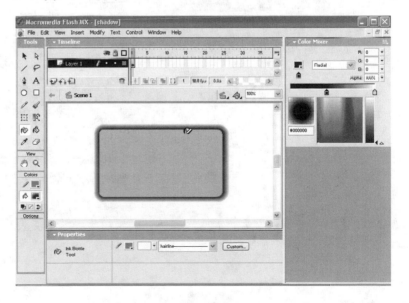

2. With the arrow tool, select the vertical stroke at the left of the rectangle, copy it, paste in place, move it to the right, and scale it to about 200%.

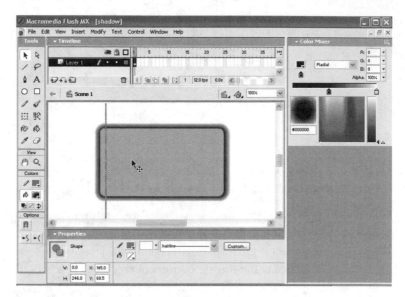

3. With Snap to Objects on, attach the line to where the top curve meets the horizontal line.

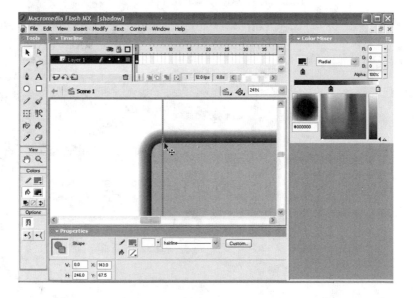

4. Repeat steps 2–3 to create guidelines for the right, top, and bottom sides of the rectangle.

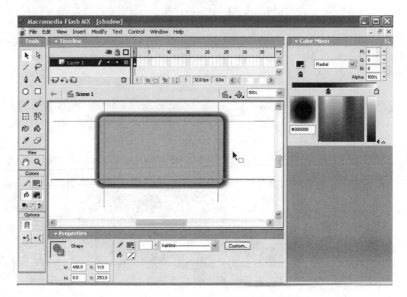

5. Create your highlight gradients: Make a linear gradient from #3399FF at 100% alpha to #92C9FF at 100% alpha, and add it to the Color Swatches panel. Then make a radial gradient from #3399FF at 100% alpha to #92C9FF at 100% alpha, and add that to the Color Swatches panel, too.

6. Grab the paint bucket tool (K) and select the linear gradient you just made. Apply it to the long top and bottom areas and to the left and right vertical areas.

   Make sure the Lock Fill button near the bottom of the main tool panel is not selected, or else when you apply your fills, they will look quite odd.

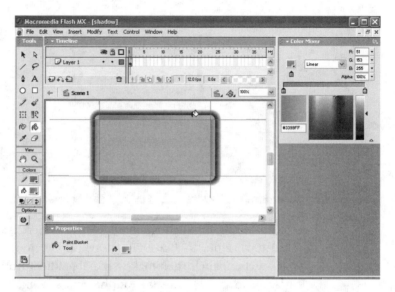

7. With the paint bucket tool still active, select the radial gradient you just made, and then apply it to all of the corner areas.

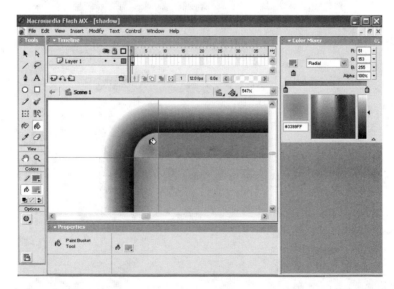

8. Select the fill transform tool (F), and edit your linear and radial gradients so that they match up seamlessly.

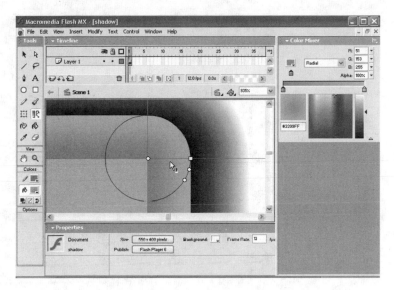

9. Use the arrow tool to select the red guidelines you made earlier, and then delete them. If the gradients don't match up perfectly, try adjusting where the colors start and stop in your gradient spectrum.

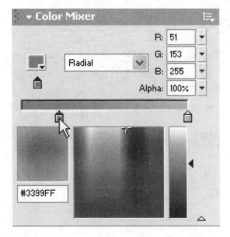

10. Select the center color, and change it to a solid fill of #3399FF so that it blends with the gradients you've just applied.

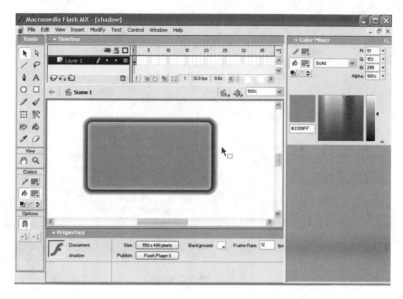

That's it! Try this technique on your user-interface items; you'll achieve that raster look with the small file sizes of vector graphics.

Putting Text in Perspective

Don't waste your time with 3D programs or third-party plug-ins trying to make killer 3D text when you can just do it in Flash! It doesn't take an artist to pull this off; just follow this easy procedure, and you'll soon be able to take a basic font and give it perspective.

1. Using the text tool, type the word "HELLO" in 40-point Arial Black, in red. Break the font elements all the way down (Ctrl-B in Windows or Command-B on the Mac) until they are just fill shapes.

2. Figure out where you want the vanishing point to be. For this example, I placed mine in the middle below the text (see the crosshairs).

VANISHING POINT

3.   Grab the line tool, and with Snap to Objects on, start connecting the points between the vanishing point and the corners of the text characters. As you go along, you can delete any lines that overlap (which just get in the way of other lines).

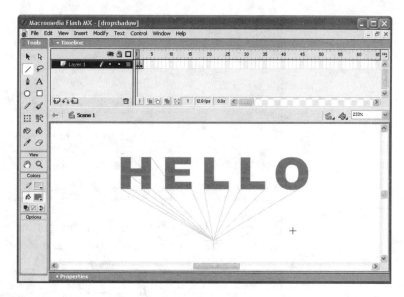

4.   Decide how thick (deep) you want the 3D text to be. Use the line tool to draw a horizontal line all the way across your stage. Apply that same thickness to the top and bottom of each letter.

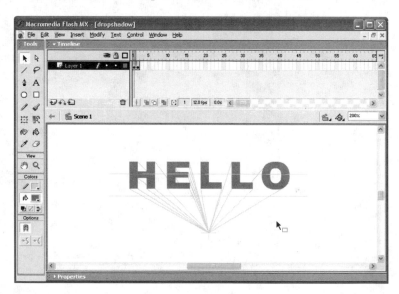

5. Use the paint bucket tool to apply color in between the guidelines you created.

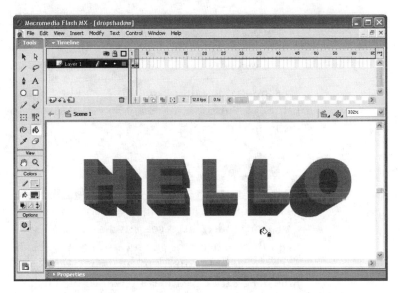

Think back to the "Light and Shadow" section—apply brighter variations of one color to signify where the light is coming from. Our example assumes that the main light source is coming from the top left. Once the fills have been applied, delete all the guidelines.

Now you have given your text some perspective, but it still seems kind of flat. Let's take it to the next level and simulate more depth and real light.

6. Using different variations on your original text colors, create and apply some linear gradients to the text.

Always keep in mind where your main light source is.

This lesson is just the beginning. Try adding some perspective to your game's user interface, or let it help you to set your perspective for a 3D environment.

Tint Change

Here's a tint-change technique that will enable you to create one graphic and, using code, edit its color as many times as you want. This is very helpful if you have one graphic that needs to be displayed in many colors. For example, in a game of 9-ball, you could create just one ball and use tint changes to make nine different-colored balls. A tint change is also very efficient in terms of file size, as it only involves one graphic. In the following example, we are going to prepare (visually, not with code) a simple ball graphic for a tint shift.

1. Grab the oval tool, and create a circle with no stroke and a fill of black.

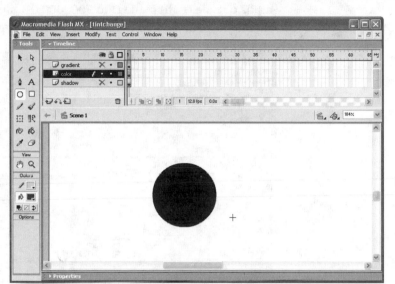

2. Select the circle you just made. With it selected, convert it into a symbol (F8) with the behavior of Movie Clip. Right-click or Control-click the circle to see the contextual menu, and choose Edit in Place. Select the circle that is inside this symbol you are now editing, and copy it. Create a new layer above the existing one and choose Edit > Paste in Place to lay down the circle you just copied. Hide the bottom layer.

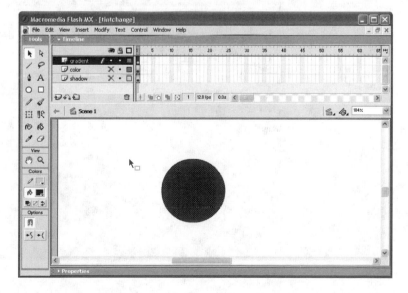

3. Open the Color Mixer; create a radial gradient from #000000 100% alpha outside (right marker) to #000000 0% alpha inside (left marker), and apply it to the new circle you just pasted.

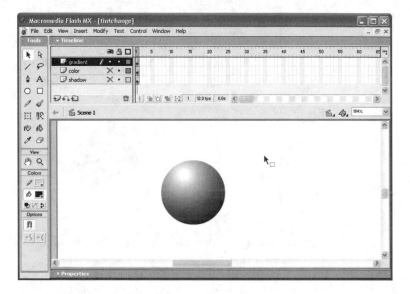

4. Grab the fill transform tool, and move the center of the gradient up and a little bit to the left. Grab the scale controller handle and move it until it touches the outside of the circle.

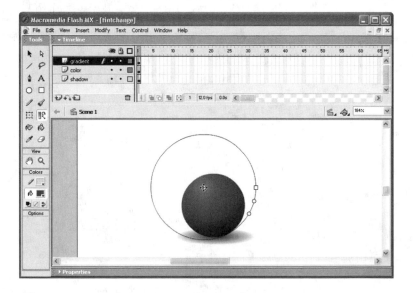

5. Hide the top layer and unhide the bottom layer. Select the black circle on the bottom layer, and convert it to a movie-clip symbol. This symbol will be the movie clip to which the ActionScript programmer will apply the tint change. (The idea is for the programmer to change only the circle with the flat color applied—the gradient can be applied, as is, to any iteration of that circle to give it the depth and dimension you want.)

That's it for the graphic aspect of this technique! All that's left is for the programmer to add the necessary code to edit the tint value of the movie clip to change its color. To see the ActionScript involved, you can open programmed_example.fla in the Chapter11 directory on the CD.

The variations on this technique are endless, and the file-size benefits are amazing. Try applying this technique to a game character that needs to appear many times but in different colors. Or use it to make elements of your game editable by the user.

Tiling

Tiles come in two shapes, to be used in two different scenarios. As shown below, for isometric games they are drawn in diamond shapes; for non-isometric games they are drawn as squares.

Tiles used in an isometric game (top row), and tiles used in a non-isometric game.

When it comes to creating the perfect tile, the most important factors to keep in mind are how well one tile flows into the next, and how to manage and control the complexity and file size of all the tiles.

The resolution of a tile typically ranges from 10 by 10 pixels to 30 by 30 pixels, and depends on the size of your game's viewable area. The recommended file size for a single tile can range from 500 bytes to 5,000 bytes! What size is best for your game? Wouldn't we all like to have an easy formula for that! But you've got to find out for yourself what works best for your game; each setup (not to mention each game) is going to be different.

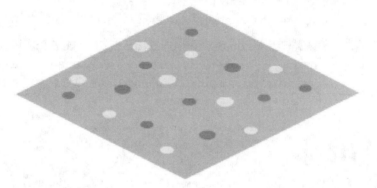

To keep your file size to a minimum, it's highly recommended that you use symbols to create the effect of textures and other repeatable patterns and elements in your designs. For example, the simple circle repeated in the figure above is a library symbol. I duplicated it throughout the diamond, and applied a tint effect to make the instances different colors. This is going to save me a lot of time and space. Still, the more symbols and vectors you add to your tile, the more processor intensive it may become, so use as few as possible to achieve the effects you want.

Sample "transition" tiles you could use to go from grass to concrete.

Now that you have an idea of how big to make your tiles and how they should be constructed, what about putting them all together? Let's say you've created a pointy grass tile and a spotted concrete tile for your game. How are you going to integrate those two tiles seamlessly in your gaming world? You will need to draw a few other types of tiles in order to make the transition from grass to concrete appear more natural.

The guidelines for tile size, resolution, and integration for vector graphics can also be applied to raster graphic tiles.

Putting it all together.

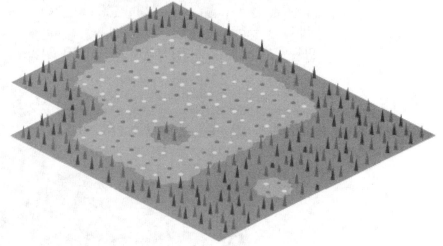

Game Animations

There are two different ways in which animations are integrated in a game: externally and internally.

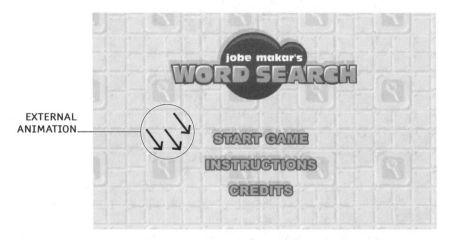

EXTERNAL ANIMATION

External animations are found on common screens of a game (such as the splash screen, instruction screen, or credit screen). For example, animations within a game introduction, on main menu areas, or in character-selection areas would be considered external. External animations do not necessarily need to be optimized or restricted to a certain resolution.

Typically, you will find internal animations in a game engine. For example, any character animations and animations with which the user interacts within the game engine are internal. Internal animations must be optimized to achieve the best possible gaming experience.

INTERNAL ANIMATION

Here we will analyze an internal animation used in the engine for the unfinished game Grave Robber, shown in Chapter 9. It is a character that the user controls with the arrow keys. This character consists of three animations: walk up, walk left, and walk down. For example purposes we will see how much we can optimize the walk-left animation.

With a movie frame rate of 24 frames per second (fps), the optimal rate for games, I started out with an eight-frame walk animation. There are a few ways you can optimize this series.

LEGS IN   LEGS OUT

FULL WALKING ANIMATION
Keyframes: 8
Original Frames: 8
File Size: 6.54 KB

OPTIMIZED WALKING ANIMATION
Keyframes: 4
Original Frames: 3
File Size: 2.60 KB

Important keyframes—Draw the fewest frames needed to achieve the motion you want to create. For example, the minimum feasible frames in a walk animation show legs in and legs out (the first and third keyframes in the Optimized Walking Animation figure above).

Extending a keyframe—By extending a keyframe for more than one frame, you can get away with using the smallest possible number of keyframes. Especially at 24 fps, the frames go by fast enough that the human eye will not notice a difference between eight individual keyframes and four keyframes extended to two frames each.

Symbols—When you create an animation, sometimes you will have to—or want to—reuse certain frames. When this happens, be sure to convert the graphics you intend to reuse into symbols, to be stored in the document's library. You'll notice in the Optimized Walking Animation above that frames 2 and 4 are both the same symbol.

With these three techniques I was able to reduce the number of frames in this animation from eight to three, with a difference of almost 4 KB. That's only one small file, but if you apply these techniques to all the animations in your game, you stand to save quite a lot more.

POINTS TO REMEMBER

- Having great communication between your art team and your programming team is key if you wish to have smooth implementation of your graphics and animation.

- Raster and vector graphics allow you to create and use very different styles of graphics, and also offer you different levels of performance.

- Identify what tools you'll need up front so that you don't have to stop midway to add another component to your workflow.

- Graphics and drawing techniques can give your game depth and life.

- Setting up flexible, code-based techniques for implementing dynamic changes such as color shifts or tiling will save you a lot of work, keep operations consistent, and improve performance.

- Taking the time to optimize your graphics will save you a lot of time and effort, and of course will improve your game's performance. Think about optimization at every stage of your game development—from the actual drawing of the figures through the prep stage, when you situate your graphics and animations within Flash, convert them to symbols and movie clips, and ready them for the programmer.

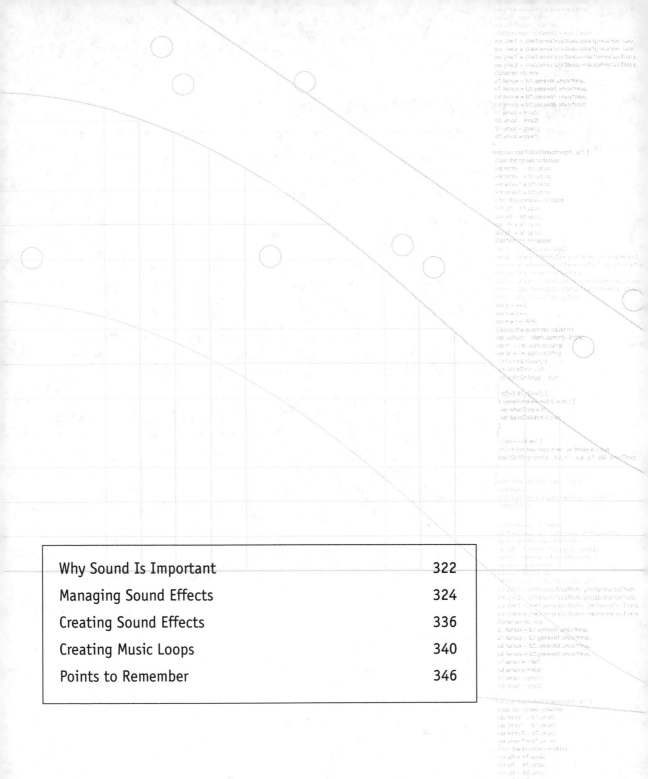

CHAPTER 12

THE SOUND OF GAMES

SOUND IS PROBABLY THE MOST NEGLECTED AREA OF FLASH GAME DESIGN. Between hatching a game idea, creating the graphical assets, programming, and debugging, it's not surprising that not much time is devoted to finding or making the perfect sounds. Sound effects and music add a lot to a game—much more than you may realize. Sounds can connect with a person on an emotional level and invoke fear, excitement, surprise, sadness, or playfulness. Used properly, sound effects and music can make a good game extraordinary. In this chapter we discuss sound effects and music loops—how to make them, and why sound should not be neglected in *your* games.

WHY SOUND IS IMPORTANT

As you develop a game, there are three senses you can use to involve a game player: touch, sight, and sound. Until computers start emitting odors and flavors, those are all we have to work with. The visuals (sight) and the control (touch) of a game tend to get a lot of attention during game design and development. In this chapter we focus our attention on the odd sense out, hearing. Sounds used in a game can be any of the following:

Songs—Full-length musical compositions created or licensed for your game. Songs can play in the background during the game or be triggered to play after something happens (for example, winning the game).

Music loops—Short pieces of music that play repeatedly. A music loop can range from about 1 second to several seconds, and have a file size that is a fraction of that of a full song.

Sound effects—Sounds triggered by the result of an action, or synchronized with a visual event.

Voice—Spoken-language clips recorded or licensed for your game. Voice can be used in animations before a game, throughout the game to show characters talking, or as a sound effect (for example, a person yelling "Ouch!" when struck by a sword).

Music and voice are not always necessary in your games, but sound effects definitely are. Here are the top three reasons why you should not neglect sound in your games:

1. **Sounds can encourage the player to feel a certain way.** This is usually achieved through songs or music loops. For instance, in a murder mystery, eerie music would help most people get into the spirit of the game. If instead of eerie music, carnival music were playing, then the mood would be decidedly different. For a racing game you would probably choose upbeat music—something that makes the players feel that they need to react quickly. Adding music is one major step in getting someone immersed in the game.

2. **Sounds can evoke immediate emotional responses such as surprise, fear, and laughter.** To use the murder mystery example again, imagine you are sleuthing in a dark room when suddenly a chandelier falls to the floor next to you. Unless you have your speakers turned off, this loud crash will probably startle you—a response intended by the game developer. Another, smaller-scale example of this is collecting coins in a typical side-scrolling adventure game like Super Mario Brothers. You may not jump for joy every time you collect a coin, but somehow that "ding" gives you a good feeling.

3. **Sounds can convey information.** A sound can let you know that your character has just been hurt or that a secret door has been opened. Two of the most common uses of sound to convey information are to let you know that your character has just collected an item, and to give you an idea of how far away something is (depth).

Sometimes, if you play your cards right (so to speak), sounds can achieve two or more of these goals at the same time. For example, let's say you're playing a game in which you must solve a puzzle somewhere in a house. When you do, you get to open a locked door to another room, and a short, cheerful tune is played. The sound conveys the information that "hey, you did something right!" as well as helps to create or elicit an emotional response of satisfaction or excitement.

After playing a good game, I rarely find myself thinking, "Wow, the sounds in this game are great!" This isn't because of bad sound; if the sounds are doing their job, then they will most likely not stand out. It's often the same in movies. There are many scenes in which the frantic music enhances the suspense or action. You probably don't notice how much of an effect the sound has. If someone doesn't really notice the sound in your game, then the sound is most likely doing its job properly. More often than not, sounds that stand out are sounds that do not belong.

In the rest of this chapter we will talk about how to use and create sound effects and loops, and how to use ActionScript with sound files to create effects.

MANAGING SOUND EFFECTS

There are two ways to use sound effects in Flash. You can place a sound directly on a frame, or you can pull it from the library with ActionScript using attachSound(). Using frames to hold your sounds is easy and pre-dictable; the sound plays when that frame is reached. The advantage of using this technique is that you can control the volume and other sound properties in the authoring environment. With attachSound(), the sound can be started or stopped using ActionScript. Further, you have control over the volume and panning of the sound in real time. With sounds placed on a frame, however, you cannot change these properties (pan and volume) of the sound after they have been set in the authoring environ-ment—the game player's actions are not going to affect the properties. In short, as always, there are advantages and trade-offs either way. In this sec-tion we discuss both ways of using sound effects in your games through the use of several example files.

Sound Placed on Frames

I've seen the source files for many Flash games over the last few years, and one thing I often find is that people put their sounds all over the place. For example, in one of these files, the sound for each object was inside the movie clip for that object—a character-hopping sound was inside the char-acter movie clip, the gunfire sound was inside the gun movie clip, and so on. There is nothing wrong with using sounds in this way, but it's not very efficient. Keeping track of your sounds is difficult, and it's not always easy to add new sounds.

Here is an easy way to keep all of your sounds in one location so that you can easily add multiple sound effects to your game. (This is also going to make it easy to create a sound on/off toggle.)

The technique is simple. We create a movie clip whose sole purpose is to hold sounds. There is one sound on each frame. Each frame has a frame label and an action that sends the playhead in that movie clip back to frame 1. We then create a function outside of this movie clip, which I usually call playSound(). This function accepts a parameter that should be the name of the sound or the label of the frame that needs to be played. It then tells the sound-effects movie clip to play that specific frame. That's it!

Now—since it's so easy, and since I want to introduce you to it before we jump into the example file—let's set up the toggle. As you can guess, a sound on/off toggle is a button that a game player can click to turn the game sound on and off. If you spend a lot of time finding the best sounds for your game, then you probably want people to hear them (and they probably want to, too). But the truth is (sssshhh!) that many players will play your game over the Internet when they are in the office, and they won't want anyone to hear that they aren't working. There are plenty of other situations in which a person might not want the sound to play. So all in all, it's a good idea to provide the game player a way to turn the sound on and off.

Let's look at an example. Open missiles.fla in the Chapter12 directory. This is a simple game (never completed). The triangle at the bottom of the screen is a ship. You can move the ship left and right with the left and right arrow keys, and you can make it fire a shot vertically by pressing the space-bar. The object is to shoot as many bubbles as possible. In this file we only have two sounds—the sound of the ship firing and the sound of a bubble popping. To the left of the stage you will see a movie clip called soundFX.

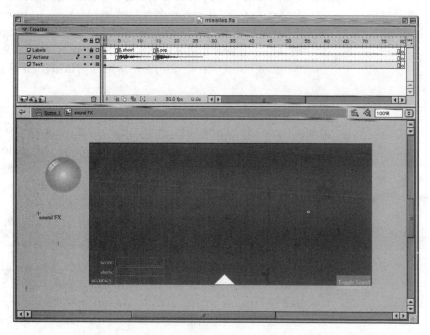

Double-click this movie clip to look inside. There are three layers in it. You can ignore the bottom layer, Text. It is only there so that we can find the movie clip on the stage. Without the text inside this movie clip, we would have a hard time locating it. The top layer, Labels, contains two frame labels, shoot and pop. The layer in the middle, Actions, contains actions on three frames. On frame 1 there is just a stop() action, so the movie clip doesn't play until told to. The actions on the two labeled frames are the same: this.gotoAndStop(1). When a sound plays, the playhead immediately moves back to frame 1 and waits for further instructions.

At the top of frame 1 on the main timeline you'll find the function playSound():

```
1   function playSound(name) {
2       if (soundOn) {
3           soundFX.gotoAndPlay(name);
4       }
5   }
```

This function accepts a parameter called name. This is also the label of the frame we wish to play. An if statement in this function checks to see if the sound toggle is on or off. The action soundOn = true is on frame 1 just before this function. That sets the sound toggle to on. If that value ever becomes false, the sound will no longer play. In line 3 of the function above we tell the soundFX movie clip to go to a certain frame to play a sound. This is a very useful technique. We can now add as many sounds as we would like to the soundFX movie clip, and then play those sounds very easily.

Select the Ship movie clip at the bottom of the stage, and if it's not already open, open the Actions panel. On line 19 of the ActionScript, you will see there is the action _root.playSound("shoot"). This action is executed when the script shoots a missile (that is, when the spacebar is pressed). Now select the instance of the Bubble movie clip and open the Actions panel. On line 12 of the ActionScript you will see _root.playSound("pop"). This calls for the pop sound to be played when the bubble detects that it has been hit with a missile.

There is a button in the bottom-right part of the screen called Toggle Sound. This button has been programmed to toggle the sound on and off. Remember that the sound is considered on if soundOn has a value of true, and off if soundOn has a value of false. Here is the ActionScript on this button:

```
1    on (press) {
2        soundOn = soundOn ? false : true
3    }
```

The action in line 2 is executed when the Toggle Sound button is clicked. The action used here is a quick shortcut that is commonly used for toggling Boolean values. What you see to the right of the = sign is called a *ternary operator*. That means it's an operator with three operands, which are (in this case) soundOn, false, and true. This is a conditional statement. If the first operand has a value of true, then the entire statement takes the value of the second operand, else it takes the value of the third operand. This is equivalent to our having written an if statement like this:

```
if (soundOn) {
    soundOn = false;
} else {
    soundOn = true;
}
```

The one-line conditional statement syntax used here is used occasionally through the games programmed in the third section of this book. It's an easy way to toggle a value in one line of code rather than five.

You have just seen a very simple technique for adding sounds to games. In the next section we'll show another technique for adding sounds to games using ActionScript.

Sound Controlled with ActionScript

To control a sound with ActionScript, you pull it from the library and attach it to a sound object using attachSound(). To pull a sound from the library, you must give it a linkage identifier, just as you would do with a movie clip when it's to be used with the attachMovie() function (as we discussed in Chapter 5, "Collision Detection"). The advantage of using ActionScript to control sounds rather than placing them on a frame is that ActionScript gives you much more control. You can change the sound's volume or pan at any time. Also, you do not have to start playing a sound at its beginning—you can start it anyplace. For instance, you can start a sound that is 4 seconds long at the third second, and as a result you'll hear just the last second of the sound. In this section we will look at three example uses of controlling sounds with ActionScript.

Controlling sound based on object speed

For our first example, open ball.fla from the Chapter12 directory on the CD. In this file you'll see a ball and four walls. The ball has been given an initial velocity, and it falls under gravity. The result is a ball that bounces off the walls, much as a basketball would, eventually stopping. This file uses a sound effect called bounce.wav, with a linkage identifier named bounce. The sound's volume depends on how hard the ball hits each wall. The *pan* of the sound—that is, the amount and volume that the sound plays in each speaker—depends on the ball's *x* position. You've already seen the ActionScript used to bounce the ball around in Chapter 4, "Basic Physics"; Chapter 5, "Collision Detection"; and Chapter 6, "Collision Reactions." What is new in this file is the function called playSound(), for which the ActionScript is shown below.

```
1   function playSound(x, speed) {
2       if (soundOn) {
3           var ballX = x-left;
4           var factor = ballX/(right-left);
5           var pan = -100+factor*200;
6           var maxSpeed = 15;
7           var minSpeed = 1;
8           var speed = Math.abs(speed);
9           var factor = speed/(maxSpeed-minSpeed);
10          if (speed<minSpeed) {
11              var factor = 0;
12          }
13          var volume = factor*100;
14          if (volume>0) {
15              bounce = new Sound();
16              bounce.attachSound("bounce");
17              bounce.setPan(pan);
18              bounce.setVolume(volume);
19              bounce.start();
20          }
21      }
22  }
```

This function is called whenever a collision is detected. The *x* position of the ball is passed into this function so that we can determine how much to pan the sound. The speed of the ball when it collided with the wall is also passed into this function, so that we can determine the volume needed. The speed passed in is the speed affected by the collision. For example, when the ball hits the floor, we pass in the *y* speed (not shown), since the *x* speed is unaffected. In line 3 we set a variable called `ballX`. The *x* position passed into this function is of the ball on the main stage. What we need to know in order to properly set the pan is the ball's *x* position with respect to the walls. The variable `ballX` stores the position of the ball with respect to the left wall. In line 4 we set a variable called `factor`. The concept illustrated here is a very useful one called *normalization*. The variable `factor` is a *normalized* number; that means it will always be between 0 and 1. We are looking for the ball's distance from the left wall in normalized terms. If `factor` is 1, then the ball is all the way over on the right wall; if it is 0, then the ball is on the left wall. If it is between 0 and 1, then the ball is somewhere in between the two walls. You find a normalized value by taking the value you want to normalize, in this case `ballX`, and dividing it by its maximum possible value, which in this case is the total distance between the left and right walls.

Next we set a variable called `pan` to store the pan amount (line 5). A pan of –100 means that all of the sound comes out of the left speaker, and a pan of 100 means that the sound comes completely out of the right speaker, for a total possible difference of 200 between left pan and right pan. We can set the pan value by starting with –100 and adding to it the value of `factor*200`. If `factor` is 1, then `pan` is 100, so the sound will play from the right speaker. If `factor` is 0, then `pan` is –100, and the sound will play completely from the left speaker.

In lines 6–9 we determine another `factor` variable, this one for speed. We will use this normalized number to determine the volume settings. If `factor` is 1, then the volume is maximum; if `factor` is 0, the volume is minimum. We use the current speed and the maximum speed allowed to determine the `factor` variable. Finally, in lines 15–19 we create a sound object (line 15), attach the bounce sound to that object (line 16), set the pan of the sound (line 17), set the volume of the sound (line 18), and finally play the sound (line 19).

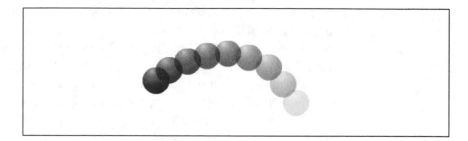

Generate a SWF from this file. You can see that the volume is dependent on the speed at which the ball collides with the wall. Also notice how the pan changes with the position of the ball.

Controlling sound based on factors other than speed

For the next example, open billiard_ball.fla in the Chapter12 directory. This file was taken directly from Chapter 6, "Collision Reactions," and modified to play a sound when a collision occurs. In this section I'm going to show how you can dynamically change the volume of the sound based on information other than speed. In the case of a ball bouncing off a wall, the volume is dependent on the speed of the ball. But imagine two billiard balls moving in the same direction very fast. If ball 1 is just a little bit faster than ball 2, then it may catch up and collide with ball 2. But even though these two balls are moving very fast, that doesn't mean the collision should be loud, since they may just barely collide. Instead of using speed, we will look at the *change* in speed. The volume of the sound is completely based on the difference between the speed before the collision and the speed after the collision.

Here is the playSound() function:

```
1   function playSound(speedDiff) {
2       if (soundOn) {
3           var maxSpeed = 5;
4           var factor = speedDiff/maxSpeed;
5           var volume = 100*factor;
6           hit = new Sound();
7           hit.attachSound("hit");
```

```
8          hit.setVolume(volume);
9          hit.start();
10     }
11  }
```

In line 3 we set a variable called maxSpeed with a value of 5. The value tells the script to play the sound at maximum volume when the speed difference hits that amount (and of course you can alter that value to suit yourself). Right now, if a speed difference of 5 occurs on a collision, then we will hear the volume at its maximum. Let's look at the two lines of code that call this function, inside the ball2BallReaction() function:

```
1   var speedDiff = Math.sqrt((b1.xmov-xVel1)*(b1.xmov-xVel1)
    ↪ +(b1.ymov-yVel1)*(b1.ymov-yVel1));
2   playSound(speedDiff);
```

In line 1 we use the Pythagorean theorem (the distance equation) to find out the difference between the speed before the collision and the speed after the collision. This value is then passed into the playSound() function (line 2).

Generate a SWF to verify for yourself that this works properly. Go back to the FLA file and change some of the velocity variables; keep retesting to convince yourself that this method works well. You can use this dynamic volume technique with a game of pool or any other game where two moving objects collide at potentially varying speeds.

Volume controlled through acceleration

Up until now we've been talking about simple speed. Now, in our third example, we'll add acceleration into the mix, and outline a simple technique used for acceleration and deceleration in racing games. Imagine a car sitting at the starting line in a racing game. When it's time to start driving, you've got to accelerate, and an acceleration sound plays. What happens if during the middle of the acceleration you decide to decelerate? Well, you need to play a deceleration sound. Sounds easy enough, right? The problem is that the sound of the deceleration would be different depending on how fast the car was moving when you started to decelerate.

Open car.fla in the Chapter12 directory. In this example we show how to handle race car–driving sounds from idle (not moving) to maximum speed, and how to handle the sounds for acceleration or deceleration at any time. This is done with four sounds:

• A loop played for the idle

• A loop played for the car when it is at maximum speed

• An acceleration sound that plays from idle all the way up to maximum speed

• A deceleration sound that plays from maximum speed all the way down to idle

The acceleration and deceleration sounds are the same length. (In fact, the deceleration sound was actually made by reversing the acceleration sound in a sound-editing program.)

When the car accelerates, we play the acceleration sound. When the player instructs the car to decelerate, we check to see the position of the acceleration sound. We then use this information to figure out where to start the deceleration sound. Likewise, if while decelerating the player instructs the car to accelerate, we check the current position of the deceleration sound and use that information to determine where to start the acceleration sound.

Got that? Now let's inspect the ActionScript. First we use the following actions to create a sound object for each of the four sounds, and to attach a sound to each object:

```
1   accel = new Sound();
2   accel.attachSound("accel");
3   decel = new Sound();
4   decel.attachSound("decel");
5   hi_loop = new Sound();
6   hi_loop.attachSound("hi_loop");
7   low_loop = new Sound();
8   low_loop.attachSound("low_loop");
9   accel = new Sound();
10  accel.attachSound("accel");
11  decel.attachSound("decel");
```

And here are the functions that play the sounds:

```
1   function playAccel(offset) {
2       accel.setVolume(vol);
3       accel.start(offset);
4       accel.onSoundComplete = accelDone;
5       playing = "accel";
6   }
7   function playDecel(offset) {
8       decel.setVolume(vol);
9       decel.start(offset);
10      decel.onSoundComplete = decelDone;
11      playing = "decel";
12  }
13  function accelDone() {
14      accel.stop();
15      hi_loop.setVolume(vol);
16      hi_loop.start(0, 100000);
17  }
18  function decelDone() {
19      decel.stop();
20      low_loop.setVolume(vol);
21      low_loop.start(0, 100000);
22  }
```

The first function, playAccel(), is used to play the acceleration sound. All
of these functions accept a parameter called offset that is used to offset
the starting point of the sound they will play. If the duration of the sound
is 10 seconds and the offset is 3 seconds, then the ActionScript will skip the
first 3 seconds of the sound and start playing it immediately. In line 4 we
set an event handler for the acceleration sound. When that sound is finished playing, it will call the function accelDone(). This allows us to easily
tell when the acceleration has finished playing, so we know when to start
playing the maximum-speed sound loop. On line 7, the next function,
playDecel(), plays the deceleration sound. When it has finished playing,
it calls the function decelDone() so that the idle sound loop can start playing. These onSoundComplete events only fire if the sound is allowed to
reach completion. If, for instance, the acceleration sound is stopped before
it has finished playing, then accelDone() will not be called.

The final part of the ActionScript in this file captures all the user actions and handles the starting and stopping of sounds that result from those user actions. It also includes the controls for the bar, which is not really related to the functioning of the sounds.

```
1   _root.onEnterFrame = function() {
2       if (playing == "decel" || playing == null) {
3           bar._yscale = (1-decel.position/decel.duration)*100;
4           if (Key.isDown(Key.UP)) {
5               if (playing == null) {
6                   var start = 0;
7               } else {
8                   var start = (accel.duration-
                        ↩ decel.position)/1000;
9               }
10              decel.stop();
11              low_loop.stop();
12              playAccel(start);
13          }
14      }
15      if (playing == "accel" || playing == null) {
16          bar._yscale = accel.position/accel.duration*100;
17          if (Key.isDown(Key.DOWN)) {
18              if (playing == null) {
19                  var start = 0;
20              } else {
21                  var start = (decel.duration-
                        ↩ accel.position)/1000;
22              }
23              accel.stop();
24              hi_loop.stop();
25              playDecel(start);
26          }
27      }
28  };
```

This is an `onEnterFrame` event that executes two main conditional statements in every frame. They check to see if the car is currently accelerating or decelerating. If the car is decelerating (line 2), then the bar movie clip on the stage is scaled to show what the car is doing. This movie clip has nothing to do with the sounds themselves; it is just giving us a visual idea of what is happening. Then the script checks to see if the up arrow key is being pressed. If it is, then the script starts the sound at position 0, or if the car is already in motion, it calculates what the sound offset should be. The *sound offset* is the reverse of the position of the deceleration sound. If the deceleration is 10 seconds long and is at the position of the third second, then the acceleration offset is 7 seconds. In lines 10 and 11 we stop sounds that could be playing, and in line 12 we start the deceleration sound by calling `playAccel()`. The second `if` statement (line 15) does the same thing as the first one, except that it checks to see if the car is currently accelerating. If the car is accelerating and the down arrow key is pressed, then the deceleration sound is played.

Generate a SWF from this file. Press the up arrow key. You should hear the car start to accelerate. If you let the acceleration reach maximum, then you will hear the maximum speed loop, hi_loop, start playing. At any time you can press the down arrow key to have the deceleration sound kick in. If you let the deceleration continue to completion, the idle sound, low_loop, will play.

CREATING SOUND EFFECTS

If you are reading this, then you are probably not a professional sound designer. As such, you probably don't own a $2,000 microphone with tube preamp and top-notch digital conversion. But chances are you do have a Sound Blaster card (from Creative Technology, Ltd.) or something similar, and the $3 plastic microphone that came with your computer. This may very well be all you need to capture the necessary sound effects for your games. So let's set up shop! In the following section, we'll give you some practical advice from the trenches on proper setup, recording dos and don'ts, ways to make your own sounds, and where to find pre-recorded sounds.

Setting Up

Before capturing sounds, take at least a few minutes to be sure that every-thing is set up properly for the task at hand. Make sure the microphone is properly plugged into your sound card, and unmute the microphone in your sound manager/mixer. I recommend temporarily plugging in head-phones where your speakers are, because you are likely to spawn a feed-back loop if you record while the speakers play back. (You are probably familiar with the loud shriek of feedback usually experienced at the high school dance or church picnic when someone memorably points the microphone toward the speakers.) Or you might just unplug the speakers while you record and then plug them back in to hear. It's up to you, but remember—it's *your* ears.

Use whatever sound-editing software you choose (see Appendix E), and start by just recording yourself speaking. Take note of how your micro-phone sounds, as this will be what determines how your sound effects will go into the computer. Does it pick up other sounds in the room? If so, try to isolate your recording area with blankets or any other reflection-absorb-ing (or echo-absorbing) material.

Also check proximity to the microphone—talk into it and note how close you are and what the sound is like at that point. For example, test as you move back in very small increments, saying, "Check 1 inch, check 3 inches, check 6 inches...." Most run-of-the-mill cheap computer microphones will not pick up much beyond 6 inches, depending on volume.

And that's the other big thing—volume. Set the volume level carefully so that you get your sound as loud as possible *without passing 0 dB* (usually indicated by a red line or clip on your decibel meter).

The Golden Rule of Digital Sound

Digital sound is measured in negative numbers going up to 0 dB (decibels). If the sound passes 0, digital clipping occurs. Digital clipping is like trying to run through a metal barred gate at top speed—and it sounds that bad, too. So the golden rule of digital recording is: Don't go over 0 dB! And don't be a cowboy thinking this is like *Ghostbusters* ("Don't cross the streams"). Even if the marshmallow monster is eating your sister, *don't* go over 0 dB. It might make a cool distortion sound on *your* computer, but it won't on most.

Recording

The second important rule of recording your own sounds (after the golden one discussed above) is to always do several takes. Trust me: You may have absolutely nailed that punch-in-the-mouth sound effect, but the truth is, you don't know how good it really is until you've heard it over the background music and other sounds in your game. This is why you should have several takes to choose from. The more sound design you do, the more you realize how important it is to have several options. There are many complex factors at play once you start combining sounds (not to mention sound and animation), so don't be surprised if what you originally thought was the best take ends up being your worst, and vice versa. If there is only one take to choose from, then you could be in trouble.

Many beginners make the mistake of recording each take as a separate file. While there is nothing wrong with this, the more productive way to go about it is to just hit Record and make your sound repeatedly in various fashions. This is where the editing software comes in really handy—you can just trim your one big recording down to the parts you like and save/cut/paste the takes as files later.

When you're stockpiling takes, it's best to have a good variety. So if you usually swing from the right to make your swinging-punch sound, do two from the right, two from the left. Do two close to the microphone, and two a little farther away. Again, you never know which will sound best until later, so it's better to have some choices.

"That's not the right sound!"

I think we're all pretty well aware that the punching sounds we hear in TV shows do not even closely resemble what a punch sounds like in real life. However, the way the mind perceives action in the two-dimensional world dictates that we need something a little more dramatic than the real thing to get the point across. This is the art of sound design—using your imagination to figure out how to give more emphasis or even depth to the sound (like in karate movies) so that the listener is right there with you. So don't be afraid to venture beyond the realm of what may seem logical and try a completely different sound to achieve what you're looking for.

Sound events in real life usually have a certain order, not just one simple sound. To make a punch sound more dramatic, we have first a swinging sound, and then an impact sound. And maybe, to put the frosting on the cake, we add the "Uggh!" sound of the punch victim. These must be timed correctly in order to sound realistic. They may even have to overlap some. This brings us to the concept of *layered sounds*. A basketball-game scene doesn't just have the sound of the ball bouncing. It may have squeaky sneakers, ball passes, bodies colliding, crowd talking and cheering, and the like. The sounds all happen at different times, volume levels, and positions relative to the listener. Although the layering of sounds is really an advanced sound-design concept and not for the faint-of-heart programmer who just needs a couple of sounds to add to the game, it still can be a very good thing to have in mind while you're designing.

Try to be consistent in matching the point of view with the acoustic space of your sounds. (It just doesn't work well to have a bar-scene punch followed by some guy yelling "Uggh!" in a hollow-sounding gymnasium.) Consider your scene carefully if you want effective sound in your game. Careful sound planning can pay off every bit as well as the hours spent perfecting subtleties in the GUI and game play.

Below are a few possibilities for home-grown sound design that you may find helpful. Some are realistic, some are melodramatic and cartoony. It is up to the sound designer's imagination to effectively use these ideas and come up with more.

TABLE 12.1 **Sounds from Scratch**

Desired Sound	Materials with Which to Fake It
Arrow, swinging fist, or swinging anything	Swing various-sized sticks, wires, and so on about 6 inches from the microphone.
Bushes	Broom straw rustling.
Electric shock	Two blocks of wood covered in sandpaper; make one long stroke.
Boiling water	Use a straw to make bubbles in water.
Crashes	Make a "crash box"—a wooden box (or cardboard for smaller crashes) filled with clangy metal things. Toss in some glass and even plastic containers for variety. Seal it up well, and beat it around to get the crash effect. If you were backstage in a live theater, you might see a 2-by-4-by-2-foot box attached to a crank that spins it.
Mud	Put some newspaper in a few inches of water and slosh around with your hands or feet.
Telephone voice	Use the equalizer in your sound-editing software to remove the bass. Some programs even have a preset for phone voice.
Fire	Open an umbrella really fast for a burst of flames. Crumple up thick cellophane near the microphone for the crackle.
Horses	Knock coconut shells together. Cover them with cloth for galloping on grass, and so on.
Gunshot	Slap a ruler against various surfaces, or fold a belt in half and snap it.
Thunder	The easiest, most common way of getting a large, boomy sound is to take a recorded sound (such as waving poster-board or really low piano notes) and just slow it down substantially with the sound editor, maybe adding some reverb to make it ring out.
Aircraft such as airplanes or spaceships	You can make a multitude of aircraft and space sounds using a garden-variety hair dryer. Just record the motor sound starting up and turning off, and then, with the sound-editing program, slow down the sound or speed it up—or try it in reverse!

Fact: Almost every sound in *Star Wars* was made by recording common everyday items and then making common alterations and modifications to the sounds, such as slowing them down, reversing them, or adding reverb. Try these on your recorded sounds and see what you come up with. To some extent it is even OK to use someone else's prerecorded sounds to play with and edit yourself; just be sure that you are making significant changes to the sounds, because it's not cool to steal.

You can find a brief list of online sound resources in Appendix E, "Developer Resources."

CREATING MUSIC LOOPS

Much like tiles for the background of a Web page or those in a tile-based world, a music or audio loop is an economical means of creating a larger sound or musical idea from a smaller one. The goal is to make the loop seamless and interesting. In most cases, there should not be any sense of beginning or end to your sound because this very quickly creates monotony. Looping sound has been in use since the early days of electronic music and *musique concrète* (a form developed in the early 1940s, based on the recording, mixing, and synthesizing of sounds found in nature). In the old days, loops were created by splicing the ends of a tape-recorded sound and piecing the start and end segments of the sound together with splicing tape. This looked like—you guessed it—a loop. The sound designer would then set the looped tape on the reel-to-reel and hit the Play button, and there you had your repeated sound. Needless to say, this was a very time-consuming process, and any mistakes made in the cutting of the tape were very difficult to repair. Add to this the fact that there was no way to determine exactly where to cut the tape except by trial and error with a piece of chalk to mark potential cutting points.

Thanks to the awesome help of computers, this process has been made much easier, faster, and precise beyond aural perception. In digital audio the basic process is still the same as it was with tape, only we now have the ability to "audition" the loops before making the cut, and of course there's the magical Undo button. I will discuss two ways of making looped sounds on the computer: The first one is with beat-/loop-creation software, and the other is by editing preexisting sound and music with digital-audio editing software.

Drum Loops

Drum loops are popular in games and on Web sites right now. The style is derived from electronic dance music that's been trendy since the '90s. It is also the basis of most rap and hip-hop music. For people who are not necessarily musically inclined, drum loops are really the best means of adding a sense of action to anything happening on the screen. The typical drum loop features three things:

1. A repeated rhythmic drum pattern

2. A complementary bass line

3. Miscellaneous additional atmospheric sounds, such as ambient synthesized orchestral strings

There are dozens, if not hundreds, of programs out there on the Internet for beat and loop creation. It is standard for these programs to open up to a default groove, which you can then edit to your liking. (Just don't use the default one in your game without changing it significantly first!) You can just open up the software and make a few adjustments to the default groove to create your beat. The start and end timing of the loop will already be set up when you save the sound from the program, and all you'll have to do is optimize it for Flash (more on this later).

My favorite software for beat creation is ReBirth (Propellerhead Software; www.propellerheads.se). It is very easy to learn and seamlessly sets up your beat, and you simply save. The coolest thing about ReBirth is that it has "mods." Mods are essentially skins for the drum machine. But not just graphical skins—these skins change the entire sound. You can instantly change the beat you just created from a driving rock sound to a jungle texture to anything else, just by changing the mod. The sounds change, but your beat remains intact. At first this program may look overwhelming, but the cool thing is that the beats are already set up when you open the program, and literally all you have to do is click a couple of buttons of your choice and the beat is now your own. If this is not easy enough for you, there is a Randomize Pattern button in the menu that automatically reorganizes the beat.

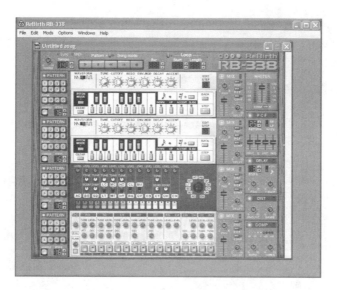

The downside of ReBirth is its very high price. The Propellerheads make a smaller, less functional version, called ReBirth One, which is a little more accessible.

There are demo versions of these products on the Web sites, so you can try them out and see if they fit your needs.

A list of popular (and more affordable) drum machines is included in Appendix E, "Developer Resources."

Editing and Preparing Audio Loops

Before importing your audio file into Flash, it will most likely need to be prepared. Much as when preparing a GIF or JPEG graphics file, there are many adjustments that should be made with audio, the most important of which is file compression. Flash is capable of compressing the audio file for you, but in many scenarios it is best to set up the compression before bringing the file into Flash so you can get the desired sound-quality-to-file-size ratio. There are countless audio-editing programs available. The professional standard is Sound Forge (Sonic Foundry; www.sonicfoundry.com), but the one that many non-musical audio types use is Cool Edit (Syntrillium Software; www.syntrillium.com). If you can get a used copy of Sound Forge version 4 or later for a good price, do it, because it is far more powerful than Cool Edit.

Here's a basic checklist to use in preparing your audio for Flash or any other Internet use. Of course it's just a starting point, but it will give you some pretty good ideas and reminders.

1. Length (2.5 seconds, for example).

2. Volume (overall, as close to 0 dB as possible—not too loud, not too soft).

3. Dynamics (moment-to-moment volume level should be consistent).

   This is the most common rookie oversight! Don't taunt your listeners with 2 seconds of quiet violin sounds and then blast them with a crash cymbal. They will hate you, and you might as well put your entire project on a neon-yellow background with white writing.

4. Sample rate and bit depth (22 kHz/8-bit, 44.1 kHz/16-bit, and so on).

   The sample rate is a representation of how many times per second a sound is sampled for digital storage (just like the frame rate for video or animation). A sound sampled at 8 kHz will take up less memory than a 44.1 kHz sound but will be much noisier. Bit depth represents the chunk of numbers used to describe each sample. Eight-bit sound files take up less space than 16-bit but don't sound as good. For reference, CDs are 44.1 kHz and 16-bit. If you can sample your sound file at 44.1 kHz/16-bit without it becoming too large for your Flash project, by all means do so.

5. File type (WAV, AIFF, or MP3).

   These are the recommended file formats for Internet use. The WAV and AIFF formats are uncompressed. The MP3 format is compressed, with a small amount of loss in audio quality.

To simplify the choices and numbers in items 4 and 5 above, the smallest file size with the poorest sound quality would be an MP3 at 8 bits and 11 kHz, whereas the largest file size would be a WAV or AIFF at 16 bits or more and a sample rate of 44.1 kHz or more, and would have superior sound quality.

Audio editors like Cool Edit and Sound Forge allow you to edit your sound files graphically. On the next page you'll see the "dashboards" of Cool Edit and Sound Forge. A cursory study of these interfaces will show you their essentials.

The straightforward interface of Sound Forge actually allows you the most sophisticated controls around.

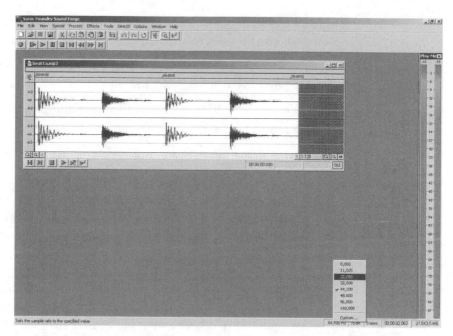

Cool Edit Pro also offers you many ways to control and manipulate any sounds.

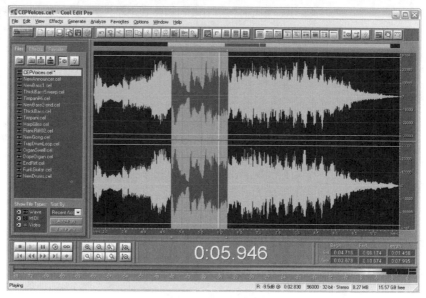

As you can see from these images, both programs allow for extremely precise editing of the sound data. When checking the length of the data (item No. 1 above), keep in mind that you *must* check your loop to make sure it's continuous and clean. Both Cool Edit and Sound Forge allow you to loop playback so that you can test the length for proper fit. There is really no way to ensure that your loop will be seamless except by good old-fashioned trial and error. However, I can give you a couple of tips. First, listen carefully to the very beginning and very end of the loop. How does the end work? Does it lead up to the beginning hit? Does the ending fade out? Is that what you wanted? If the sound is repetitive throughout (for example, "Boom boom bap, boom boom bap, boom boom bap"), you will be able to see that very easily on the editing screen. Take note of the timing (in seconds, tenths of seconds, and so on). Zoom in to make sure that the sound ends exactly before the next hit, and adjust as necessary. (You don't want it to be "Boom boom bap, boom boom bap, boom boom b—.") There are options for processing the sound to make it louder or softer, to pan left or right, and more. These programs allow you to adjust the sample rate and bit depth right there on screen, but you can also use the Save As command and choose the sample rate and bit depth there.

You can see a list of popular audio-editing software in Appendix E.

Sound is a very important part of a game. In this chapter we have outlined several reasons why you should give sounds a lot of attention when developing your games. Hopefully you will take the time to look for or create sounds that fit well with your game.

POINTS TO REMEMBER

- Sound effects and music can make a good game extraordinary.

- Sound effectively contributes to the environment and atmosphere of your game, and can guide the game player to feel a certain way.

- You can compose or license songs specifically for your game.

- Well-crafted and well-chosen sounds are not usually noticed; that is the mark of a good sound track. Sounds that stand out are often sounds that do not belong.

- You can place a sound directly on a frame in the timeline, or you can attach and play a sound using ActionScript. Each of these techniques provides different advantages.

- Keeping all of your sounds in one movie clip makes it easy to manage them and to add sound effects to your game whenever necessary.

- A sound on/off toggle is a feature that users will appreciate.

- You can change the volume of a sound in a game based on dynamic values, such as the speed of an object or the change in momentum of an object (during a collision).

- With very little equipment (which you probably have already), you can make the majority of sound effects you need by yourself.

- When recording digital sound, don't go over 0 dB.

- Record more takes of a sound than you think are necessary, and keep them in the same file until you begin editing.

- Consider beefing up real-world sounds in a creative or dramatic manner to help convey a stronger image of the event.

- Try to match a sound's environment acoustic to the kind of environment or room in which the action is supposed to be taking place.

- An audio loop is an economical means of creating a larger sound or musical idea from a smaller one.

- Run your file against a checklist before you import it into Flash to make sure it's properly compressed, has the right specs, and is as seamless as you want it to be.

CHAPTER 13

DISSECTING A CHAT

IN THE GAMING INDUSTRY, A CHAT IS NOT JUST THE ACT OF COMMUNICATING, but an online place where people can go to talk to each other using text messages. Some people visit chats just to pass the time, to get information, or to try to meet new people. For our purposes, a chat serves as a meeting ground for users who want to participate in multiplayer games. Before you attempt to create a multiplayer game, it is important to set up a chat, because users need a place where they can talk to each other and decide whom they want to play in a game and, of course, what to play.

Not only is it important to have that chat, it's important to understand how the chat works, so that you'll be able to add or change the chat's features (or build a chat from scratch). It's very difficult to modify a chat if you don't understand how it works. And believe me, once you get started with multiplayer gaming, it's pretty much a given that you'll want to create a chat from scratch or modify the one we discuss in this chapter.

To fully understand how this chat works, you should know all of its features, how they work in the finished file, the structure of the source file, and the ActionScript used. And by the end of this chapter, you will.

INTRODUCTION TO THE CHAT

A typical game chat allows you to perform the following actions:

- Send and receive messages (duh!).

- Send and receive private messages (ones that are sent to a specific user).

- Join any room in the room list.

- Create a room. The room is then added to the room list, and others can join it.

- Challenge another user to a game.

- Cancel a challenge you sent.

- Accept or decline a challenge that has been sent to you.

The chat analyzed in this chapter lets you do all of those things and is the one we use with the multiplayer games in Part 3 of this book.

Let's first review this chat's technical situation: what it connects to, what form of information it sends, how you prepare the information, and so on.

The chat application—which consists of a single SWF file—needs to connect with a *socket server*. A socket server is a software application that connects several people together to enable things like chats and multiplayer games. In this book we are going to use the ElectroServer socket server application, which was created for multiplayer games in Flash. In order for you to successfully run the chat file we'll describe in this chapter, you'll need to have ElectroServer up and running. So we will assume that you have installed it and know how to start it up. (To learn how to do this, see Appendix B.)

The main screen of the chat.

A big job—already done for you

Flash talks to the socket server over an XML socket. This means that the messages sent and received are XML formatted. It's no easy task to build an application from scratch that understands which XML-formatted messages to send, and why and when to send them. Not only that, but the application would have to know how to interpret the incoming messages. That's why I created the ElectroServerAS object. This ActionScript object makes creating chats and multiplayer games in Flash a lot easier. With it you can easily do things like log in to the server or send a message by calling one simple method. You don't need to worry about formatting XML or remembering all of the complicated syntax—the ElectroServerAS object does all that for you. It has more than 40 methods and properties. You can even install them into the Actions panel in Flash. The ElectroServerAS object is contained within the ElectroServerAS.as file found in the AppendixC directory on the CD. This object can be included in any Flash file by using the #include action.

All of the methods and properties contained in the ElectroServerAS object are defined in Appendix C, which also includes information on their installation and setup.

The ElectroServerAS object is a powerful piece of ActionScript that functions as the "command center" for running an online chat or multiplayer game—managing, interpreting, sending, and delivering messages. It connects with the server, formats the messages appropriately, and informs you of the status of the connection and of the chat. But with the ElectroServerAS object, you can do many other things beyond these. Most of the additional functions apply directly to multiplayer games. For instance, in multiplayer games we can make use of *server variables*. A server variable is one that is stored by the socket server, and one that you can create from Flash. They are particularly useful for storing game information that everyone in the game can see, such as the card order in a shuffled deck.

With the ElectroServerAS object you can also send ActionScript objects between game players. For instance, one player can send an array of information that contains the position of a character. The other player then receives this array. You will see this done when we create multiplayer games in Part 3 of this book.

HANDS-ON TOUR OF THE CHAT

We have already discussed the chat's main features. In this section we will test-drive the actual chat file to see the features perform, and then inspect the source files and the ActionScript.

The Features

Start ElectroServer, and make sure it is listening on port 1024. If you have not already done so, see Appendix B for help on this. Open chat_fullfeatured.fla in the AppendixC directory on the CD. Publish a SWF file from this file (File > Publish).

You should be all set to start testing. The socket server is running and listening for connections, and the chat file has been created. Now open the SWF file you just created. You will see, probably just for an instant, the word "Connecting." If the SWF connected properly to ElectroServer, you'll see the log-in screen. If the SWF failed to connect, then you'll get a "Connection Failed" message, and you should check to make sure that ElectroServer is configured properly.

From the login screen, enter a user name and then click Login. There are only two situations that could cause you to receive an error message when logging in: if the user name is already in use by someone else currently connected, or if the user name contains a word from the bad-word list (see "Language Filter" in Appendix B) that's configurable with ElectroServer.

If your login failed, ElectroServer will display the reason why and ask you to try again. You can easily test this by opening more than one SWF and trying to log in with the same user name in two windows.

After you have logged in successfully, you'll get to the main chat screen and you automatically join a room called Lobby. This screen shows you a list of all users in your room, a list of all the rooms, the chat window for displaying all of the chat messages, and a text-input box for you to use when sending a message. There is also a text field at the top of the screen showing the name of the room you're in.

Send a few messages to the room. You'll notice that the messages are colored. The name of the user that sent the message is one color, and the body of the message is another.

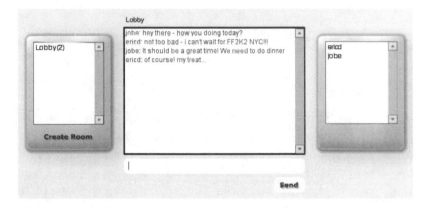

Open at least one other copy of the chat SWF and create another user, so that you will have at least two chat windows open. Send a few messages back and forth. Notice that if you run your mouse pointer over the name of another user in the chat window, it turns into the hand cursor. When you see the hand cursor, you can click the user name to send a private message to that user. A pop-up box appears, containing a text field. You can then type the message into that text field and send it. The format of that message will be slightly different from the regular room message, so the user knows that it's a private message.

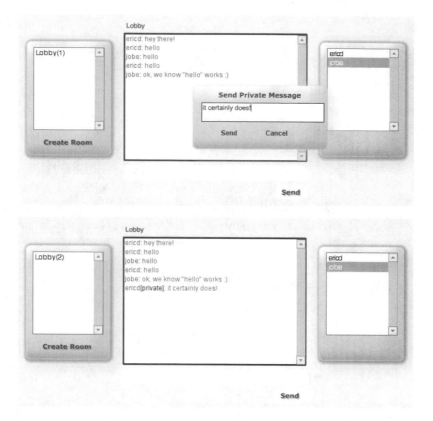

In one of the chat windows, click the Create Room button and enter a room name. Notice that there are now two rooms in the room list and that you are the only one in the user-list window. You can move to the other chat window and click on the new room to join it. Now there are two people in the new room. The original room you were in, the Lobby, has been removed. Currently ElectroServer does not support *persistent* rooms (rooms that always exist)—when there are no people left in a room, it is removed.

That's it for the major features of the main chat. Another feature—which you won't use until you're working with actual multiplayer games—is to challenge a user to a game. (You will be able to test multiplayer games on your own machine, but not until we reach the multiplayer-game chapters in Part 3.) Click on a user name (other than your own) in the user-list window. You will see a pop-up window that says you are waiting for a response from the other user. The second user sees a pop-up window that says that he has been challenged to a game and that presents him with the option to accept or decline the challenge. If he accepts, then both he and the challenger are taken to the screen where the game will take place. If the challengee declines, then the challenger is notified of that fact.

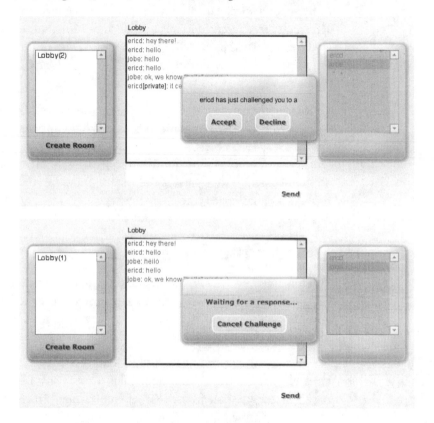

In a multiuser gaming environment there are going to be lots of variables and situations that occur between players and potential players. Your chat structure—as the interface between those players—has to be able to handle all of those situations. The ElectroServerAS object has been programmed to anticipate and manage these interactions, and to prevent problems that can occur from receiving multiple challenges, through the use of its intricate internal event system.

For example, imagine that there are several people in the room—say, user1 through user3. User1 challenges user2. While user2 is considering what she wants to do and has not yet responded, user3 challenges user1. The ElectroServerAS object knows when a player has been challenged but has not yet responded, and it knows when a player has challenged someone but has not yet received a response. So if a user receives a challenge during an unresolved moment such as this, the ElectroServerAS object automatically sends a special decline message to the second challenger (user3). This message is received as an "autodecline," not as a regular, user-generated decline. Thus user3 will know that user1 did not initiate the decline, but rather that it was a product of the situation. Is smoke coming out of your ears yet?

Here is another situation: user1 challenges user2. But before responding, user2 leaves the room or leaves the chat. What happens then? The ElectroServerAS object is programmed to handle this as well. The challenger (user1) receives an autodecline, alerting him to the general unavailability of user2. If user1 leaves the system, then the challengee (user2) receives a "Challenge Cancelled" message.

The File Structure

You have seen everything this chat has been programmed to do. Now let's look at all of the frames and movie clips used in the file. Once you have a good understanding of how this file is structured, it'll be a lot easier to understand the ActionScript.

Open chat_fullfeatured.fla from the Chapter13 folder, if you have not already done so. The main timeline has three layers: Labels, Actions, and Assets. There are three frame labels here: Loader, Chat System, and Game. The Loader frame (and the unlabeled frame after it) handle displaying the loading progress of the movie. The Chat System frame contains a movie clip that contains all of the screens used in the chat, such as the log-in screen and the chat screen. This frame also contains all of the ActionScript used to build the chat (more on this frame in a moment). The Game frame is only a placeholder for where a multiplayer game will reside at a later time. We will not talk about this now. In Part 3 of this book we cover some multiplayer games, and there'll you'll see this frame used.

Scrub the playhead to the Chat System frame. The movie clip in this frame has an instance name of chat. Double-click this movie clip to see what's inside. You'll see that it also has three layers: Labels, Actions, and Assets (the same layer names as on the main timeline), and four frame labels: Connection Failed, Login, Login Failed, and Chat. The first frame in this timeline is unlabeled and contains text that says "Connecting." This frame is displayed when the chat is attempting to connect to ElectroServer. The Connection Failed frame (which contains text with those same words) displays when an attempted connection to ElectroServer does not succeed. The Login frame is where you log in to the server. It contains an input-text field and a button that says Login. You see the Login Failed frame when a log-in attempt is not successful. This frame displays a text field that tells the reason for the failure, and a Try Again button that takes you back to the Login label.

The Chat label contains the majority of the assets used in the chat. There is a large text field at the top of the screen with an instance name of window. This is where the chat messages are displayed. A ScrollBar component attached to this text field has been given an instance name of bar.

Above the window field is a text field with an instance name of room. This text field displays the name of the room you are in. It is updated whenever you change rooms. Below the window field is an input-text field with an instance name of message. This is where you type the chat message you would like to send. To send the message, you can click Send, or press the Enter or Return key.

On the left and right side of the screen there are ListBox components (which are available directly within the Flash program). The one on the right has an instance name of userList and is used to display the list of users in the room. The one on the left has an instance name of roomList and is used to display the list of available rooms. Below the room list is a button called Create Room. When clicked, it opens a pop-up window that prompts you to enter a new room name.

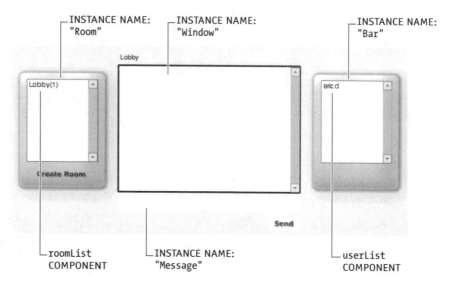

There are three movie-clip instances on the stage (above the window field) with instance names of popup, popup2, and popup3. The popup instance handles the four necessary screens for challenging and being challenged. The popup2 instance handles the screen needed to create a room. The popup3 instance handles sending a private message to a user. All three of these movie clips have blank first frames so that they don't show all the time.

The ActionScript

Now that you have seen all the features of this chat and understand the structure of the chat file, it's time to explore the ActionScript.

A Real Code-Saver

Normally a chat like this would take about 1,000 lines of code to create properly (800 or more for the functions themselves, including the WDDX_mx.as file, and easily another 150 to create the components). But by using Flash components for the chat window and the list boxes, and by using the `ElectroServerAS` object to add functionality, we are able to build this fairly robust chat in fewer than 150 lines of code! This allows you to concentrate on building the application, and not on worrying about the annoying behind-the-scenes code.

See Appendix C for more information about the `ElectroServerAS` object and the WDDX_mx.as file.

Move to the frame labeled Chat System in the root timeline. Select the frame in the Actions layer, and open the Actions panel. Notice the first line of ActionScript: `#include "ElectroServerAS.as"`.

This crucial line includes all of the ActionScript that runs behind the scenes in the `ElectroServerAS` object. That means that when the SWF is initially created, all of the ActionScript contained in both the ElectroServerAS.as and WDDX_mx.as files is pulled into the SWF and stored on that frame.

Now let's look at the ActionScript at the bottom of the frame. We look at this first because it is the part that does the `ElectroServerAS` object configuration; it associates functions with events and sets the needed properties to connect to the ElectroServer socket server.

```
1    ES = new ElectroServerAS();
2    ES.ip = "localhost";
3    ES.port = 1024;
4    ES.onConnection = this.connectionResponse;
5    ES.loginResponse = this.loginResponse;
6    ES.chatReceiver = this.messageArrived;
```

```
7   ES.roomListChanged = this.roomListChanged;
8   ES.userListChanged = this.userListChanged;
9   ES.challengeReceived = this.challengeReceived;
10  ES.challengeAnswered = this.challengeAnswered;
11  ES.challengeCancelled = this.challengeCancelled;
12  ES.connectToServer();
```

Line 1 creates a new instance of the ElectroServerAS object. Doing so is necessary in order to use this object. We are giving this instance a reference name of ES (short for ElectroServer). Then we set the object's ip property. This is the IP (Internet Protocol) address that ElectroServer is bound to. When you are running it on your own computer, this IP address should be "localhost" or can be alternatively written as 127.0.0.1. If ElectroServer were running on a computer anywhere else in the world, then you would include the IP of that remote computer. In line 3 we configure the port that ElectroServerAS should use when attempting a connection with ElectroServer. Flash can connect to any port that is 1024 or higher, but in order to successfully connect to ElectroServer, you must use the same port it is listening on. You can configure which port ElectroServer listens on in the ElectroServer.properties file. See Appendix B for detailed information about IPs, ports, and configuring ElectroServer.

Lines 4–11 define *event handlers*—functions that get called when a special event occurs. What you see on the right side of the = sign in each of those lines is a reference to a function, created on this frame, that we have not yet discussed but that will be obvious from its name. For instance, the onConnection event is fired when a connection is established. (If any of these events aren't clear to you, then flip to Appendix C to look them up.) Line 12 of the ActionScript above tells ElectroServerAS to try to establish a connection with the server. When a response has been received (either success or failure), the onConnection event is fired. When that happens, the connectionResponse() function is called, so we'll look at that next.

TIP

The syntax you see in line 2 is a code shorthand in which, in an if statement, (success) means the same thing as (success==true).

```
1   function connectionResponse(success) {
2       if (success) {
3           chat.gotoAndStop("Login");
4       } else {
5           chat.gotoAndStop("Connection Failed");
6       }
7   }
```

The parameter success is passed in and contains either true or false. If true, then the connection was successful and the user is taken to the Login frame. If false, then the connection was not a success and the user is taken to the Connection Failed frame.

From the Login frame, as you already know, the user enters a name and clicks the Login button. The following function is executed when the button is pressed:

```
1   function login(username) {
2       ES.login(username);
3   }
```

The name that the user entered is passed into this function, which then calls the method on the ElectroServerAS object login(). Doesn't this look easy? That's the whole point of the ElectroServerAS object!

When the server sends a response (one way or the other) about the log-in attempt, it activates the loginResponse event. Then the following function is called:

```
1    function loginResponse(success, reason) {
2        if (success) {
3            ES.joinRoom("Lobby");
4            chat.gotoAndStop("Chat");
5            chat.room.text = "Lobby";
6        } else {
7            chat.gotoAndStop("Login Failed");
8            chat.reason.text = reason;
9        }
10   }
```

Two parameters are passed in, success and reason. If the log-in was a success, then the value of success is true. In this case, we invoke the joinRoom() method of the ElectroServerAS object to join (or enter) the Lobby. We are then taken to the Chat frame, and the room text field is given a name to display. If success is false, then the log-in attempt failed, and the reason parameter contains the reason why it failed. In this case you are taken to the Login Failed frame, where the reason is displayed.

From the Chat frame you can send a chat message. To do this, you type in the input-text field and click Send. The message is passed into this function, and it is executed:

```
1   function chatSend(info) {
2       ES.sendMessage(info, "room");
3   }
```

The parameter info contains the text message you're trying to send. We then invoke the sendMessage() method of the ElectroServerAS object. The second parameter, "room", specifies that we want to send this message directly to the room. If instead of "room" that parameter contained a user name, then the message would be sent to a specific user (that is, it would be a private message, which we'll get to in a little while).

When a message is received from the server, the chatReceiver event is fired and this function is called:

```
1   function messageArrived(info) {
2       var from = info.from;
3       var body = info.body;
4       var type = info.type;
5       if (type == "public") {
6           var msg = formatFrom(from)+":
          → "+formatBody(body)+"<br>";
7       } else if (type == "private") {
8           var msg = formatFrom(from)+"[private]:
          → "+formatBody(body)+"<br>";
9       }
10      chat.window.htmlText = ES.addToHistory(msg);
11      chat.bar.setScrollPosition(chat.window.maxscroll);
12  }
```

This function is called whenever a message is received. The info parameter is an object that contains three properties: from, body, and type. The from property is the person who sent the message. The body property is the main part of the message. The type property is either "public" or "private". If it's "public" (which most will be), then it is a message to the room. If it's "private", then it is a message to you specifically. In line 5 of the code above there is a conditional statement that looks to see if the message is "public". If it is, then the message is HTML-formatted for display in the chat window. If the message is private, then the message is also HTML-formatted, but with the word *private* appended to the user name. The functions formatFrom() and formatBody() in lines 6 and 8 take what is passed in and return a formatted HTML string. We'll look at these functions next.

In line 10 we add the message to the chat history and then display this in the chat window. Then we set the scroll bar to its maximum possible position so that the most recent chat message is always shown.

Now let's look at the functions formatFrom() and formatBody():

```
1   function formatFrom(from) {
2       return "<a href=\"asfunction:_root.privateMessage,"
        → +from+"\"><FONT face=\"arial\" size=\"12\"
        → color=\"#0033FF\" >"+from+"</FONT></a>";
3   }
4   function formatBody(body) {
5       return "<FONT face=\"arial\" size=\"12\"
        → color=\"#336600\" >"+body+"</FONT>";
6   }
```

Look at the function formatFrom() in line 1 above. This function accepts a parameter, a user name, which it HTML-formats. The color and font size of this user name is set in the HTML. Also, the user name is made into a hyperlink by using the <a> tag with asfunction in it. When you click the name, the function _root.privateMessage() will be called, and the user name will be passed in.

The formatBody() function does the same thing as formatFrom(), only it applies a different color and does not make the text a hyperlink.

Now let's look at privateMessage(). Here is the function:

```
1   function privateMessage(who) {
2       chat.popup3.who = who;
3       chat.popup3.gotoAndStop("Private Message");
4   }
```

This function is called when someone clicks a user name in the chat window. The who parameter contains the user name of the person whose name is clicked. Then popup3 is sent to a specific frame so that you can type in the message to send. When you click the Send button, the following function is called:

```
1   function sendPrivateMessage(msg, who) {
2       ES.sendMessage(msg, who);
3   }
```

This function has two parameters. The first one is the actual message to send, and the second is to whom to send the message. We invoke the sendMessage() method of the ElectroServerAS object to send this private message.

When you join a room, the server adds you to the user list in that room. Whenever the user list changes (when someone enters or leaves the room), the server sends a message to everyone in the room containing the list of users. As a result of receiving the incoming-user-list message from the server, the roomListChanged event is fired. Here is the function that is called:

```
1   function roomListChanged(roomList) {
2       var path = chat.roomList;
3       path.removeAll();
4       path.setChangeHandler("roomClicked", _root);
5       for (var i = 0; i<roomList.length; ++i) {
6           var name = roomList[i].name;
7           var item = name+"("+roomList[i].total+")";
8           path.addItem(item, name);
9       }
10  }
```

The roomList parameter is an array of objects. Each element in the array is an object with the properties name and total that describe a room. Name is the name of the room, and total is the number of people in that room. In line 5 we use the for loop to loop through the entire array and create items in the ListBox component that has an instance name of roomList. We also set it so that when a room is clicked, the function roomClicked() is called. Here is the roomClicked() function:

```
1   function roomClicked(path) {
2       var name = path.getValue();
3       chat.room.text = name;
4       ES.joinRoom(name);
5   }
```

When this function is called, the path to the list box item that was selected is passed in. We use that to extract the name of the room and then use the joinRoom() method to join that room.

If you click the Create Room button, then popup2 is told to go to a specific frame where you can enter a new room name. When you've entered the name and clicked the Create button, the following function is executed:

```
1   function createRoom(room) {
2       chat.room.text = room;
3       ES.joinRoom(room);
4   }
```

This function simply takes the parameter passed in and joins the user to that room.

Now let's focus on the userList ListBox component. This component displays the list of users in your room. Every time the user list changes, the userListChanged event fires and this function is executed.

```
1   function userListChanged(userList) {
2       var path = chat.userList;
3       var enabled = path.getEnabled();
4       path.setEnabled(true);
5       path.removeAll();
6       path.setChangeHandler("personClicked", _root);
7       for (var i = 0; i<userList.length; ++i) {
8           path.addItem(userList[i].name);
9       }
10      path.setEnabled(enabled);
11  }
```

It may seem like overkill to use an object to store just one property, but this is good architecture for the future. Revisions of the ElectroServerAS object may store more than just a user's name—it may also include her email address or favorite game, for instance. So this way, we're just being prepared.

The parameter userList is an array. Each element in the array is an object that represents a user. Each of these objects has only one property—name. In line 2 above we create a reference called path to the userList list box. In line 3 we create a variable called enabled to store the enabled property of the userList ListBox component.

What we're doing here is not that tricky, but it is worth some attention and discussion so that you can understand all you need to about the enabled, getEnabled(), and setEnabled() properties. The value of the enabled property of a ListBox component is either true or false. If true (which is the default setting), then the list box is active. If false, then the list box is not active and you cannot select any items in it. When you tested the chat earlier and you clicked on another user to challenge him, you may have noticed that the userList list box was disabled (so that the user doesn't challenge another person until the current challenge is accepted, declined, or cancelled). Once you decline the challenge, the box becomes enabled again. Every time the userListChanged() function is called, we completely rebuild the userList list box. If the enabled property is false, then the list box cannot update when we attempt to change its contents. So if you receive a challenge and then a user-list update comes in, then the user list will not update properly because the enabled property is false. To avoid this problem, we store the enabled property in a variable called enabled. We then set the list box's enabled property to true (line 4). After that, we set the enabled value back to what it was before the update. This allows the userList list box to get updated even when it is disabled (line 10). In lines 7–9 we loop through the array of users to add items to the list box. Whenever you click a user name, the function personClicked() is called. Here's the code for that function:

```
1   function personClicked(path) {
2       var name = path.getValue();
3       if (name != ES.username) {
4           chat.popup.gotoAndStop("Waiting");
5           chat.userList.setEnabled(false);
6           ES.challenge(name, "Fake Game");
7       }
8   }
```

When this function is executed, the path to the name item in the list box is passed in. From the path reference we can get the value of that list item, which is a user name. The objective of this function is to challenge the selected user to a game. First we check to make sure that you are not trying to challenge yourself (line 3). If you are not, then we are clear to proceed. In line 4 we send the popup instance to the Waiting frame. Then we disable the userList list box (so that you cannot challenge anyone else yet). Finally, the challenge() method of the ElectroServerAS object is called. This method takes two parameters—the user name of the person you want to challenge and the name of the game you want to play. When the user receives your challenge request, the challengeReceived event is fired.

```
1   function challengeReceived(from, game) {
2       var msg = from+" has just challenged you to a game of
     →  "+game+"!";
3       chat.userList.setEnabled(false);
4       chat.popup.gotoAndStop("Challenged");
5       chat.popup.msg.text = msg;
6   }
```

Two parameters are passed in, from and game. The from parameter is the name of the challenger, and game is the name of the game you are being challenged to. In line 2 we create a message to show to the challengee. Then the userList list box is disabled (line 3). In line 4 the popup movie clip is sent to the frame labeled Challenged, and in the next line the message is displayed in the text field. When this function is finished, the user should see a message displayed saying that he has been challenged. At this point he has the choice to either accept or decline the challenge. If he clicks the Accept button, then acceptChallenge() is executed. Here's the code for that function:

```
1   function acceptChallenge() {
2       chat.userList.setEnabled(true);
3       chat.popup.gotoAndStop(1);
4       ES.acceptChallenge();
5       this.gotoAndStop("Game");
6   }
```

When executed, the userList list box is enabled again, the popup instance is sent back to frame 1, and the acceptChallenge() method is called. The acceptChallenge() method sends a message to the challenger to let him know that you have accepted the challenge. Then, in line 5, we move from the current frame to the Game label. The Game frame is just a placeholder for a multiplayer game you will later use.

If a user clicks Decline instead of Accept, then this function is executed:

```
1   function declineChallenge() {
2       chat.userList.setEnabled(true);
3       chat.popup.gotoAndStop(1);
4       ES.declineChallenge();
5   }
```

When executed, the userList list box is enabled, the popup instance is sent back to the first frame, and the declineChallenge() method is executed. The declineChallenge() method of the ElectroServerAS object sends a message to the challenger to let him know that you have declined the challenge.

When the challenger receives a response to a challenge, the challengeAnswered() function is called:

```
1   function challengeAnswered(response) {
2       if (response == "accepted") {
3           _root.gotoAndStop("Game");
4       } else if (response == "declined") {
5           chat.popup.gotoAndStop("Declined");
6           chat.popup.msg.text = "The challenge has been
              › declined.";
7       } else if (response == "autodeclined") {
8           chat.popup.gotoAndStop("Declined");
9           chat.popup.msg.text = "The challenge has been
              › automatically declined.";
10      }
11      chat.userList.setEnabled(true);
12  }
```

The response parameter contains a string that says the challenge was
"accepted", "declined", or "autodeclined". If it was accepted, then the
ActionScript takes you to the Game label. If it was declined, then the popup
instance is sent to a frame that tells you the request has been declined. If
the request was automatically declined (for any number of reasons), then
the popup instance is sent to a frame that tells you why.

We are almost done with all of the ActionScript. There are just two more
functions left to discuss—perhaps not quite as central as the others, but
certainly important. When you challenge a user to a game, it is possible—
and not unlikely—that the user will not reply to your challenge request for
a while. You can cancel your challenge if you don't want to wait any
longer. There is a Cancel Challenge button on the frame that says "Waiting
for a response...." If you click this button, then the following function is
executed:

```
1   function cancelChallenge() {
2       ES.cancelChallenge();
3       chat.userList.setEnabled(true);
4   }
```

When executed, the cancelChallenge() method of the ElectroServerAS
object is executed, after which the userList list box is enabled. The
cancelChallenge() method sends a message to the opponent saying that
the challenge has been canceled, and the challengeCancelled event is

fired for that user. Here is the function that is executed when the challengee has been informed of a challenge cancellation:

```
1    function challengeCancelled() {
2        chat.userList.setEnabled(true);
3        chat.popup.gotoAndStop("Cancelled");
4    }
```

This function enables the userList list box and sends the popup instance to the Cancelled frame, where the challengee is informed about the cancellation.

POINTS TO REMEMBER

- A chat is a meeting place for people who want to play multiplayer games.

- You've got to understand how to build and edit a chat if you are going to want to add features to your game setup later.

- Using `ElectroServerAS` greatly reduces the amount of work needed to create a chat or multiplayer game.

- You need to familiarize yourself with socket servers in order to properly understand and manage the chat (see Appendix B).

- You can test the features of the chat by opening more than one chat window on your own computer.

PART 3:
THE GAMES

Computer Terms

```
J G Y Z W S F C N A N O V P W R E
Z I D G X T D C I C O N Z S J B U
M B T G D R A O B Y E K A R A G L
L E H V D C G Z V C I X K O M N Y
I M N O I T U L O S E R N T D K V
R A Y U I D G V O V H M A I E R Z
J C G J E R O M H M Z Z T N D O A
Y I P O P A E Q O P P O O O D W A
U N I Y U O X O Y R Z I R M E T C
M T J Q Z B P G N T D Y T S R E X
Z O V G M R O C Y L M C C I R N R
L S U V D E T O M T I V E I J R Y
J H E S L H K E F T E N L S R E E
C K V Q E T S Z R D W W E R B T U
F X P L Z O E B V A G G F Z I N O
A M F I H M D G E T Q A G W R I R
M O E C E I L N N L K W F R I Y Z
```

Look for these words

MOTHERBOARD
KEYBOARD
MONITOR
RESOLUTION
MOUSE
ELECTROTANK
CDROM
MACINTOSH
INTERNET
DESKTOP
MENU
ONLINE
NETWORK
ICON

RESTART   SHOW ANSWERS   BACK

CHAPTER 14

WORD SEARCH

WORD GAMES ARE ONE OF THE MOST POPULAR TYPES OF CASUAL GAMES on the Internet. Word Search is a word game that has you search for words hidden among what appears to be a random pool of letters.

While a very simple-looking game, Word Search requires some complicated ActionScript. If you have read through most of this book, then there shouldn't be any surprises in the code that pulls this game together. However, if you have just turned to this chapter, you'll probably need an intermediate-or-higher grasp of ActionScript to fully understand what is done here.

Prerequisites

Chapter 7, "Tile-Based Worlds." Word Search is not a tile-based world; however, you should be familiar with the tiling technique for adding movie clips to the stage in a grid using nested loops. Also, you should be familiar with the simple math trick used to determine which tile a point is over.

Strong familiarity with two-dimensional arrays and using objects to store data.

Appendix D, "XML Basics in Flash." The word lists for this game are loaded from an external XML file.

Game Overview

As someone who loves physics, I usually like to create games that have a lot of physically realistic movement, like pool, pinball, or miniature golf. But one day I noticed my wife playing a word-search game from a tiny book she'd just bought. She jokingly asked me, "Why can't you make a game like this?" So I did, and this is it!

Before beginning the task of creating Word Search, I thought, how hard can it be? It turns out that although it wasn't too terribly difficult, it was much harder than I had initially thought. It took me quite a bit of time to come up with a plan for coding this game.

The game of Word Search is easy to understand. It has a grid of letters that can be any size. In this game we use 17 by 17 letters. There is a list of words that can be found within this grid. Words may be positioned vertically, horizontally, or diagonally (and either spelled forward or backward in any of these directions). In this Flash Word Search version, I have enabled words in all directions except diagonal stretching from upper right to lower left.

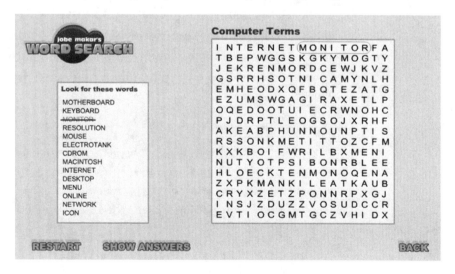

When playing a word-search game on paper, you typically circle a word when you find it, or you mark through it. You also mark it off the list so that you can easily see which words you still have left to find. It's the same in this Flash version. When you find a series of letters you wish to select, you click and hold the first letter, and drag toward the last letter you want to include. As you drag, an oval is drawn along your path of movement. When you reach the last letter, you release the mouse button. If the letters you selected match a word from the word list, then the oval you drew stays on the grid, and the word from the word list is marked through and its color is changed. (If you've tried to select a group of letters that isn't on the word list, the oval disappears.)

Now that you have a basic understanding of how the core of the game functions, I'll tell you about the rest of the game. Open wordsearch.swf in the Chapter14 directory.

The first thing you see is the main menu (also called the *splash screen*). This is the screen from which the player should be able to reach all major areas of the game. This basic splash screen has just three buttons: Start Game, Instructions, and Credits.

Where is the content for the Instructions and Credits pages?

In wordsearch.fla I have included all of the graphical assets and ActionScript needed for the complete game of Word Search. However, I have left the credits and instructions screens blank, because it will be easy enough for you to fill them in, and you can do it in your own way. Unless you take this game completely unmodified and put it on your Web site, chances are you will have made enough changes to the way things work that you should write your own instructions on how to play the game. You can easily list the instructions for this game in a text field on the instructions page. And on the credits page you can list yourself and whoever helped you create the word lists (and even me if you want to!).

When you click Start Game, you are immediately taken to a new screen. On this screen you can scroll through a roster of word lists. Each category contains 14 words that will be hidden in the Word Search grid. To select a category, click the category name and click the Play button. You are then taken to the game screen. A list of words is displayed on the left. Each of those words is hidden among the pool of letters in the grid. Unlike what happens in the paper version of this game, if you get stumped, you can click the Show Answers button. This will make all of the letters invisible except those that fall within a word from the word list.

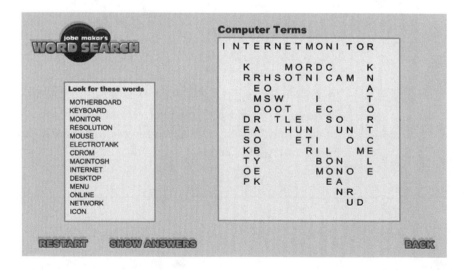

Every time a game starts, the grid is randomly created. The words are placed randomly and the filler letters are chosen randomly. The end result is this: You can play the same word list thousands of times and never get the same grid configuration. If you click Restart, the game will be restarted with a new grid configuration, but with the same word list.

That's it for the basic tour of the game. There is one more important thing to note, though. The word lists are stored in a single XML file called wordlists.xml. To fully understand how Flash loads an XML file and parses it to extract the necessary information, see Appendix D, "XML Basics in Flash." But even without much knowledge of XML, you can still modify the word lists very easily. You can add or remove lists, or just change what is there.

Open wordlists.xml from the Chapter14 directory. (As you probably know by now, you can open an XML file in almost any text editor.) The format of the XML in this file is very basic and should be easy to understand. The root node—the lowest level of the XML structure—is `<lists>`. There can be any number of `<list>` nodes that are children of `<lists>`. Each `<list>` contains 14 `<word>` nodes (to correspond to the 14-word format we've chosen for this game). Following is an example of what the entire XML file could contain if there were only two word lists.

```
<lists>
    <list category="Classic Films">
        <word>casablanca</word>
        <word>africanqueen</word>
        <word>wizardofoz</word>
        <word>bodysnatchers</word>
        <word>redplanet</word>
        <word>vertigo</word>
        <word>suspicion</word>
        <word>charade</word>
        <word>musicman</word>
        <word>lifeboat</word>
        <word>showboat</word>
        <word>thinman</word>
        <word>palerider</word>
        <word>blob</word>
    </list>
    <list category="Greek Mythology">
        <word>zeus</word>
```

```
            <word>hera</word>
            <word>hermes</word>
            <word>minerva</word>
            <word>apollo</word>
            <word>artemis</word>
            <word>aphrodite</word>
            <word>poseidon</word>
            <word>hades</word>
            <word>cronos</word>
            <word>gaia</word>
            <word>ares</word>
            <word>atlas</word>
            <word>demeter</word>
      </list>
</lists>
```

Other than my choices for classic films, this example file should be fairly easy to understand. You'll notice that there is an attribute called `category` on the `<list>` nodes. This is the name you will see in the scrolling list on the Start Game screen of the game. You should also note that it doesn't matter if the words are capitalized or lowercased (except in the category attribute), because in the game all of the letters are going to get capitalized. Finally, you cannot use any characters in the `<word>` tags that are not letters. That means no spaces, dashes, numbers, or any symbols that are outside the realm of A–Z. As an example, "Wizard of Oz" is written above as `wizardofoz`. With this information, you can easily create your own word lists!

GAME LOGIC

In this section we will discuss the logic involved in all aspects of the game, from choosing a word-list category to generating the grid and selecting words. In certain cases we will specifically look at code, but in most cases I will explain what each function does without taking you through it line by line.

Choosing a Category

Before you can choose a category (which is just any one of the word lists in the wordlists.xml file), the file must be loaded and the information extracted. Let's look at the ActionScript on frame 1.

```
1    doc = new XML();
2    doc.ignoreWhite = true;
3    doc.load("wordlists.xml");
```

First we create an XML object called doc in which we want to load the file. Then we load it using the load() method of the XML object. Since we can't do anything in the game until this file is loaded, we add a condition to the pre-loader for the game. You can see this on frame 2.

```
1    factor=(_root.getBytesLoaded()+doc.getBytesLoaded())/
     → (_root.getBytesTotal()+doc.getBytesTotal());
2    percent.text=Math.floor(factor*100)+"%";
3    if (factor>=1 && doc.loaded) {
4        _root.gotoAndStop("Splash");
5    }
```

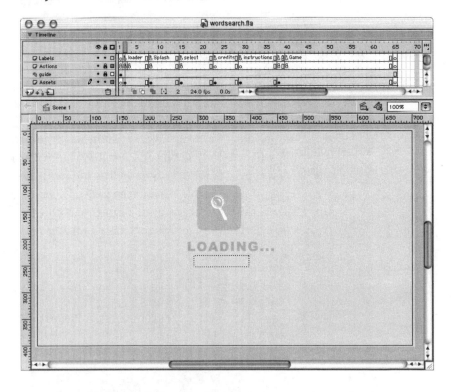

Imagine that the XML file is very large, say 50 KB. Then adding this XML file to your pre-loader would be a necessity. If you did not, then the game file would display the main menu, and the user could attempt to start playing a game before the words were even loaded! In line 1 above, we create a variable called factor. It is the total number of bytes loaded, divided by the total number of bytes in the file. When factor is multiplied by 100, the result is the percentage that has been loaded. So, for instance, if word-search.swf is 80 KB and wordlist.xml is 20 KB, then the denominator of that ratio is 100. If at one point wordsearch.swf has 60 KB loaded and wordlist.xml has 10 KB, then the numerator is 70. So then the percentage loaded at that time is (70/100)*100 = 70%. In line 3 we check to see if factor is greater than or equal to 1 and if doc is fully loaded. When doc is fully loaded, its loaded property is true. If both of these conditions are met, then everything is finished loading and it is OK to proceed to the Splash frame. Otherwise, the playhead moves to the next frame and then back to this frame again for another check.

From the Splash frame the user can click Start Game and get taken to the Select frame. Here we interpret the XML in the doc object and build and display the categories in a ListBox component. Here are the first few lines of ActionScript:

```
1   words = {};
2   words.lists = [];
3   playButton._alpha=50;
```

First we create an object called words. This object will be used to store the word lists and eventually will be used to store all of the information about the game. In line 2 we create an array in the words object called lists. This array will contain one object for each category. The object will contain the list of words in that category as well as the category's name. Next we set the _alpha property of the playButton to 50. This is to give a visual indication that you cannot proceed until a category is chosen. When a category is chosen, playButton's _alpha is set back to 100.

Next, the following function is created and then executed:

```
1   function init() {
2       var temp = [];
3       var temp = doc.firstChild.childNodes;
4       scrollingList = [];
```

```
5     for (var i = 0; i<temp.length; ++i) {
6         var tempList = temp[i].childNodes;
7         var category = temp[i].attributes.category;
8         var wordArray = [];
9         for (var j = 0; j<tempList.length; ++j) {
10            var word = tempList[j].firstChild.nodeValue;
11            wordArray.push(word);
12        }
13        words.lists.push({wordList:wordArray,
              category:category});
14        scrollingList.push({label:category, data:i});
15    }
16    scrollList.setDataProvider(scrollingList);
17    scrollList.setChangeHandler("myHandler");
18 }
19 init();
```

This function steps through the XML in the doc XML object and extracts all of the information we need. An array of words is created for each category (line 11) and then stored in an object that describes that category (line 13). Also stored in that object is a property called category that stores the category's name. This object is pushed into the lists array. For example, the object for the first category, Types of Fruit, is stored as the first element in the lists array, lists[0]. This object, lists[0], contains the property category whose value is "Types of Fruit", and an array called wordList, whose values are the words of the category. By the time the function gets to line 16, all of the information from the XML has been extracted and stored properly. The ListBox component on the stage has an instance name of scrollList. In line 16 we set a data provider for this list by pointing it to the scrollingList array, which contains the name of each category. The ListBox component then takes this information and automatically populates the list. Then, in line 17 we change the function that is called when an item is selected. We do this with the setChangeHandler() method and pass in the name of the function we would like to have called. So when a category is clicked, the myHandler() function is called.

Up to this point you have seen the ActionScript needed to load the XML file, parse it, store the data logically, and display the categories in a list. Now let's look at what happens when a category is selected.

```
1    function myHandler() {
2        playButton._alpha = 100;
3        playButton.enable = true;
4        var categoryIndex = scrollList.getSelectedItem().data;
5        words.words = words.lists[categoryIndex].wordList;
6        words.category = scrollList.getSelectedItem().label;
7    }
```

The function above, myHandler(), is called whenever a category is selected. First the playButton is given an _alpha value of 100 so that it appears to be enabled. Then we set a variable in the playButton instance called enabled to true. An if statement on the button in the playButton instance checks to see if enable is true before it (the button) responds to being clicked. In line 4 we set a variable called categoryIndex. This variable stores a number—the number of the category that was selected in the list. Then, in line 5 we create an array in the words object called words. The value of this array is set by using categoryIndex and pointing to the wordList array on the object that represents that category. In short, this line creates an array of the words that will be in the game from the category selected. In line 6 we store a property on the words object called category. The value of category is the string name of the category selected. So, if Types of Fruit were selected, then words.category would be "Types of Fruit".

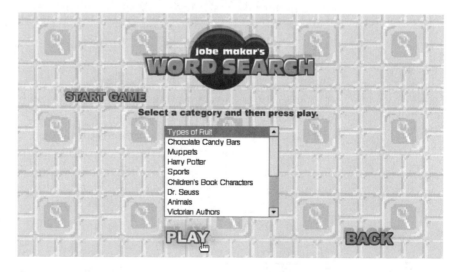

After a category has been selected, we have (as seen above) an array of words called words and the name of the category both stored in the words object. We can now safely move the frames needed to build the board.

Generating the Grid

Creating the grid layout from the list of words is the toughest part of this game. Words can be written forward or backward; can be vertical, horizontal, or diagonal; can even cross through each other. The logic used to do all of this is not too complex—but it's not that easy, either! What is complex is the tall function, approximately 130 lines, that handles the bulk of this logic. In this section we will pick up where we left off in the previous section and look at everything needed to create a unique word-search grid on the screen.

We left off in the previous section after a category was selected. Once this is done, it is OK for the user to click the Play button. When Play is clicked, the game is taken to a frame called Generate. This frame contains all of the movie clips needed for the game screen. Here are the two actions in this frame:

```
1   generating._visible=true;
2   play();
```

There is a movie-clip instance on the stage called `generating`. We set its `_visible` property to `true`. The first time you reach the Generate frame, the generate movie clip is already visible. However, when the game is restarted and this frame is visited again, `generate` is not already visible, so we make it visible with this action. We want this movie clip visible while the game is computing the grid layout, so that the game player knows what is going on. Line 2 above just tells the timeline to keep playing. Two frames later we reach the Game label and stop there.

The Game frame is the location of all the ActionScript that handles creating the grid, detecting word selections, and restarting the game. We will look at four functions in this section: `scrambleWords()`, `displayList()`, `createBoard()`, and `restart()`.

ScrambleWords() takes the word list in memory and randomly maps those words into the board layout. It is the large function mentioned above and handles all of the logic needed to create the grid in memory. This function does not perform any physical placement of movie clips or text fields on the stage.

CreateBoard() takes the results from `scrambleWords()` and actually builds the board layout with all of the movie clips, adding random letters to fill all the blank spaces.

DisplayList() creates the list of words that shows on the left side of the screen. This function is also called whenever a correct word has been selected; it handles marking off a word in the list after it's been found.

Restart() simply removes all circle movie clips that have been created, if any, and then sends the movie back to the Generate frame label.

But first, let's look at the initial actions that need to happen to get this game going. The following ten lines of ActionScript, at the bottom of the Game frame, are not contained within a function.

```
1   scrambleWords();
2   if (scrambledOK) {
3       wordList.createEmptyMovieClip("lines", 1);
4       category.text = words.category;
5       generating._visible = false;
6       displayList();
7       createBoard();
8   } else {
9       restart();
10  }
```

When the Game frame is reached, these actions are performed. First, the scrambleWords() function is called. We will talk about that function in detail below, but for now just assume the following: If scrambleWords() does its job successfully, then the variable scrambledOK is set to true. If it does not succeed, then scrambledOK is set to false. If false, then the game is restarted, and the movie will keep looping between the Game frame and the Generate frame until scrambleWords() does its job successfully. (We will talk about what determines success below.) If scrambledOK is true, then lines 3–7 are executed. Line 3 creates an empty movie clip within the wordList instance. The wordList movie clip is the one that will contain the list of words that are in the grid. The empty movie clip, called lines, is where the lines will be drawn through any words in the list that have been selected in the grid. We will discuss this in the next section. In line 4 we simply display the name of the category in a text field. Next, we set the visibility of the generating movie clip to false, since the generating is finished. We execute the displayList() function so that the list of words is shown on the left, and then call the createBoard() function so that the grid is made visible on the screen. You may recall that before createBoard() is called, the board exists only in memory.

What you have just seen is the big picture. First we attempt to create the board in memory. If we can't, then we restart and try again. If we can, then the board is created on the stage.

scrambleWords()

Now let's look at what the `scrambleWords()` function does. Here is pseudo-code that represents what is done in the function:

```
1    set maxTime to 5000
2    set scrambledOK to true
3    create two-dimensional letters array
4    create listings array
5    set now to getTimer()
6    for each word in words.wordList
7        randomly choose alignment
8        randomly choose direction
9        set tempWord from the word
10       set wordLength to tempWord.length
11       push object which stores tempWord, direction, and alignment
         → onto listings
12       if direction is backward
13           reverse tempWord
14       if alignment is horizontal
15           set notDone to true
16           while notDone
17               row = random row
18               startx = random(boardsize-wordlength)
19               notDone = false
20               for each letter in tempWord
21                   set tempLetter to current letter
22                   if grid spacing contains something and it's not
                     → tempLetter
23                       notDone=true
24               if notDone is false
25                   store the word letters in the letters array
26               if getTimer() - now > maxTime
27                   set scrambledOK to false
28                   break
29       else if alignment is vertical
```

```
30          set notDone to true
31          while notDone
32              column = random column
33              startY = random(boardsize-wordlength)
34              notDone = false
35              for each letter in tempWord
36                  set tempLetter to current letter
37                  if grid spacing contains something and it's not
                    → tempLetter
38                      notDone=true
39              if notDone is false
40                  store the word letters in the letters array
41              if getTimer() - now > maxTime
42                  set scrambledOK to false
43                  break
44      else if alignment is diagonal
45          set notDone to true
46          while notDone
47              startX = random(boardsize-wordlength)
48              startY = random(boardsize-wordlength)
49              notDone = false
50              for each letter in tempWord
51                  set tempLetter to current letter
52                  if grid spacing contains something and it's not
                    → tempLetter
53                      notDone=true
54              if notDone is false
55                  store the word letters in the letters array
56              if getTimer() - now > maxTime
57                  set scrambledOK to false
58                  break
```

This function is pretty well commented in the actual ActionScript in the FLA file. With the explanation of the pseudo-code given here and the function itself, you should be able to understand what is going on in `scrambleWords()`.

First we set a variable called `maxTime` to 5000. This number serves as a cutoff for the amount of time we will allow the function to run. In this function we place words randomly. But if you've ever tried to make your own word jumble or crossword puzzle on paper, you'll know that this procedure is not foolproof; sometimes the script places words in positions that make it impossible to place any more words! In the case of the code we've written for this particular game, the loops in scrambleWords() would continue indefinitely looking for available slots that do not exist. To prevent this happening, we set this maxTime variable. During every while loop, we check to see how long the function has been running. If it has been running for a longer time than maxTime, then we break out of the loop and the function. This is when we would consider the scrambleWords() function not to have been successful, and as a result, the restart() function will be called.

Next, we set scrambledOK to true. This variable is set to false if maxTime is ever reached. We then create a two-dimensional array called letters on the words object. Each element in this array corresponds to a letter in the grid. The letters are inserted into the array as we place the words. At the end of the scrambleWords() function the only letters in the array are the ones from the words. So there are many blank elements. It is not until the createBoard() function is called that we fill in the remaining empty spaces.

In line 4 we create an array called listings. This array will contain one element for each word that is placed in the grid. The element is an object that stores information about the word. Next, we set a variable called now to store the current time. We can use that later to determine how long the function has been running.

The rest of the code, lines 7–58, is performed for each word in the wordList array. We randomly choose an alignment for a word (horizontal, vertical, or diagonal). Then we randomly choose a direction for the word to be spelled (forward or backward). Then, in line 9, we create a variable called tempWord, which stores the current word. We also create a variable, called wordLength, to store the length of the word. In line 11 we create an object that stores tempWord, the alignment, and the direction of the word and pushes it onto the listings array. This array is used later to determine if a word has been selected. We will see more of this in the next section. If the direction randomly chosen is backward, then we reverse the order of the letters in tempWord (line 12).

What happens next depends on the alignment that's been randomly chosen. There is a giant conditional with one branch for each of the three possible alignments. Each of these three branches works quite similarly. I will explain what happens in the horizontal branch and then mention the minor differences in the other two branches.

If the script has chosen horizontal alignment, then the "horizontal branch" (lines 15–28) is executed. We set a variable called notDone to true. Then we execute a while loop that will keep looping until notDone is no longer true. In the loop we randomly choose a row for this word to appear in. We then randomly choose an *x* position for the word's starting point. This random starting position isn't *completely* random, though; we base it on the width of the grid minus the length of the word. So if the grid's width is 20 and the word's length is 7, then we can start the word on row 13 or earlier. At this point we have a row in which to place the word and a starting *x* position, which is the equivalent of choosing a random column. Next, we loop through each letter in tempWord and compare the letter with the grid spacing in which this letter can be placed. If that space contains nothing or if it already contains this same letter, then we continue on and check the next letter. However, if we find a letter in that grid spacing other than the one that we are currently using, then we abort this loop and start over with new random starting positions. The script runs through this loop until it finds an acceptable position in the grid. If the loop takes too long (as previously discussed), then the entire function is aborted and the restart() function is called.

The branches of the conditional that handle vertical and diagonal alignments are very similar. The vertical alignment randomly chooses a column and then randomly chooses a starting *y* position based on the grid size and the length of tempWord. The while loop is then performed in the same way as it was for the horizontal alignment. For the diagonal branch of the conditional statement, the only difference is in choosing the starting position; both the starting *x* position and the starting *y* position are chosen from random numbers, based on the grid size and the word length.

The scrambleWords() function is well commented throughout the ActionScript, so don't worry about being able to follow along with it.

createBoard()

The createBoard() function takes the randomly placed words from the scrambleWords() function and places movie clips on the screen to represent them. Then, if a grid spacing is blank (as most of them are), createBoard() assigns a random letter to that position.

```
1   function createBoard() {
2       path = this.board;
3       path.depth = 0;
4       path.circles = 0;
5       gridSpacing = 17;
6       for (var i = 0; i<boardSize; ++i) {
7           for (var j = 0; j<boardSize; ++j) {
8               var clipName = "letter"+i+"_"+j;
9               path.attachMovie("letter", clipName,
                → ++path.depth);
10              path[clipName]._x = i*gridSpacing;
11              path[clipName]._y = j*gridSpacing;
12              var tempLetter =
                → words.letters[i][j].toUpperCase();
13              if (tempLetter == undefined || tempLetter == "") {
14                  var tempLetter = chr((random(26)+65));
15                  words.letters[i][j] = tempLetter;
16                  path[clipName].dummy = true;
17              }
18              path[clipName].letter.text = tempLetter;
19          }
20      }
21  }
```

In line 2 we create a reference to the board movie clip called path. The
board instance is where we will attach all of the movie clips to hold the letters. It will also contain the circles, when they get drawn. Next we set the
variable depth to 0 in the board movie clip, using the path reference. This
number will be incremented for every movie clip attached and used to
assign each of those movie clips a unique depth. In line 4 we set circles
to 0. When circles are drawn in the board instance to select a word, a new
movie clip is created to hold that circle, and this variable is incremented.
After the game is over, we can then easily remove all of the circles, because
this variable tells us how many there are. In line 5 we create a variable
called gridSpacing. This will represent the distance we need to have
between the registration points of each letter. The registration point is the
top-left corner of the movie clip called letter, which will be attached for
each letter. It has a linkage-identifier name of letter.

Next, we perform a nested loop to make the grid. In line 8 we create a name for each movie clip we are about to attach. We'll use the same naming convention as we did in Chapter 7, "Tile-Based Worlds," but with a slight variation: We'll use "letter" instead of "cell" as the naming stem, and we'll start the counting from 0 instead of 1. (It is common, when accessing arrays, to count from 0, since array values start at index 0.) For instance, `letter3_5` is found in column 4 and row 6. Next, we add the new instance of the letter movie clip to the grid and position it. In line 12 we set a local variable called `tempLetter` from the element sitting in the corresponding spot in the two-dimensional array called `letters`. If that spot was occupied by a letter from one of the randomly placed words, then it will contain a letter. Otherwise it will contain nothing.

In line 13 we check to see if a letter in column i and row j exists. If it doesn't, we generate one randomly. Every character—even tabs and carriage returns—can be represented by a numeric value. This number is called an ASCII value. The ASCII numbers 65–90 represent the letters A–Z (A=65, B=66, and so on). The ASCII numbers 97–122 represent the letters a–z. Flash contains a function called `chr()` that returns a letter from an ASCII value. So, `chr(65)` returns "A." Using this expression, `chr((random(26)+65))`, we can have a random letter from A to Z returned (line 14). That is how we populate the blank grid spacings. In line 15 we take this new letter and store it in the two-dimensional `letters` array. Then we store a variable called dummy on the new letter movie clip with a value of `true`. We use this variable later when determining if selected text belongs to a word.

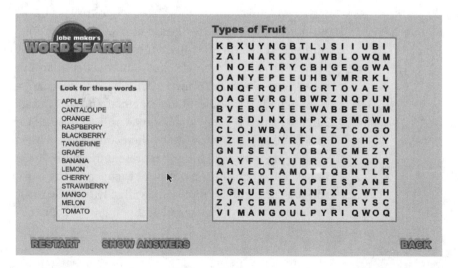

displayList()

This function handles the creation of the list of words to be displayed on the left side of the game screen. If a word has been selected in the game, it is crossed out in this area.

```
1   function displayList() {
2       _root.tempFormat = new TextFormat();
3       _root.tempFormat.font = "arial";
4       _root.tempFormat.size = 12;
5       var tempValue = "";
6       for (var i = 0; i<words.listings.length; ++i) {
7           var tempWord = words.listings[i].word;
8           if (!words.listings[i].found) {
9               tempValue += "<font color=\"#000099\">"+
                → tempWord+"</font><br>";
10          } else {
11              tempValue += "<font color=\"#009999\">"+
                → tempWord+"</font><br>";
12              _root.wordList.list.htmlText = tempValue;
13              var width = _root.tempFormat.getTextExtent
                → (tempWord).width+15;
14              var y = _root.wordList.list.textHeight-5;
15              _root.wordList.lines.lineStyle(2, 0x990000, 100);
16              _root.wordList.lines.moveTo(0, y);
17              _root.wordList.lines.lineTo(width, y);
18          }
19      }
20      _root.wordList.list.htmlText = tempValue;
21  }
```

It's not hard to understand the big picture of what this function does. It uses HTML-formatted text to display the word list in an HTML text field. If a word has not yet been selected, it appears as one color; if it has, it appears as another color with a line marked through it. In this function we loop through the list of words in the listings array. If you remember, the listings array contains objects that represent each word. If there is a property on a word object called found that has a value of true, then the word has been marked as found.

In the first few lines we create a new text format. This text format is not to be applied directly to a text field. We create it for the sole purpose of being able to use the getTextExtent() method of the textFormat object. With getTextExtent() we can find out how wide a certain phrase of text will be. We use that information when drawing a line through a word to cross it out (lines 13–17). If you're using a Macintosh and the cross-out line extends all the way across the stage, it's not your eyes going bad—it's a bug we haven't traced yet.

After every word in the listings array has been inspected and formatted in the tempValue variable, we set this value in the text field (line 20).

restart()

This function was discussed briefly at the beginning of this section. It is very short and simple. It removes all of the circle movie clips and then sends the movie back to the Generate frame label.

```
1   function restart() {
2       for (var i = 0; i<=board.circles; ++i) {
3           board["circle"+i].removeMovieClip();
4       }
5       _root.gotoandPlay("generate");
6   }
```

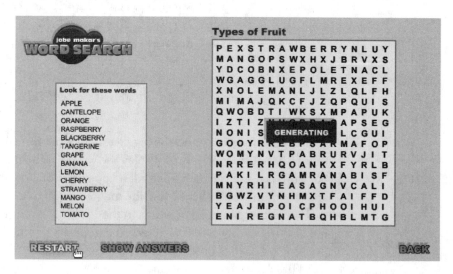

The for loop uses the value of the circles variable to know how many circle movie clips need to be removed. In line 5 the movie is instructed to go back to the Generate frame label. The game has now been restarted.

Detecting a Choice

When you click anywhere on the grid, a blue circle appears. If you keep the mouse button pressed and move the mouse around, one end of the circle (or, more accurately, the oval) stays pinned in the original spot but can freely rotate. The other end of the oval stretches to match your mouse position. The result is that you appear to be circling a group of letters. I am not going to discuss the ActionScript needed to move this circling movie clip around; I think you'll be able to easily understand it by looking at the ActionScript on the circler movie clip. (There's an instance of that movie clip to the left of the stage in the main timeline on the Game frame.) What you should know, though, is that when you (as a user) attempt to select text, the circler movie clip calls the selected() function and passes in the mouse's initial and end positions. From these two positions, the selected() function can tell which letters were selected. It then checks these selected letters against the list of words, using a function called checkList(). If the word is found, then a permanent circle is created around the word and the displayList() function is called to update the list, now showing the found word crossed out.

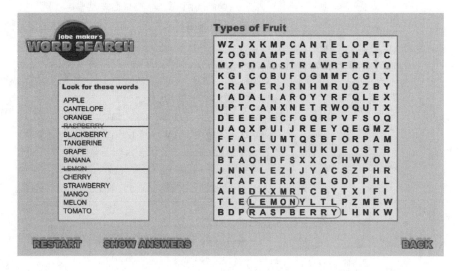

Here is the selected function:

```
1  function selected(downX, downY, upX, upY) {
2      var x1 = Math.floor(downX/gridspacing);
3      var y1 = Math.floor(downY/gridspacing);
4      var x2 = Math.floor(upX/gridspacing);
5      var y2 = Math.floor(upY/gridspacing);
6      var tempWord = undefined;
7      if (y1 == y2) {
8          if (x2>x1) {
9              for (var i = x1; i<=x2; ++i) {
10                 tempWord += words.letters[i][y1];
11             }
12         } else if (x1>x2) {
13             for (var i = x2; i<=x1; ++i) {
14                 tempWord += words.letters[i][y1];
15             }
16         }
17     } else if (x1 == x2) {
18         if (y2>y1) {
19             for (var i = y1; i<=y2; ++i) {
20                 tempWord += words.letters[x1][i];
21             }
22         } else if (y1>y2) {
23             for (var i = y2; i<=y1; ++i) {
24                 tempWord += words.letters[x1][i];
25             }
26         }
27     } else if (x1 != x2 && y1 != y2 && Math.abs(x1-x2) ==
       ↪ Math.abs(y1-y2)) {
28         var xSign = (x2-x1)/Math.abs(x2-x1);
29         var ySign = (y2-y1)/Math.abs(y2-y1);
30         var steps = Math.abs(x2-x1);
31         for (var i = 0; i<=steps; ++i) {
32             tempWord += words.letters[x1+xSign*i][y1+ySign*i];
33         }
34     }
35     if (tempWord != undefined) {
36         if (checkList(tempWord)) {
37             var x1 = x1*gridspacing+gridspacing/2;
```

```
38        var x2 = x2*gridspacing+gridspacing/2;
39        var y1 = y1*gridspacing+gridspacing/2;
40        var y2 = y2*gridspacing+gridspacing/2;
41        var rise = y2-y1;
42        var run = x2-x1;
43        var angle = Math.atan2(rise, run)*180/Math.PI;
44        var distance = Math.sqrt(rise*rise+run*run);
45        var name = "circle"+(++board.circles);
46        board.attachMovie("circler", name, ++board.depth);
47        var clip = board[name];
48        clip._x = x1;
49        clip._y = y1;
50        clip._rotation = angle;
51        clip.right._x = distance;
52        clip.lineStyle(0, 0x000099, 100);
53        clip.moveTo(0, 9.3);
54        clip.lineTo(distance, 9.3);
55        clip.moveIo(0, -9.3);
56        clip.lineTo(distance, -9.3);
57        clip._alpha = 50;
58        displayList();
59     }
60   }
61 }
```

First, we determine from the mouse positions the grid spacings that the mouse was over when the mouse button was pressed and when it was released. (This is a simple math trick that was explained in Chapter 7, "Tile-Based Worlds"; "spacing" from that chapter works the same as "grid spacing" here.) We then check the coordinates of these spacings against three conditions. There are three valid relative positions of these coordinates: They can be in the same column (vertical); that is, x1 is the same as x2. They can be in the same row (horizontal); that is, y1 is the same as y2. Or they can be diagonal, in which case the absolute value of the difference in x1 and x2 is the same as the absolute value of the difference in y1 and y2. If none of these conditions are met, then the selected letters are not a valid choice. If one of these conditions is met, then the user has made a selection in an appropriate way, but we still need to check to see if the letters form a word in the word list.

In each of the three conditions above, we use `for` loops, moving from the starting position to the end position, to build the selected word from the individual letters. We store this built word as `tempWord`. In line 35 we check to see if `tempWord` has a string value. If it doesn't, then the function is over, and the user sees nothing happen (except that the circle that he or she attempted to draw disappears). If `tempWord` has a value, then we check it against the list of words using the function called `checkList()`. This function just loops through the available words and checks it in both forward and reverse directions. If the word matches, then a result of `true` is returned; otherwise `false` is returned. If `true`, lines 37–58 are executed. They add an instance of the circler movie clip and draw a circle around the selected text using Flash's drawing API. This leaves a permanent circle on the board to mark what the user has already found. In line 58 the `displayList()` function is called. This rebuilds the list on the left side of the screen so that it shows the newly found word crossed out.

You have seen the majority of what makes this game work. There are several little functions used to handle things like mouse-down and mouse-up events that we aren't discussing in this chapter but that should be easily understood.

POINTS TO REMEMBER

- Word games are one of the most popular types of games on the Internet.

- Externalizing content into an XML file makes it easy to modify and update.

- Flash components like the ListBox make scrolling lists very easy to create.

- Keeping track of how long a loop has been running is a good way to determine if a loop is taking too long. In our case we restart the game if it takes too long to generate the board.

- The Flash drawing API can come in handy for tasks like drawing circles around words and crossing out words in a list.

Menu   Sound

CHAPTER 15

ICE WORLD: A PLATFORM GAME

YOU ARE PROBABLY FAMILIAR WITH SUPER MARIO BROTHERS—ONE OF THE most popular games ever created. While Super Mario Brothers was not the first platform game, it is certainly the one on which most platform games are based. Even though advancements in game technology allow for fully interactive 3D multiplayer games, this basic style of 2D side-view game is still very popular. In this chapter we dissect Ice World, a platform game whose rules were inspired by those of Super Mario Brothers. A *platform* is an object on which a character can stand, and a *platform game* is a game that features many such objects. You will get an inside look at the ActionScript used for a game like this. There is a lot of ActionScript, but for the most part it is organized into several very simple functions. I have also created a level editor for this game, with which you can easily create levels for Ice World. We will not discuss the ActionScript in the editor, but we will look at how to use the editor.

Prerequisites

Chapter 4, "Basic Physics." The main character in this game runs, jumps, and slides. You need an understanding of velocity, "good-enough" gravity, and "good-enough" friction to fully understand the ActionScript in this game.

Chapter 5, "Collision Detection." In this game the character can run and jump onto floating platforms, run into or jump onto enemies, and collect ice cubes. You need collision detection to perform these tasks. In reviewing Chapter 5, pay attention to the most simple collision-detection techniques, such as hitTest() and rectangle-rectangle, since those are the only ones used here.

Chapter 11, "Graphics in Games." This chapter is important if you want to understand how the graphics for this game were created. However, it is not necessary for understanding the ActionScript.

Appendix D, "XML Basics in Flash." For complete flexibility, each level in Ice World is stored as XML-formatted data in individual XML files. Knowing how the XML is formatted and parsed by the game is not crucial to understanding the game itself, but it is important for understanding how you can easily make dozens of levels for a game.

GAME OVERVIEW

The objective of Ice World is to grab the flag at the end of each level, while squashing as many enemies as possible and collecting as many of the ice cubes as possible along the way. You've got to be careful, though—you have only a limited number of lives, which are lost by falling in a gap or by running into an enemy. When creating this game, I focused on the ActionScript, not the story. So, unlike Super Mario Brothers, this game has no grand objective, such as saving a princess.

Let me introduce each of the graphic objects. Each object is followed by a description of its properties.

This is the character you control. We will call him the hero. You can make him walk left or right by using the left and right arrow keys, jump by pressing either the spacebar or the up arrow key, or crouch by pressing the down arrow key.

The lowest point in any level is the ground, which is created from the floor movie clip. There are gaps in the ground that the hero can fall through—watch out for those!

Don't be fooled by how cute and harmless this guy looks—he is your enemy (also called a baddy). In each level you will find several of them. You jump on them to squash them. If you run into one (not by jumping), then you lose a life.

These ice cubes are the collectible items in this game. You collect them by running into them.

This cube is the most common platform found throughout the levels. Cubes are solid on all sides. You can jump onto them to stand there or to position yourself for gaining access to another area. Some of these cubes contain secret ice cubes. If you bump one from underneath, it may expose an ice cube that gets automatically collected.

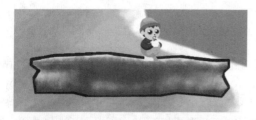

This type of platform may be stationary, or it may move (horizontally, vertically, or both). I will call this the "ice platform." By jumping onto one, you can be transported to a new spot to find secret items or get closer to another platform you need jump onto.

When falling from above, you can land on the "tree platform." However, it is not solid from the sides or from underneath. In terms of the collision properties, I will call the other platforms "solid" and this type of platform a "cloud."

This is what you're aiming for on each level. You collect this flag by running into the pole. Once you collect the flag, you've completed the level, and you move up to the next level.

Now that you have been introduced to the game elements, you should play the game a few times to get a feel for everything. Open ice_world.swf in the Chapter15 directory. When you see the menu, select Start Game. After the first level has been loaded, you will see a Play button. Click that, and you will find yourself on level 1. Use the directional arrow keys to navigate the world. Collect the ice cubes, squash the enemies, and collect the flag at the end. You will see that, as you would expect, the levels get more difficult as you progress.

Speed Boost for Windows Users

As you are probably aware, the Flash Player has gained in popularity at an amazing rate because of its small file size (read: fast download). But that small file size also meant that there are a few things Macromedia could not fit in the Flash Player, like powerful graphics-rendering ability and faster code execution. Plug-ins like the Shockwave Player for Director are much more powerful than Flash's, but they have large file sizes and hence are less popular. For most Web applications, Flash's level of power is acceptable, but to the game developer it can pose a problem. As the number of graphics and calculations per frame increases in a game, the Flash Player slows down dramatically. Luckily there is a new product (Wndows only) that can help with one of these two deficiencies—graphics rendering—Design Assembly's swfXXL (www.swfxxl.com).

swfXXL takes a Flash projector file (which is output from the Publish settings in Flash) and creates a new executable file from it. The new file runs in full-screen mode and takes advantage of Microsoft DirectX for the graphics. This is great news for Windows game developers. It doesn't necessarily speed up any code, but it frees up much of the processor resources that were being devoted to graphics rendering, which can then be used by the Flash Player for code execution. The result is that you can easily create games that run at up to 60 frames per second (the frame rate of most professional non-Flash games). Check out the file called platform_standalone.exe in the Chapter15 directory. It is Ice World after being modified with swfXXL. It plays full screen, and it plays fast.

THE XML AND THE LEVEL EDITOR

When you create a game that has multiple levels, each of which reuses the same graphic assets, it makes sense to build a level editor. The goal is to represent each level using XML-formatted data. That way, you can create as many XML files as you like (one for each level) without having to edit the game itself. You can use a level editor to visually build what the level will look like and to generate the XML used to represent that level. This is the simple, top-level process for building a level:

1. **Open the level editor (we will talk in detail about this and the next step later).**

2. **Build the level.**

3. **Click the Generate XML button.**

4. **Copy the XML generated in the Output window and paste it into a new text file.**

5. **Name the text file using the appropriate or subsequent level number (level1.xml, level2.xml, level3.xml, and so on).**

Before we get to exactly how to use the level editor, you should be familiar with the XML format chosen for this game.

The XML Format

For more informa-
tion on XML, see
Appendix D.

You may be thinking, "I have a level editor, so why do I need to under-stand the XML?" Well, you have a point. If you only want to make levels using what I have provided in this game, you don't need to understand the XML. But if you want to modify or extend this game idea to include more features, then you *will* need to understand how the XML is formatted. If you were to add, for instance, a second type of enemy, you would need to add some extra attributes to the enemy nodes to specify the type of enemy, or create a new section of the XML document. Or even if you want to do something simple like specify the background or the music to use for each level, you need to understand how the XML is set up so that you can mod-ify it to include this information.

Here is the basic format, with no actual data being stored. I'm initially showing it to you like this so that you can have an overview of the entire document. You will see some real data farther down.

```
1   <level>
2       <blocks />
3       <grounds />
4       <baddies />
5       <collectables />
6   </level>
```

As you know, every XML document must have exactly one root node. For us, with this game, that's the `<level>` node. It will be used to store the position of the flag that must be captured (it will store that position as attributes). The `<blocks>` node will store the positions and properties of all the three types of platforms (cubes, ice platforms, and trees). It will store information for each of these platforms in `<block>` nodes, which are children to the `<blocks>` node. The `<grounds>` node stores child nodes that describe areas of the ground. To put it another way, every area of the ground that is not contained within the `<ground>` child nodes of the `<grounds>` node is a gap in the ground. The `<baddies>` node stores `<baddy>` child nodes that represent the enemies. Each `<baddy>` node contains the position of the enemy as well as its speed and the initial direction in which it will walk. The `<collectables>` node simply stores the positions of each of the collectable movie clips—the ice cubes—in separate `<collectable>` nodes.

Here is an example that has very few nodes but contains actual level data:

```
1    <level flagx="1742" flagy="332" >
2        <blocks>
3            <block x="340" y="210" type="solid" graphic="cube"
             → container="true" containerCounter="3" />
4            <block x="385" y="210" type="solid" graphic="cube"
             → container="false" />
5            <block x="430" y="210" type="solid" graphic="ice platform"
             → container="false" mover="yes" xspeed="2" yspeed="0"
             → maxxmov="150" maxymov="0" />
6            <block x="475" y="210" type="cloud" graphic="tree"
             → container="false" />
7        </blocks>
8        <grounds>
9            <ground xstart="0" xend="940" />
10           <ground xstart="1020" xend="4800" />
11       </grounds>
12       <baddies>
13           <baddy x="646" y="330" breadth="200"
             → start_direction="right" speed="2" />
14           <baddy x="1362" y="330" breadth="100"
             → start_direction="left" speed="1" />
15       </baddies>
```

```
16        <collectables>
17            <collectable x="362" type="ice cube" y="193" />
18            <collectable x="405" type="ice cube" y="192" />
19            <collectable x="451" type="ice cube" y="191" />
20        </collectables>
21    </level>
```

In line 1 you see that we have two attributes within the <level> node—flagx and flagy. This is where the flag will be positioned in the level. In lines 3–6, four platforms, each slightly different, are described:

Line 3 describes a cube platform that will contain three collectable items. The container attribute indicates whether the platform will contain a collectable item, and the containerCounter attribute indicates how many items this platform will contain. Line 4 describes a basic cube platform, containing nothing (so the container attribute is false). Line 5 describes the ice platform. We give it an attribute of mover with a value of "yes", meaning that the platform will move. We also give it several attributes that contain how the platform will move. The attributes xspeed and yspeed control the speed at which the platform will move in those directions. The maxxmov and maxymov attributes specify how far the platforms will move in those directions. Most commonly, maxymov and yspeed are 0, so the platform only moves horizontally. Line 6 describes a tree platform. I usually give the tree platform a type attribute of "cloud". That is so the hero can jump from underneath (if the tree is set up over ground) through the leaves and then land on top of the tree.

Lines 8–11 describe the valid pieces of the ground. In line 9 the <ground> node contains two attributes: xstart, with a value of 0, and xend, with a value of 940. This means we are defining a valid walkable area that spans $x = 0$ to $x = 940$. Before $x = 0$ (that is, <0) there is no ground. In line 10 we have a <ground> node that specifies valid ground between $x = 1020$ and $x = 4800$. Putting both of these pieces (lines 9 and 10) together conceptually, we can see that we are defining ground between 0 and 4800 with a gap in the middle between 940 and 1020.

The enemies are defined in lines 12–15. Each <baddy> node must contain these attributes: x, y, breadth, start_direction, and speed. The x and y values specify the enemy's starting position. The breadth attribute tells how far the enemy should walk before turning around and coming back. The start_direction tells which direction (either "left" or "right") he should start moving in, and the speed attribute specifies the speed at which the baddy should move.

In lines 16–20 we describe where all of the collectable items should be. Each collectable node contains three attributes: x, y, and type. The attributes x and y specify the collectable item's position; the type attribute specifies which collectable item you would like to use. In this game we are using only one collectable item, but it is easy to modify the game to add more. The ActionScript uses the value of the type attribute to pull a movie clip from the library (the linkage identifier has the same name as the collectable). So you could easily add a movie clip to the library, give it a linkage identifier, and then specify it here in the XML file.

Code-Graphics Independence

Throughout this book I have been pushing the idea of not tying your ActionScript specifically to one movie clip or graphic, and have pointed out several advantages of this method along the way. If you play around with this XML file a bit, you'll find another advantage. As you can see above and from playing the sample Ice World game, cubes tend to be "solid" and can sometimes contain collectables. Ice platforms tend to be solid and to move. Trees tend to be clouds (meaning there is only detection from above). However, there is nothing in the XML to stop you from making a tree move, or from turning a cube into a cloud. I didn't tie the code to any specific graphic, so you can come up with many different combinations if you want to. For example, sometime you might only want one little tiny cube to movie vertically, not the whole clunky ice platform.

The Level Editor

As I mentioned earlier in this chapter, we are storing the data used to build each level as separate XML files. The level editor's purpose is to assist in the creation of these XML files. With this level editor, you can visually drag and drop elements onto the game world. Once they are in the world, the properties of these elements can be edited. When you are happy with what you see, you can generate the XML, copy it, and paste it into a text file.

Open platform_editor.fla in the Chapter15 directory. I will not discuss the ActionScript in this file, but rather explain how to use it. Press Ctrl-Enter (Windows) or Command-Enter (Macintosh) to watch this movie in test mode. (As it currently stands, this file must be used in Test Movie mode because the XML that is generated is displayed from a trace action in the Output window.

You now have the SWF running in Test Movie mode. Before launching into the details of how to build a map, let me take you on a quick tour of this simple interface. In the top-left corner of the screen you can see the level dimensions written out. The level is 4800 wide and 4000 tall. These dimensions are not configurable, but you don't have to fill the space completely, either. (I didn't completely fill in any of the sample levels on the CD.) To the right of the dimensions are some directional arrows. By clicking the arrows you can move the level around so that you can see other areas of it. That navigation can become frustrating when you're trying to move large distances, so I also included support for the keyboard arrow keys. I suggest using the arrow keys for easy level movement. On that note, skip over to the bottom-right corner of the screen just for a moment, to the reposition button. When you click that button, the world moves back to its starting position.

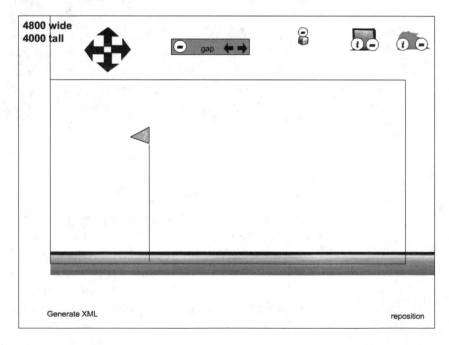

To the right of the directional arrow keys are four items, each of which is draggable. You can click and drag any item over the level and then release it. Note that you can only drag these items into the area within the black lines on the stage. The first item has the word "gap" written on it. By default, the entire ground from $x = 0$ to $x = 4800$ is a walkable area. To add areas of no ground—that is, gaps—you drag and drop this movie clip. You should note that a gap has no y position, so when you drop this movie clip onto the stage, you don't have to worry about placing it exactly over the ground; all that's necessary is to place it horizontally where you want it. There are three buttons on the gap movie clip: a left arrow, a right arrow, and a minus sign. The arrows are for controlling and adjusting the width of the gap: The left arrow shrinks the movie clip horizontally. The right arrow makes it wider. The minus sign is something you'll see on all four of the elements. It allows you to remove an item from the stage. If you placed the item but no longer want it on the stage, click the minus sign button and the item will be removed.

The next element is the collectable ice cube item. This is an easy one, as it has no configurable properties. Just drag it to the position where you want it.

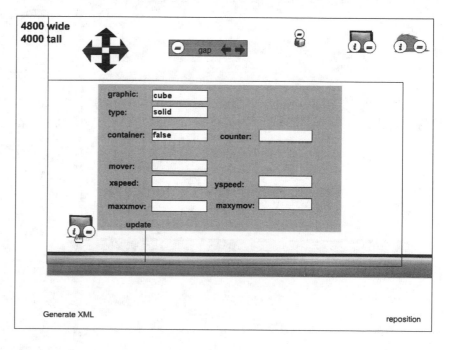

Then we have the platform movie clip. Notice that there is only one of these, not three. That is because this one movie clip can be configured to display any of the three types. Drag the clip out onto the level. Click the i button on it (the i stands for "info"). This opens an information-display window, where you can edit all of the `<block>` node attributes. The graphic field can contain any of three values: "cube," "ice platform," or "tree." The type field can contain either of two values: "solid" or "cloud." (The behavior of the rest of the attributes was explained above in the XML.) As soon as you click the update button (or press the Enter or Return key) the element is updated and the display window closes. The platform will not start moving on the stage (if set to move) but will display the correct graphic.

Finally, we have the enemy movie clip. Drag one onto the stage and click the now-familiar i button. There are only three editable fields for this movie clip: the direction for it to start walking, its speed, and its breadth.

Remember that when the flag is captured, the level has been completed. The flag is already on the stage, since there can only be one flag. You can drag it to any position.

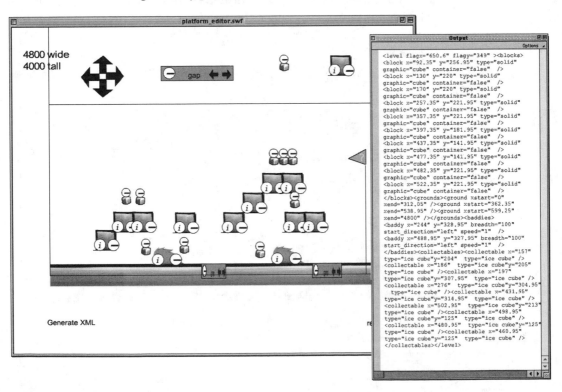

Notice the Generate XML button in the bottom-left corner of the screen. When clicked, it takes all of the level data and generates an XML-formatted document for that level, and displays it in the Output window. You can then copy it from the Output window and store it in a text file. You can name that text file anything you like (such as level1.xml). When testing new levels, the procedure I usually follow is this:

1. *Rename level1.xml to something else (like level1_.xml) so as not to ruin the original.*

2. *Build a level using the editor, and copy the XML.*

3. *Without closing the level editor, open a text editor and paste the level XML data into it, and then save it as level1.xml.*

4. *Open the ice_world.swf file (the standalone one, not in Test Movie mode) and test this level. It is quick and easy to test, because it is now level 1.*

Note that while you are testing the game, it will appear to be playing more slowly than you would expect. This is because the editor is still open.

5. *To make any changes, close the game and go back to the editor, which is still open. Since the editor was open during the testing period, capturing all key presses, chances are good that the level's position is not where you left it. Click the reposition button to reset to the starting position. You can then move the level to the area that you want to edit. Once you have edited the level again, return to step 3.*

6. *Repeat steps 3–5 as needed. When you are happy with the level, do a Save As, using the real level number that you want for this file (for example, level7.xml). Then rename level1_.xml back to level1.xml.*

One major deficiency of this level editor is that it doesn't load in level files that you can then modify to create a different level file. You must start from scratch every time. Other than that problem, this level editor should provide you with everything you need to create some very interesting levels!

GAME STRUCTURE AND RESOURCE FILES

In this section we are going to look at the game's structure and at the individual movie clips used in the levels (such as the hero, the platforms, and the ground).

The Game Structure

Open ice_world.fla in the Chapter15 directory. The game's main timeline is set up in the same way as used in the other games in this book; the game itself resides on the Game frame. Click the Game frame label. You will see one movie clip in that frame (called game board); double-click it to enter it.

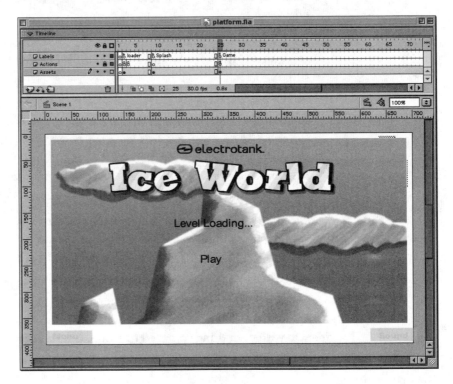

The Layers and Frames

There are two frames and four layers in this movie clip. The layers are as follows:

Actions—Contains all of the ActionScript for the game. Notice that it is on the second of the two frames. This is because we need the movie clips in this timeline to be fully instantiated (that is, any ActionScript on the first frame of any of these movie clips needs to be loaded) before we try to do anything with them. If the ActionScript was on the first frame, we might try to do something with a movie clip that had not fully been instantiated.

Border—Contains a simple white outline of the game area and two buttons. One button toggles the sound (either on or off), and the other takes you back to the menu.

Waiting Screen—In this layer we have a movie clip, with an instance name of waitingScreen, that contains all of the screens that display during the changeover between levels. It tells you when a level file is loading, when the game is over (and if you won or lost), and when the next level is finished loading and ready to be played.

Game Clip—This layer contains a movie clip with an instance name of gameClip. It contains the hero, the flag, the ground, the background, and all of the other movie clips that will be added to the game. We will discuss this in more detail next.

The gameClip instance

The gameClip movie clip instance (with a library name of game) contains (or will contain, once they are attached by the main game ActionScript) all of the level graphics. Double-click the movie clip to enter it. There are three layers within. The top layer is a mask layer that masks the two layers beneath it. It masks an area of 680 by 350, which is the amount of area we intend to see at any time in the game. The two layers beneath it each contain one movie clip, with instance names of bg and overlay. The bg instance contains the background movie clip, which is quite large. Notice that its registration point is the upper-left corner and is at (0, 0). The overlay movie clip instance contains the hero and will contain every attached movie clip when a level is created. The instance name of the hero movie clip is man.

As the hero moves to the right (in an actual game), the overlay instance will be moved left so that the character is always near the center of the screen. As the character moves up, the overlay instance moves down. Also, the bg movie clip instance moves in the opposite direction from the character in a subtler way. The goal is to keep the character in the middle of the screen as much as possible. The one exception is when the character reaches the boundaries of the level. At the beginning of the level, the hero is at the left boundary (which means the bg and overlay instances can't scroll any further), and the hero does not have to stay in the center of the screen. But after the hero moves far enough away from the boundaries, the screens start to scroll.

At this time you might want to open up the game and play it again, paying attention from the perspective of someone who now knows the movie-clip structure. Notice that the overlay and bg instances move independently and at different rates. Notice what happens at the boundaries.

Supporting Movie Clips

Now let's look at the rest of the movie clips used in the game, the ones that illustrate or animate individual pieces of the game. Open up the library and take a look inside the clips described below.

man

This movie clip contains the hero. There is only one movie clip inside, with an instance name of animation. Notice that its registration point is in the center at the feet of the hero. When the hero is walking in one direction, we face him in that direction. When he turns around, we just reverse his _xscale property so that he is facing the other direction.

man animation

While in the man clip above, double-click the animation instance inside. Now you're in the man animation clip. You will see that this is the movie clip that contains the five states of the hero: standing, walking, crouching, jumping, and dead. (Each of these states has a frame label and an area in the timeline of its own, except for standing, which is the first frame and has no label.)

platform

The platform movie clip has three frame labels, one for each platform type. There is one movie clip in this timeline that spans all three of the frame labels. It has an instance name of item, and it contains the collectable object (the ice cube). This is the collectable item that can be contained within a platform. If the hero jumps from underneath a platform and hits it, and a collectable item comes out from the top, then it did so using this internal movie clip. Also notice that we have two black lines on each of the three frame labels. Their placement determines the platform's boundaries. If you want to adjust the boundaries of a platform, then move those lines around. The left boundary is determined by the $x = 0$ position, and the top boundary is determined by the $y = 0$ position. This movie clip has a linkage identifier of platform.

ice cube

This movie clip, with a linkage identifier of ice cube, has two frame labels: Display and Capture. The Display frame is shown for the ice cubes that are just sitting around. When an ice cube is captured (by the hero either running into it or bumping a platform from below), the Capture frame is played.

floor

This movie clip simply contains the graphic of the ground and has a linkage identifier of ground. It can be tiled with multiple instances of itself to give the feeling of long stretches of ground.

ground corner

This movie clip helps the edge of the ground appear smooth where there is a gap. This is not mandatory; it's just more pleasing to the eye than a sharp cliff. It has a linkage identifier of corner.

end flag

This is the flag the game player must capture to complete a level. It has a linkage identifier of flag. The first frame shows the flag at full mast. After the player runs into the flagpole, this movie clip plays an animation. On frame 20, a function is executed:

```
where.levelComplete()
```

This serves as a simple time delay to end the level and display the "level complete" message. The `where` reference is set from the main code area, as you will see in the next section.

baddy

This is the movie clip of the enemy. It contains two movie clips. One contains the animation of the enemy walking and dying, and has an instance name of `animation`. The other one is a box, which becomes invisible when the game starts, that is used to detect a collision between the hero and the enemy itself. It has an instance name of `hitArea`.

GAME CODE

This game has a lot of ActionScript. Don't be intimidated by it, though, because there is not much in the way of techniques that you haven't seen before, and for the most part the code is simple. It's just that in this game, many things can happen that we have to use code to check for. For instance, when detecting a collision of the hero with a platform, we need to do the following:

1. *Check the left side. If hitting, reposition the hero.*

2. *Check the right side. If hitting, reposition the hero.*

3. *Check the top. If the hero is on the top, then do we also need to move him a little bit if the platform is moving?*

4. *Check the bottom. If the hero hits from underneath, are there collectable items hidden in there? If so, how many? Is the hero crouched under the platform? If so, move him out.*

None of those things are difficult—there are just many situations to cover. Those are only a few of the platform-detection questions answered with code. Above I didn't even include cloud properties that we need to check for (such as a tree)!

This game takes a very *object-oriented* (OO) approach. I used my fledgling knowledge of OO programming to create this game, and I'm happy with the results. The code is easy to understand and can be extended without having to rewrite it.

Object-Oriented Programming

Over the last few years there has been a big push for Flash coders to start coding in an object-oriented (OO) way. OO coding, also known as Object-Oriented Programming (OOP), contains no syntax with which you are not already familiar. It is more a state of mind and adherence to some structures. We have been using many techniques throughout this book that are considered OO—for instance, the A* algorithm, the isometricAS object, and the ElectroServerAS object (which you see in Chapter 13, "Dissecting a Chat"; and in the multiplayer game chapters 17 and 18, "Tic-Tac-Toe: Your First Multiplayer Game" and "9-Ball"). When you see something coded in an OO way, it is usually pretty easy to understand. For instance, in Ice World we have a game object, which contains a hero object (make sense so far?). The hero object contains certain methods, like jump(), walkLeft(), and crouch(). That is as complicated as it gets in this game! OO coding is just a structured way of programming things to work.

Let me give you a comparison. If I did not use OO, then I might just have a function called jump() on the timeline. But what if the enemy also could jump? Then I would have to rename that function to, let's say, heroJump(), and create a second function called enemyJump(). OO coding makes it much easier and more intuitive to give each object the ability to perform the function. So it would be enemy.jump() and hero.jump().

OO tends to be easily extended (that is, you can easily add a method, such as hero.explode(), without colliding with other code), easy to conceptualize, and easy to understand. But it has one big problem: performance. For games like Ice World, performance is not that big of an issue. But for games that require a lot of calculations done very frequently (like 9-ball), OO may be too verbose. You might have to optimize in a non-OO way to gain performance.

My knowledge of OOP is growing every day, but I still have much to learn. There are many concepts I've read about or heard about in lectures that I'm sure I will eventually adopt. If you are interested in OOP in Flash, you should participate in forum discussions (or just read them) on Flash resource sites such as Ultrashock.com (www.ultrashock.com).

If you don't already have ice_world.fla open, then open it now. We are going to go through some of the major pieces of ActionScript, but not all of it. (As a reminder, we're looking at the game board movie clip.)

ActionScript Not Found in a Function

There are about 50 lines of ActionScript in this game that are not contained within a function (or the `onEnterFrame` event). These perform the tasks that only need to occur once within the game. We will look at these actions here.

The game object

The game object is the container for all of the information in the game. This includes, but is not limited to, the level data (once it's been loaded from an XML file), the hero object, and all of the constants used throughout the game, such as friction and gravity. The game object is defined first:

```
game = {};
```

The bg object

The bg object is created to store information about the background image. The background image is scrolled subtly as the hero runs around the level. In order to calculate how much to scroll the background, we need to know the width and height of the background. All of this information is stored in the following lines of ActionScript:

```
1   game.bg = {};
2   game.bg.clip = gameClip.bg;
3   game.bg.x = 0;
4   game.bg.y = 0;
5   game.bg.height = game.bg.clip._height;
6   game.bg.width = game.bg.clip._width;
```

The overlay object

This object is used to store information about the `overlay` movie-clip instance inside the `gameClip` instance. That is the movie clip that contains the hero as well as all of the other level elements except the background.

We create an object for the overlay so that we can keep track of its position in an OO way.

```
1    game.overlay = {};
2    game.overlay.clip = gameClip.overlay;
3    game.overlay.x = 0;
4    game.overlay.y = 0;
```

You can see in lines 3 and 4 that we initially give the overlay object *x* and *y* positions of 0. This is because it starts at that position. When the hero moves around the level, the overlay will also move, and its *x* and *y* positions will be updated.

The hero object

The hero object serves many functions. It represents the hero character of the game, and it stores a lot of information about the hero, such as his position, his dimensions, and the number of lives he has. In addition to what you see here, we will define a lot of methods onto this object later in the code. Those methods will allow for events like jumping, walking, and crouching.

```
1    game.hero = {};
2    game.hero.clip = gameClip.overlay.man;
3    hero = game.hero;
4    hero.lives = game.numLives-1;
5    clip = game.hero.clip;
6    hero.xmov = 0;
7    hero.startx = 50;
8    hero.starty = 320;
9    hero.standingHeight = 50;
10   hero.crouchingHeight = 30;
11   hero.width = 23;
12   hero.height = hero.standingHeight;
13   hero.ymov = 0;
14   hero.minXmov = .75;
15   hero.maxXmov = 12;
16   hero.groundWalkIncrement = 1.7;
17   hero.airWalkIncrement = .85;
18   hero.pushSpeed = 4;
```

```
19  hero.walkIncrement = hero.groundWalkIncrement;
20  hero.jumpSpeed = 23;
21  hero.clip.swapDepths(1000000);
```

Notice that in line 3 we define a shortcut to the hero object. This is done as a convenience and is not required. It is just easier to type *hero* than *game.hero*. In line 9 we set a property to the hero object called standingHeight. This is the height of the hero when he is standing. In the next line we set a property called crouchingHeight. This is the height of the hero when he is crouching. When the hero is on the level and he crouches and then stands, internally the code switches the hero.height property between standingHeight and crouchingHeight. This allows the hero to fit into places when crouched that he couldn't when standing.

In line 14 we set minXmov. When the hero is moving at a speed less than this number, we set his speed to 0. In the next line we set maxXmov. This is used as a speed cap—we don't let the hero move at an *x* speed faster than this number.

In line 16 we set a property called groundWalkIncrement. This is the amount added to your *x* speed in each frame in which you have the left or right arrow key pressed. Notice that the next line sets a property called airWalkIncrement, and its number is a little smaller than the value in groundWalkIncrement. We do this because you should have control over your character in the air, as in other popular platform games—but not quite as great control as if you were on the ground. (In line 19 there is a walkIncrement property whose value gets changed from the groundWalkIncrement value to the airWalkIncrement value based on the location—ground or air—of the hero).

In line 18 we set a property called pushSpeed. If there is a platform you can only move under by running, crouching, and sliding, then we need to make it so that you can't get stuck. So if you are under a platform and you are crouched, then you slowly get pushed in a certain direction, based on a speed of pushSpeed.

Next we set jumpSpeed. This is the initial speed at which you move upward on the screen when you jump. Finally, we swap the hero movie clip to a very high depth. At this new depth, the hero will always be above everything else.

Miscellaneous Property Definitions of the Game Object

These are the rest of the properties on the game object. Except for lines 6–11, this ActionScript should be easily understood with no further explanation.

```
1    game.level = 1;
2    game.numLevels = 5;
3    game.runDecay = .85;
4    game.depth = 10000;
5    game.floor = 330;
6    game.viewableHeight = 350;
7    game.viewableWidth = 680;
8    game.walkAbleWidth = 4800;
9    game.walkAbleHeight = 4000;
10   game.xScrollFactor = (game.bg.width-game.viewableWidth)/
     → game.walkAbleWidth;
11   game.yScrollFactor = game.bg.height/game.walkAbleHeight;
12   game.gravity = 2;
13   game.windResistance = .92;
14   game.numLives = 3;
```

Let's look at lines 6–11. The goal in these lines is to determine how much the background needs to be scrolled when the hero moves. We do this by storing the dimensions of what we can see and the dimensions of what we can't see. In lines 6 and 7 we store the viewable dimensions of the level. This tells us that at any given time we can see 680 pixels across and 350 pixels up and down. The next two lines define how far (at a maximum) we will allow the hero to walk both horizontally and vertically. These numbers are arbitrary; you can pick any that you want. The idea is, though, that if the character were to walk from one side of the defined area all the way to the other side, then the background image will have scrolled one full scroll … so I'd recommend using large numbers as I did here. The large number will make it so that the background won't scroll too fast and will appear to be moving fairly naturally or realistically. If you think the background is still scrolling too fast, then make these numbers even larger. In lines 10 and 11 we determine the scrolling factors based on a ratio of the background-image dimensions to the walkable areas.

levelLoaded()

The ActionScript used in this function deals almost entirely with parsing through the XML, which is beyond the scope of this book. For information on XML parsing, please see Appendix D, "XML Basics in Flash." But here, we should at least go over the big picture of what this function does. Once the level XML file is loaded, this function is executed. It parses through the XML and creates a few objects and some arrays, and then adds the movie clips to the level. Here are the objects and arrays it creates:

game.flag—This object is used to store the x and y positions as well as a movie-clip reference of the flag.

game.platforms.column—This array stores an object for each platform that contains information about that platform, including the x and y positions, type of platform, width and height of the platform, and a reference to the movie clip.

game.baddies—This array contains an object for each enemy. It contains the enemy's position as well as a reference to the enemy's movie clip.

game.collectables—This array contains an object for each collectable item; the object stores the x and y positions of the item and a reference to its movie clip.

game.grounds—This array stores objects representing the areas of the ground that are walkable (meaning that they are not gaps in the floor).

The onEnterFrame Event

As with most games, in Ice World we have an onEnterFrame event that is set up to repeatedly call a series of functions. Here it is:

```
1    this.onEnterFrame = function() {
2        if (game.inPlay) {
3            if (!hero.dead) {
4                listenForKeys();
5            }
6            addFrictionAndGravity();
7            createTempPosition();
8            if (!hero.dead) {
```

```
9              baddyDetection();
10             platformDetect();
11             collectableDetect();
12             detectFlag();
13             checkFloor();
14         }
15         renderScreen();
16     }
17 };
```

There is an if statement that contains all of the function calls. It executes the actions within the if statement if game.inPlay is true. The inPlay property of the game object is set to true when the startLevel() function is called.

There is a property on the hero object called dead. When the hero dies, dead is set to true; otherwise it is false. Line 4, listenForKeys(), is executed if hero.dead is not true. The listenForKeys() function checks to see if any of the arrow keys or the spacebar is currently pressed. If one of those keys is pressed, the hero's movement is affected. Lines 6 and 7 decrease the horizontal movement due to friction (either air friction or ground friction) and increase the hero's y velocity by the gravitational amount.

In line 8 we check (again) to see if the hero is dead. If he's not, then we execute lines 9–13. In line 9 we check for collisions between the hero and the enemies. In line 10 we execute platformDetect(), which checks for collisions between the hero and the platforms. We then check for collisions between the hero and the collectable objects by executing collectableDetect() in line 11. In line 12 we check to see if the hero has reached the flag, and in line 13 we check to see if the hero has fallen far enough to stand on the floor.

listenForKeys()

This function is called in every frame by the onEnterFrame event. It checks to see if the directional arrow keys or the spacebar is pressed. If any of those hero-control keys are pressed, then the hero's current state may change (for example, walking changes to a jump). If you think about it from a programming point of view, you can see that controlling the hero and making him look as real as possible can get a little confusing. Here are some rules and behaviors for Ice World.

- The hero can only jump if he is currently on the ground or on a platform. (In some games the hero can jump in mid-air, but not in this game.)

- The hero can jump when crouching, but cannot walk when crouching.

- While in the air (crouching or not), the hero can be controlled to move left or right.

- The controllability of the hero is less sensitive while in the air. That means that if the hero jumps, the game player can control the hero's direction, but not as easily as if the character were on the ground.

When you can look at a bulleted list of rules, as above, then the functionality doesn't seem as confusing to code. Still, there are a few things that can be tricky to control. For instance, when you press the down arrow button, the hero should crouch. But what if the hero ran, then crouched and slid underneath a platform, and then you released the down arrow button? The hero would then stand up if you (as the programmer) did not foresee this situation. What happens in this situation (in this game and in other similar games) is that the hero stays crouched but is slowly pushed (by code) to one side of the platform or the other. When the hero reaches the edge, he is automatically un-crouched. You will see more about this in the platformDetect() function.

Here is the listenForKeys() function:

```
1   function listenForKeys() {
2       hero.wasCrouching = hero.isCrouching;
3       if (hero.inAir) {
4           hero.walkIncrement = hero.airWalkIncrement;
5       } else {
6           hero.walkIncrement = hero.groundWalkIncrement;
7       }
8       if (Key.isDown(Key.RIGHT) && (!hero.isCrouching ||
        → (hero.isCrouching && hero.inAir))) {
9           hero.xmov += hero.walkIncrement;
10          hero.walkRight();
11      } else if (Key.isDown(Key.LEFT) && (!hero.isCrouching ||
        → (hero.isCrouching && hero.inAir))) {
```

```
12          hero.xmov -= hero.walkIncrement;
13          hero.walkLeft();
14      }
15      if ((Key.isDown(Key.SPACE) || Key.isDown(Key.UP)) &&
     → okToJump) {
16          okToJump = false;
17          if (!hero.isJumping && !hero.inAir) {
18              hero.inAir = true;
19              hero.ymov -= hero.jumpSpeed;
20              hero.jump();
21          }
22      } else if (!Key.isDown(Key.SPACE) &&
     → !Key.isDown(Key.UP)) {
23          okToJump = true;
24      }
25      if (Key.isDown(Key.DOWN)) {
26          hero.crouch();
27      } else {
28          hero.unCrouch();
29      }
30  }
```

The first thing we do (line 2) is store the current crouching state of the hero. We do this to help with the situation described above (sliding under a platform and then trying to stand). In the platformDetect() function we will use this stored crouching state, hero.wasCrouching, to determine if the hero should be pushed out.

Next, in lines 3–7, we change the hero.walkIncrement property depending on whether the hero is on the ground or platform, or in the air. The value of hero.walkIncrement determines the character's sensitivity (that is, its acceleration).

In lines 8 and 11 we check for similar conditions. If the right arrow key is pressed and the hero is not crouching, we move the hero to the right. If the right arrow is pressed and the hero is crouching and is in the air, we also move the hero to the right. If any other situation is happening, we do not move the hero to the right. In line 11 we do the same check, except with the left arrow key.

Lines 15–24 control the hero's jumping. In line 15 we check to see if either the spacebar or the up arrow key (both of which control jumping) is pressed, and if okToJump is true. The variable okToJump is set to true when neither the spacebar nor the up arrow key is currently pressed. This makes it so that you cannot just hold down the spacebar or the up arrow key and have the hero jump automatically as soon as he touches the ground—you have to release the jump key and press it again for the hero to jump again. Notice that when the conditions exist for a jump to occur (that is, the condition in line 15 is fulfilled), hero.inAir is set to true. We keep track of when the hero is in the air and when he is on the ground.

In lines 25–29 we check to see if the down arrow key is pressed. If it is, then we tell the hero to crouch by invoking hero.crouch(); otherwise we call hero.uncrouch(). If you are thinking ahead, you may wonder if this interferes with the scenario of sliding under the platform and then un-crouching mentioned above. It doesn't affect it, because we check for this condition in a function that is called *after* the platformDetect() function. If we detect that the hero should still be crouching, then we call hero.crouch() and the game player never sees the hero stand up (until appropriate).

platformDetect()

If you take the time to understand any one function in this game, let it be this one. It is pretty long (77 lines) but not too difficult. As mentioned earlier in this chapter, there are many situations we have to take into account when our hero is colliding with a platform. This function does all of that. It not only detects if he is colliding with a platform, but it determines the properties of the platform (such as solid, cloud, moving) and makes the hero react accordingly. Here it is:

```
1    function platformDetect() {
2        var oldOnPlatform = hero.onPlatform;
3        var onPlatform = false;
4        for (var i = 0; i<game.platforms.column.length; ++i) {
5            var platform = game.platforms.column[i];
6            var px = platform.x;
7            var py = platform.y;
8            var pw = platform.width;
9            var ph = platform.height;
10           var type = platform.type;
```

```
11      for (var iteration = 1; iteration<=
        → game.totalIterations; ++iteration) {
12          hero.tempx = hero.x+
            → (hero.xmov/game.totalIterations)*iteration;
13          hero.tempy = hero.y+
            → (hero.ymov/game.totalIterations)*iteration;
14          if ((hero.tempx+hero.width>px) &&
            → (hero.tempx<px+pw) &&
            → (hero.tempy-hero.height<py+ph) &&
            → (hero.tempy>py)) {
15              // find which side he hit.
16              if (hero.tempy>py && hero.y<=py+.01 &&
                → hero.tempy<py+ph && hero.ymov>0) {
17                  //landed on top
18                  //the .01 is for a comparison error
19                  var onPlatform = true;
20                  var platformTop = py;
21                  landOnPlatform(platformTop);
22                  if (platform.mover == "yes") {
23                      var xinc = platform.xspeed+
                        → hero.xmov*.5;
24                      hero.x += xinc;
25                      hero.y += platform.yspeed+
                        → hero.ymov*.5;
26                      hero.tempx = hero.x;
27                      hero.tempy = hero.y;
28                  }
29              } else if (type != "cloud" &&
                → hero.tempy-hero.height>py &&
                → hero.tempy-hero.height<py+ph &&
                → hero.tempx+hero.width/2>px &&
                → hero.tempx<px+pw-hero.width/2 &&
                → hero.ymov<0) {
30                  //hit from underneath
31                  var newy = py+ph+hero.height;
32                  bounceOffOfBottom(newy);
33                  if (platform.container) {
34                      platform.clip.item.gotoAndPlay
                        → ("Display");
```

```
35              display.num2 = Number(display.num2)+1;
36              playSound("collect");
37              if (--platform.containerCounter<=0) {
38                  platform.container = false;
39              }
40          }
41      } else if (type != "cloud" &&
        → hero.tempx+hero.width>px &&
        → hero.tempx+hero.width<px+pw) {
42          //hit the left side of the platform
43          if (!hero.wasCrouching) {
44              var newx = px-hero.width;
45              bounceOffOfPlatform(newx);
46          } else {
47              hero.crouch();
48              var crouchMove = true;
49              var left = true;
50          }
51      } else if (type != "cloud" && hero.tempx>px
        → && hero.tempx<px+pw) {
52          //hit the right side of the platform
53          if (!hero.wasCrouching) {
54              var newx = px+pw;
55              bounceOffOfPlatform(newx);
56          } else {
57              hero.crouch();
58              var crouchMove = true;
59              var left = false;
60          }
61      }
62  }
63  }
64  }
65  hero.onPlatform = onPlatform;
66  if (crouchMove) {
67      if (left) {
68          hero.tempx -= hero.pushSpeed;
69      } else {
70          hero.tempx += hero.pushSpeed;
```

```
71          }
72      }
73      if (!hero.onPlatform && oldOnPlatform) {
74          //he just left a platform
75          hero.inAir = true;
76      }
77  }
```

First we store the current state of the onPlatform property of the hero object as oldOnPlatform. We use this at the end of the function to determine if the hero has just left a platform without jumping. Next we set the local variable onPlatform to false. We assume that the hero is not on a platform. Then, through the loops and conditions that follow we determine if the hero is actually on a platform.

In line 4 we initiate a for loop that loops through the platform objects in the column array (which stores the objects that represent the platforms). In line 5 we create a reference to the current object in the column array called platform. Then we create some local variables to store some of the properties of this platform (lines 6–10).

In line 11 we do something that may not be immediately obvious. If you remember the description of frame-dependent collision detection in Chapter 5, "Collision Detection," it is like a snapshot in time. If one or both of the objects are moving fast enough, then they can pass through each other without being detected. That is a possibility in this game, too. In fact, I ran into that issue while programming this game and had to implement the technique I'm about to describe. Here is what happens in line 11: We take the position where the hero was on the last frame and the position where he is on this frame, and then divide that distance into steps. We then run through the collision-detection routines on each step. If a collision is found, we stop the looping. Most of the time, you'll find that one loop is enough. It is just when the hero is moving over a certain speed that we need to use more than one loop. So the property that controls the number of loops, game.totalIterations, is controlled in every frame by the createTempPosition() function. That function changes game.totalIterations based on the hero's speed.

If the condition in line 14 is met, then the hero is colliding with a platform. At that point, more conditions must be checked to determine exactly what needs to be done with the hero. If the condition in line 16 is met, then the hero has landed on top of the platform. We also check to see if this platform is one that moves, and if it is, we move the hero a little bit.

In line 29 we check to see if the hero hit the platform from underneath. If he did, then we also check to see if that platform contains a collectable item, and if so, then we display it.

In lines 41 and 51 we check to see if the hero is colliding with either the left or right side of the platform. If he is, and he wasn't just crouching, we move him to the boundary of the platform. If he was just crouching, we keep him crouching and slide him to one side or the other (see lines 66–72).

If the condition in line 73 is met, the hero has just left the platform without jumping. We then set the hero.inAir property to true.

baddyDetection()

This function is called in every frame. It determines whether there is a collision between the hero and an enemy, by using the hitTest() method of the movie-clip object.

```
1   function baddyDetection() {
2       for (var i = 0; i<game.baddies.length; ++i) {
3           var baddy = game.baddies[i];
4           if (hero.clip.hitTest(baddy.clip.hitArea)) {
5               if (hero.ymov>game.gravity) {
6                   //baddy squashed
7                   hero.tempy = hero.y;
8                   hero.ymov = -10;
9                   killBaddy(baddy, i);
10              } else {
11                  //hero died
12                  hero.ymov = -20;
13                  hero.xmov = 15;
14                  hero.die();
15              }
16          }
17      }
18  }
```

Each enemy is represented by an object. These objects are stored in the baddies array. In this function we loop through the baddies array, checking for a collision between the hero and each enemy. If the condition in line 4 is met, there has been a collision between the hero and an enemy. But then we have to determine who dies—the hero or the enemy. If the hero's *y* velocity is greater than that of gravity (that is, the hero is falling and not standing), then the enemy dies. Otherwise, the hero dies. That's all there is to this detection!

collectableDetect()

In every frame, we call this function and loop through the list of collectable items on the screen to determine if the hero is touching any of them:

```
1   function collectableDetect() {
2       for (var i = 0; i<game.collectables.length; ++i) {
3           var ob = game.collectables[i];
4           if (hero.clip.hitTest(ob.clip) && !ob.captured) {
5               display.num2 = Number(display.num2)+1;
6               playSound("collect");
7               ob.captured = true;
8               ob.clip.gotoAndPlay("Capture");
9           }
10      }
11  }
```

The collectable items are stored in an array called collectables. We loop through this array and use hitTest() to determine whether a collision is occurring. If the hero is colliding with a collectable, then the item should be collected, and so we animate the item and play a sound.

POSSIBLE GAME ENHANCEMENTS

With a game like this, there are many opportunities for improvements. Your own imagination is the best source for enhancing this game, but here are a few ideas for making this platform engine more interesting, or just better:

- Add more types of enemies.

- Create a boss at the end of each level that the hero must find a way to defeat.

- Come up with a story line that can get the game player more involved. Give the hero some sort of motive for what he is doing. Why is he collecting things? Why is he killing enemies? Where is he going?

- Create more graphics for different types of platforms.

- Add angled slope areas that the hero can slide down.

- Give the hero some sort of gimmicky behavior, such as flipping, super speed, or a special type of weapon (like shooting fire).

- Spice up the visuals with several different types of backgrounds.

- Add another level of visual parallax. (For example, add something between the background and the foreground, which scroll at different rates.)

- Create more types of collectable items, including rare ones.

- Make the code more efficient. Currently the game code has one major disadvantage—it is checking for collisions between objects that are not even close to it! You can use the tile-based approach or some other type of "zoning" that will allow you to only have to detect collisions between objects that are in close proximity.

- Enhance the level editor so that it can load in levels and then let you edit them that way so that you don't have to build from scratch every time.

- Enhance the level editor by including a "test" button or other method for getting to a test state. You can easily write the XML document to a shared object and launch the game file to automatically test the level.

POINTS TO REMEMBER

- Any platform object can be either solid or a "cloud," and can move.

- Level editors are a must in a game like this. Without one, you will spend too much time hand-typing XML files.

- This game is coded in a very OO way. This allows for the game to be easily extensible (meaning that you can add features without much trouble).

- The background image moves independently of the foreground (the overlay movie-clip instance). The hero is contained within the overlay instance.

- We use an iterative-stepping technique to work around Flash's snapshot frame-dependent collision-detection nature. Using this technique, we look at where the hero was in the last frame and where he is now, and then divide this distance into steps.

- This game can be easily enhanced with any number of creative features.

CHAPTER 16

PINBALL

IT'S WILD, IT'S FLASHY, IT'S GOT REALLY ANNOYING SOUND EFFECTS, IT'S pinball! In this chapter we dissect a basic version of this very popular game. You may want to review the chapters on collision detection and collision reactions, because this chapter uses a lot of both. We will focus on the construction of the game, not the techniques used for collision detection and reaction.

Prerequisites

Chapter 5, "Collision Detection." Pinball involves a lot of objects with which a ball can collide. Understanding collision detection is imperative to understanding this game.

Chapter 6, "Collision Reactions." In this chapter we are going to use wall collisions, ball-line collisions, and ball-ball collisions. To fully understand the game, you need to understand how the ball reacts to these collisions.

Chapter 10, "Using a High Score List." In pinball we are going to use the High Score List movie clip, covered in that chapter. Understanding how a high score list works is not important for understanding pinball, but it is for understanding all aspects of the game file.

GAME OVERVIEW

Before discussing the game play and the rules, let's take a look at the pinball table and the terminology associated with its various parts.

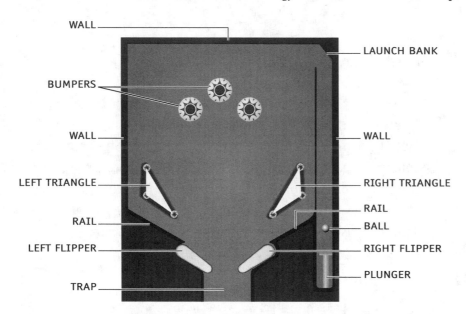

When a game begins, the ball falls from above the plunger down onto it, bounces a few times, and slowly comes to rest. When the ball has stopped bouncing, you can retract the plunger by holding down the spacebar. When you release the spacebar, the plunger accelerates toward the ball, hitting it upward. The ball bounces off the launch bank and into the main table area. The ball's trajectory is affected by its collision with any number of objects. If the ball approaches the trap, you can attempt to deflect the ball away using the flippers. The left flipper is controlled by the Shift key, and the right flipper is controlled by the Ctrl key (Windows) or Command key (Macintosh).

In this basic game of pinball, the object is to score as many points as possible. Points are gained by bouncing the ball off the bumpers, the flippers, and the inner edges of the left and right triangles. Here's how points (and bonus points) are awarded in this game:

TABLE 16.1 **The Pinball Award System**

When you do this:	You get:
Hit the ball with a flipper	150 points
Bounce the ball off a bumper	300 points
Bounce the ball off the inner edge of a triangle	200 points
Earn 2000 points	500-point bonus Special sound played
Earn 19,000 points	1000-point bonus Special sound played An extra ball

One other thing to note about this version of pinball is that it has a high score list. This game uses the High Score List movie clip developed in Chapter 10, "Using a High Score List." There have been no ActionScript modifications to that movie clip, only slight graphic changes.

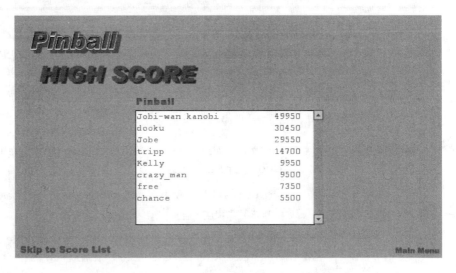

The Skinny on Pinball

Before building any game I didn't invent, I research it. I try to get information on the specific rules and terminology, and in some cases the dimensions, weights, or colors of the objects used. I found that I—probably like many of the readers of this book—had a misconception about pinball. I thought it was simply a game in which you launch a ball and then try not to let it fall down the trap by hitting it with the flippers (and making a lot of lights blink along the way). Well, it turns out that pinball games are much more complicated than that. The goal of the game is to get the highest score possible, but you knew that much. In a full game of pinball (not the one created in this chapter), there are many gadgets, slides, holes, and sensors that the ball can interact with. The object is to send the ball into various locations on the table in a certain order. If you do this correctly, you are rewarded with a lot of points and possibly extra balls. Also, on some tables, by hitting a certain sequence you can open up other secret areas of the table that were previously inaccessible. The basic game in this chapter plays more like the average person's expectation of pinball: You smack the ball around to gain points. That's as complicated as the game play gets.

GAME CODE

Pinball uses a lot of code you've already seen in earlier chapters. The game requires frame-independent collision detection for ball-ball and ball-line collisions, and employs the appropriate collision-reaction code for both of these. The bulk of the code you haven't yet seen, and may not be able to easily understand at first glance, is the code that handles the following functions:

- Creating the table geography in memory—specifically, the angled lines (including the flippers)

- Detecting if a collision has occurred between the ball and a flipper at the instant a flipper is flipped

In this section we will discuss several pieces of the game, including the two functions listed above. It is assumed that you can easily follow the remaining ActionScript, such as the functions that play sounds, increment the score, detect collisions, and capture key presses.

Before we look at the ActionScript, let's take a quick look around the pinball.fla file in the Chapter16 directory. This file has a frame setup that's similar to the one used in all the other games in this book. The game itself is on the Game frame in the movie clip called game. Move to the Game frame label and double-click the movie clip to view the contents. There are three layers in this movie clip: Actions, Assets, and Table. The Table layer contains the background graphics for the pinball table. The Assets layer contains all of the other assets, including game graphics, menu button, and score text field. The Actions layer contains the ActionScript used to make this game.

ActionScript Not Found in a Function

The ActionScript in this frame is contained mostly within functions. However, there is also an area where we initialize some variables, objects, and arrays that is not within a function. This ActionScript is used to initialize the variables, arrays, and objects that only need to be created one time. There is also an onEnterFrame event, but we will discuss that in the next section. Here is this loose ActionScript:

```
1  inPlay = false;
2  soundOn = true;
3  makeLinesVisible = false;
4  left_tester._visible = false;
5  right_tester._visible = false;
6  ball = {};
7  ball.clip = this.pb;
8  ball.x = ball.clip._x;
9  ball.y = ball.clip._y;
10 ball.radius = ball.clip._width/2;
11 ball.mass = 1;
12 ball.xmov = 0;
13 ball.ymov = 0;
14 airDecay = .99;
15 gravity = .2;
16 depth = 100;
17 runPatch = 0;
18 bumperArray = [];
19 buildMap();
```

First, a variable called inPlay is set with a value of false. This means that the game has not yet begun. When the game is started, inPlay will be set to true. When the game is over, it will again be set to false. Next, we set the soundOn variable to true. This variable, as you know by now, controls the playing of sounds. If soundOn is false, then no sounds will be played. In line 3 we set a variable called makeLinesVisible with a value of false. This is used for testing, debugging, and graphics-placement reasons. When it's true, the lines that are drawn in memory (the flippers, rails, and launch bank) are shown on the screen. When it's false, these lines are not shown. I set this variable to true when developing this game (before I had the graphics from an artist) so that I could see the physical borders for all of the objects. After I placed the flippers, triangles, rails, walls, and launch bank, I took a screen shot and sent this wireframe of the pinball game to the graphic artist. He created assets that I could place over the wireframe. Once I verified that the placement of the graphics was good, I set the makeLinesVisible variable to false so that all we see are the intended pinball graphics. As you may remember from the collision-detection and collision-reactions chapters (which detailed the development of the createLine() function), each line is contained within a dynamically created movie clip. These lines are the only dynamically created movie clips in this game.

In lines 4 and 5 we set the visibility of two movie clips to false. You can see these two white movie clips on the stage, above (that is, on top of) the left and right triangles. Most of the time we have what appears to be perfect collision detection and collision reactions. However, there can be odd behavior when a ball collides at an interface between two lines, so when the ball collides with any of the three vertices of either of the two triangles, the ball can be sent *into* the triangle instead of away from it. Therefore, we include these movie clips and use hitTest() as a fail-safe so that the ball never has to get stuck inside. (For the very same reason, we will use a similar patch() function in Chapter 18, "9-Ball.") Future revisions of this game will hopefully include a better solution to this edge-effect problem.

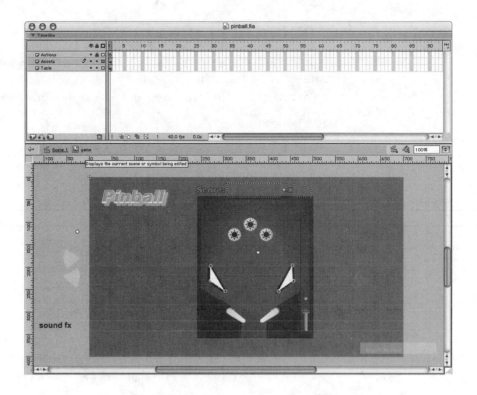

In lines 6–13 we create an object called ball to store information about the ball. The instance name of the ball movie clip is pb. Next, we create a variable called airDecay. This controls the percentage of slowdown of the ball as it moves along the table. The gravity variable is set next, with a value of .2. In every frame, .2 will be added to the ball's *y* velocity. In line 16 we create a variable called depth with a value of 100. This gives us a starting depth for placing movie clips dynamically. The only movie clips we will be adding dynamically are the lines that can either be visible or invisible. In line 17 we set runPatch to 0, to start its counter. As in the 9-ball game, we don't execute the patch() function every frame, but rather once every 20 or 30 frames. We then create an array called bumperArray. This array will be used to store objects that represent the several bumpers on the screen. We will see more of this in the addBumper() function. Finally, buildMap() is called. This function places the walls and objects in memory and then starts the game.

The onEnterFrame Event

At the bottom of the Actions frame is an onEnterFrame event. This event handles calculation of the ball's new position, collision detection, capturing of key presses, and rendering of the ball's new position onscreen.

Here is the function:

```
1   this.onEnterFrame = function() {
2       //now=getTimer();
3       if (inPlay) {
4           if (animate) {
5               animatePlunger();
6           }
7           collided = false;
8           getTempPositions();
9           captureKeys();
10          if (!collided) {
11              bankCollisionDetect();
12          }
13          if (!collided) {
14              bumperCollisionDetect();
15          }
16          checkForWalls();
17          render();
18          patch();
19      }
20      //trace(getTimer()-now);
21  };
```

First, notice the two lines of ActionScript that have been commented out—lines 2 and 20. They serve the same purpose as the ones seen in the 9-ball game. When uncommented, they trace the amount of time spent on each frame. With this trace you can better analyze the efficiency of your ActionScript. If too much time is being spent on each frame, then you know that you may have to simplify the ActionScript or possibly remove a few objects from the stage.

The bulk of the ActionScript in this event is contained within a large if statement that simply checks to see if inPlay is true. If it is true, the actions within are executed; otherwise, nothing happens. In lines 4–6 we check to see if a variable called animate is true. If it is, that means we are supposed to be animating the plunger. When the plunger has reached its destination (when being fired), then animate is set to false. Next, we set a variable called collided to false. When a collision with a line, circle, or flipper is detected, we then set collided to true. We want to avoid multiple collision detections and reactions in one frame, and by setting this variable we can do that. In line 8 we set the temporary position of the ball in memory by calling getTempPositions(). In the next line we capture key presses by calling captureKeys(). This function checks to see if the Ctrl key (Windows), Command key (Mac), Shift key, or spacebar is pressed. You will see more about this function later.

In the final lines of the onEnterFrame event, we call collision-detection routines (if no collision has yet been found), check for wall collisions, and then call the patch() function.

buildMap()

This function places all of the objects and defines the walls in memory. What is done in this function is crucial—and also confusing at times. In this function, we

- Initialize some variables that will be used throughout the game, such as score and numBalls.

- Create variables that store the positions of the pinball table's four walls.

- Create the several lines in memory needed for the flippers, rails, triangles, and launch bank. (This is the confusing part.)

- Add bumpers to the map in memory.

Here is the function:

```
1   function buildMap() {
2       numBalls = 3;
3       score = 0;
4       lastScoreLevel = 0;
5       lastBigScoreLevel = 0;
6       startx = 250;
7       starty = 50;
```

```
8    width = 225;
9    height = 300;
10   var heightFromBottom = 100;
11   //left triangle
12   var diagLength = 70;
13   var diagAng = 60;
14   var cosAng = Math.cos(diagAng*Math.PI/180);
15   var sinAng = Math.sin(diagAng*Math.PI/180);
16   //left triangle, inner wall
17   var x = startx+20;
18   var y = starty+height-heightFromBottom-55;
19   l = createLine(x, y, diagAng, diagLength, 2,
     → left_triangle, "laser");
20   var sx = l.x2;
21   var sy = l.y2;
22   //left triangle, left wall
23   var x = l.x1;
24   var y = l.y1+diagLength*sinAng*.6;
25   l = createLine(x, y, 269, diagLength*sinAng*.6, 1);
26   //left triangle, bottom wall
27   var ex = l.x1;
28   var ey = l.y1;
29   var ang = Math.atan2(ey-sy, ex-sx)*180/Math.PI;
30   l = createLine(sx, sy, ang, 42, 1);
31   //right triangle
32   var diagAng = 300;
33   var cosAng = Math.cos(diagAng*Math.PI/180);
34   var sinAng = Math.sin(diagAng*Math.PI/180);
35   //right triangle, inner wall
36   var x = startx+width-diagLength*cosAng-20;
37   var y = starty+height-heightFromBottom-
     → diagLength*sinAng-55;
38   l = createLine(x, y, diagAng, diagLength, 2,
     → right_triangle, "laser");
39   var sx = l.x1;
40   var sy = l.y1;
41   //right triangle, right wall
42   var x = l.x2;
```

```
43    var y = l.y2-diagLength*sinAng*.6;
44    l = createLine(x, y, 90.1, diagLength*sinAng*.6, 1);
45    //right triangle, bottom wall
46    var ex = l.x1;
47    var ey = l.y1;
48    var ang = Math.atan2(ey-sy, ex-sx)*180/Math.PI;
49    l = createLine(ex, ey, ang+180, 42, 1);
50    //launch bank
51    launchBank = createLine(startx+width+20, starty+20, 230,
    → 30, 1);
52    //flippers and rails
53    var length = 80;
54    var angle = 30;
55    var xstep = length*Math.cos(angle*Math.PI/180);
56    var ystep = length*Math.sin(angle*Math.PI/180);
57    l = createLine(startx, starty+height-heightFromBottom,
    → angle, length, .5);
58    createFlipper(l.x2, l.y2, "left");
59    var x = startx+width-xstep;
60    var y = starty+height-heightFromBottom+ystep;
61    l = createLine(x, y, 360-angle, length, .5);
62    createFlipper(l.x1, l.y1, "right");
63    //bumpers
64    bounciness = 10;
65    addBumper(tempB1._x, tempB1._y, tempB1._width/2,
    → bounciness, tempB1);
66    addBumper(tempB2._x, tempB2._y, tempB2._width/2,
    → bounciness, tempB2);
67    addBumper(tempB3._x, tempB3._y, tempB3._width/2,
    → bounciness, tempB3);
68    addBumper(tempB4._x, tempB4._y, tempB4._width/2, 2,
    → tempB4, true);
69    addBumper(tempB5._x, tempB5._y, tempB5._width/2, 2,
    → tempB5, true);
70    addBumper(tempB6._x, tempB6._y, tempB6._width/2, 2,
    → tempB6, true);
71    addBumper(tempB7._x, tempB7._y, tempB7._width/2, 2,
    → tempB7, true);
```

```
72    addBumper(tempB8._x, tempB8._y, tempB8._width/2, 2,
      → tempB8, true);
73    addBumper(tempB9._x, tempB9._y, tempB9._width/2, 2,
      → tempB9, true);
74    --numBalls;
75    initializeShot();
76  }
```

First the numBalls variable is set. This stores the number of balls you start with when a new game begins. (When you reach certain score amounts, you are awarded another ball by the incrementing of this variable.) Then the score is set to 0, since when you first begin the game, you have not yet earned any points. The next two variables—lastScoreLevel and lastBigScoreLevel—are used to measure relative score. They start at 0. Whenever the score is incremented (using the addScore() function), we check to see if the score is a certain amount of points higher than each of these two variables. If it is, then we do … something, like award an extra ball or extra points. Then, for whichever of the two variables' values was reached, we set that variable to the current score, so the counting starts over again. The end result is that a new ball can be awarded every, say, 19,000 points, and some other bonus is given at, say, every 2000 points.

The next four variables (lines 6–9), startx, starty, width, and height, define the table's dimensions. They give the position of the upper-right corner of the table and then the table's width and height. The variable heightFromBottom is the amount of space we want to have between the bottom of the table and the top of the rails. That variable is used as a relative starting place to add the triangles, rails, and flippers.

Now we start adding lines in memory. In lines 11–30 we add the left triangle to the table. First we set a variable called diagLength, which is the length of the side of the triangle that faces toward the middle of the table (the right side). Next we set diagAng, which is the angle that this side of the triangle should be, with respect to the x-axis. This angle is 60°. We then calculate and store the values of the sine and cosine of this angle. Those values will be used for creating the other sides of the triangle. In lines 17 and 18 we store the x and y starting positions of this line we are about to create. The y position is calculated by finding the y position of the bottom wall (starty + height) and stepping back by heightFromBottom, and then stepping back again by an arbitrary amount of 55. (I chose the number 55 because to my eye it made the triangle look better.) The x position is found by starting with the left wall (startx) and moving to the right a little bit—say, 20.

In line 19 we create the line by calling the createLine() function. This is the same function used in Chapter 5, "Collision Detection," and Chapter 6, "Collision Reactions," to create lines, and is used here to create several lines on the pinball table. We have modified it slightly to do things like play a sound when a line is hit. We will not look at those differences in this chapter; they are simple and can be understood at a glance. But let's look at the parameters of the createLine() function on line 19. Here are all seven of them, in order:

x—The starting x position of the line.

y—The starting y position of the line.

angle—The angle at which the line will point (measured from the x-axis).

length—The length of the line.

decay—A normalized factor, showing the percentage by which the ball's speed will be changed when a collision occurs. This is usually between 0 and 1. A value of .5 would mean a 50 percent decrease in speed. However, on the inner triangle lines, we want there to be a dramatic bounce, so we use a value of 2, which sends the ball away at 200 percent of its collision speed.

clip—This is an optional parameter for playing a movie clip when this line is collided with. For most lines in this game, this parameter will be left out. (When the ball collides with the inner line of the triangle, we want the animation to play, so we include a reference to the appropriate movie clip. But we don't want any animation when the ball collides with either of the other two sides of the triangle, so we don't give the clip an instance name when creating those lines.)

sound—This also is an optional parameter. It specifies the name of a sound you want to play when a line is collided with. In this game, this parameter will only be used for the two inner-triangle lines. When the line is collided with, it calls the playSound() function and passes in the string name of the sound, which is then played in the soundfx movie clip.

You should also notice in line 19 that when using the createLine() function, we also set a reference, called l, to the object that represents that line. That way we can easily access values on that object while creating the next line. In the lines that follow (all the way to line 51) we create the rest of the lines in this triangle and also those in the right triangle and in the launch bank. Notice that in line 51, when creating the launch bank, we set a reference called launchBank to the object that represents it. We do this because after we launch the ball, we disable the launchBank so that we don't have to (needlessly) look for collisions with it—the ball should not collide with it. When it's time for the ball to be launched again, launchBank is turned back on.

In lines 53–62 we add the two rails and flippers. To create a flipper, we must execute the createFlipper() function and pass in the *x* and *y* starting positions for it, as well as which flipper it will be (left or right). We will look at the createFlipper() function next.

Next, in lines 64–73, we add nine bumpers to the table. At first glance, you will notice only three bumpers. But in the quest to keep the pinball from entering the left and right triangles (due to edge effects), we add a tiny bumper on each of the two triangles' vertices—that accounts for six bumpers to add to the three that you see at regular size on the stage. The three at the top of the stage are named tempB1, tempB2, and tempB3. The others are named tempB4 through tempB9. We add a bumper in memory by calling the addBumper() function.

Like the createLine() function, the addBumper() function has a lot of parameters. Here they are (in order):

x—The *x* position of the center of the bumper.

y—The *y* position of the center of the bumper.

radius—The radius of the bumper.

reflection speed—The speed at which the ball should be deflected away from the bumper. The speed at which the ball was moving when it collided with the bumper has no effect on the reflection speed. The angle of the reaction does depend on the incident angle, but not the incident speed.

clip—This is a reference to the bumper movie clip. It is used to play an animation (in our case, only for the three bumper instances on our table that we have chosen to animate).

turn invisible—This is an optional parameter. If `true`, then the bumper is turned invisible. This is useful for the tiny bumpers that are on the left and right triangles. If left blank, or if `false`, then the bumpers are left visible.

In line 74 we decrement the `numBalls` variable. This game player will get the correct number of balls; it is just that the ball that is currently on the plunger is not counted in the `numBalls` variable. We decrement this variable because we are adding the ball to the table in the next line, `initializeShot()`. From now until the end of the game, the `numBalls` variable will only be decremented when a ball falls down the trap.

createFlipper()

This function takes *x* and *y* positions passed in, as well as a direction (either left or right), and creates a flipper in memory at that position. The ActionScript is straightforward enough that I don't think you need to see it dissected line by line. But it's worth noting how we detect collisions with the flipper. There are three possible states of the flipper: down, moving up, and up. When the flipper is down or up, there is a line in memory (exactly like all of the other lines we've created) that checks for collisions. At the instant that the flipper is flipping up, we disable the lines in memory that describe the flipper and do something a little tricky: We use a wedge-shaped movie clip and perform a `hitTest()` between the ball and the wedge. If the `hitTest()` is `true`, then we calculate a realistic reaction. As you know if you've read the collision-detection chapter, `hitTest()` is not good for all that many things. In this case it is only barely acceptable. (And just as soon as I have the time, I will create a frame-independent ball-rotating line collision-detection routine.)

When creating the left and right flippers, this function also creates references to the line objects that represent each flipper, `leftFlipper` and `rightFlipper`. These references can be used by other functions to read properties of the flipper (such as its angle) or to change the flipper's properties, such as during a flip action.

Keeping Track of Weaknesses

So far, you have learned of two weaknesses in this game. It is important to remember what they are if you are going to try to make this a better game.

- At the interface between two lines, such as the vertices of the triangles, there are odd edge effects. These can cause the ball to do things we don't expect or want.

- During a flip of the flipper we use hitTest(), along with a wedge-shaped movie clip, to detect if a collision is taking place.

initializeShot()

This function is called at the end of the buildMap() function, and also whenever the ball falls down the trap. It is used to enable the launch bank, initialize some variables, and position the pinball above the plunger. When this function is executed, the pinball is ready to be launched.

```
1   function initializeShot() {
2       inPlay = true;
3       launchBank.enabled = true;
4       launchBank.counter = 0;
5       rightWallOn = false;
6       shotYet = false;
7       ball.xmov = 0;
8       ball.ymov = 0;
9       ball.x = cradle._x;
10      ball.y = cradle._y-100;
11      ball.tempx = ball.x;
12      ball.tempy = ball.y;
13      shotPower = 0;
14      shotMax = 30;
15  }
```

In line 2 we set inPlay to true. This is so that the collision-detection routines get executed (think back to the onEnterFrame event). We then enable the launch bank. Remember that we set a reference to the launch bank in line 51 of the buildMap() function? Well, this is why! This way, we can easily enable or disable it.

One thing to note about disabling a line is that it re-enables itself when its counter property reaches 5. This was added to give the ball enough time (after a flipper collision) to move out of the way before looking for more collisions with that same flipper. Also notice that there are actually two right walls—the far-right wall (to the right of the plunger) and the right wall that is at the edge of the main part of the table. This inner right wall is what we actually consider the right wall. In line 5 we set rightWallOn to false. When it's false, we do not detect collisions with this wall. This is so that we can let the pinball pass through it when launched. After the pinball has passed through it, we set rightWallOn to true. This is done from the checkForWalls() function.

Next we set a variable called shotYet to false. This variable is set to true as soon as the ball bounces off the launch bank. When it's true, the plunger will not respond if you press the spacebar. In lines 7–12 we set the initial velocity of the ball to 0 and position the ball above the plunger. We then set the power range for the plunger. Its minimum power is 0 and maximum is 30. This refers to the initial speed of the ball as it is launched.

flip()

This function accepts two parameters, which and dir. The which parameter tells which of the flippers to flip, either left or right. The dir parameter specifies whether to flip up or down.

What this function does is simple. When a flipper is moving either up or down, the function must redraw the flipper line in memory so that the ball will be able to react to the flipper's new rotation. Also, when it's flipping up or down, this function tells the graphic asset that represents the flipper on the stage (either left_paddle or right_paddle) to go to the correct frame to display the flipper at the proper rotation. Further, when it's flipping up, this function also runs the checkCollision() function, which checks to see if the ball is currently colliding with the wedge-shaped movie clip. If it is, then a reaction is calculated.

checkCollision()

When this function is called, it simply checks for a collision between the ball and the wedge-shaped movie clip, using hitTest(). If the collision is occurring, then the following steps happen:

1. The angle of the imaginary line formed between the stationary rotating point of the flipper and the ball's current position is found using Math.atan2(). This is the angle that the flipper would have been at when a collision occurred.

2. The angle at which the ball was moving is used with the angle found in step 1 to find the deflection angle for the ball.

3. This deflection angle is run through a simple filter. Through testing, I found that sometimes the ball came off the flipper moving at a horizontal angle straight toward the other flipper or at an extreme angle toward the wall. So there are some if statements to check to see if the angle is within a certain range. If the angle is out of that accepted range, then the value of the angle gets changed.

4. The speed at which the ball gets deflected depends on the ball's distance from the flipper's stationary rotation point. If the ball collides at the far end of the flipper, then it should fly away at a maximum speed. If the ball is hit really close to the rotation point, then it should fly away at a lower speed.

I mentioned earlier in the section that this function also disables the flipper when a collision is detected. We disable the flipper so that on the same frame or the next frame, the flipper line itself does not collide with the ball. The flipper will enable itself after just a few frames.

POSSIBLE GAME ENHANCEMENTS

There are so many possible additions to this game that it's hard to even find a starting place. Here are just a few things that can greatly improve it:

- Resolve the edge-effect issue. That is, of course, easier said than done.

- Develop a frame-independent rotating line-ball collision-detection routine for the flippers. This is another thing easier said than done, but it is possible and not as difficult as it might seem.

- Add in the "order of events" aspect of the typical game of pinball that we did not attempt here. For a complete game you would definitely need to add that feature. (See "The Skinny on Pinball" early in this chapter for a discussion of the general procedures and characteristics of a full game of pinball, including the order of events.)

- Add in other typical pinball gadgets such as sunken holes, two sets of flippers, and tiles that can be knocked over.

- Tilt the game to a slight 3D perspective to give it the illusion of being more real. Most of the better computer pinball games are rendered that way.

- Add in a ramp to a second level. The ball can travel up the ramp and then score points by hitting objects on the second level.

- Find or make some crazy sounds. Just about anything goes in pinball, so you should not have much trouble finding some great sounds to add to this game.

- Add lots of blinking lights and flashy animations to the table. In a game of pinball, the table is almost never static. There is always something blinking.

- Add the ability to have more than one ball on the table at a time. This is another addition that would not be that difficult.

POINTS TO REMEMBER

- Understanding collision detection (specifically wall, ball-line, and ball-ball collisions) is imperative to understanding this game.

- While the goal of the game is to get the highest score possible, in a full game of pinball the object is to send the ball into various locations on the table in a certain order.

- Using the `createLine()` function, we draw lines in memory with which the ball can react.

- At the interface between two lines, such as the vertices of the triangles, there are odd edge effects, which cause undesirable and unexpected behaviors in the ball's motion. We have used certain tricks in this game to compensate for these odd behaviors. For example, we use invisible movie clips over visible graphic elements to help us deflect these edge-effect problems.

- As in the 9-ball game, we don't execute the `patch()` function every frame, but rather once every 20 or 30 frames, to check on the edge-effect problem mentioned directly above.

- The critical `buildMap()` function places all of the objects and defines the walls in memory.

- The fairly straightforward `createLine()` function has been modified to include the ability to play a sound when the ball hits a line.

- Disabling objects that are clearly not needed at certain times—for instance, collision detection on the launch bank when the game ball is already in play on the table—is a good way to speed up and streamline the game.

- You can use small and/or invisible bumpers to limit the ball's movements (around objects it shouldn't enter, for example), using the `addBumper()` function.

- The limited-use function `hitTest()` can be used to determine a collision between the ball and the flipper. We have used a wedge-shaped movie clip with `hitTest()` to determine these collisions.

- There are a lot of improvements—some simple, some not—you could make to this game!

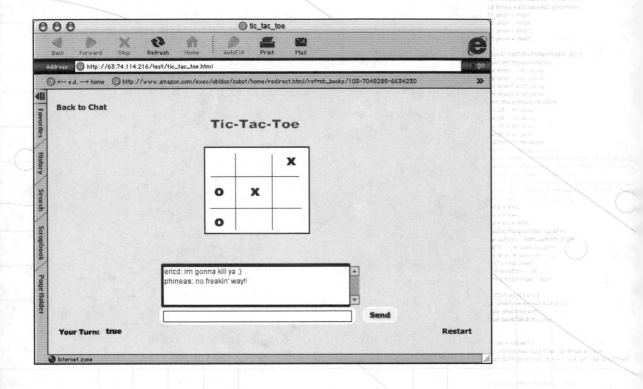

CHAPTER 17

TIC-TAC-TOE: YOUR FIRST MULTIPLAYER GAME

THIS CHAPTER IS INTENDED TO SHOW YOU HOW TO CREATE A VERY simple multiplayer game using the commonly known contest of tic-tac-toe. I have chosen a very simple game so that we can focus on the multiplayer concepts and multiplayer code involved without having to deal with the immense code usually found in more challenging games (like 9-ball). By the end of this chapter you should have a pretty good understanding of how to use the ElectroServerAS object effectively for multiplayer games.

Prerequisites

Chapter 13, "Dissecting a Chat"

Appendix C, "The ElectroServerAS Object." Use this as a quick reference for definitions of the methods and properties of the ElectroServerAS object.

Appendix B, "Multiuser Servers." Read this appendix to gain an understanding of multiuser servers, and specifically to understand ElectroServer and its capabilities, and how to install it. You need to know how to start ElectroServer so that the game file in this chapter can connect to it.

GAME OVERVIEW

You are probably familiar with the common game of tic-tac-toe. For this chapter I have created a version of the game that can be played by two people over the Internet (or a network). As you probably already know—and should, by now!—a game that can be played in this way is called a *multiplayer game*. Tic-tac-toe is played on a simple board (or a piece of paper) that displays a 3-by-3 grid. Each player has a letter that he or she can place in a grid space; this is usually either *X* or *O*. After a move is made, the other player can then make a move. The winner of the game is the first person to establish a horizontal, vertical, or diagonal straight line of three of the same letters. If the board is filled and there has been no match, then there is no winner of this game but the game is over.

Here is how a game of multiplayer tic-tac-toe would typically be initiated and played. There are at least two people in a room in the chat. One of them decides to challenge another. The challenge is made by clicking the user name in the user list. Let's call the challenger Player 1. The person who was challenged, Player 2, can then either accept or decline the challenge. If Player 2 accepts the challenge, then both players are immediately taken to the game screen.

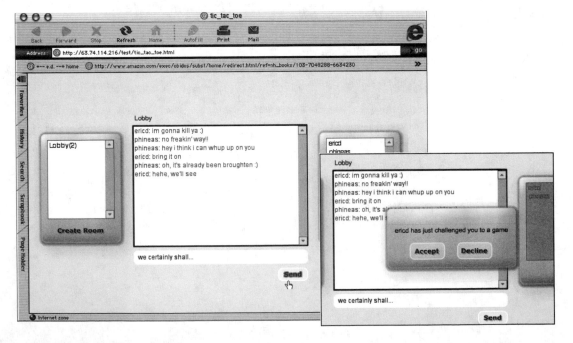

When both players get to the game screen, they are prompted with a pop-up box that tells them the game has begun. Player 1 is informed that it is his turn, and Player 2 is informed that it is her opponent's turn. To move, Player 1 must click any of the nine tiles. When he does this, the letter X appears in that spot, and Player 2 is informed of this move. It is then Player 2's turn, and she can click any of the remaining eight tiles to add an O. The first player to establish three of his or her own letters in a vertical, horizontal, or diagonal straight line wins the game. When the game has been won, a pop-up box displays a little message telling the players if they have won or lost the game. If the board is filled and no one has won, then the game ends in a tie. In this event, a pop-up window tells both players that the game has no winner. Either player can restart the game by clicking the Restart button at the bottom-right part of the screen. When a game is restarted, the board is reset so that it contains no letters, and Player 1 gets the first turn again.

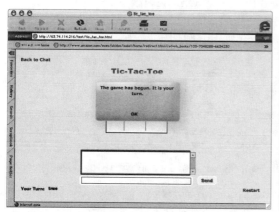

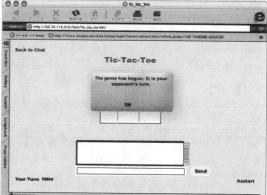

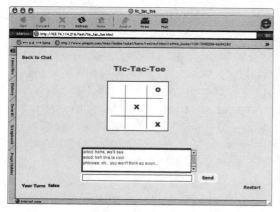

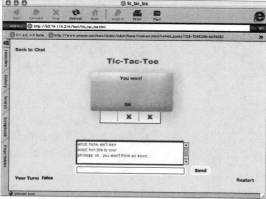

There is a chat window on the screen so the players can still chat. One of the toughest things to do in a multiplayer game is to find room on the stage for the chat window. In tic-tac-toe this is not an issue, but in many games it can cause layout problems.

The Flash file used for this game is called tic_tac_toe.fla and is located in the Chapter17 directory on the CD. This file was created by taking the chat_full_featured.fla file from Chapter 13, "Dissecting a Chat," and creating the tic-tac-toe game on the Game frame label. Everything up to the Game label was discussed in Chapter 13, so we will not cover it again here but will skip right to the ActionScript and movie clips that are on the Game label. In the next section we talk about the multiplayer actions needed to make this game work. Then, in the final section, we go over the ActionScript that controls the game's rules and interactivity.

To test this game, you need to start ElectroServer on port 1024. This game file is configured to connect to localhost, which is the same as the IP address 127.0.0.1, on port 1024. Both of these properties can be changed easily in the file's Chat System frame if needed.

Turn-Based Games vs. Real-Time Games

Tic-tac-toe and all of the multiplayer games in this book are *turn-based*. In a turn-based game, only one player at a time can make a move. In chess, for example, Player 1 makes a move. Then Player 2 makes a move. At no time can both Player 1 and Player 2 make a move at the same time.

A *real-time* game is one in which both players can make moves simultaneously. A good example of this is a Mortal Kombat–style fighting game. Both players can move, jump, kick, punch, and eviscerate simultaneously. This type of game is not impossible with Flash, but it is very difficult for several reasons. To name one, network latency is a big issue. Let's say that at time1, Player 1 punches Player 2. At precisely that instant, out there on his own computer, Player 2 moves out of the way. Due to network latency, the information about Player 2's moving has not yet reached Player 1. Likewise, the information about Player 2's getting punched has not yet reached Player 2, and he is now out of the way. This presents a problem. There are workarounds for this issue, but they are beyond the scope of this book.

THE MULTIPLAYER ASPECT

In this section we are going to look at the ActionScript needed to handle the multiplayer aspect of this game. Also, we will examine one major issue that we solve easily using room variables. Open tic_tac_toe.fla from the Chapter17 folder on the CD.

As you may remember from Chapter 13, after two people have agreed to play a game, they are taken to the Game frame. Let's look at the ActionScript on this frame in the Actions layer now. Here are the last few lines of that ActionScript:

```
1    ES.moveReceived = this.moveReceived;
2    ES.onRoomVarChange = roomVarChanged;
3    ES.chatReceiver = this.messageArrived;
4    ES.joinGame();
5    iAmIn();
```

In the first three lines we define the event handlers. In line 1 we define the moveReceived event handler so that a function is executed whenever a move is received. We will see this function later. In the next line we define the onRoomVarChange event handler. (Remember that with ElectroServer we can store variables in a room on the server.) When a variable is created, modified, or deleted, this event fires. We define the onRoomVarChange event handler so that we know when we can check for new information. In line 3 we redefine the chatReceiver event handler, which we defined with a different function on the Chat System frame. Next, in line 4, we join the game. This method joins you to a room in which the ElectroServerAS object chose for you to play your game. (You do not need to know the name of this room; the ElectroServerAS object always chooses it.) Make sure you don't use the joinRoom() method until you have defined all of the event handlers; otherwise, you may receive information about your game that does not trigger the right events. Finally, in line 5, iAmIn() is executed. This function, which we will discuss below, creates a variable in your room indicating that you are there. Here is the iAmIn() function:

```
1    function iAmIn() {
2        var name = "player"+ES.player;
3        var val = "here";
4        ES.createVariable(name, val);
5    }
```

This function creates a variable in your room on the server called player1 or player2 (depending on which player you are). When you challenge someone, a property on the ElectroServerAS object called player is set to 1. If you are the person who was challenged, then this property is set to 2. It is accessed to create the name of the variable in line 2 above. The value of this variable is "here" (line 3). In line 4 we create the variable on the server by invoking the createVariable() method of the ElectroServerAS object. Next we will discuss the roomVarChanged() function and why we set these room variables in the first place.

This is the roomVarChanged() function:

```
1   function roomVarChanged(ob) {
2       if (ob.player1 == "here" && ob.player2 == "here") {
3           locked = false;
4           if (!initializedYet) {
5               initializedYet = true;
6               startGame();
7           }
8       } else {
9           locked = true;
10          if (initializedYet) {
11              popup.gotoAndStop("player left");
12          }
13      }
14  }
```

This function is called whenever a variable is created, modified, or deleted in your room. An object is passed in containing every variable that your room contains. There are some other optional parameters we don't use here that give information about which variable was modified or deleted. (See Appendix C, "The ElectroServerAS Object," for information on those, specifically the variable onRoomVarChange.) As you can see in line 2, we check to see if player1 and player2 have a value of "here". If they do, that means, of course, that both players are in the room and are ready to play. We then set the value of the variable locked to false. The value of locked is true before we verify that both players are there. We use this variable to keep a player from making a move before both players are ready. You will see this used again later. In line 4 we check to see if the variable initializedYet is not true. If it is not true, then we set it to true and call the startGame() function. The initializedYet variable is used to determine when a player has left. In line 10 you can see that if `initializedYet` is `true` and either `player1` or `player2` does not have a value of `"here"`, then a player has left the game.

Being able to correctly determine when a player has left the game has been a major issue in Flash games. It is more difficult than it should be to determine this. It can be done with traditional multiplayer servers, but it usually requires tedious user-list comparisons. You would compare the current user list with an older user list to see who has entered the room or who has left the room. With this room-variable technique you can very easily tell when your opponent is in the room. If the opponent leaves the room, the server deletes his variable from the room and you are informed. You then know that he is no longer in the game.

We have now covered the ActionScript needed to arrive at the Game frame, join the game, set a variable to the room to indicate that you are there, and determine when both players are available. Now we will look at the ActionScript needed to send a move to your opponent. In order to understand what is happening when sending the move, we must also cover a bit about the game itself (which we would ideally leave for the code section later in the chapter). What we don't cover about the game ActionScript here we will cover in the next section.

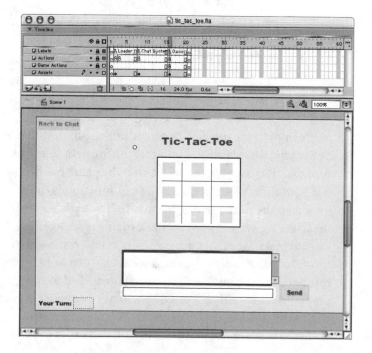

The game of tic-tac-toe has nine tiles (which are movie clips) in three rows and three columns. Using a naming convention similar to what we have used throughout this book, the tiles are named piece1_1 through piece3_3. The first number in the name is the column number; the second is the row number. So the piece found in column 1 and row 2 is piece1_2. Each of these movie clips contains three keyframes. The first one (frame 1) contains an invisible button (an invisible button contains only a hit state). The second (labeled X) shows the letter X, and the remaining frame label, O, shows the letter O. We will be looking at the ActionScript on the button.

```
1   on (release) {
2       _root.iGotClicked(this);
3   }
```

When the piece has been clicked, the function iGotClicked() is called, and a reference to the movie clip is passed in. Now let's look at iGotClicked().

```
1    function iGotClicked(who) {
2        if (!locked && gameInPlay && myTurn) {
3            myTurn = false;
4            who.gotoAndStop(myLetter);
5            who.letter = myLetter;
6            var ob = {name:who._name, type:"move"};
7            ++moves;
8            checkForWin();
9            sendMove(ob);
10       }
11   }
```

A reference to the movie clip containing the button that was clicked (one of the nine tiles) is passed into this function. In line 2 we check to make sure that the game is not locked, that the game has been started, and that it is your turn. When the startGame() function is called, which we'll look at in the next section, the gameInPlay variable is set to true. When the game is over, the gameInPlay variable is set to false. So in line 2 we look to make sure that gameInPlay is true—otherwise you shouldn't be trying to make a move. In line 3 we set myTurn to false. Next, we tell the movie clip that contains the button you clicked to move to a frame to display your letter (either X or O). We then store your letter in this movie clip as the variable letter (line 5). This is done so that when the script is checking to see if the game is over, it can easily look in each movie clip to find out which letter it is displaying. By inspecting the letter in all nine movie clips, we can tell who won the game. In line 6 we create an object called ob with the properties name and type. The name property contains the name of the movie clip that contains the button you clicked. The type property contains the string value "move". This object is what will be sent to your opponent (line 9). When your opponent receives this move, then moveReceived() is called on his computer. (We'll talk about the moveReceived() function next.) In line 7 a variable called moves is incremented. This variable is used by the checkForWin() function, which we will talk about in the next section.

Here is the moveReceived() function:

```
1   function moveReceived(ob) {
2       if (ob.type == "move") {
3           myTurn = true;
4           var name = ob.name;
5           _root[name].gotoAndStop(hisLetter);
6           _root[name].letter = hisLetter;
7           ++moves;
8           checkForWin();
9       } else if (ob.type == "restart") {
10          restart();
11      }
12  }
```

To see the moveReceived() function in action in other games, see Chapters 18 and 19.

This function is called when you receive a move from your opponent. The parameter ob is an object that has been sent to you from your opponent. This is the first time you have seen ElectroServerAS's ability to send an ActionScript object from one Flash client to another. It is one of the most powerful uses of the ElectroServerAS object; it allows for even very complicated moves to be sent easily. However, in the case of tic-tac-toe, we are using just about the simplest moves possible—we've only got "move" and "restart." In other games we might have several types of moves. (Understand that I am using the term *move* generally—restarting a game isn't really a move, but it just enables us to easily consider restarting a move.) In line 2 we check to see if the move type is "move". If it is a "move" move, then we do several things. We set the myTurn variable to true. Since your opponent just moved, it is now your turn. We extract the name property from ob and store it as the local variable name. It is used to tell a specific movie clip—the one your opponent clicked—to move to the frame to display your opponent's letter, hisLetter. We increment moves and call the checkForWins() function. If the move type is "restart", then we call the restart() function.

You have now seen the absolute basics of a multiplayer game using ElectroServer and the ElectroServerAS object. You can chat, challenge, create room variables, and send moves to your opponent. This is a very powerful toolkit! Next we will look at the rest of the code needed to make this game function.

GAME CODE

Wow—think of all the information needed to get to this point. You have learned about multiplayer servers, a little bit about networking, how to create a chat, and the basics of multiplayer gaming in Flash. After all that, this section should be a breeze! We'll discuss the code needed to start a game of tic-tac-toe, restart the game, and detect if the game is over and who (if anyone) won—all of which is pretty basic.

As mentioned in the last section, in tic-tac-toe there are nine tiles on the screen, one for each possible move, or space. There is also a movie clip with an instance name of popup. This movie clip contains four keyframes. The first one is blank. The next, labeled Game Started, is displayed when a game first starts; it informs the player that the game is under way and whose turn it is. The next keyframe is labeled Game Over. When the game has finished, this frame is displayed. It can display any of three messages: "You won!," "You lost!," or "Game over. There is no winner." The final keyframe is labeled Player Left. This frame appears when your opponent leaves the game (either by leaving the room or by leaving the chat).

Select the Game frame in the Game Actions layer and open the Actions panel. The first line is this:

```
gameInPlay = false;
```

This means that a game has not yet started. When a game is started, as you will see, this variable is set to true. When it's false, a user cannot get a response by clicking the tiles.

Next in the frame is this conditional statement:

```
1   if (ES.player == 1) {
2       myLetter = "x";
3       hisLetter = "o";
4       myTurn = true;
5   } else {
6       myTurn = false;
7       myLetter = "o";
8       hisLetter = "x";
9   }
```

What this conditional does is simple but important. If you are Player 1 (meaning that the value of the player property is 1), then myLetter is set to contain "x" and hisLetter is set to contain "o". Also, myTurn is set to true. This means that if you are Player 1, then you get to move first and your letter is X. If you are not Player 1, then we assume (since this is a two-player game) that you are Player 2. In this case, myTurn is set to false, myLetter is set to "o", and hisLetter is set to "x".

Here is the startGame() function:

```
1    function startGame() {
2        moves = 0;
3        gameInPlay = true;
4        popup.gotoAndStop("Game Started");
5        if (myTurn) {
6            popup.msg.text = "The game has begun. It is your
             → turn.";
7        } else {
8            popup.msg.text = "The game has begun. It is your
             → opponent's turn.";
9        }
10   }
```

This function is called when it has been determined that both players have arrived. (It is also called from the restart() function.) It sets the value of moves to 0. This variable is incremented every time a move is made. When this value reaches 9, then no more moves can be made. It is used by the checkForWin() function. Next, the gameInPlay variable is set to true. When it is true, one of the several conditions needed to allow a player to move is met (the others are that locked is not equal to true, and myTurn is true). The pop-up movie clip is sent to the Game Started frame. In lines 5–9 we determine whether to display text informing the user that it is his turn or his opponent's turn. We use the myTurn variable to determine this. Once this function is called, the game has been started, and it is now OK for Player 1 to make the first move.

When the Restart button is clicked, the restart() function is called on both players' computers.

```
1   function restart() {
2       for (var i = 1; i<=3; ++i) {
3           for (var j = 1; j<=3; ++j) {
4               var name = "piece"+i+"_"+j;
5               this[name].gotoAndStop(1);
6           }
7       }
8       if (ES.player == 1) {
9           myTurn = true;
10      } else {
11          myTurn = false;
12      }
13      startGame();
14  }
```

Lines 2–7 simply tell each of the nine tile movie clips to go back to frame 1. In lines 8–12 we reinitialize the myTurn variable. If you are Player 1, then it is your turn, so myTurn is set to true. In line 13 the startGame() function is executed. Once this is done, the game has been successfully restarted: The board's previous state has been erased and a new game has begun.

Here is the checkForWin() function:

```
1   function checkForWin() {
2       var win = false;
3       var letter = null;
4       if (piece1_1.letter == piece2_1.letter &&
        → piece2_1.letter == piece3_1.letter) {
5           var letter = piece1_1.letter;
6       }
7       if (piece1_2.letter == piece2_2.letter &&
        → piece2_2.letter == piece3_2.letter) {
```

```
 8          var letter = piece1_2.letter;
 9        }
10        if (piece1_3.letter == piece2_3.letter &&
        piece2_3.letter ==1 piece3_3.letter) {
11            var letter = piece1_3.letter;
12        }
13        if (piece1_1.letter == piece1_2.letter &&
        piece1_2.letter == piece1_3.letter) {
14            var letter = piece1_1.letter;
15        }
16        if (piece2_1.letter == piece2_2.letter &&
        piece2_2.letter == piece2_3.letter) {
17            var letter = piece2_1.letter;
18        }
19        if (piece3_1.letter == piece3_2.letter &&
        piece3_2.letter == piece3_3.letter) {
20            var letter = piece3_1.letter;
21        }
22        if (piece1_1.letter == piece2_2.letter &&
        piece2_2.letter == piece3_3.letter) {
23            var letter = piece1_1.letter;
24        }
25        if (piece3_1.letter == piece2_2.letter &&
        piece2_2.letter == piece1_3.letter) {
26            var letter = piece3_1.letter;
27        }
28        if (letter != null) {
29            if (letter == myLetter) {
30                gameOver(true);
31            } else {
32                gameOver(false);
33            }
34        } else if (letter == null && moves == 9) {
35            gameOver("tie");
36        }
37    }
```

While long, this function does a very simple thing: It checks to see if there is a winner or if the game is over and there is no winner. In tic-tac-toe there are eight possible ways to win. You can align three like letters vertically in any of the three columns (that's three possibilities), you can align three like letters horizontally in any of the three rows (there's another three), or you can align three like letters diagonally (two possibilities). What we do in lines 4–25 is check, with eight different if statements, to see if any of the eight conditions just described are being met. If any one of them is, then the variable letter is set with the value of the letter that is involved in this match. In line 28 we check to see if letter has a value. If it does, then we determine if it is the current player's letter or his opponent's letter. If it is the current player's letter, then he won the game, so we call gameOver(), passing in true. If the opponent has won, then we call gameOver(), passing in false. If letter is null and moves is 9, then the game is over but there is no winner. In this case we call gameOver() and pass in "tie".

Here is the gameOver() function:

```
1   function gameOver(iWon) {
2       gameInPlay = false;
3       popup.gotoAndStop("Game Over");
4       if (iWon) {
5           popup.msg.text = "You won!";
6       } else if (iWon == "tie") {
7           popup.msg.text = "Game over. There is no winner.";
8       } else {
9           popup.msg.text = "You lost!";
10      }
11  }
```

The parameter iWon can be true, false, or "tie". First we set gameInPlay to false. This keeps anyone from making any more moves. We then send the pop-up movie clip to the Game Over frame and display some text. The text displayed depends on the value of iWon: If true, then we display "You won!". If false, then we display "You lost!". If the game was a tie, then we display "Game over. There is no winner."

You have now been introduced to all of the functions necessary for creating a very simple multiplayer game in Flash! Using the basic concepts outlined in this chapter, you can now create any number of turn-based multiplayer games. A game of checkers or chess will easily fit into this same multiplayer structure. Games that involve more animation and movement, like pool, require a few more tricks. Check out Chapter 18, "9-Ball," for more on this.

POINTS TO REMEMBER

- Make use of room variables to keep track of which players have arrived.

- Using the sendMove() method of the ElectroServerAS object, you can very easily send information to your opponent.

- The sendMove() method allows you to send objects. It is a good idea to use a property on the object, such as type, to concisely describe why the object is being sent. For instance, in checkers you might have a special move for making a checker a king. In this case, the type property would be "king". For other moves it would probably just be "move".

- Don't forget to use the joinGame() method when you have reached the frame that displays the game; otherwise you'll be playing a game in a regular chat room!

- Turn-based games are easier to build in Flash than real-time games; however, real-time games are possible.

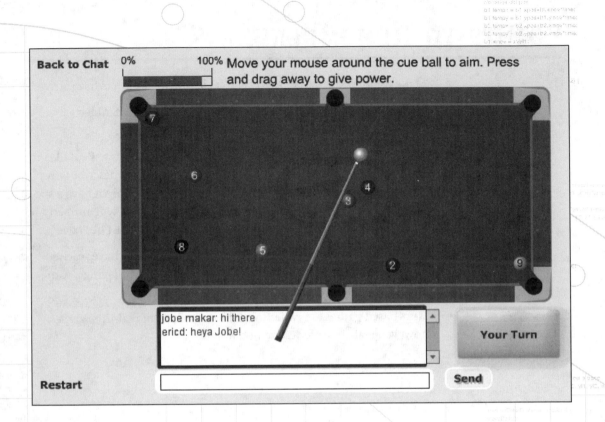

CHAPTER 18

9-BALL

NINE-BALL IS JUST ONE OF THE MANY TYPES OF POOL GAMES BUT IS probably the most popular among professional pool players. Most nonprofessionals, at least in the United States, tend to be more familiar with 8-ball. I programmed 9-ball instead of 8-ball because 9-ball only uses 10 balls, as opposed to the 16 used in 8-ball. Through my tests I determined that having 16 balls is much too CPU intensive in Flash. You may remember that in Chapter 2, "The Plan: From Idea to Design," we listed this very problem as a possible programming deterrent; having too many balls on the table could cause a problem that we would have needed to work around. The workaround, in that case, was changing the game.

This game requires more knowledge than just about any other game in this book: knowledge of physics, collision detection, collision reactions, and multiplayer systems. If you have trouble understanding the ActionScript used in this game, I recommend that you review the prerequisite chapters.

Prerequisites

Chapter 4, "Basic Physics"

Chapter 5, "Collision Detection"

Chapter 6, "Collision Reactions"

Chapter 13, "Dissecting a Chat"

Chapter 17, "Tic-Tac-Toe: Your First Multiplayer game." That chapter takes you through the basics of creating your first multiplayer game. The multiplayer-specific techniques used there are also used here. They are much easier to understand in a basic game than they are in a complicated game like 9-ball.

Appendix C, "The ElectroServerAS Object." Use this as quick reference for definitions of the methods and properties of the ElectroServerAS object.

Appendix B, "Multiuser Servers." Read this appendix to gain an understanding of multiuser servers, and specifically to understand ElectroServer and its capabilities, and how to install it. You are expected to know how to start ElectroServer so that the game file in this chapter can connect to it.

GAME OVERVIEW

Before getting into the rules of the game, let me introduce the equipment and some terminology.

The structure on which the game is played is called the *table*, or *pool table*. There are a total of ten balls on the table—the cue ball and balls numbered 1 through 9. The cue ball is a completely white, blank ball. As in all pool games, a stick called the *cue* is used to strike the cue ball into other balls.

Before a game can begin, the table must be set up. You do this by racking the balls. The nine numbered balls are arranged in a diamond shape, with the 1 ball closest to the middle of the table and the 9 ball in the middle of the diamond. The racked balls (see the image below) are placed on one side of the table. That side is then called the *foot* of the table. The opposite side of the table is called the *head*. There are six notches marked on the sides across the length of the table. An imaginary line across the two second notches from the head of the table is called the *head string*. The four inner walls of the pool table are called *cushions* (or *rails*, or *walls*). There are six holes, called *pockets*, around the perimeter of the table.

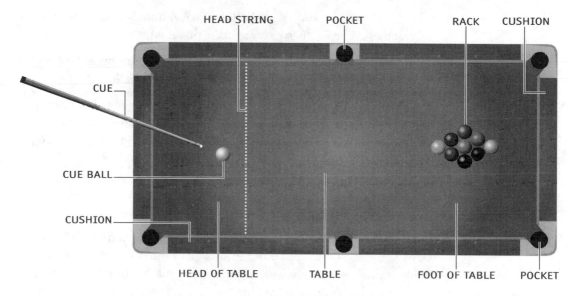

Nine-ball is a two-player game. In real life, Player 1 is chosen by what is called *lag* (or *lagging*). Each player does the following:

1. Place the cue ball somewhere behind the head string.

2. Use the cue to hit the cue ball to the other end of the table, intending for the cue ball to rebound and to come to a rest as close to the head cushion as possible.

The person who gets the cue ball closest to the head cushion is Player 1. If you wish to enhance this Flash game, you can implement a similar selection process. However, in this version of 9-ball, I've set it up so that the challenger is Player 1.

I need to mention two more terms before discussing the rules: breaking and ball-in-hand. The act of hitting the cue ball into the rack is called *breaking*. Player 1 breaks by placing the cue ball anywhere behind the head string and then hitting it toward the rack. *Ball-in-hand* is when a player is allowed to manually place the cue ball anywhere on the table. On break, Player 1 gets ball-in-hand behind the head string. All other occurrences of ball-in-hand are not restricted to the head of the table.

Here are the rules of 9-ball:

1. The game ends when the 9 ball is pocketed.

2. If the player who sinks the 9 ball does so without losing his turn, then that player wins. Otherwise, the other player wins.

3. When shooting, the cue ball must hit the lowest numbered ball on the table before hitting any other balls. It can hit the walls first.

4. If the cue ball gets pocketed or if the lowest numbered ball is not the first ball *hit*—not sunk—then the player is said to have *scratched*. When a player scratches, he loses his turn and his opponent gets ball-in-hand.

5. If a player sinks a ball without scratching, then that player keeps his turn and can shoot again.

6. If a player fails to sink a ball, then that player loses his turn.

Those are the only rules! Some things should be inferred from the rules above. The goal of the game is not to sink all of the balls—it is to sink the 9 ball without losing your turn. As long as you hit the lowest numbered ball on the table, no matter what ball goes in (except the cue ball), you keep your turn. So it is conceivable to win the game very early by hitting the 1 ball into the 9 ball and sinking the 9 ball. It is also possible—and likely—that one player can sink balls 1–8 and then lose his turn. Then the opponent sinks the 9 ball and wins the game.

One note about the rack: When the balls are racked, the 1 ball should be closest to the cue ball. When Player 1 breaks, he must hit the 1 ball or he will have scratched. It is possible, although unlikely, to either win or lose the game on the break.

Now that you know the rules, let's walk through an example experience (from chat to game). Start ElectroServer on port 1024. Open the pool.fla file, found in the Chapter18 directory. This is the game file. If ElectroServer is running, you should be able to publish a SWF from the pool.fla file and enter the chat. For our example, open two instances of the published SWF and log in with two different names; let's say they are Frank and Estelle.

You can talk to your alter ego back and forth between. windows (which is good therapy sometimes).

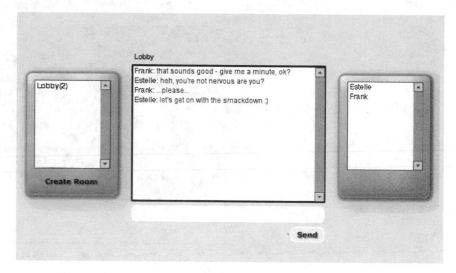

In Frank's window, click Estelle's name in the user list. This will send her a challenge request. In Estelle's window, accept the challenge. Both players will be pulled into the game. Since Frank was the challenger, he is Player 1. So when he is pulled into the game, and when both people are verified to be in the game, then a message pops up in Frank's window, saying, "The game has begun. It is your turn." In Estelle's window the message reads, "The game has begun. It is your opponent's turn." Click OK in both windows.

Move to Frank's window. You should see that the cue ball is following your mouse around. You can place the cue ball anywhere on the table as long as it's behind the head string. You place the ball on the table by clicking the spot where you want it. Once the ball is placed, you can't pick it up and move it again. After you have clicked to place the cue ball, the cue appears. As you move your mouse, the cue rotates to follow. There is a faint line that acts as a guide for aiming the cue ball. When you find the direction in which you want to shoot, press and hold down the mouse button. Now you can move your mouse, and the stick will move toward or away from the cue ball. What you are doing is setting the amount of power at which you want to shoot the ball. On the top left of the table you can see a power meter. When you have adjusted the stick to the power you want, release the mouse button, and the cue ball will move in the direction you specified.

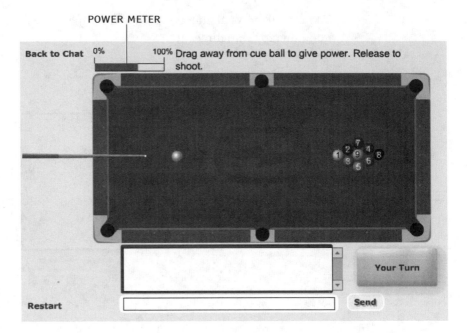

If Frank's shot first hits the 1 ball and then another ball sinks without scratching, then he gets to take another shot. Otherwise, it is Estelle's turn. Frank and Estelle take turns like this until one of them pockets the 9 ball. When the game is over, the pop-up message appears again, telling each player whether he or she has won or lost.

MULTIPLAYER ASPECTS OF THE GAME

In Chapter 17, "Tic -Tac-Toe: Your First Multiplayer Game," we discussed all of the basic multiplayer techniques that are used in Flash multiplayer games covered in this book:

- Creating room variables on the server to keep track of when both players have arrived and when a player has left the game

- Sending a move to your opponent and creating a property called type, which specifies the type of move being made, on the object you send to your opponent

- Joining the game room at the right time

If you have not yet read Chapter 17, you should probably do so now, as we are not going to go over those topics again here. However, there is one multiplayer issue, not seen in tic-tac-toe, that we need to discuss in this section. After you have read through this, you will probably think "No duh!", but it took me a good six months to realize that what we explain here is a necessity.

Synchronization: A Multiplayer Problem and Solution

Imagine this situation. Frank and Estelle are playing a game of multiplayer 9-ball created in Flash. Frank has a top-of-the-line computer, the fastest available. Estelle, on the other hand, is using an old computer that she picked up back in college. It is so slow that she can only run one or two applications at a time.

Frank is Player 1, so he breaks. He hits the cue ball into the rack at top speed. Within about 30 seconds, he's pocketed two of the balls (from the hard break), and the rest of the balls roll to a stop. Estelle's computer is having trouble computing the ActionScript at the intended frame rate. All of the actions will be calculated precisely the way they are on Frank's computer; it's just that they will take two to three times as long. Around 1 minute goes by before the balls stop rolling on Estelle's computer. According to Frank's computer, after the first 30 seconds it is still his turn and the balls have stopped rolling, so he takes another shot. Do you see the problem? Frank just tried to take a shot before the balls have stopped on Estelle's computer. If we allow this to happen, then the multiplayer game will break down at that point. At the time of Frank's shot (30 seconds after the break), only one screen—Frank's—is showing the correct configuration of the balls. If he had waited a full minute, then Estelle's computer would have caught up and both screens would show the correct configuration of the balls.

What I have just described causes a synchronization issue—a multiplayer game programmer's worst nightmare. I described the situation using two computers with extremely different processing speeds to highlight the discrepancy. More likely the two computers will be fairly similar in their specifications, but there will still be a few seconds during which the screens won't be completely in sync. For example, say both players have screamingly fast computers, but Frank has three Web windows open, plus Adobe Photoshop and Macromedia FreeHand. His fancy computer will be a little bit slower to process the information than Estelle's computer and will lag behind.

They say hindsight is 20/20, and I believe it. I don't know how I missed this issue for so long … but I did. You will encounter it when you create or play turn-based multiplayer games in which animation or some other timed factor plays a part. In games like tic-tac-toe, checkers, and chess, we would not see this issue. Now that you understand what the problem is, and before you let it get you down, let's talk about the solution. The solution is to not let a player move unless both players are ready. We do this in a very simple way. As you might remember from the tic-tac-toe chapter, we set room variables to help us determine when the users are in the game room or if one of them has left. We can also use room variables to store the status of each user's window. (By "window" I mean one user's instance of the entire game.) For example, when Player 1's screen is ready to send or receive a move, we set a room variable called `player1stopped` with a value of `"yes"`. When Player 2's screen is ready to send or receive a move, we set the room variable `player2stopped` with a value of `"yes"`. As soon as a player sends or receives a shot, his game automatically sets the server variable `player1stopped` or `player2stopped` with a value of `"no"`.

Remember that whenever a room variable is created, modified, or deleted, that causes the `onRoomVarChange` event to be fired. When this event is fired, an object that contains all of the room variables is passed in. We check the values of `player1stopped` and `player2stopped` on this object. If they both have a value of `"yes"`, then we are at a point where we can allow another move.

The Multiplayer Actions

If you don't already have pool.fla open, then open it now. This game file is identical to that of tic -tac-toe, except for the contents of the Game frame on the main timeline. Click that frame now, on the Actions layer. The ActionScript on this frame that is used to handle chatting is precisely the same as that used for the chat window in tic-tac-toe.

Double-click the movie clip in that frame to enter it. You will see three layers in this movie clip—Multiplayer Actions, Actions, and Assets. The Assets layer contains all of the graphics and movie clips needed in the game. The Actions layer contains the ActionScript used for everything in the game except the transfer of data from player to player (for example, sending and receiving moves). The Multiplayer Actions frame contains all of the ActionScript needed to send and receive moves; create, change, and receive room variables; and initialize the game. It is the code on this frame that we will look at now. Most of this code will be just briefly mentioned because of its similarity to that used in the tic-tac-toe game.

Here is the ActionScript found at the bottom of that frame:

```
1   ES = ElectroServer;
2   player = ES.player;
3   initializedYet = false;
4   ES.onRoomVarChange = roomVarChanged;
5   ES.moveReceived = moveReceived;
6   ES.joinGame();
7   createVar("player"+player, "here");
```

In line 1 we simply create a shortcut to the ElectroServer instance of the ElectroServerAS object. This is done purely out of laziness (it's easier to type ES than to type ElectroServer!). Next we set a variable called player to store your player number. If you are the challenger, then your player number is 1; otherwise it is 2. In line 3, initializedYet is set to false. This is the variable that tells us whether both players have ever both been in the room. We start with a value of false, and then the first time player1 and player2 have values of "here", we set initializedYet to true. (This is the same thing we saw in the tic-tac-toe chapter.)

In line 4 we set the onRoomVarChange event handler to call roomVarChanged() when room-variable information comes in. Likewise, in the next line we set the moveReceived event handler to call the moveReceived() function when a move arrives. Now that all of the event handlers have been set, it is safe to join the game. We do so in line 6. Remember that the order in which you do this is very important. It is important enough for me to mention again: If you were to join the game before defining the event handlers, then you would run the risk of receiving data about the room or your opponent before you were equipped to handle it. In the final line we create a room variable for your player and give it a value of "here".

We are about to look at all of the functions on this frame. Before we do that, I want to mention the different types of moves in this game. You'll remember from the tic-tac-toe chapter that when we sent a move, we sent an object to our opponent. We added a property to the object called type, which stores a string value of the move type. In tic-tac-toe we only had two types, "move" and "restart". Here are the move types we have in 9-ball:

Shot—This move sends your opponent the information that will replicate your shot on her screen, including the *x* and *y* positions of the ball, the speed at which it has been shot, and the angle at which it has been shot.

Place_cue—When you have placed the cue ball from ball-in-hand, this move is sent to your opponent. When it's received, the cue ball position is updated on your opponent's screen. Currently this is only sent when the cue ball has been placed. However, you can modify it to be sent while you move the cue ball, for more of a real-time feel.

Restart—This move is sent to your opponent when you click the Restart button. When your opponent receives it, the entire game will be restarted.

If you want to make this game more polished, you can add other types of moves. For instance, as a player rotates the stick around the ball or slides the stick away from the ball to adjust the power, you can send that information. These kinds of refinements can give the game more of a real-time effect. The three moves that have been implemented in this game are the minimum needed to get it working.

Now let's look at the moveReceived() function:

```
1    function moveReceived(ob) {
2        if (ob.type == "shot") {
3            game.ball1.x = ob.x;
4            game.ball1.y = ob.y;
5            shoot(ob.speed, ob.angle);
6        } else if (ob.type == "place_cue") {
7            game.ball1.x = ob.x;
8            game.ball1.y = ob.y;
9            game.ball1.clip._x = ob.x;
10           game.ball1.clip._y = ob.y;
11       } else if (ob.type == "restart") {
12           restart();
13       }
14   }
```

This function is called when a move is received. An object containing the information your opponent sent is passed in. For the "shot" type of move, we extract the cue ball's *x* and *y* positions, and set its position based on them. The cue ball is represented by the `ball1` object, which is stored on the game object. (You will see more about this later.) We then call the `shoot()` function, passing in the speed and angle. The `shoot()` function, which handles shooting the ball, will be discussed later. When a move is a `"place_cue"` move, we update the cue ball's position both in memory and on the screen. And if the move is a `"restart"` move, then we call the `restart()` function.

Now let's look at the three separate functions used to send these types of moves:

```
1   function sendShot(speed, angle) {
2       var ob = {speed:speed, angle:angle, x:game.ball1.x,
        ⇢ y:game.ball1.y, type:"shot"};
3       ES.sendMove(ES.opponent, ob);
4   }
5   function sendCuePlacement() {
6       var ob = {x:game.ball1.x, y:game.ball1.y,
        ⇢ type:"place_cue"};
7       ES.sendMove(ES.opponent, ob);
8   }
9   function sendRestart() {
10      var ob = {type:"restart"};
11      ES.sendMove(ES.opponent, ob);
12  }
```

As you can see, sending a move is simple. First an object is created to store the information you want to send, and the object is sent. In `sendShot()`, in addition to the `type` property, we send the speed and position of the cue ball as well as the angle at which it was shot. In `sendCuePlacement()` we just send the ball's position in addition to the type. And in `restart()` we simply send the name of the move.

We create two types of room variables in this game: one to flag a player as being in the room, and one to flag a player's game instance to be able to send or receive a move. The latter resolves the synchronization issue covered earlier in this chapter. Here are the functions used to create variables:

```
1   function createVar(name, value) {
2       ES.createVariable(name, value);
3   }
```

```
4   function flagStopped(val) {
5       createVar("player"+player+"stopped", val);
6   }
```

The createVar() function simply takes the name and value parameters passed in and uses them to create a room variable. This function is called when the frame first loads, as we saw above, to set a variable for the player. If you are Player 1, then the variable set from your SWF to the room is player1 with a value of "here"; otherwise it is player2 with a value of "here". It is also called from flagStopped(). This function changes player1stopped or player2stopped to "yes" or "no" when appropriate. Let's say you are Player 1. As soon as shoot() is called, flagStopped() is then called, and player1stopped is given a value of "no". When all of the balls on the table come to a stop, player1stopped is given a value of "yes" by calling flagStopped() and passing in "yes". A player cannot move unless both player1stopped and player2stopped have a value of "yes".

That brings us to the roomVarChanged() function, which is called whenever a room variable is created, modified, or deleted.

```
1   function roomVarChanged(ob) {
2       if (!initializedYet && ob.player1 == "here" &&
        → ob.player2 == "here") {
3           initializedYet = true;
4           startGame();
5       } else if (initializedYet && (ob.player1 != "here" ||
        → ob.player2 != "here")) {
6           popup.gotoAndStop("player left");
7       }
8       if (ob.player1stopped == "yes" &&
        → ob.player2stopped == "yes") {
9           locked = false;
10          display.gotoAndStop(game.myTurn ? "myturn" :
            → "notmyturn");
11      } else {
12          locked = true;
13          display.gotoAndStop("sync");
14      }
15  }
```

This function is almost identical to its tic-tac-toe counterpart. What's different is the second `if` statement. This is where we handle locking and unlocking the game screen. If both `player1stopped` and `player2stopped` have a value of `"yes"`, that means it's OK for somebody to shoot. In that case, we set `locked` to `false`, which allows the current player to make a move. Otherwise we set `locked` to `true` because the balls on one of the screens are not yet stopped. In either case, we tell a movie clip with an instance name of `sync` to go to a specific frame. This movie clip tells us what's going on. If it is on the sync frame, then the movie clip displays the word "Synchronizing." If it is someone's turn, then it either displays "Your Turn" or "Not Your Turn."

You have now seen all of the actions that control the multiplayer nature of this game. Next we'll tackle the ActionScript for controlling the state of the game screen itself.

GAME CODE

The amount of code used in the Actions frame of the game movie clip in this file is intimidating. There are nearly 700 lines of code used to make this game work. But don't despair—a large chunk of this code is from functions you've already seen throughout the book. For instance, we use frame-independent collision detection and ball-ball collision reactions. Both of those were explained in detail earlier in the book and are fairly lengthy functions.

In this section I'm going to give you an overview of how the code in this game works. Then we'll talk about some specifics.

General Overview

After both players are in the game, Player 1 has ball-in-hand. When Player 1 places the ball, Player 2 is updated with the cue ball's new position. Player 1 can then aim and break. As soon as Player 1 releases the mouse button to shoot, Player 2 is informed of the shot and the balls begin moving on both players' screens. As the shot plays out, each player's game keeps track of whether any rules have been broken. We watch to see if a ball is scratched, if the lowest-numbered ball was hit first, and if a ball is pocketed. If a ball gets pocketed, then we check to see if it was the cue ball or the 9 ball. If it was the 9 ball, then the game is over. If it was the cue ball, then only the turn is over. Play continues in this manner until the 9 ball sinks.

This code is lengthened by the inclusion of some optimizations I've come up with. This is the fourth time I've created a game of 9 ball. (One thing you'll find as you program more games is that by the time you're finished programming a game, you already have ideas about how to do it better next time around.) Every time I've programmed this game, the code gets longer—but there are fewer bugs and the game play is smoother.

The one major enhancement I've included in this version of the game is how the code determines if it should detect the collision between two balls. In previous versions of 9 ball, the code constantly checks for collisions between every ball. So, for instance, if you were to hit the cue ball into the 3 ball and all of the other balls remained untouched, the code would still do collision detection between balls 5 and 6. There is no reason why I should check for a collision between balls 5 and 6 if neither of them is moving—a collision isn't possible!

In this version of 9 ball I've created two arrays, called `moving` and `notMoving`. The names pretty much tell all: The `moving` array contains references to the balls that are moving, and the `notMoving` array contains references to balls that are not moving. When a ball is hit, it is removed from the `notMoving` array and placed in the `moving` array. When a ball stops moving, it is removed from the `moving` array and placed in the `notMoving` array. When the `moving` array is empty, that means that all balls have stopped and the turn is over. This technique helps me to more efficiently determine which balls should have collision detection. I check every moving ball against every other moving ball, and every moving ball against every stationary ball. When many balls are moving, this detection can run a little slow. But for most shots there are only going to be a few balls moving, and so we greatly reduce the number of collision-detection checks.

Optimization Analysis

It is important to understand why 10 balls in the game of 9-ball is a more reasonable number for us to use than the 16 required for a game of 8-ball. Common sense dictates that if you have a smaller number of balls, then the number of collision-detection checks goes down. That is true. And collision detection is the "expensive" script we are looking to minimize.

Flash actually doesn't have much trouble moving that many balls around. The problem is with the intensity of calculations. A ten-ball game is not just a little faster—it is substantially faster. If all of the balls on the table are moving in a game of 9-ball, we have 45 collision-detection checks per frame. If we add just six more balls, this flies up to 120 collision-detection checks per frame—nearly three times as many checks for just six more balls. Through my tests I found that a 13-ball game still runs at a reasonable speed. That takes 78 collision checks per frame. Remember, though, that these are the maximum numbers of collision checks per frame if all balls are moving. When just a few balls are moving, this number is greatly reduced because of the optimized way in which we check collisions in this game (described above in this section).

When you code something that appears to be taking a lot of CPU power, it is very important to spend some time trying to understand why the code is so intense. There are usually ways to reduce a script's CPU load by analyzing why the script is slow and guessing at alternative ways to code it. If you can come up with a great way in this pool game to, say, divide the balls (in memory) into four quadrants of the table and only perform collision detections based on table location, then you might be able to drop the CPU load enough to make a game of 8-ball that runs well!

Who's on First?

I have implemented another technique in this game that I have never used before: collision order. It is entirely possible for more than two balls to collide during the same frame. In fact, it is possible to detect that two balls have collided when they shouldn't collide. Let me explain. Imagine that there are three balls moving on the table. Balls 1 and 2 are moving toward each other from opposite sides of the table and are on a collision path. Ball 3 is moving perpendicular to these two balls on a collision path with ball 1. Because of the way we normally perform loops to detect collisions, we may erroneously detect a collision between balls 1 and 2, even though ball 1 actually collides with ball 3 a fraction of a second earlier. If ball 1 collides with ball 3 first, then it will probably be deflected out of the way of ball 2, and so what seemed an inevitable collision with ball 2 will never happen. Our collision-detection scripts look at the collision possibilities between two balls and don't even consider the fact that other balls exist. Do you see the problem? We may detect three collisions with ball 1 in one frame, but which is the real collision? After all, a ball can only collide with one other ball at a time. Here is the solution.

1. We run through all of the possible collision-detection comparisons. This means that we check every ball in the moving array against every other ball in the moving array, and then every ball in the moving array against all of the stationary balls in the notMoving array.

2. For every collision determined, we temporarily store in an array the time of this collision and the names of the balls involved in the collision. Remember this from the frame-independent collision-detection scripts we developed in Chapter 5, "Collision Detection": When a collision is detected, we are given the amount of time that has passed from the previous frame to the time of the collision. If this number is .2, then one-fifth of a frame passed before the balls collided. We do not perform any collision reactions here; in this step we are simply collecting times and ball names.

3. When the collision-detection script is done, we sort the array so that the collision with the shortest time is at the 0th index in the array. This is the collision that was the first to occur.

4. We calculate a collision reaction for the first collision to occur. Since this collision can affect whether any of the other collisions are valid, we abort the script here and start it over (back up to step 1).

We perform these four steps in a loop until there are no collisions on the table, or until we abort the loop for any other reason.

The Functions

At this stage in your career as a Flash developer (or at least as a reader of this book so far), you have seen just about all of the functions that make this game run, or similar versions of them. In this section we will mention most of the major functions and what they do, and in some cases we will look at the ActionScript.

Open the Actions panel, and look at the ActionScript on the Actions layer. (Remember, we're still in the game movie clip of pool.fla, not back on the main timeline.) Before the script defines any functions, it lists several lines of code initializing some variables and objects that will be used in the game. Here are the first few lines:

```
1   soundOn = true;
2   radius = 8.5;
3   mass = 1;
4   decay = .98;
5   runPatch = 0;
6   inPlay = false;
```

Line 1 simply creates a variable that controls whether a sound is played or not. It sets the value of soundOn to true. If true, then when the balls collide, a sound will be played. If false, then the sound will not be played. We did not include a sound on/off toggle in this file, but if you decide to add your own sound toggle button, all you have to do is toggle the soundOn variable's value. In line 2 we create a variable called radius. This is the radius of the pool balls. Next we set the mass of the balls to 1. We then create a decay variable, which is used to slow the balls down over time so that they eventually come to a stop. In line 5 we set runPatch to 0. It is used by the patch() function, which we will talk more about later. Finally, we set inPlay to false. This variable is used in the onEnterFrame event to determine if we should run the movement and collision-detection functions.

A few more things happen in the ActionScript on this frame before the function definitions begin. We create an object called game that will be used to store most of the information about the game. On the game object we create several other objects, including one for each ball, called ball1 through ball10, and one for the cue stick called stick.

startGame()

Now let's look at the startGame() function:

```
1   function startGame() {
2       flagStopped("yes");
3       inPlay = false;
4       if (player == 1) {
5           game.myTurn = true;
6       } else {
7           game.myTurn = false;
8       }
9       sinkList = [1, 2, 3, 4, 5, 6, 7, 8, 9];
10      currentBall = sinkList[0];
11      game.moving = [];
12      game.notMoving = [];
13      rack();
14      if (game.myTurn) {
15          ballInHand("partial");
16      }
17      moveVariables();
18      popup.gotoAndStop("game started");
19      if (game.myTurn) {
20          popup.msg.text = "The game has begun. It is your
            → turn.";
21      } else {
22          popup.msg.text = "The game has begun. It is your
            → opponent's turn.";
23      }
24  }
```

This function is called when both players first arrive and when a game is restarted. First, the flagStopped() function is called. This creates a room variable saying that this user is ready to send or receive a move. Next, the inPlay variable is set to false. This variable is used in the onEnterFrame event to determine if some function should be executed. If false, the functions are not executed. It is set to true when the cue ball is shot. Then, using the player variable, we determine whose turn it is. If it is Frank's turn, we set game.myTurn to true in Frank's game instance; otherwise we set it to false.

In line 9 we create an array called sinkList. Remember that the lowest-numbered ball on the table always has to be hit first. The number of the lowest-numbered ball on the table is sinkList[0]. Whenever a ball is pocketed, its number is removed from the sinkList array. In this way, sinkList[0] will always contain the lowest-numbered ball on the table. In line 10 we set a variable called currentBall, which is used to store the number of the lowest ball on the table, to sinkList[0]. This stores the number of the lowest ball on the table. Next we create new moving and notMoving arrays. They are used to store the objects that represent the balls that are moving and the balls that are not moving. When a ball starts moving, it is removed from notMoving and inserted into moving. Likewise, when a ball stops moving, it is removed from moving and inserted into notMoving.

We then position the balls correctly on the table by calling the rack() function. Then, in line 15, if it is Estelle's turn, she is given ball-in-hand by calling the ballInHand() function. The string "partial" is passed into ballInHand(). That string signifies that she has ball-in-hand behind the head string. If "full" was passed in, then she gets ball-in-hand with no restrictions. The final few lines in this function are straightforward: The moveVariables() function is called (it initializes some variables and is called before every shot). Then the pop-up graphic appears and informs you that the game has begun.

onEnterFrame

At the bottom of the Actions frame there is an onEnterFrame event:

```
1   this.onEnterFrame = function() {
2       //l = getTimer();
3       if (inPlay) {
4           moveBalls();
5           keepGoing = true;
6           timer = 0;
7           while (keepGoing && ++timer<10) {
8               ball2Ball();
9           }
10          detectWalls();
11          patch();
12          renderBalls();
13          if (game.moving.length == 0) {
```

```
14              moveDone();
15          }
16      }
17      //trace(getTimer()-1);
18  };
```

The actions in this event are executed in every frame, if inPlay is true. That variable is set to true when the cue ball is shot. In line 4 we do something that you have seen all throughout this book: update the positions of the objects in memory, but not on the stage. Next, we set keepGoing to true and timer to 0. Earlier in this chapter we discussed the way we are performing collision detection in detail. We store all collisions, sort the array, and then calculate a collision reaction for the first collision in the array. In lines 7–9, we run through the collision-detection script again and again, until all collisions have been detected. When no more collisions have been found, the ball2Ball() function sets keepGoing to false, and the loop terminates. However, you've probably already noticed that we've put another limit on this loop as well—we don't let it execute more than ten times per frame. I chose the number 10 as the upper limit (called a *loop cap*) by experimentation. I played several games of pool using various loop caps and watched the physical results versus the amount of time the loop took to execute. In the end, a cap of ten loops gave the optimal physical performance with little loop-time overhead. In line 10 we run the script that checks for collisions between the balls and the cushions. If a ball is colliding with a cushion, we also check it for a collision with a pocket, using the detectPocket() function. Checking for pocket collisions with every ball on every frame would use needless overhead processing, so we only check when a ball is colliding with a wall. That helps reduce the amount of code being executed every frame.

In line 11 we execute the patch() function. Why a patch? With all of the math and physics used in this game to give the high level of realism, there is still a nonrealistic reaction problem that can occur. Approximately 1 out of every 50 or 100 shots results in two balls' sticking together—just a bit, but unmistakably touching. This is a bug that I will undoubtedly solve on the next build of this game, but as of this writing I'm stumped. As a last resort for a situation like this, I've built a special time-based function to check for problems. This function has an internal timer that only lets it execute about once every 20 frames. When it executes, it checks for hitTest() between the actual ball movie clips. No two balls should ever be touching—that, of course, constitutes a collision. If the hitTest() returns true, then the balls are touching and our bug is happening. We then slightly nudge the balls to the side so that they break apart. As mentioned above, this doesn't happen very often, but when it does happen, we are prepared.

In line 12 we take the positions of the balls in memory and place them on the screen. If the length of the moving array is 0, then all of the balls are stopped and the turn is over. When that happens, moveDone() is called, which analyzes the results of your shot and determines whose turn it is now.

Analyzing Code-Execution Time

Did you notice the two lines that are commented out in the ActionScript above (lines 2 and 17)? When uncommented, they trace the amount of time in milliseconds (ms) that it takes for everything in the onEnterFrame event to completely execute. Approximately 24 times per second, this trace puts a new number in the output window. This is one of my most often-used tools when looking for optimizations in a game. I use it when I'm trying to find out what is the slowest part of the script. I can watch the numbers as the pool rack is broken and as the cue ball is being placed with ball-in-hand to see if things are executing at a reasonable speed. What is considered reasonable? You will have to use your own experience to make that call. But here is a starting place: We are working at 24 fps. There are 1000 ms in 1 second—approximately 41 ms per frame. If the trace time for your onEnterFrame event is greater than 41 ms, then the movie will not play at the full frame rate. So you would want to do your best to try to keep the number below 41. I would consider it reasonable to have occasional spikes above 41 (such as when breaking in pool), but not to average above 41.

moveDone()

This function handles the logic to determine if you get to keep your turn or if the game is over. When you shoot the cue ball, several game actions are tracked. If you collide with the correct ball first, then correctFirstHit is set to true. If you sink a ball, then ballSank is set to true. If the cue ball sinks, then cueBallSank is set to true. If the 9-ball sinks, then nineBallSank is set to true. These four Boolean values can determine if you get to keep your turn and if the game is over. If the game is over, then this script will also determine who the winner is:

```
1   function moveDone() {
2       roundPositions();
3       flagStopped("yes");
4       inPlay = false;
5       var loseTurn = false;
6       var gameOver = false;
7       var scratch = false;
8       if (nineBallSank && !cueBallSank && correctFirstHit) {
9           var gameOver = true;
10      } else if (nineBallSank && (cueBallSank ||
    → !correctFirstHit)) {
11          var loseTurn = true;
12          var gameOver = true;
13      } else if (!nineBallSank && (cueBallSank ||
    → !correctFirstHit)) {
14          var loseTurn = true;
15          var scratch = true;
16      } else if (!nineBallSank && !cueBallSank &&
    → correctFirstHit && !ballSank) {
17          var loseTurn = true;
18      } else if (!nineBallSank && !cueBallSank &&
    → correctFirstHit && ballSank) {
19          //you did good
20      }
21      if (gameOver) {
22          if (loseTurn) {
23              if (game.myTurn) {
24                  iWin = false;
25              } else {
26                  iWin = true;
27              }
28          } else {
29              if (game.myTurn) {
30                  iWin = true;
31              } else {
32                  iWin = false;
33              }
34          }
35          popup.gotoAndStop("game over");
```

```
36          if (iWin) {
37              popup.msg.text = "You win!";
38          } else {
39              popup.msg.text = "You lose!";
40          }
41      } else if (loseTurn) {
42          game.myTurn = game.myTurn ? false : true;
43          if (scratch) {
44              game.ball1.x = (game.middle+game.left)/2;
45              game.ball1.y = (game.top+game.bottom)/2;
46              game.ball1.clip._x = game.ball1.x;
47              game.ball1.clip._y = game.ball1.y;
48              game.ball1.clip._visible = true;
49          }
50      }
51      moveVariables();
52      if (game.myTurn && !gameOver && !scratch) {
53          initializeStick();
54      } else if (game.myTurn && scratch) {
55          ballInHand("full");
56      }
57  }
```

The first thing we do in moveDone() is call the roundPositions() function. (See the sidebar on page 498 for a description of why that function is needed.) We then set player1stopped or player2stopped to "yes" on the server. Remember that that variable represents the status of the screen. When it's "yes", that means both screens are in sync and stopped. After initializing several variables used by the function, we launch into a large conditional statement. We run through a series of conditions (lines 8–20) to determine the result of the shot that was just made. If the 9 ball sank *and* the lowest ball was hit first *and* you didn't scratch, then the game is over and you win! If the 9 ball sank but either you scratched or you didn't hit the correct first ball, then the game is over and you lose. If the 9 ball didn't sink and you scratched, then you lose your turn. If you sank a ball and didn't scratch, it's still your turn.

We then have another conditional statement that checks to see if the game is over (lines 21–50). If the game is over and whoever shot lost his turn, then that player loses. If the player who shot did not also lose his turn, then

Why the roundPositions() Function Is Necessary

In the second line of the moveDone() function, you see the roundPositions() function. The purpose of this function is to eliminate the minor math calculation discrepancies between different Flash clients.

Multiplayer gaming comes in at least two flavors. One type is called *authoritative server*, in which the server calculates everything for the client (that is, your game) and tells the client where to put the objects. In Flash we use the other type of multiplayer gaming, called *authoritative client,* in which the server is just there to route the information correctly and is ignorant of the game's details. We pass the minimal amount of information from one client to another and hope that Flash calculates precisely the exact same outcome on both machines. In 9-ball, this means that we can pass the cue ball's position as well as the angle and speed at which to hit the cue ball; and your opponent's game instance can take that information and precisely re-create the same outcome as what occurred on your own machine. We rely on the fact that given the same initial state, both clients will calculate precisely the same results from identical input.

But I'm here to tell you not to rely on this too heavily. While both clients appear to give the same results, those results are ever so slightly different. I played several games of this version of 9-ball while developing it. After 10 or 15 shots, I saw that the positions of the balls on the two screens were a little bit off from each other. I then put on my sleuthing hat and decided to get to the bottom of it. It turns out that even after the very first shot, the balls were not in precisely the same place on both machines! They were very close, though. Want to know how close? Flash calculates numbers out to 15 decimal places, and it was at the 15th decimal place where the positions were different. After the first shot or two, this is still a negligible difference. But because of propagation of error, this discrepancy increases with every shot. After about 10 shots, the difference becomes visible—possibly even enough for a ball to sink on one screen and not the other.

This brings up two questions: Why do we have a discrepancy, and what can we do about it? I don't know the answer to the first question. I can only speculate that it is some sort of a rounding error, or that at 15 decimal places there are some sort of random variations from machine to machine (variations that Macromedia didn't know about or didn't think would ever be a problem). But I do know that the solution to the second question is quite simple: We round all positions to three decimal places, which is accurate enough for us, by including the roundPositions() function on line 2, as we've done in the moveDone() function above. Since the discrepancies are never even close to three or four decimal places after the first shot, we will always be able to round predictably on both clients. This means that after every shot, the balls will be positioned in precisely the same spot on both players' machines.

he wins. If the game isn't over but the current player has lost his turn, then we change whose turn it is (line 42). Also, if that player scratched, then we center the cue ball behind the head string (lines 43–49).

In line 51 we reset some variables by calling moveVariables(). This function was also called from the startGame() function. Finally, we either initialize the cue stick to rotate around the cue ball, or we give the player ball-in-hand.

shoot()

We have talked a lot about the functions that move the balls around. But let's look at the function that tells the cue ball to move in the first place:

```
1    function shoot(speed, angle) {
2        if (!inPlay) {
3            flagStopped("no");
4            game.stick.moveStick = false;
5            game.stick.rotateStick = false;
6            game.stick.clip._visible = false;
7            line._visible = false;
8            inPlay = true;
9            var ob = game.ball1;
10           var cosAng = Math.cos(angle);
11           var sinAng = Math.sin(angle);
12           ob.xmov = speed*cosAng;
13           ob.ymov = speed*sinAng;
14           addMoving(ob);
15           var message = "Table locked!";
16           changeMessage(message);
17       }
18   }
```

This function is called after the angle and the power (speed) of the shot have been set. Both of these values are passed in. We call flagStopped() and pass in "no". This locks the screen so that it can't receive any moves. In the next few lines we toggle several variables that allow the user to rotate the stick and set the speed. We then set inPlay to true so that the onEnterFrame event can do its job. Next we calculate the ball's speed, set the speed on the cue ball's object, and add it to the moving array by calling addMoving(). In the last couple of lines we create a message on the screen saying "Table locked!"

Possible Game Enhancements

This is a pretty advanced Flash game. However, several things can be added or modified that would improve the game even more—if they are done well! If you put your mind to it, you can probably come up with a few more important features or effects to make this a more perfect game. Good luck!

Rolling balls—In a perfect version of this game, rather than appearing to slide (as they do here) the balls would have some sort of rolling animation that coincided with the direction in which they were rolling.

Angular velocity—If you decided that you wanted to do the rolling animations mentioned above, you'd need to know that the physics for rolling balls is different from that of sliding balls. The rotation of a ball is handled using *angular velocity*—that is, angles divided by time. (Think about it: If velocity equals distance per time, so should angular velocity equal angles per time.) We did not cover angular velocity or the moment of inertia for rigid bodies in this book (maybe in the next revision). But in a perfect game of 9-ball, they would be accounted for. These principles also directly apply to the next point.

English—*English* describes the spin put on the cue ball when it is hit off-center. If you put bottom English on the cue ball and hit another ball dead-on, then the cue ball may rebound back toward your stick. Or if you put top English on the cue ball, then it will follow the ball that it just struck. English can help you better position the cue ball after a shot and make shots that would not otherwise be possible. The English on the cue ball affects how it bounces off a cushion and imparts some of its own spin onto every other ball that it touches.

Real friction—While the "good-enough" friction used here (and introduced in Chapter 4) looks, well, good enough, it doesn't simulate exactly the look of a real game of pool. In a better version of this game, the friction would look more real. Note also that treating the balls as three-dimensional rolling objects using angular velocity and adding English would not be possible without using real friction.

More sounds—A complete and perfect game of 9-ball would include many sounds. You would have soft sounds for balls hitting the cushions, and different sounds for other events, such as the stick hitting the cue ball, the balls getting racked, and a ball being pocketed.

POINTS TO REMEMBER

- Don't let a player make a move until both he and his opponent are ready to receive a move. Otherwise, the game's synchronization will be affected.

- Given the same input on two SWF instances of the same game, Flash may not calculate the exact same result twice, although the numbers will be very close to each other. In some cases, like 9-ball, rounding will help you avoid synchronization issues.

- All of the possible collisions during a frame are calculated, stored, and sorted from earliest time to latest time . Then the script goes back and calculates the reaction for the first collision (lowest time). We run the collision-detection script again to see if there are any more collisions. This is done until there are no more collisions, or ten times— whichever comes first.

- For speed optimization, we use two arrays to store the state of the balls—a moving array and a notMoving array. We then perform collision detection between every ball in the moving array and then between every ball in the moving array with the balls in the notMoving array. We do not check for collisions between balls in the notMoving array.

- When the moving array is empty, the turn is over.

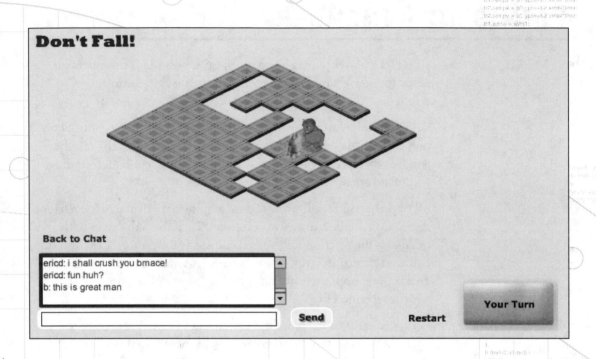

Don't Fall!

Back to Chat

ericd: i shall crush you bmace!
ericd: fun huh?
b: this is great man

Send   Restart   **Your Turn**

CHAPTER 19

DON'T FALL!

IN THIS CHAPTER WE DISSECT A VERY SIMPLE BUT ORIGINAL ISOMETRIC, tile-based, turn-based, multiplayer game. If you have read through the other two multiplayer-game chapters (see "Prerequisites"), then this one should be a breeze. The game is very simple, although it uses many underlying concepts—concepts you've learned throughout this book, including multiplayer techniques, 3D, character animations, and creating tile-based worlds.

Prerequisites

Multiplayer

Chapter 17, "Tic-Tac-Toe: Your First Multiplayer Game." That chapter takes you through the basics of creating your very first multiplayer game and uses the same techniques that are used here. I think they are easier to understand within the context of a basic game like tic-tac-toe. (The tic-tac-toe chapter has its own list of prerequisites that must be met to understand it.)

Chapter 18, "9-Ball." Read the section "Synchronization: A Multiplayer Problem and Solution." The rest of Chapter 18 is not needed to understand this chapter, but a major multiplayer issue that arises with 9-ball is also a factor in this game, so we employ the same solution, which is explained in detail in that chapter.

Game Engine

Chapter 7, "Tile-Based Worlds." Comprehension of tile-based worlds is needed to fully understand this tile-based game.

Chapter 8, "The Isometric Worldview." This game was created by taking the main example file from Chapter 8, iso_world.fla, and modifying it. It is assumed that you have read through Chapter 8 and understand the movie-clip architecture and the ActionScript used.

GAME OVERVIEW

Don't Fall! is a very simple but fun game. It uses an isometric tile-based world as the game board. As far as multiplayer games go, there is very little going on at once, and there isn't much opportunity for synchronization issues. This game is just waiting for someone to customize it, to make it more interesting (stay tuned at the end of the chapter for some ideas on this).

Before launching into the rules, let me lay out the basic setup of the game. There are two characters, one for each of the two players. Each of the characters is a monster—one green, one blue. The fact that the characters are monsters lends to the theme of the game but changes nothing about the game play itself—of course they could be any sort of characters you want.

The world is a tile-based, isometric, 10-by-10 grid. The grid's size does not play that important a role, either; changing the grid size should not affect game play much.

For the sake of explanation, let's assume that Player 1 is always the green monster, and Player 2 is always the blue monster.

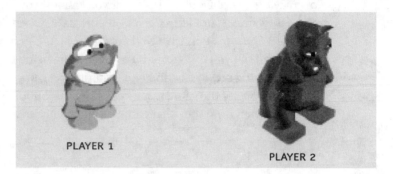

PLAYER 1

PLAYER 2

Here are the rules of this game:

1. Players start the game on diagonally opposite corners of the world, which is a grid of tiles suspended in the air.

2. The green monster (Player 1) gets the first turn.

3. The monster with the current turn can step on any adjacent tile. This is done by simply clicking that tile.

4. The tile that the monster just left falls downward and disappears off the screen. Since this tile has fallen away, it cannot be stepped on again.

5. After a monster has moved, it becomes the other monster's turn to move.

6. A tile must have at least one of its four sides touching another tile. If it does not, then it, too, falls. Just having one of its corners touching the corner of another tile isn't enough to keep it up.

7. If a monster is on a tile that falls, then that monster loses the game and the other wins the game.

8. If both monsters fall at the same time, they both lose the game.

From the rules you should be able to guess that the object of the game is to stay standing longer than your opponent. The steps you choose to take can force your opponent into taking steps where he doesn't want to go. This game can become addictive. You will start to see that there is some strategy involved.

Now play a game of Don't Fall! so that you can fully understand the controls of the game. Start ElectroServer on port 1024. Open dont_fall.fla in the Chapter18 directory. Publish a SWF from this FLA. Open two instances of the dont_fall.swf you just created. Log in to both, using two different user names. As in the previously discussed multiplayer games of tic-tac-toe and 9-ball, from one of the game instances, click your opponent's name to challenge him. Then from the other game instance, click to accept the challenge.

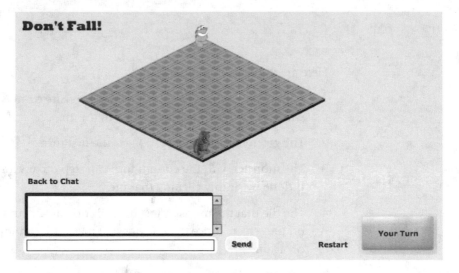

At this point you will find that both game instances have moved to a screen that displays the game of Don't Fall! The green monster is Player 1. So move to the game instance that belongs to the green monster. As you move your mouse over the tiles, you'll notice that a little circle appears if your mouse moves over any tiles that are adjacent to the one on which the green monster stands. You can then click any of those tiles. Once you click, the green monster walks to that tile, and the tile he was just on falls. It is now the blue monster's turn. Move to the game instance belonging to him. You should immediately see that this game instance shows exactly what the other one does—the green monster in a new spot and one tile missing.

You can now click a tile adjacent to the blue monster to move him. Keep moving both monsters until someone wins. And there you have it—a simple but addictive game.

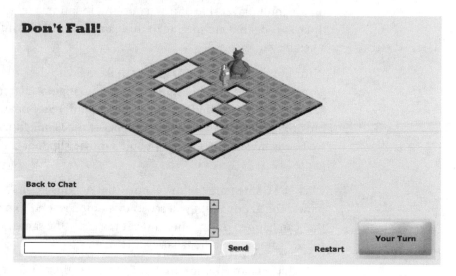

For the rest of the chapter, we will discuss the multiplayer ActionScript, the game ActionScript, and some possible game improvements for Don't Fall!

MULTIPLAYER ACTIONS

In the tic-tac-toe and 9-ball chapters we discussed all of the basic multiplayer techniques that are used in Flash multiplayer games:

- Creating room variables on the server to keep track of when both players have arrived and when a player has left the game.

- Sending a move to your opponent and creating a property called type, which specifies the type of move being made, on the object you send to your opponent.

- Joining the game room at the right time.

- Creating room variables on the server to keep track of when both players' game instances are ready for the next move. (See the "Synchronization: A Multiplayer Problem and Solution" section of Chapter 18, "9-Ball," for details on this.)

If you have not yet read Chapter 17, "Tic-Tac-Toe: Your First Multiplayer Game," you should probably do so now, as we are not going to go over these topics again here. However, we will briefly review what is happening on the multiplayer side of this game and mention a few pieces of the multiplayer code that are specific to this game (such as the information sent in a sendMove() action).

Return to the main stage of dont_fall.fla. As with the other multiplayer games discussed, this file is made from the original chat file dissected in Chapter 13, "Dissecting a Chat," with the difference between this file and the original chat file being the contents of the Game frame. On that frame, we have some chat ActionScript and a movie clip that contains all of the game assets.

Click the Game frame in the Game Chat Actions layer. Open the Actions panel. The ActionScript you see in this frame is used to handle the chatting that can happen during the game. It is exactly the same ActionScript used for the game chat in tic-tac-toe and 9-ball.

Also in the Game frame you'll find a movie clip that contains all of the game assets and game ActionScript. Double-click this movie clip to view the contents. You'll see four layers: Multiplayer Actions, Iso Object, Game Actions, and Assets. The only layer we need to concern ourselves with here is Multiplayer Actions.

Click the Multiplayer Actions layer and open the Actions panel. This ActionScript is very similar to the ActionScript found in the Multiplayer Actions layer of 9-ball. When this frame is first visited, we do the following:

1. Define the event handlers for moveReceived and onRoomVarChange.

2. Join the game room.

3. Set a room variable that flags a player as being in the room and ready to play.

The onRoomVarChanged function is called when a room variable is created, modified, or deleted. Room variables contain information telling us if both players are in the room and if they are both ready to receive a move. If they are both in the room, and this is the first time we have determined that they are both in the room, then we call the startGame() function. If they are both ready to move, then we unlock the game by setting locked = false.

The sendMove() function sends whatever object we pass in from the current player to the opponent. The moveReceived() function is then called in the opponent's game instance. Here is the moveReceived() function:

```
1   function moveReceived(ob) {
2       if (ob.type == "move") {
3           clickAccepted(ob.xm, ob.zm, ob.x_cell, ob.z_cell);
4       } else if (ob.type == "restart") {
5           restart();
6       }
7   }
```

As you can see from this function, there are only two types of moves—an actual game move and a restart move. When a move of type move is received, four variables are extracted from the object and passed into the clickAccepted() function. These values describe the end position of where the character should walk to, and the row and column number of the end tile. They will be discussed more in the "Game Actions" section.

There are no multiplayer surprises in this chapter. All of the techniques used have been seen in the previous chapters. The code discussed here is almost identical to what you have seen before.

GAME ACTIONS

By now you can probably tell what's coming next. It's time to look at the game movie clip itself. In the game movie clip there are four layers. The Multiplayer Actions layer was discussed in the previous section. Here we will discuss the rest.

As you know, Don't Fall! is a game that's seen in the isometric view. The Iso Object layer contains the ActionScript needed to translate coordinates from 2D to 3D and back to 2D. It also gives us the depth to use for each tile so that we don't have to worry about z-sorting. All of this is done through the isometricAS object found in the Iso Object layer. In Chapter 8, "The Isometric Worldview," we talk about the isometricAS object and its methods in detail. The isometricAS object used here is exactly the same as the one found in Chapter 8, so we don't need to talk here about how it works.

The Game Actions layer contains the ActionScript needed to build the game itself. We will talk about this frame in detail below. But first let's look at the Assets layer.

The Assets layer contains some user-interface elements. There is the Restart button, the little status window at the bottom right, and the pop-up movie clip that displays information like "You won!" and "Your opponent has left." Also in this frame is a movie clip off the left of the stage, with an instance name of soundfx. This movie clip contains two frames that have sounds on them: One of them has a sound of a tile falling, the other has the sound of a monster falling.

At this point you might be wondering where the monsters and tiles are hiding, since they are not on the stage. Good question! We are using attachMovie() to add the monsters and tiles; you'll find them in the library with linkage identifiers of character1, character2, and tile. There is one other movie clip we attach, with the linkage identifier of grid. This movie clip just serves as a container to hold all of the other movie clips we attach. That way, when it comes time to restart the game, we can just remove the container—the grid movie clip—and all of the tiles and monsters inside are automatically removed. The grid is then built again from scratch.

Now let's look at the ActionScript on the Game Actions layer of the game movie clip.

ActionScript Not Found in a Function

On the Game Actions frame there are several functions defined. But there are also some actions that are not defined as functions, because they need only be called once (in the process of setting up the game for each game session). You'll find them at the bottom of the frame. Here they are:

```
1    maxx = 10;
2    maxz = 10;
3    iso = new isometricAS(maxx, maxz);
4    buildWorld(maxx, maxz);
5    popup.swapDepths(10);
6    soundOn = true;
```

The first two lines define the size of the grid—ten tiles in the *x* direction and ten in the *z* direction. (There is no need to define the size of the grid in the *y* direction because the grid is only two-dimensional [*x* and *z*] and it sits at the *y* position of 0.) Then we create a new instance of the isometricAS object and give it a reference name of iso. In line 4 we call the buildWorld() function, which creates the objects used to store information about the game. The buildWord() function calls the functions that add the tiles and the monsters. In line 5 we simply move the pop-up movie clip to a depth that is higher than everything else. That way it will not be covered by the movie clip that is attached in the buildWord() function (which is attached at a depth lower than 10).

onEnterFrame

This simple onEnterFrame event for this movie clip is the one that actually positions the characters in each turn; in that sense, it's sort of the "bread and butter" event of the game.

```
1    this.onEnterFrame = function() {
2        moveCharacter();
3        if (inPlay) {
4            positionCharacter();
5        }
6    };
```

The moveCharacter() function is called in every frame. This function will only move a character if the character has not yet reached its destination. In that sense, it shuts itself off when it isn't needed. The positionCharacter() function is called only if the inPlay variable is true. The inPlay variable is set to true when the game is started, and set to false when the game is over. This function renders the position of the character onto the stage using the positions in memory set from the moveCharacter() function.

buildWorld()

The buildWorld() function is called when the frame first loads (as you saw above) and is also called from the restart() function. It handles creating the monsters, the tiles, and the container movie clip to hold them all. It also defines an onMouseMove and onMouseDown event onto the container clip, which is given an instance name of floor. Here is the function:

```
1   function buildWorld(maxx, maxz) {
2       this.attachMovie("grid", "floor", 1);
3       world = new Object();
4       world.depth = 10000;
5       world.maxx = maxx;
6       world.maxz = maxz;
7       world.cellWidth = 29;
8       world.width = maxx*world.cellWidth;
9       world.length = -maxz*world.cellWidth;
10      world.path = this.floor;
11      var path = world.path;
12      buildFloor(path);
13      if (ES.player == 1) {
14          name1 = ES.username;
15          name2 = ES.opponent;
16      } else {
17          name2 = ES.username;
18          name1 = ES.opponent;
19      }
20      buildCharacter(path, name1, 1, 1, 1);
21      buildCharacter(path, name2, 10, 10, 2);
22      floor.onMouseDown = function() {
23          if (!locked && myTurn && inPlay) {
24              this._parent.worldClicked(this._xmouse,
                   → this._ymouse);
25          }
26      };
27      floor.onMouseMove = function() {
28          updateAfterEvent();
29          if (!locked && myTurn && inPlay) {
30              this._parent.over(this._xmouse, this._ymouse);
31          }
32      };
33  }
```

The function starts off by attaching the movie clip from the library that
has a linkage identifier of grid and giving it an instance name of floor.
It is attached at a depth of 1. All other movie clips that will be created
are attached inside of floor.

Over the next several lines (3–10), the world object is created and is used to store information about the world. This is done just like it was in Chapter 8, "The Isometric Worldview." The path property stores a reference to the floor movie clip. In line 12 the buildFloor() function is called and the path reference is passed in. That function creates all of the tiles and uses path to know where to put them.

Lines 13–21 are used to create a monster for each player. First, two variables are created—name1 and name2. The values of these two variables are the user names of the two players. We then call the buildCharacter() function, once for each of the two names. We pass the name to call the monster, the path reference, the x- and z-coordinates of the tile on which to place the monster, and the type of monster to use. There are only two monsters, so the type of monster can be either 1 (for the green monster) or 2 (for the blue monster).

The last thing the buildWorld() function does is define onMouseMove and onMouseDown event handlers for the floor movie clip. When the mouse is clicked, the onMouseDown event handler calls the worldClicked() function. The worldClicked() function determines if the character can walk where you just asked it to (by clicking). If the character can walk there without breaking the rules, then it is instructed to do so. When the mouse is moved, the onMouseMove event handler calls the over() function, which determines if your mouse is currently over a tile that your character can legally walk to. If it is, then a little circle animation is played over that tile.

buildCharacter()

This function is called from the buildWorld() function. It creates the object that stores information about the character that is being created, attaches a character movie clip from the library, and then calls the positionCharacter() function to place the movie clip over the correct tile. Here is the function:

```
1   function buildCharacter(path, name, x_cell, z_cell, type) {
2       var clip = world.path.attachMovie("character"+type,
         ↪ name, ++world.depth);
3       world[name] = new Object();
4       world.char = world[name];
```

```
5       world.char.tempx = world.cellWidth*x_cell-
→ world.cellWidth/2;
6       world.char.tempy = 0;
7       world.char.tempz = -(world.cellWidth*z_cell-
→ world.cellWidth/2);
8       world.char.speed = 4;
9       world.char.xmov = 0;
10      world.char.zmov = 0;
11      world.char.moving = false;
12      world.char.clip = clip;
13      world.char.x_cell = x_cell;
14      world.char.z_cell = z_cell;
15      currentOver = world.tiles[world.char.x_cell]
→ [world.char.z_cell];
16      positionCharacter();
17  }
```

The first thing that happens in this function is that a character movie clip is attached from the library. As mentioned earlier, there are two characters in the library, character1 and character2. The character that is attached is decided by the type parameter passed in, which can be either 1 or 2. The name of the character movie clip being created is set from the name parameter passed in. The name parameter is also used to create an object that is used to store information about the character on the world object (line 3). In lines 5–7 we set the character's starting x, y, and z positions. We then initialize the speed variable, which controls how far the character walks in each frame until it reaches the destination (line 8). In lines 9 and 10, the character's initial velocity in the x and z directions is set to 0. We set the moving property on the character's object to false. That means the character is not moving. In line 12 a reference to the character movie clip is set on the object as clip. We also store the x_cell and z_cell values that are passed into this function on the character's object. These two values represent the current cell that the character is over. In line 15 we set a reference called currentOver. Remember that there is an array called tiles on the world object. Each element in this array is an object that represents a tile. The currentOver reference points to the object representing the tile that the character is currently over.

startGame()

This function is called when it is determined that both players are in the room, or when the restart() function is called.

```
1    function startGame() {
2        flagStopped("yes");
3        inPlay = true;
4        if (ES.player == 1) {
5            myTurn = true;
6            world.char = world[ES.username];
7            var msg = "The game has started. It is your turn!";
8        } else {
9            myTurn = false;
10           world.char = world[ES.opponent];
11           var msg = "The game has started. It is your
             → opponent's turn!";
12       }
13       popup.gotoAndStop("Game Started");
14       popup.msg.text = msg;
15       me = world[ES.username];
16       you = world[ES.opponent];
17   }
```

First we flag the game instance as being able to send or receive a move (line 2). We then set the inPlay variable to true. This tells some other functions, such as positionCharacter(), that it is OK to execute. Then we set the turn so that Player 1 can move first.

It is important to note what is happening in lines 6 and 10. We set the reference world.char to point to the character whose turn it is. When the current turn is over, we set the world.char reference to point to the other character object. We create this reference and flip-flop what it points to as a convenience. In many of the functions you will see that we use world.char to access and modify values. This way we can easily change the object to which the reference points and still use the same functions. Also as a convenience, we set other references to the character objects in lines 15 and 16. These are used by the fall() function discussed later.

worldClicked()

The worldClicked() function is called when a tile is clicked. In it we map the mouse position into the isometric world. From that position we determine which tile area was clicked. We then check to see if that tile exists (if the tile has fallen, then it no longer exists). We also check to see if the tile that was clicked is adjacent to the one on which your character currently stands. If the tile exists and is adjacent to the character's tile, then we accept the click and call the function clickAccepted().

Here is the function:

```
1    function worldClicked(xm, ym) {
2        var temp = iso.mapToIsoWorld(xm, ym);
3        var xm = temp[0];
4        var zm = temp[1];
5        var x_cell = Math.ceil(xm/world.cellWidth);
6        var z_cell = Math.ceil(Math.abs(zm)/world.cellWidth);
7        var xm = x_cell*world.cellWidth-world.cellWidth/2;
8        var zm = -(z_cell*world.cellWidth-world.cellWidth/2);
9        var x_cell_diff = world.char.x_cell-x_cell;
10       var z_cell_diff = world.char.z_cell-z_cell;
11       if (!world.char.moving && world.tiles[x_cell][z_cell].
         → exists && (x_cell_diff != 0 || z_cell_diff != 0) &&
         → ((x_cell_diff == 0 || Math.abs(x_cell_diff) == 1) &&
         → (z_cell_diff == 0 || Math.abs(z_cell_diff) == 1))) {
12           clickAccepted(xm, zm, x_cell, z_cell);
13           sendMove({type:"move", xm:xm, zm:zm, x_cell:x_cell,
             → z_cell:z_cell});
14       }
15   }
```

Take a look at lines 12 and 13. In line 12, clickAccepted() is called and the values for the mouse position and tile that was clicked are passed in. In line 13 we send the move to the other player. When the other player's game instance receives the move, then the moveReceived() function is called on in that player's instance. That game instance then calls the clickAccepted() function and passes in the information needed to move the character.

The clickAccepted() function rotates the character to walk in the direction that you clicked, and then starts the character moving in that direction.

determineFall()

When a character is set to move, the moveCharacter() function determines the next step for the character to take, and moves it there in memory. If it determines that the character has reached its destination, it calls determineFall(). This function tells the tile (the one that the character just left) to fall. It then checks the surrounding tiles to see if any of them have been destabilized enough to fall. (Remember that a tile needs to have at least one full side touching another to stay in the air.)

Here is the function:

```
1    function determineFall() {
2        var x = world.char.old_x_cell;
3        var z = world.char.old_z_cell;
4        var ob = world.tiles[x][z];
5        fall(ob);
6        checkTile(x-1, z);
7        checkTile(x, z+1);
8        checkTile(x+1, z);
9        checkTile(x, z-1);
10   }
```

In lines 2 and 3 we set variables that store the position of the last tile that the character was over. In line 4 we create a reference to the object that represents that tile. Then a function called fall() is executed, and the tile object reference is passed in. That function handles making the tile fall. We will talk about that next. We then call the checkTile() function for each of the four neighbors of the tile that just fell. The checkTile() function checks to see if it is time for that tile to fall.

fall()

This function is called when it has been determined that a tile must fall. A reference to the object that represents the tile is passed in. We check to see if either of the monsters is on the tile. If one or both of the characters is on the tile, then we instruct the character to fall, and the game is over. Here is the function:

```
1   function fall(ob) {
2       if (ob.x == me.x_cell && ob.z == me.z_cell) {
3           var clip = me.clip;
4           clip.ymov = 0;
5           clip.gravity = 1;
6           clip.char = true;
7           clip.onEnterFrame = fallFunction;
8           playSound("scream");
9           iFell = true;
10          end = true;
11      }
12      if (ob.x == you.x_cell && ob.z == you.z_cell) {
13          var clip = you.clip;
14          clip.ymov = 0;
15          clip.gravity = 1;
16          clip.char = true;
17          clip.onEnterFrame = fallFunction;
18          playSound("scream");
19          youFell = true;
20          end = true;
21      }
22      playSound("drop");
23      ob.exists = false;
24      ob.clip.ymov = 0;
25      ob.clip.gravity = 1;
26      ob.clip.onEnterFrame = fallFunction;
27  }
```

In lines 2–11 we check to see if the character whose game instance is running this code is on that tile. If so, then we play a scream sound and give the character an onEnterFrame event that makes it fall. Also, we set the variable iFell to true and end to true. Lines 12–21 do the exact same thing as 2–11, but for the other character. If that other character falls, then youFell is set to true and end is set to true. In either case, the drop sound is played (line 22) because the tile is falling. We set the exists property on the object that represents this tile to false. We do this so that if this space is clicked again, a character can't walk there. We then give the tile movie clip some initial variables and an onEnterFrame function so that it animates itself downward to imitate falling.

The moveCharacter() function uses the variables end, iFell, and youFell to determine if the game is over and who won. Here are the possible combinations.

TABLE 19.1 ## Who wins?

Event	Game Instance Settings		Winner
	Player 1	**Player 2**	
Player 1 falls	iFell=true	youFell=true	Player 2
Player 2 falls	youFell=true	iFell=true	Player 1
Both fall	iFell=true, youFell=true	iFell=true, youFell=true	Neither

checkTile()

This function is called from the determineFall() function, as seen above. It checks to see if the tile specified should fall.

```
1   function checkTile(x, z) {
2       var ob = world.tiles[x][z];
3       if (ob.exists) {
4           var ob1 = world.tiles[x-1][z];
5           var ob2 = world.tiles[x][z+1];
6           var ob3 = world.tiles[x+1][z];
7           var ob4 = world.tiles[x][z-1];
8           if (!ob1.exists && !ob2.exists && !ob3.exists &&
              → !ob4.exists) {
9               fall(ob);
10          }
11      }
12  }
```

First we set a reference to the tile specified, called ob. If ob.exists is true, then we know that it is possible for the tile to fall. If ob.exists is not true, then the tile has already fallen or never existed in the first place. In lines 4–7 we set references to the four tiles that touch any of this tile's sides. If none of them exist, then this tile must fall. If any of them exist, then the tile can stay.

POSSIBLE GAME ENHANCEMENTS

You have seen the inner workings of this simple yet addictive game. At one point I had this game on my site, and thousands of people played it. They kept coming back to play (which is always a good thing), but many requested more interesting additions. We at Electrotank are working on some new additions to this game to make it more interesting. Check out GameBook.net (www.gamebook.net) periodically if you are curious to see what we come up with! Here are a few simple suggestions for what you can do to make game play more engaging:

- Allow more than two players to play simultaneously. This is a topic that I did not have time to cover for this book. Introducing more than two players into a game adds a new level of complexity to game design, but if you can accomplish it, it's also sure make this game more interesting. Check out www.gamebook.net, the Web site for this book, from time to time. I may get around to providing a source file for a game that can support more than two players simultaneously.

- Add more creative tiles. Make it so that some tiles can be stepped on two times, or three times. Maybe some tiles do something interesting and unexpected, like warp you to another tile of the same type.

- Add collectible and destructive items. Perhaps you can pick up a land mine. Then when you land on a certain tile—one on which you can step multiple times—you can place the land mine there. This land mine can be invisible to other players and will explode (taking a few tiles with it) if an opponent comes within a certain distance. But watch out—your opponent may have placed one, too!

- Use multiple vertical levels. You can have more than one floor in this game. Using steps or elevators or warps, you can allow players to move from one level to another.

These are just a few of the many possible alterations to this game that can make it much more interesting. With each added feature, though, comes added complexity and greater chances of introducing bugs. So be prepared to do some multiplayer debugging!

POINTS TO REMEMBER

- Make use of room variables to keep track of which players have arrived.

- Using the sendMove() method of the ElectroServerAS object, you can easily send information to your opponent.

- The sendMove() function allows you to send objects. It is a good idea to use a property like type on the object, to concisely describe why the object is being sent. For instance, in checkers you might have a special move for making a checker a king. In this case the type property would be "king". For other moves it would probably just be "move".

- There are two characters used in this game, automatically chosen based on which player you are.

- The world.char reference is used to point to the character whose turn it is.

- The fall() function determines if a character is on a tile. If this is the case, the function tells the character to fall, and the game is over.

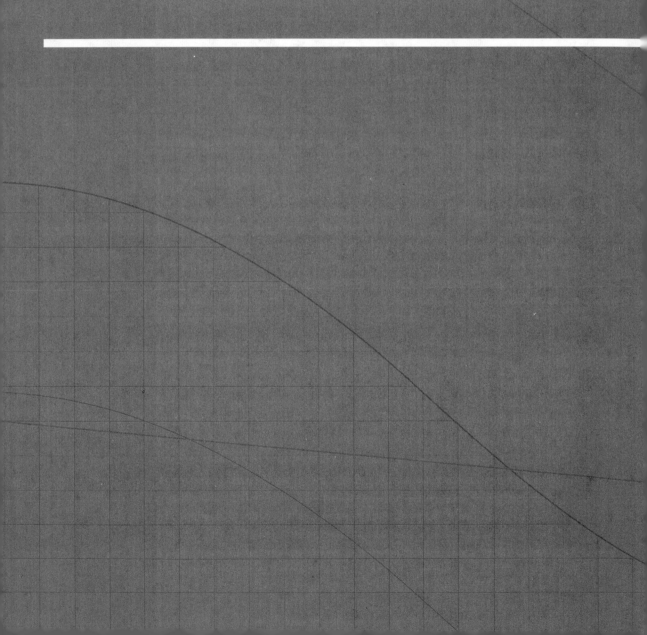

APPENDIXES

APPENDIX A

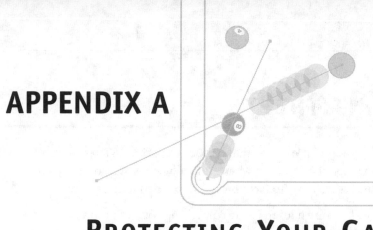

PROTECTING YOUR GAMES

WHILE THE INTERNET IS A WONDERFUL PLAYGROUND AND RESOURCE, IT IS also a new medium for thieves. Theft of content has been a problem for as long as the Internet has been around. Luckily for us, there are things we can do to help protect all our hard work. Here we'll discuss the vulnerabilities of SWF files and the choices you have for protecting these files.

THEFT AND ANTITHEFT

Picture this: You find a Web site that has dozens of cool Web games. You are browsing through the game list when suddenly you see … one of yours! Sound unlikely? It's not—in fact, this has happened to me several times.

You have worked very hard to create something you are proud of. You should spend a little extra time taking steps to help prevent its being stolen. Listed below are the three major vulnerabilities of your SWF files and what you can do to eliminate them.

Vulnerability: Downloading the SWF

Someone can download your SWF file or copy it from his browser's cache to his own hard drive. He can then play the game on his own computer or upload it to his own server for other people to play. This is the most common SWF theft problem.

Deterrent(s)

There is nothing you can do to prevent someone from taking the SWF file. But you can do several things to help prevent this game from working properly when downloaded.

_url

This is a property that has been in Flash since version 4 and has never gotten much attention. I'd now like to give it the attention it deserves. This little guy can help you in a tremendous way: It returns the absolute path to the SWF itself. For instance, if the SWF file is being run from the location http://www.electrotank.com/minigolf.swf, then the _url property returns `http://www.electrotank.com/minigolf.swf` as a string. For example:

```
myURL=_url;
```

This line of code sets a variable whose value is the absolute path to the SWF file. Now let's see how this is going to help you protect your game.

```
1   myURL=_url;
2   okDomain="www.electrotank.com"
3   if (myURL.indexOf(okDomain) != -1) {
4       _root.gotoAndStop("game screen")
5   } else {
6       _root.gotoAndStop("warning message");
7   }
```

Line 2 above sets a string called okDomain, whose value is a single domain
that is allowed access to the file. Then, on line 3, the indexOf string
method is used to see if the allowable domain is part of myURL. If it's being
run from the correct server, the game goes to the frame labeled *game screen;*
otherwise it goes to the frame labeled *warning message.* If someone (illegally) downloads a SWF file that has this sort of script in it, he will not be
able to view the content properly. Mission accomplished!

Multiple Files

Structuring your game to use multiple files is a natural sort of theft protection. This good coding practice makes it easier for you replace your content,
and harder for someone to take it. For instance, let's say you have a jigsaw
puzzle that loads in images dynamically. A thief can easily read the HTML
in your Web page to find the name of your SWF file, but how will this person know the names of your image files? In Entry 3 below, I'll list one way
for a person to find out these filenames, but the fact that there are multiple
files provides a level of protection that will deter most nefarious types.

ActionScript Review: indexOf

The method used above, indexOf, is a method of the string object. It
checks to see if the parameter passed into it exists in the string to
which it was applied. If this search string does exist, then the position
of this search is returned. If the search string does not exist, then the
number −1 is returned.

Vulnerability: Embedding the SWF through HTML

A person can write an HTML page that embeds your SWF file even though it's on another server. When visited, this HTML file loads the SWF, and viewers of the page will think the content belongs to the owner of this site.

Deterrent

Sadly, there is not a good solution to prevent this. Technically, your files are not being stolen. One common technique people use to circumvent this problem is to rename their files frequently. This can be a hassle, but it works. If Web sites are pointing to your games and you rename your file(s), those Web pages will no longer show your file. The administrator of that Web site will have to look through your HTML again to find the new name. If you find a Web site that consistently updates its own pages every time you rename your files, you may want to try contacting the owner's ISP (Internet service provider—information on this is listed later in this appendix).

Vulnerability: Expose the ActionScript

A hacker can download your SWF files and open them with software designed to read ActionScript. With this software, your code is exposed, as are the names of files that you may be loading in. This can be a huge issue if you have trade secrets or just plain don't want to give away your code. Also, an advanced hacker can use a program that will allow him or her to edit binary files, such as a SWF. That means the hacker can remove the protections you had in your file, such as the `_url` property protection, and then resave it.

Deterrent

There is nothing that you can do to keep a serious villain from reading the ActionScript in your file. But there is something that will make you smile and the evil-doer grimace: obfuscation. To obfuscate something means to make it confusing or hard to understand. An obfuscator is an application that will take your file, read through every bit of code, and replace the code names with gibberish. The ActionScript still works—it just uses oddly named variables and other references. Here is an example of a function that has been obfuscated.

```
1   function F_]}•êaŸTÖ (ÈŒüm_P, Á_Qîî, F, O1/4C_,
    → mù__, Fü_O, Fü__) {
2       var eval ("ÈX_");
3       var eval ("_O");
4       var eval ("_m");
5       var eval ("_§");
6       var eval ("På");
7       var eval ("…_");
8       var eval ("PŸ");
9       var eval ("mŸ");
10      var eval ("b_]_P");
11      var eval ("È") = new Array ();
12      eval ("b_]_P") = 0.0174532925199433;
13      eval ("På") = Math.sin(eval ("Á_Qîî") * eval ("b_]_P"));
14      eval ("…_") = Math.cos(eval ("Á_Qîî") * eval ("b_]_P"));
15      eval ("È")[0] = new Array ();
16      eval ("È")[1] = new Array ();
17      eval ("È")[2] = new Array ();
18      eval ("È")[3] = new Array ();
19      var W = 0;
20      while (W < 4) {
21          eval ("_O") = eval ("ÈŒüm_P")[W][0];
22          eval ("_§") = eval ("ÈŒüm_P")[W][2];
23          eval ("_m") = (-eval ("ÈŒüm_P")[W][2]) * eval ("På");
24          eval ("_§") = eval ("_§") * eval ("…_");
25          eval ("ÈX_") = F / (eval ("_§") + F);
26          eval ("È")[W][0] = eval ("O1/4C_") + (eval ("ÈX_") *
            → eval ("_O"));
27          eval ("È")[W][1] = eval ("mù__") - (eval ("ÈX_") *
            → eval ("_m"));
28          W++;
29      }
30      eval ("F_]fgôü_H")("ôü_H0", eval ("È")[0][0], eval
        → ("È")[0][1], eval ("È")[1][0], eval ("È")[1][1]);
31      eval ("F_]fgôü_H")("ôü_H1", eval ("È")[1][0], eval
        → ("È")[1][1], eval ("È")[2][0], eval ("È")[2][1]);
```

```
32      eval ("F_]fgôü_H")("ôü_H2", eval ("È")[2][0], eval
     →  ("È")[2][1], eval ("È")[3][0], eval ("È")[3][1]);
33      eval ("F_]fgôü_H")("ôü_H3", eval ("È")[3][0], eval
     →  ("È")[3][1], eval ("È")[0][0], eval ("È")[0][1]);
34      eval ("F_]fgôü_H")("é__PPÑôü_H", eval ("01/4C_") - eval
     →  ("Fü_0"), 35 eval ("mù__"), eval ("01/4C_") + eval
     →  ("Fü_0"), eval ("mù__"));
35      this.eval ("Úü____")._x = eval ("01/4C_");
36      this.eval ("Úü____")._y = eval ("mù__");
37      this.eval ("Úü____")._xscale = 40;
38      this.eval ("Úü____")._yscale = 40 * eval ("På");
39    }
```

Can you understand what the function above was designed to do? Probably
not, and that's the point! Not only is it almost impossible to understand,
but if you pasted this into the Actions panel and tried to create a SWF, Flash
would give you an error. There is an amazing obfuscator created by Robin
Debreuil specifically for Flash, available at www.debreuil.com/vs/. At the
time this book was written this obfuscator only worked with Flash 5, but a
Flash MX version was in the works. So chances are that a Flash MX version
is at the above URL waiting to obfuscate something for you.

The battle of software theft has been around for a long time and may never
go away. If security is an important issue to you, I recommend that you
stay informed about the latest developments in security holes and
enhancements. A good way to do this is to subscribe to popular Flash
mailing lists, or to frequent message boards (see Appendix E for recom-
mendations). If you keep up-to-date on these issues, you'll be safe from
most casual hackers.

SO YOU FOUND YOUR GAME ON ANOTHER WEB SITE?

For whatever reason (most likely an unprotected or hacked SWF), your game is sitting on another server illegally, and you want it removed. Here are some things you can do.

Email the Webmaster

Almost all Web sites have a "Contact" or "About Us" page. On one of those pages you're most likely to find a contact email address. Write something like this:

> IIi,
>
> *My name is Jobe Makar, and I'm from Electrotank (http://www.electrotank.com). I have noticed that you are using a game of mine without my permission. Software piracy is a crime, but I would like to resolve this without involving my attorney. Please remove the game immediately. If it has not been removed within 24 hours, I will be forced to take legal action. Thank you for your immediate removal of this game.*
>
> *Jobe Makar*
> *Electrotank*
> *www.electrotank.com*
> *Phone: (555) 555-5555*
> *Fax: (555) 555-5555*

Email or Call the ISP

If you get no response from the Webmaster, you can involve the site's Internet service provider (ISP). I have contacted the ISPs of more than a dozen Web sites to have content removed and find it very effective—they don't want to be associated with any illegal activity and are quick to take action. Here is how you find out the ISP of a Web site.

1. *Go to www.networksolutions.com.*

All domains must be registered, and most of them are registered at Network Solutions.

2. *Click the WHOIS tab.*

This is where you search for information about a domain.

3. *Type in the domain name you're investigating, and click GO!*

4. *Analyze the results.*

You may see personal information about the owner of the domain (such as phone number and address). Toward the bottom you will see information about the domain servers—and that's how you find the site's ISP. For instance, if NS.MEDIA3.NET is the domain server, then www.media3.net is the ISP. You can then visit the ISP's Web site and contact the ISP by phone or email.

Here is an actual letter I once wrote to an ISP after days of ineffective letters to the Web site's owner.

> *My name is Jobe Makar, President of Electrotank, Inc., in the USA. It has just come to my knowledge that a Web site (http://www.wwwww.com) is hosting dozens of games illegally. The only one that Electrotank is really concerned with is our own, and it can be found here: http://www.wwwww.com/minigolf.htm.*
>
> *I am sure that [This Company] does not support software piracy. Electrotank would be grateful if you would assure us that our game will be removed from this Web site immediately. If wwwww.com is not one of your clients, then I apologize, but our research seems to indicate that it is.*
>
> *Thank you for your swift action.*
>
> *Jobe Makar*
> *Electrotank, Inc.*
> *www.electrotank.com*
> *Phone: (555) 555-5555*
> *Fax: (555) 555-5555*

The matter was resolved in under an hour after I sent this!

Take Legal Action

Happily for me, this is something I haven't experienced. Every letter to an ISP has been effective. However, some day you may encounter your content on a Web site that is its own ISP (or has some other reason for not removing the game). In this case, look in the phone book (or on the Internet, of course!), or start polling your savvy friends, for an attorney specializing in Internet law.

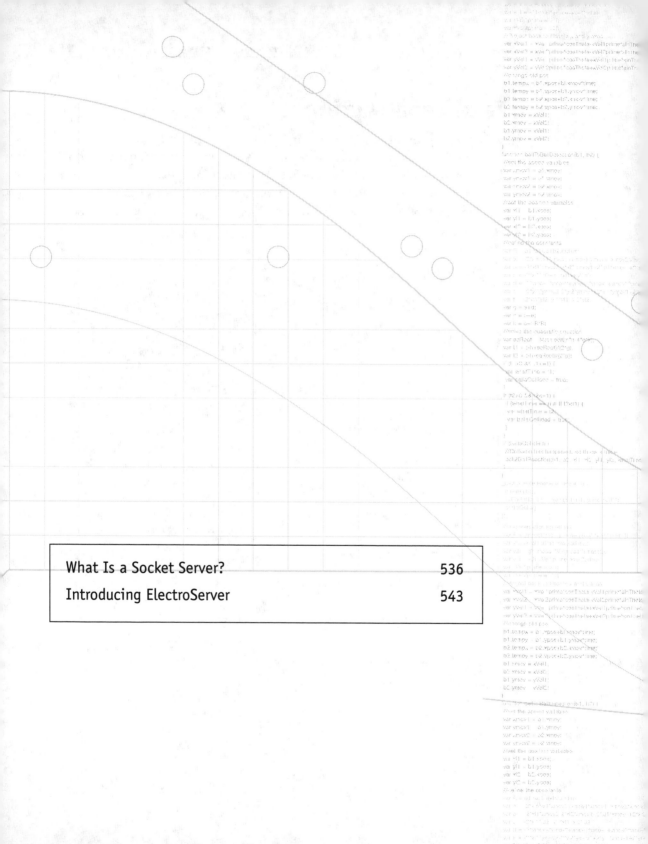

APPENDIX B

MULTIUSER SERVERS

THROUGHOUT THIS BOOK WE HAVE DISSECTED MANY DIFFERENT GAMES, some of which were multiplayer. When we work with multiplayer games, we use a *socket server* called ElectroServer, along with an ActionScript object called ElectroServerAS. In this appendix, we discuss what a socket server is, how one works, and how you can use one for your own games. More specifically, we talk about ElectroServer. We also discuss how to install ElectroServer on almost any computer, from a desktop model to a multiprocessor Sun server.

WHAT IS A SOCKET SERVER?

Before we can get into the details of installing and using a socket server, it's important to understand what a socket server is. Put simply, a socket server—also called a *multiuser server*—is a server that listens for inbound client connections on a port and allows those clients to communicate with each other over a common protocol (which in the case of ElectroServer will be XML). That's quite a mouthful! Let's break this concept down into more digestible parts. We'll start with a review of the Internet basics on which a socket server depends.

Internet Basics

While I'm sure everyone reading this uses the Internet just about all the time, it's surprising to learn how little most developers know about how it actually works. I've always felt that the more knowledge you have about something, the more effective you can be in using it. In the case of socket servers, this knowledge can help you avoid the sticky deployment and security issues that so many people run into.

IP Address

While the Internet Protocol (IP) address isn't even close to being the lowest level of networking on the Internet, it's the lowest layer we need to worry about. An IP address means just what it says: It's essentially the address of a computer on the Internet. While there are exceptions, it's easiest to assume that each computer on the Internet has a unique IP address. An IP address, coupled with some other Internet technologies, is enough to let any machine find and communicate with any other machine over the Internet.

An IP address typically takes the form

XX.XX.XX.XX

where each segment can be a one, two, or three-digit number. For example, one of the Web servers for Macromedia.com is

65.57.83.12

These numbers are called *dotted quads* or just *IPs*. A single number in the IP is called an *octet* because its maximum size is 2^8, defined as a range of 0–255. At first glance, it may seem as if the number of IP addresses available is huge and we will never run out; but in reality we are already getting uncomfortably close to the limit. The current IPv4 specification allows for about 4.3 billion addresses, but with the explosive growth of users on the Internet, more and more IPs are needed every day.

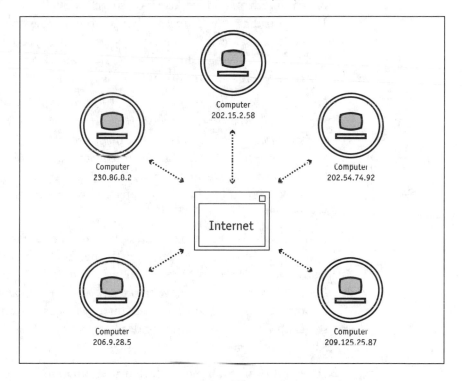

To this end, a new version of the IP specification called IPv6 is in the works. This specification adds improved multimedia streaming and better performance. But most important, it increases the IP address size from 32-bit to 128-bit.

How do you get an IP? In the case of home users, you are assigned an IP address when your machine connects to your ISP. If you are on dial-up, this means that every time you connect to the Internet, you typically get a new IP address. For the most part, cable and DSL modems work the same way, but as you are always connected, your IP usually won't change unless you reboot your machine. There are some exceptions to this, however. Many DSL providers are using a technology named PPPoE (Point-to-Point

Protocol over Ethernet), which allows you to disconnect and reconnect with your machine still running. When this happens, you could be assigned a new IP address. Also, it is possible to "release" your current IP address and get another one, but the method for doing so depends on your operating system and there is no guarantee that it will be a new IP address.

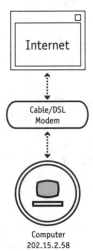

Computer
202.15.2.58

The illustration at left shows the typical home computer setup with a DSL or cable modem. You can also have something called a *static IP address*. This means that your IP doesn't change from one day to the next but stays the same even after your connection goes down or you have to reboot. Servers on the Internet almost always have static IP addresses, and there are few cases where you wouldn't want one.

So do you have to be online to get an IP address? Not at all! Any machine that supports TCP/IP (the protocol the Internet uses) always has an IP available to it. This is a reserved IP called the *loopback IP*, and you can connect to it using the IP 127.0.0.1 or the host name *localhost*. This IP is used for diagnostics and testing but can also be used by us Flash developers to run socket servers locally without anyone else's being able to access them. We will talk more about this later.

I said previously that each computer on the Internet has a unique IP address, and also that this is not strictly true. You've probably heard of firewalls and routers. These devices can be used to hide IP addresses from the Internet in various ways. Now before any of you groan and skip ahead, know that I bring this up because it directly relates to running a socket server on your home machine and getting people to see it on the Internet. Kind of important!

Here's a real-life example to illustrate the situation. If a small corporation wanted to provide its 20 employees with Internet access from their workstations through the company's dedicated ISDN line, how would it do this? One possible way would be to contact the company's ISP and have 20 IP addresses made available to its network. This constitutes a maintenance headache and a lot of administrative overhead. A simpler way would be to use a technology called Network Address Translation (NAT). NAT allows one computer to act as a gateway to the Internet for other computers. This computer would have one connection to the Internet with an externally available IP address, and another connection to the internal network with an internal address. This is usually accomplished by having two network cards. By "internal address," I mean an IP that only the internal network will understand. Often these start with *10* in the first octet. Each computer on the internal network would also have its own unique internal IP and would understand that to connect to the Internet, it needs to go through the gateway.

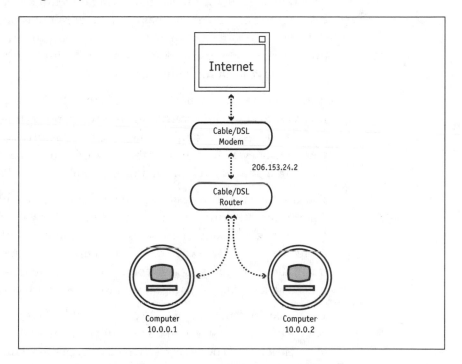

I bring this up because many people with cable modems or DSL access use small router/firewall appliances made by companies such as Linksys, 3Com, or Intel. When you use one of these appliances, you cannot run a socket server on the internally designated IP address and expect people on the external Internet to see it without some configuration changes. Specifically, you can start the server without any problems, but when you give out your IP and port, people will not be able to connect to it. If this happens, you may need to use the DMZ, port, or IP forwarding feature of your appliance to allow external clients to connect to your server. A DMZ allows your computer to be in an unsecure location on your network, and thus the firewall allows anyone in. Port and IP forwarding are ways to tell your firewall to send all IP requests on a given port to your server rather than blocking them. One other solution to this problem is to open up that port on your firewall so that it is not restricted. Implementing any of these solutions is beyond the scope of this appendix. Look in your router/firewall appliance's documentation to see which will work best for you.

Ports

Thus far, we have talked about a computer's address on the Internet. This is a valid analogy on the surface, but it still needs some refinement. The typical computer on the Internet has one IP address but is often running many different Internet-related applications at the same time. As you know, Web browsers, instant messengers, email clients, multiplayer games, and other applications can all run simultaneously.

With only one address, how does your computer know which application needs the data you are receiving? This is where ports come into play. For every IP address on a computer there are 65,536 ports associated with it. If you think of every IP address as the real-world address of an apartment building, a port would be an apartment number.

This means that, theoretically, your desktop computer could be talking to 65,000+ remote computers at the same time without getting confused. (Realistically, a desktop machine couldn't handle that, but some servers are more than able to.) So when talking to a remote computer, you use not just the IP address but also a specific port to uniquely identify both the computer *and* the service/application with which you wish to communicate.

You would think that with 65,536 ports available, there would be enough for every service imaginable. And for the most part, there are—but still, you have to be careful. Many ports are reserved for a specific functionality, such as HTTP, FTP, POP, SMTP, and many others. The general rule of thumb is that you should never use any port below 1024 for your own applications. In the case of Flash with XMLSocket, this is a hard rule—Flash is unable to use a port below 1024. Below is a table of common ports used by various services.

TABLE 1 **Commonly Used Ports**

Internet Service	TCP Port
HTTP	80
HTTPS	443
SMTP	25
POP3	110
FTP	21
Telnet	23
NMTP	119

Sockets

A socket is simply one endpoint of a two-way connection over a network. Any socket is defined by an IP and a port. When a server application is running, it "listens" on a socket for inbound connections from a client. A client, such as a Web browser, knows the IP or host name and port number of the server, and attempts to connect. If all goes properly, the server accepts the connection and then moves the client's connection to a different socket, which it picks internally. This is so that the server can continue listening for clients on the original socket, in order to accommodate more than one client at a time. Once they are connected through the internally picked socket, both the client and the server are able to communicate with each other directly.

Let's follow through with our example of a Web browser. You open your favorite Internet browser and type in http://www.macromedia.com. Through the wonder of DNS (that's a Domain Name Server, which maps an IP address to a domain name), that domain name gets translated to 65.57.83.12. The browser knows you are using HTTP; therefore it knows the port is 80. This is enough information to attempt to establish a socket connection to 65.57.83.12:80. Internally, the Web browser does exactly that. The Macromedia Web server accepts the connection and shuffles your browser to a different socket on its side. At this point, your browser is able to request a Web page. Once you have finished getting the page you want, your browser automatically closes the connection to the server and is able to move on. This is only a very simple description of what happens, but it gives you the basic idea.

Where Does Flash Fit In?

We have now talked about the basic underlying technologies used to establish TCP connections between computers on the Internet, and how a common application handles this transaction. Now, how does Flash accomplish this? Easy—exactly the same way!

Flash does not handle sockets any differently than your Web browser does. The only difference is the protocol that's used. In a Web browser it's HTTP. When you receive email, it's POP3 or IMAP. For sending email, it's SMTP. In Flash it's XML, which you define yourself to best customize it to your task. (And Flash hasn't chosen a specific port number, so you can pick whatever port you want, as long as it's above 1024.)

Now that you have all that background material under your belt, we will talk specifically about socket servers and how they work with Flash.

Socket Servers

A socket server is just a server that listens on a socket for a connection from a Flash client, and accepts those connections when it hears them. That seems straightforward enough, but now you are probably thinking: What makes a socket server different from a Web server? Well, two things specifically: A socket server uses a different protocol, and its connections are state-full.

A *state-full* connection is one that remembers the user between interactions. This critical difference dramatically extends Flash's abilities over an application based on the HTTP protocol. The HTTP protocol is not state-full. There are many clever methods to make it *appear* to remember a client between requests, but in reality a Web page doesn't know if you visited it five minutes or five days ago. It is always up to the non-state-full application (any Web application using HTTP) to determine who you are, as well as to store any data it needs to remember about you. Conversely, the connections to a socket server are held open until you explicitly close them with code, or until you close the Flash application. This means that many transactions can occur over one connection, and that the server can remember you between transactions with little difficulty. This is necessary for chat functionality such as game history, accurate counts of people in a room, and so on.

The protocol for a Web server is HTTP. The high-level protocol for a socket server, as we've said, is XML. This is where the power and flexibility of a socket server come into play. By using XML as the high-level protocol, you are able to define your own specific (that is, user-defined) protocol for the application at hand. The multiuser game chapters in Part 3 will explain this in some detail.

Introducing ElectroServer

As you can see, a socket server is a simple yet powerful communication tool. The specific implementations of a socket server may vary, but the basic idea is the same. There are several major socket servers available for Flash and quite a few minor ones. Here we'll introduce you to the one we know best, and which, of course, is best suited for the online gaming environment: ElectroServer. ElectroServer is a high-performance socket server designed by your friends at Electrotank (www.electrotank.com) with multiplayer Flash games in mind. Throughout this book, the multiplayer games have all used ElectroServer and its various features. Over the next few pages, we will discuss those features and how you can install, use, and administer ElectroServer for your own use.

If you're planning to run the server, make sure to read "Properties File" in the "Configuring ElectroServer" section below.

On the CD we have included a full version of ElectroServer and a demo license key. The demo license key is limited to five concurrent connections but will work on any IP address. This means that up to five people can be connected to the server at once. ElectroServer running in demo mode *must* be able to connect to the Internet every time it is started, or it will shut itself down. For the most recent information on ElectroServer, or if you are interested in a copy that accepts more than five concurrent connections, visit www.electrotank.com/ElectroServer.

Features

ElectroServer has several unique abilities that other socket servers don't support, and that allow for some sophisticated game functionality. We will start with the basic features and work toward the more advanced ones. Many features are configurable via a properties file (which we'll discuss in "Configuring ElectroServer" below).

Rooms. ElectroServer supports a room model for all chatting and games. This means that when you connect to the server, you are not automatically in a room, and you must join one to do anything.

Rooms can be either visible or hidden (in which case they don't show up on the room list). The ElectroServerAS object used in this book (and discussed in further detail in Appendix C) takes care of this for you. Making a game room invisible keeps people from attempting to join it.

When the number of users in a room changes, all rooms set to receive updates will be notified of the new room size. This is useful for getting a count of users in any given room. But rooms can also be configured to ignore these updates for performance reasons, and many people prefer that configuration.

Room list. All clients (users) receive an accurate list of all visible rooms on the server. This list contains the quantity of users in all rooms as well. It does not contain rooms that have been marked invisible.

User list. Within each room is a list of users for that room. This list is updated every time someone enters or leaves the room, so it is always up-to-date.

Private messages. ElectroServer supports the ability for users to send private messages to any specific player on the server.

Administrators. ElectroServer supports the concept of administrators. Administrators are users who have access to the kick and ban functionality (discussed below). To create or remove an administrator account, you use the built-in administrator console application (explained later).

Kick user. If a user is acting up (and believe me, this happens a *lot*), then you can kick the user from the server. This does not work in the same way as a kick in IRC (which only removes you from a room). In ElectroServer, the kick command disconnects a user totally from the server and gives him a message about why he was booted. This command is only available to users who have administrator-level status.

Ban user. If a user is being particularly bad, you can ban her from the server. Ban is based on the user's IP address, so it is not foolproof. But it is permanent—if you ban her and restart the server, she is still banned from the system. An administration tool is provided to remove users from the ban list. The ability to ban is only available to users who have administrator-level status.

Logging. ElectroServer provides extensive logging functionality to ensure smooth operation. When the server starts, it initializes all necessary components and logs that information to the screen. Once the components are started and the server is listening for users, it starts logging instead to whatever location is specified in the properties file. If requested, the server will roll log files—rename the old file and start a new one with the original name—at startup. The server supports configurable levels of logging, allowing you to determine how much or how little information you want to capture. All error, kick, and ban messages are logged no matter what.

Language filtering. ElectroServer supports the ability to determine if a player is using words that are prohibited on the site. The prohibited words are listed in a text file specified in the properties file. This feature can be enabled or disabled and has many configurable options, including the ability to kick the offenders from the server.

System messages. A system message is one transmitted to all users in all rooms, regardless of their status. It can be used to inform users of events about to occur, such as a server restart or a celebrity chat. Only administrator-level users can send out system messages.

Room variables. A room variable is defined at the room level by a user. These variables have various configurable behaviors. For instance, a room variable can be configured to remove itself when the user who created it leaves the room. A room variable can be locked to protect it from being overwritten, or it can be persistent and maintained even when the user who created it leaves the room. Room variables are automatically sent to all users when they are created, modified, or deleted. A user gets all the room variables in a room when he joins the room. Room variables are one of the features that make ElectroServer especially well suited for games.

Object serialization. This powerful ElectroServer feature actually stems from its client-side object. The ElectroServerAS object supports the ability to take most ActionScript objects not bound to physical resources (such as movie clips and sound clips) and send them to the room the user is in, or even use them as room variables. This makes it quick and easy to send complicated data structures to anyone you wish.

Detect updates. ElectroServer supports the ability to automatically check for updates to its code over the Internet. When the server first starts, it makes an HTTP connection to www.electrotank.com and checks the available versions. It determines if the version online is newer than your current version and notifies you.

Administration. ElectroServer supports several console-based administration applications to ease administering the server. You can manage the administrator accounts, as well as the banned-user lists, from simple console applications.

Installing ElectroServer

While this is a production-quality server, you can very easily run it on your local workstation. In fact, that is the recommended way to develop multi-user applications.

There are several ways to install ElectroServer. As ElectroServer is written completely in Java, it will run on any platform that supports the 1.3.1 Java Virtual Machine. Sun Microsystems currently has downloads for Windows, Solaris, and Linux; and many other platforms support Java as well, such as Mac OS X and HPUX.

The first thing you need to do, regardless of platform, is install the Java Virtual Machine. For Windows, Solaris, or Linux you can find it at Java.Sun.com (http://java.sun.com). For Mac OS X, you can find it at Mac OS X Java Runtime Environment (http://developer.apple.com/java).

Follow the directions listed with the download and install the Java environment. When you are completely finished, you should be able to type *java* from a command prompt and get a response that looks something like this:

```
C:\WINDOWS\Desktop>java
Usage: java [-options] class [args...]
        (to execute a class)
  or  java -jar [-options] jarfile [args...]
        (to execute a jar file)
```

This is how it looks for the 1.4 JVM, so yours might look a little different. At this point, your computer should be able to run Java applications, and you should be able to proceed with the actual installation of ElectroServer, which should be very simple.

Windows Installation

Run the Windows installer (setup.exe) for ElectroServer from the CD included with this book. You'll find it in the Demos\ElectroServer\Windows folder. Run this application as you would any other, and follow the onscreen prompts to finish installing ElectroServer. This installation will create a Start-menu group as well as a script you can use to start and stop the server as needed. The setup application also creates an uninstaller.

Unix Installation

Locate the Demos\ElectroServer\Unix folder on the CD. Copy the files in that directory to the location from which you want the server to run. Usually it's something like /usr/local/ElectroServer, but that is completely at your discretion. Then execute the Setup.sh script. It will extract the contents of the .tar file into your current directory. The server should now be installed correctly.

Other Platform Installation

Locate the Demos\ElectroServer\Generic folder on the CD. Take the .zip file in that folder and manually extract it to wherever you want the server to execute.

The difference you will see between this installation and the other installation methods is that this one won't create easy-to-use start and stop scripts for you.

Configuring ElectroServer

Now that you have the server and Java installed, you need to configure it to reflect your desired environment, startup options, and features. Configuring ElectroServer is quite simple; everything you need to manage or change can be done through either an easy-to-use console application or the text-based properties file.

Properties File

Most of the ElectroServer configuration occurs through the Electro-Server.properties file that is created in the installation directory. You can open this file in any text editor, such as Notepad or VI. The various configuration options for the ElectroServer.properties file are documented right in the file, so we will not cover that information here. Any changes to the properties file require you to restart the server.

There are two configurations that are crucial to starting the server. The first is

```
General.LicenseFileLocation
```

This option points to the ElectroServer license file in the installation directory, without which the server cannot start. By default, it points to the demo license file, which lets you run the ElectroServer on any IP address and port, but with a maximum of five connections at once. This license also requires the server to be able to connect to the Internet, or it will not start. If you have any settings in the properties file that don't match your license file, the server will inform you of that, and shut down.

The second crucial configuration is

```
ChatServer.IP
```

This setting is used for the chat server's IP address. By default, it is set to 127.0.0.1. This is the loopback IP for your machine, as we discussed previously. You will have to change this if you want other people on the Internet to connect to the server.

Administrator Accounts

If you wish to have administrators for your chat server, you have to set the ChatServer.AdministrationEnabled setting in the properties file to true. Once this is done, you will need to run the ElectroServer administration tool to add administrators. Here's how you can run the tool in various platforms.

Windows—Either choose the Start Administrator option from the Start menu or go to ElectroServer's installation folder and run the file StartAdministrator.bat.

Unix—From ElectroServer's installation folder, run StartAdministrator.sh.

Other platforms—From ElectroServer's installation folder, run

```
java -cp ElectroServerV2.jar com.electrotank.electroserver
→ .admin.ElectroAdmin
```

Please note that no matter how this looks onscreen, it's one command line.

Once in the tool, choose the Manage Administrator Accounts option and follow the onscreen prompts.

Language Filter

The Language filter manages a customizable list of any words you want blocked on your chat server. You simply specify the location of the bad-word list in the ElectroServer.properties file. This list is a plain-text file in this format:

```
Badword1
Badword2
...
Badword10
```

You can change this file at any time, but you need to restart the server in order to see those changes.

Banned IPs

If some IP addresses have been banned on the server and you want to remove them from the restricted list, you will need to run the ElectroServer administration tool. You can run the tool in the same way you did for administering admin accounts. Once in the tool, choose the Manage Banned IP Addresses option, then follow the onscreen prompts.

Running ElectroServer

Running ElectroServer is similar to running the Administrator—very simple. As you can imagine, the server must be started before you can jump into testing, playing, or chatting.

Starting the Server

Windows—Choose the Start ElectroServer option from the Start menu, or go to the ElectroServer installation folder and run StartElectroServer.bat.

Unix—Run StartElectroServer.sh from the ElectroServer installation folder.

Other platforms—Run

```
java -cp ElectroServerV2.jar com.electrotank.electroserver
→ .ElectroServer ElectroServer.properties
```

from the ElectroServer installation folder.

Stopping the Server

Windows—Choose the Stop ElectroServer option from the Start menu, or go to the ElectroServer installation folder and run StopElectroServer.bat.

Unix—Run StopElectroServer.sh from the ElectroServer installation folder.

Other platforms—Run

```
java -cp ElectroServerV2.jar com.electrotank.electroserver
.StopES ElectroServer.properties
```

from the ElectroServer installation folder.

ElectroServer has been around from almost the beginning of Flash 5 and has seen a lot of use for many different applications. It has been used by multiple companies on many platforms with great success. With a little effort, you should have no trouble adapting it for your needs.

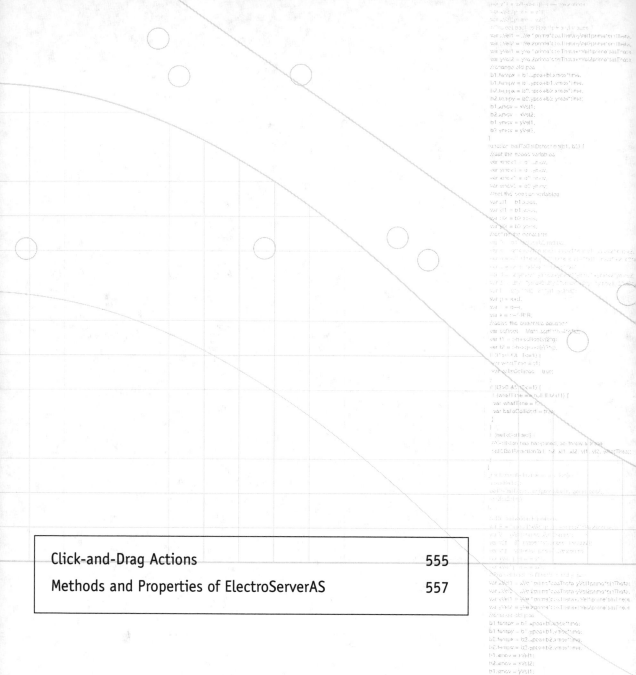

APPENDIX C

THE ELECTROSERVERAS OBJECT

THE `ElectroServerAS` object ALLOWS YOU TO EASILY CREATE CHATS, multiplayer games, and any other types of multiuser entertainment applications you are interested in developing. It is an ActionScript object that has tons of properties and methods to make your job as a Macromedia Flash developer much easier. With this object, you do not need to write a single line of XML to talk to the ElectroServer socket server; it does that for you!

For instance, if you want to send a chat message, all you need to do is execute a line of ActionScript like this:

```
ElectroServerAS.sendMessage(info, "room")
```

The `info` variable contains the message you wish to send. The second parameter, `"room,"` specifies whether you want to send the message to the room at large or as a private message to another user. When this line of ActionScript is executed, the `ElectroServerAS` object takes the information passed in, determines which XML tags are necessary, formats the data, and sends it to the server.

But the `ElectroServerAS object` can do more than just send and receive messages. It can create variables at the room level on the server itself. Also, to make multiplayer games easier to program, we have enabled the `ElectroServerAS` object (with the help of the WDDX_ms.as script, created by Branden Hall of Fig Leaf Software) to send objects to other users. This is a big advantage over other multiuser server systems (server and Flash client working together), because it means that when a player makes a move in a game, instead of having to format an awkward string or XML packet with a zillion attributes, she can just send the object itself. Also, if you find it useful, which I'm sure you will, you can create variables in a room on the server. Whenever these variables are created, updated, or deleted, everyone in the room is informed. This makes creation of a card-based game like poker or hearts (which involves shuffling the deck and informing the players of the card arrangement) more elegant. Without this feature, you'd need a round-robin type of procedure—which I find very annoying—in which everyone messages everyone else privately. Room variables get around this and enable some really cool possibilities in games.

Earlier, I mentioned that ElectroServer's ability to send ActionScript objects to other users gives it a great advantage over other multiuser servers. I want to also make it clear that there is nothing keeping other multiuser servers from doing this, since it is actually a feature of the `ElectroServerAS` object and not the socket server. If you use a socket server other than ElectroServer, you can add this ability yourself, but it will take quite a bit of time to write.

In order to use much of the `ElectroServerAS` object's functionality, you must understand *event handlers*. An event handler is a function that is called when an event occurs. There are many multiuser events that can occur, such as receiving a chat message, receiving a move in a game, receiving an update of the room list, and receiving a game challenge from another user. While you probably won't ever need to use all of the methods and properties `ElectroServerAS` offers, you will want to know they are there—and how to use them. In this appendix we will list and describe every method and property of the `ElectroServerAS` object.

TIP

You can certainly develop chats and multiplayer games without the use of the ElectroServerAS object, but it would require a lot of work—writing and parsing XML documents—as well as numerous hours of debugging.

Evolution Is Ongoing!

Just as with every innovation that makes our lives easier, we are always finding new ways to increase the usefulness of the ElectroServerAS object. To download the most recent version of this object (and any—gulp—bug fixes or documentation fixes), please visit Electrotank's ElectroServer page (www.electrotank.com/ElectroServer).

In the AppendixC folder on the CD-ROM, you'll find two functional chats that were created using the ElectroServerAS object. Chat_fullfeatured.fla has all the features of a good chat. Chat_barebones.fla has the absolute minimum features needed to create a working chat.

CLICK-AND-DRAG ACTIONS

We've mentioned that there are a lot of methods and properties in the ElectroServerAS object, and many of them are going to be really useful for your game development. But don't think you have to remember the syntax for even the ones you use all the time. You can install these actions directly into the Actions toolbox in the Actions panel in Flash (that's a lot of Action!), and drag and drop them into the script pane whenever you want to use them. This installation will also enable color-coding for all ElectroServerAS actions.

1. *Open Flash.*

2. *Locate the install.swf file in the AppendixC directory, and open it inside the Flash environment (as a SWF—don't import it!).*

3. *Click the Install ElectroServerAS Object Actions button.*

   The actions are now installed. Close the SWF and look in the Actions panel. You'll see that the ElectroServerAS object is now an option in the Actions panel. Currently there is no documentation (reference help) installed with these actions; this appendix will serve as the documentation. However, by the time this book is published, there will probably be an updated installer for these actions (see www.electrotank.com/ElectroServer) that should contain the reference help.

4. *For the color-coded version, close Flash and then reopen it.*

In order for all of these actions to work, you must include the file ElectroServerAS.as within the Flash file that is to make use of the ElectroServerAS object. ElectroServerAS.as is a text file that contains all of the ActionScript used to define the methods and properties of the ElectroServerAS object. You don't ever need to open or edit this file (unless you want to extend the object's capabilities).

To include ElectroServerAS.as with your movie (which you must do to make use of its actions) follow this simple procedure:

1. *Copy the ElectroServerAS.as file into the directory where your Flash movie is saved.*

2. *Copy WDDX_mx.as into that same directory.*

   This file enables the ElectroServerAS object to send ActionScript objects.

3. *Add this line of ActionScript to the main timeline anywhere before you need to start using the* ElectroServerAS *object:*

   ```
   #include "ElectroServerAS.as"
   ```

That's it. Now when you create a SWF movie, all of the information in the ElectroServerAS.as file will be pulled into it. You do not need to insert an include action for WDDX_mx.as, because ElectroServerAS.as does that for you automatically.

METHODS AND PROPERTIES OF ELECTROSERVERAS

And now, without further ado, here is the list of all events and functions that the ElectroServerAS object can perform.

Please note that all of the methods included here are intended to be used with Flash Player 6; the version that supports and correctly interprets them is Flash Player 6.

ElectroServer works with Flash 5 and with Flash MX. However, the ElectroServerAS object works only with Flash MX, because of the function scoping changes that are new to Flash MX.

ElectroServerAS.addToHistory

Usage: ElectroServerAS.addToHistory(message)

Parameters: message   This parameter is the string to add to the chat history.

Returns: Nothing.

Description: Method; appends a string to the history property, ElectroServerAS.history.

Example: The following line adds a chat message to the history property:

ElectroServerAS.addToHistory("Anyone for a game of golf?")

ElectroServerAS.ban

Usage: ElectroServerAS.ban(who, why)

Parameters: who   This is the user name of the person whom you wish to ban.

why   This parameter shows the reason why you wish to ban this user.

Returns: Nothing.

Description: Method; disconnects a user from the ElectroServer socket server and bans him or her from connecting from that IP address again. This method is only available to users with administrator-level access. See also ElectroServerAS.login.

Example: The following line bans a user:

```
ElectroServerAS.ban("meanie", "Offensive language")
```

ElectroServerAS.cancelChallenge

Usage: `ElectroServerAS.cancelChallenge()`

Parameters: None.

Returns: Nothing.

Description: Method; cancels the challenge request you sent out. The `ElectroServerAS.challengeCancelled` event is fired on the challengee's side.

ElectroServerAS.challenge

Usage: `ElectroServerAS.challenge(who, game)`

Parameters: who   This is the user name of the person whom you wish to challenge.

         game   This parameter is a string that is the name of the game to which you are challenging a user.

Returns: Nothing.

Description: Method; challenges a user to a game. The `ElectroServerAS.challengeReceived` event is triggered on the challengee's computer. The property `ElectroServerAS.challenging` is set to `true`.

Example: The following line is an example of how to challenge a user:

```
ElectroServerAS.challenge("jobem","Mini Golf")
```

ElectroServerAS.challengeAnswered

Usage: `ElectroServerAS.challengeAnswered(which)`

Parameters: which   This is a string value indicating the response from the person challenged ("accepted", "declined", or "autodeclined").

Returns: Nothing.

Description: Method; a callback function invoked by the `ElectroServerAS` object when a person you have challenged responds to that challenge. If the user accepts your challenge, which is `"accepted"`. If the user declines your challenge, which is "declined". If for any number of reasons the user's Flash client declines your challenge automatically, which is "autodeclined".

Example: The following lines create a function to be called when a challenge request is answered:

```
function challengeAnswered(which) {
    if (which == "accepted") {
        _root.gotoAndStop("game");
    } else if (which == "declined") {
        trace("declined");
    } else if (which == "autodeclined") {
        trace("auto declined");
    }
}
ElectroServerAS.challengeAnswered = this.challengeAnswered;
```

ElectroServerAS.challengeCancelled

Usage: ElectroServerAS.challengeCancelled

Parameters: None.

Returns: Nothing.

Description: Method; a callback function invoked by the ElectroServerAS object when a challenge request that has been sent to you is cancelled.

ElectroServerAS.challengeReceived

Usage: ElectroServerAS.challengeReceived(who, game)

Parameters: who   This is the user name of the person who challenged you.

          game   This is the game you were challenged to.

Returns: Nothing.

Description: Method; a callback function invoked by the ElectroServerAS object when a challenge is received. You can be challenged to a game by other users. The who parameter contains the user name of the person who challenged you, and the game parameter contains the name of the game.

ElectroServerAS.challenging

Usage: ElectroServerAS.challenging

Description: Property; this is a Boolean value. If true, then a challenge has been sent and no response has yet been received. If, while this is true, you are challenged, then an automated decline message is sent back to the challenger. If challenging is not true, then you can receive challenges. This property is used internally by the ElectroServerAS object.

ElectroServerAS.chatReceiver

Usage: ElectroServerAS.chatReceiver(info)

Parameters: info   An object containing the properties from, type, and body.

Returns: Nothing.

Description: Method; a callback function invoked by the ElectroServerAS object when a chat message is received. When this method is called, an object is passed in. The properties of this object are from, type, and body. The from property is the user name of the person who sent the message. The type property is the type of message that arrived. If type is "public", then it is a message to the room; if type is "private", then it is a private message to you. The body property is a string value that contains the chat message.

Example: The following lines create a function that is to be called when a message is received:

```
function messageArrived(info) {
    var from = info.from;
    var type = info.type;
    var body = info.body;
    if (type == "public") {
        var msg = from+": "+body+newline;
    } else if (type == "private") {
        var msg = from+"(private): "+body+newline;
    }
    chat.window.text = ES.addToHistory(msg);
    chat.bar.setScrollPosition(chat.window.maxscroll);
}
ElectroServerAS.chatReceiver = this.messageArrived;
```

ElectroServerAS.connectToServer

Usage: ElectroServerAS.connectToServer()

Parameters: None.

Returns: Nothing.

Description: Method; this method uses the ElectroServerAS.port and ElectroServerAS.IP properties, and initializes a socket connection with the ElectroServer socket server. See ElectroServerAS.port and ElectroServerAS.IP for more information.

Example: The following line makes a connection with the ElectroServer socket server:

ElectroServerAS.connectToServer()

ElectroServerAS.createVariable

Usage: ElectroServerAS.createVariable(name, value, deleteOnExit,
→ lock)

Parameters:	name	The name of the server variable you wish to create in your current room.
	value	The string value of the variable.
	deleteOnExit	Either true (or "True") or false (or "False"). If true, then the variable is deleted when you exit the room. If false, then the variable is not deleted when you exit the room.
	lock	Either true (or "True") or false (or "False"). If true, then the variable cannot be updated. If false, then the variable can be updated. The variable can be deleted using ElectroServerAS.deleteVariable() no matter what value lock has.

Returns: Nothing.

Description: Method; creates or updates a variable in your current room on the socket server. Whenever a variable is created, updated, or deleted, all users in that room are informed via the ElectroServerAS.roomVariablesChanged event. All room variables are stored in an object on the ElectroServerAS object called roomVars.

Example: The following line creates a room variable:

```
ElectroServerAS.createVariable("secret_door","door3",true,false)
```

ElectroServerAS.deleteVariable

Usage: `ElectroServerAS.deleteVariable(name)`

Parameters: `name`   The name of the room variable you wish to delete.

Returns: Nothing.

Description: Method; deletes a room variable of the name you specify. The variable is deleted even if it is locked (see `ElectroServerAS.createVariable()`). Once it's deleted, all users in that room are informed.

Example: The following line deletes a room variable:

```
ElectroServerAS.deleteVariable("secret_door")
```

ElectroServerAS.disconnectFromServer

Usage: `ElectroServerAS.disconnectFromServer()`

Parameters: None.

Returns: Nothing.

Description: Method; closes the connection between Flash and the ElectroServer socket server.

Example: The following line disconnects the Flash client from the ElectroServer socket server:

```
ElectroServerAS.disconnectFromServer()
```

ElectroServerAS.getHistory

Usage: `ElectroServerAS.getHistory()`

Parameters: None.

Returns: The string `ElectroServerAS.history`.

Description: Method; returns the chat history. The chat history is stored as a string in `ElectroServerAS.history` and gets added to using the `ElectroServerAS.addToHistory()` function.

Example: The following line sets a variable from the chat history:

```
myHistory = ElectroServerAS.getHistory()
```

ElectroServerAS.getRoomList

Usage: `ElectroServerAS.getRoomList()`

Parameters: None.

Returns: An array of objects.

Description: Method; returns an array. Each element of the array is an object that describes a room and has two properties: `name` and `total`. The property `name` is the name of the room; the property `total` is the number of people in that room.

Example: The following ActionScript loops through the room list and shows the names and number of people in each room in the output window:

```
var theRooms = ElectroServerAS.getRoomList();
for (i in theRooms) {
    trace(theRooms[i].name);
    trace(theRooms[i].total);
}
```

ElectroServerAS.getUserList

Usage: `ElectroServerAS.getUserList()`

Parameters: None.

Returns: An array of objects.

Description: Method; returns an array. Each element of the array is an object that describes a user and has only one property: name. The property name is the user name of one person in your room.

Example: The following ActionScript loops through the room list and shows the names and number of people in each room in the output window:

```
var theUsers = ElectroServerAS.getUserList();
for (i in theUsers) {
    trace(theUsers[i].name);
}
```

ElectroServerAS.history

Usage: `ElectroServerAS.history`

Description: Property; this is a string value that stores the chat history. Currently this method just returns the `history` property. However, in future revisions of the `ElectroServerAS` object, the history may be stored in a different manner, in which case the `getHistory()` method will be more useful. So it would be a good idea to get into the practice of using the `ElectroServerAS.getHistory()` method.

Example: The following line is an example usage of this property:

```
myHistory = ElectroServerAS.history
```

ElectroServerAS.inGame

Usage: `ElectroServerAS.inGame`

Description: Property; this is a Boolean value (`true` or `false`). If it's `true`, then you are currently in a game. If it's `false`, then you are not currently in a game. If you receive a challenge and `ElectroServerAS.inGame` has a value of `true`, then a decline message is sent automatically. This property is used internally by the `ElectroServerAS` object.

ElectroServerAS.ip

Usage: `ElectroServerAS.ip`

Description: Property; stores the IP address of the server you wish to connect to. It (as well as `ElectroServerAS.port`) must be set before the `ElectroServerAS.connectToServer()` method will perform properly. This can be the numeric IP address of a server or the domain name (such as "23.244.81.5" or "macromedia.com").

Example:

```
ElectroServer = new ElectroServerAS();
ElectroServerAS.ip = "localhost";
ElectroServerAS.port = 8080;
ElectroServerAS.connectToServer();
```

ElectroServerAS.isResponding

Usage: ElectroServerAS.isResponding

Description: Property; this is a Boolean value (true or false) used internally by the ElectroServerAS object. If you receive a challenge, this property is set to true. If while it's true you receive another challenge, a decline message is automatically sent. Once you respond to this challenge by either accepting it or declining it, isResponding is set to false.

ElectroServerAS.joinRoom

Usage: ElectroServerAS.joinRoom(name)

Parameters: name   The name of the room you want to join.

Returns: Nothing.

Description: Method; changes the room you are in to the room specified in the name parameter. If the room does not yet exist, then it is created. The name of the room you have chosen to join is stored in the property ElectroServerAS.myRoom.

Example: The following line changes the room you are in to "Lobby":

ElectroServerAS.joinRoom("Lobby")

ElectroServerAS.kick

Usage: ElectroServerAS.kick(who, why)

Parameters: who   The user name of the person you wish to kick.

            why   The reason why you are kicking this person.

Returns: Nothing.

Description: Method; disconnects a user from the ElectroServer socket server. You must have administrator-level access to the server in order to initiate this method.

Example: The following line kicks a user from the server:

ElectroServerAS.kick("meanie")

ElectroServerAS.leaveAlone

Usage: ElectroServerAS.leaveAlone

Description: Method; this is a Boolean value (true or false); the default is false. If true, then all incoming challenge requests will automatically be declined.

ElectroServerAS.login

Usage: ElectroServerAS.challenge(name, password)

Parameters: name   This is the user name you wish to have.

          password This is an optional parameter containing a password.

Returns: Nothing.

Description: Method; logs in a user to the server. If a password is used, the log-in information is compared with the user name and passwords listed for administrator-level users. If no password is used, the user is just logged in. An administrator is created using tools provided with the ElectroServer socket server.

Example: The following line logs in the user:

ElectroServerAS.login("jobem")

The following line logs in the user as an administrator:

ElectroServerAS.login("important_person","his_password")

ElectroServerAS.loginResponse

Usage: ElectroServerAS.loginResponse(success, reason)

Parameters: success This is a Boolean value (true or false). If true, then the log-in was successful; if false, then it was not.

          reason   This is a string value saying why the log-in was not accepted.

Returns: Nothing.

Description: Method; a callback function invoked by the ElectroServerAS object when a response has been received from the server after a log-in has been attempted. The first parameter, success, is true if the log-in was a success and `false` if it was not. If the log-in failed (`success false`) then the `reason` parameter (a string value that contains the reason why the log-in attempt failed) is passed in.

Example: The following lines create a function that is to be called when a response to the log-in attempt is received:

```
function loginResponse(success, reason) {
    if (success) {
        ElectroServerAS.joinRoom("Lobby");
        chat.gotoAndStop("chat");
    } else {
        trace("reason="+reason);
    }
}
ElectroServerAS.loginResponse = this.loginResponse;
```

ElectroServerAS.moveReceived

Usage: `ElectroServerAS.moveReceived(object)`

Parameters: `object`   A custom object that an opponent created.

Returns: Nothing.

Description: Method; a callback function invoked by the `ElectroServerAS` object when an opponent sends you a move in a game. This custom object can contain any data type, including arrays, XML objects, and variables.

Example: The following lines create a function and set that function to be called when a move is received. The function simply traces the names and values of all properties of the custom object passed in.

```
function moveReceived(ob) {
    for (i in ob) {
        trace(i+"="+ob[i]);
    }
}
ElectroServerAS.moveReceived = this.moveReceived;
```

ElectroServerAS.myRoom

Usage: ElectroServerAS.myRoom

Description: Property; stores as a string the name of the room you are currently in.

ElectroServerAS.onConnection

Usage: ElectroServerAS.onConnection(success)

Parameters: success   This is a Boolean (true or false). If true, then the connection was successfully established; if false, then it was not.

Returns: Nothing.

Description: Method; a callback function invoked by the ElectroServerAS object when a connection to the ElectroServer socket server has been established and verified. A value of true is passed into the callback function if the connection was a success; a value of false is passed in if it was not. The server must successfully send a message verifying that the connection is valid before this event is fired. In other words, making the connection to the server is not enough to fire this event—you need confirmation of the connection.

Example: The following lines create a function that is to be called when a connection to ElectroServer is established and verified:

```
function connectionResponse(success) {
    if (success) {
        chat.gotoAndStop("login");
    } else {
        trace("connection failed");
    }
}
ElectroServerAS.onConnection = this.connectionResponse;
```

ElectroServerAS.onPlayersInRoomChange

Usage: `ElectroServerAS.onPlayersInRoomChange(num)`

Parameters: num   A number representing the total number of people in your room.

Returns: Nothing.

Description: Method; a callback function invoked by the `ElectroServerAS` object when the number of people in your room changes. This happens whenever a person joins or leaves your room.

Example: The following lines create a function and set it to be called when the number of people in your room changes. The function checks to see if there are two people in your room. If there are, then it is time to initialize the game (assuming it is a two-player game).

```
function numPlayers(num) {
    if (num == 2) {
        startGame();
    }
}
ElectroServerAS.onPlayersInRoomChange = this.numPlayers;
```

ElectroServerAS.onRoomVarChange

Usage: `ElectroServerAS.onRoomVarChange(roomVars, type, name)`

Parameters: roomVars An object containing variables.

        type   A string specifying the type of room-variable change that has occurred (`"list"`, `"update"`, or `"delete"`)

        name   The string name of the changed variable.

Returns: Nothing.

Description: Method; a callback function invoked by the `ElectroServerAS` object when the list of variables associated with your current room (stored on the socket server) changes or when you first enter a room. When you first enter a room, this event occurs and you are sent a list of all of the variables in that room. The type parameter is `"list"` when this happens. When a variable in your room is created or modified, then the type parameter is `"update"` and the name parameter contains a string name of the variable that changed (or was created). When a variable in your room is deleted, then the type parameter is `"delete"`, and the name parameter contains a string name of the variable that has been deleted.

ElectroServerAS.opponent

Usage: ElectroServerAS.opponent

Description: Property; stores the name of your opponent. This property is created when you and another person have agreed to play a game.

ElectroServerAS.player

Usage: ElectroServerAS.player

Description: Property; stores your "player number" within a game. If you are in a game with only two players, then this property has a value of 1 for one person and a value of 2 for the other.

Example: The following is an example of a snippet of code you might find at the beginning of a chess game:

```
if (ElectroServerAS.player == 1) {
    myChessPieceColor = "white";
} else if (ElectroServerAS.player == 2) {
    myChessPieceColor = "black";
}
```

ElectroServerAS.port

Usage: ElectroServerAS.port

Description: Property; stores the IP address of the server you wish to connect to. It must be set (as well as ElectroServerAS.ip) before the ElectroServerAS.connect() method will perform properly. This can be the numeric IP address of a server or the domain name (for example, "23.244.81.5" or "macromedia.com").

Example:

```
ElectroServer = new ElectroServerAS();
ElectroServerAS.ip="localhost";
ElectroServerAS.port=8080;
ElectroServerAS.connect();
```

ElectroServerAS.roomListChanged

Usage: `ElectroServerAS.roomListChanged(rooms)`

Parameters: `rooms`   This is an array of objects.

Returns: Nothing.

Description: Method; a callback function invoked by the `ElectroServerAS` object when the list of visible rooms changes. When it's called, an array is passed in. Each element in the array is an object representing a room with the properties `name` and `total`. The `name` property is the name of the room, and `total` is the number of people in that room.

Example: The following lines create a function and set it to be called when the room list changes. The function populates a text field with room names that take the format Lobby(32).

```
function roomListChanged(roomList) {
    roomList.text = "";
    for (var i = 0; i<roomList.length; ++i) {
        chat.roomList.text += roomList[i].name+"
        → ("+roomList[i].total+")"+newline;
    }
}
ElectroServerAS.roomListChanged = this.roomListChanged;
```

ElectroServerAS.rooms

Usage: `ElectroServerAS.rooms`

Description: Property; an array that stores information about each room. Every element in the array is an object with the properties of `name` and `total`. The `name` property contains the name of the room; `total` is the number of people in that room. It is recommended to use the `ElectroServerAS.getRoomList()` method; currently `ElectroServerAS.getRoomList()` just returns the rooms property, but in future revisions of the `ElectroServerAS` object, the room list may be stored in a different way.

ElectroServerAS.roomVars

Usage: `ElectroServerAS.roomVars`

Description: Property; an object that stores the room variables. Every time a variable is created, updated, or deleted from the server, it is also reflected in this object. If you define an event handler using `ElectroServerAS.onRoomVarChange`, you will be informed when this happens.

Example: The following example shows the names of all the server variables in the output window, along with their values:

```
ob = ElectroServerAS.roomVars;
for (i in ob) {
    trace(i+"="+ob[i]);
}
```

ElectroServerAS.sendData

Usage: `ElectroServerAS.sendData(msg)`

Parameters: `msg`   The data you would like to send to the server.

Returns: Nothing.

Description: Method; sends the information found in the `msg` parameter to the server. This method is used internally by the `ElectroServerAS` object, and it is unlikely to be needed for anything other than extending the `ElectroServerAS` object.

ElectroServerAS.sendMessage

Usage: `ElectroServerAS.sendMessage(msg, who)`

Parameters: `msg`   The chat message you would like to send.

   `who`   A string value stating to whom you would like this message to go. If the string is `"All"`, then the message will be sent to everyone in your current room. If the string specifies a user name (in any room), then the message will be sent to that user as a private message.

Returns: Nothing.

Description: Method; sends a chat message to the room or to a user. This is the method used for regular chatting and private messaging.

Example: The following line sends a message to the room:

```
ElectroServerAS.sendMessage("Good morning Raleigh!","All")
```

The following line sends a message to "jobem":

```
ElectroServerAS.sendMessage("Hey man, where've you
→ been?","jobem")
```

ElectroServerAS.sendMove

Usage: ElectroServerAS.sendMove(who, what)

Parameters: who   The player to whom you want to send the move.

         what   The object you would like to send.

Returns: Nothing.

Description: Method; sends an object to the specified user. The object is of type object and can contain any other data objects, such as arrays, date objects, or XML objects. This method is how moves are made in a game.

Example: The following sends a move to "jobem":

```
myObject=new Object();
myObject.ball_x=32;
myObject.ball_y=413;
ElectroServerAS.sendMove("jobem",myObject);
```

ElectroServerAS.sendSystemMessage

Usage: ElectroServerAS.sendSystemMessage(msg)

Parameters: msg   A string value of the message you wish to send.

Returns: Nothing.

Description: Method; sends a message to every user in every room on the server. This is only available to users with administrator-level access to the server.

Example: The following line of ActionScript sends a message to everyone connected to the server:

```
ElectroServerAS.sendSystemMessage("The server is about to be
→ rebooted. Please refresh in 1 minute.")
```

ElectroServerAS.userListChanged

Usage: ElectroServerAS.userListChanged(users)

Parameters: users   An array of objects.

Returns: Nothing.

Description: Method; a callback function invoked by the ElectroServerAS object when the list of users in your room changes. When you first enter a room, this event occurs, and you are sent a list of all the users in the room. The users parameter is an array of objects. Each object represents one user and has one property, name, which stores the user name of the user whom it represents.

Example: These lines of ActionScript create a function and set it to be called whenever the list of users in the room changes. The function uses the Flash ListBox component to display the list of users.

```
function userListChanged(userList) {
    var path = chat.userList;
    path.removeAll();
    for (var i = 0; i<userList.length; ++i) {
        path.addItem(userList[i].name);
    }
}
ElectroServerAS.userListChanged = this.userListChanged;
```

ElectroServerAS.username

Usage: ElectroServerAS.username

Description: Property; the name with which you are logged in.

ElectroServerAS.users

Usage: ElectroServerAS.users

Description: Property; an array of objects. Each object represents a user in your room with one property, name, that stores the user name of that person. It is recommended that you use ElectroServerAS.getUserList() to retrieve the user list. In future revisions of this object, the user list may be stored differently.

ElectroServerAS.usersInMyRoom

Usage: ElectroServerAS.usersInMyRoom

Description: Property; an integer that specifies the total number of people in your room.

new ElectroServerAS()

Usage: new ElectroServerAS()

Parameters: None.

Returns: Nothing.

Description: Constructor; creates a new ElectroServerAS object. You must use the constructor method to create an instance of the ElectroServerAS object before calling any of the ElectroServerAS object methods.

Example: The following line creates an instance of the ElectroServerAS object with a reference of ES:

```
ES = new ElectroServerAS();
```

APPENDIX D

XML BASICS IN FLASH

IMAGINE WHAT IT WOULD BE LIKE IF EVERY ELECTRICAL APPLIANCE IN your home had a different type of plug. Chances are, you'd end up putting most of those gizmos back in the cupboard and doing the task manually. Or what if none of the screwdrivers or wrenches in your tool shed even came close to fitting the screws, nuts, and bolts that hold your stuff together? Well, all I can say is, watch out for falling bookshelves! Fortunately, neither scenario is likely because people figured out long ago that by creating products according to guidelines, or rules of standardization, they could have far more productive societies.

In essence, rules of standardization—let's just call them *standards*—facilitate linkages between disparate items, such as batteries and flashlights; Macromedia Flash and multiuser game servers; and so on. And on the Web, where so much data gets transferred every second, having a standardized way of moving data between systems is essential. The powerful and easy-to-use XML is quickly becoming that standard.

In this appendix we'll introduce you to the XML format, and look at how to use the XML object and the XMLSocket object in Flash.

LEARNING XML BASICS

Although the name XML, for *Extensible Markup Language*, sounds a bit cryptic, it is actually quite easy to understand. In a nutshell, XML provides a way of formatting and structuring information so that receiving applications can easily interpret and use that data when it's moved from place to place.

You may not realize it, but you already have plenty of experience in organizing information. Consider, for example, the following. If you wanted to write a letter to a friend, you would structure your thoughts (information) in a format you know your friend would recognize. Thus, you would begin by writing words on a piece of paper, starting probably somewhere near the upper-left corner, breaking your thoughts into paragraphs, sentences, and words. You could, of course, use images to convey your thoughts, or write your words in circular fashion, but that would most likely just confuse your friend. By writing your letter in a format your friend is accustomed to, you can be confident that your message will be conveyed—that is, you will have transferred your thoughts (data/information) to the letter's recipient. When you want to write a different kind of letter—say, a complaint to a neighbor for her dog's behavior on your newly seeded lawn—you can use the same proven-successful format to get a very different message across.

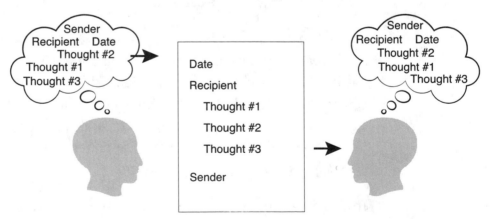

You can use XML in much the same way—as a format for conveying information. If, for instance, you wanted to send data out of Flash for processing by a Web server, you would first format that data in XML. The server would then interpret the XML-formatted data and use it in the manner intended. Without XML, you could send chunks of data to a server, but the server probably wouldn't know what to do with the first chunk, or the second, or even know how the first chunk related to the second. XML gives meaning to these disparate bits of data so that the server can work with them in an organized and intelligent manner.

XML's simple syntax resembles HTML in that it employs tags, attributes, and values—but the similarity ends there. While HTML uses predefined tags (for example, *body*, *head*, and *html*), in XML you create your own; that is, you don't pull them from an existing library of tag names. Before going any further, let's take a look at this simple XML document:

```
<MyFriends>
    <Name Gender="female">Kelly Makar</Name>
    <Name Gender="male">Mike Grundvig</Name>
    <Name Gender="male">Free Makar</Name>
</MyFriends>
```

Each tag in XML is called a *node*, and any XML-formatted data is called an *XML document*. The above document has a *root node* called MyFriends and three *child nodes*. Each XML document can contain only one root node. The first child node has a *node name* of Name and a *node value* of Kelly Makar. The word Gender in each child node is an *attribute*. Attributes are optional, and each node can have an unlimited number of attributes. You will typically use attributes to store small bits of information that are not necessarily displayed on the screen (for example, a user identification number).

XML Document

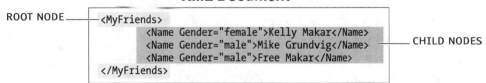

As you can see in this example, the tags (which we made up and defined) give meaning to the bits of information shown (Kelly Makar, Mike Grundvig, and Free Makar). This is why XML is so useful.

This next XML document shows a more extended use of XML:

```
<AddressBook>
    <Person>
        <Name>Kelly Makar</Name>
        <Street>121 Baker Street</Street>
        <City>Some City</City>
        <State>North Carolina</State>
    </Person>
    <Person>
        <Name>Tripp Carter</Name>
        <Street>777 Another Street</Street>
        <City>Elizabeth City</City>
        <State>North Carolina</State>
    </Person>
</AddressBook>
```

This example shows how the data in an address book would be formatted in XML. If there were 600 people in the address book, the Person node would appear 600 times with the same structure.

So how do you actually create your own nodes and structure? How does the destination (Active Server Page [ASP], socket, and so on) know how the document is formatted? And how does it know what to do with each piece of information? The simple answer is that the destination by nature has no idea what to do with this information you are sending—you (or someone else) must also program the destination script or socket server to understand the data. Thus, if we were to build an address book in Flash and wanted the information it contained to be saved in a database, we would send an XML-formatted version of that data to an ASP (or another scripted page of choice), which would then *parse* that information and insert it into the appropriate fields in a database. The important thing to remember is that the ASP must be designed to deal with data in this way. Since XML is typically used to transfer rather than store information, the address-book data would be stored as disparate information in database fields rather than as XML. When needed again, that information could be extracted from the database, formatted to XML by a scripted page, and sent along to Flash or any other application that requested it.

XML Document

```
<AddressBook>
    <Person>
        <Name>Kelly Makar</Name>
        <Street>121 Baker Street</Street>
        <City>Some City</City>
        <State>North Carolina</State>
    </Person>
    <Person>
        <Name>Tripp Carter</Name>
        <Street>777 Another Street</Street>
        <City>Elizabeth City</City>
        <State>North Carolina</State>
    </Person>
</AddressBook>
```

```
<asp>
```

ID	Name	Street	City	State
1	Kelly Makar	121 Baker street	Some City	North Carolina
2	Tripp Carter	777 Another Street	Elizabeth City	North Carolina

That said, you may sometimes use text files that contain XML-formatted information—for example, a static XML file for storing information about which ASPs should be called, or what port and IP to connect to when attempting to connect with a socket server.

To briefly recap, XML can be

- Sent to a server-side script

- Sent to a socket server

- Stored in a text file (that you can load into Flash anytime)

- Stored in a database and retrieved by requesting it from a server-side script

Now that you know the basics of the XML structure, here are some rules you need to follow when you begin using it.

- *Don't begin node names with the letters* **XML***; many XML parsers will break when they see this. For instance,* <myXML> *is OK, but* <XMLdoc> *is not.*

- *Properly terminate every node—for example, you would terminate* <Name> *with* </Name>*.*

- *Use the* escape() *function in Flash to URL-encode all odd characters. Many parsers will interpret certain unencoded characters as the start of a new node that is then not terminated properly (since it wasn't a node in the first place). An XML document with non-terminated nodes will not pass through an XML parser completely. Attributes are less forgiving than text nodes because they can fail to pass through the parser on more characters, such as a carriage return or an ampersand. If you URL-encode the text, you will not experience any trouble with this.*

- *Keep the text case consistent. Most XML parsers are case-sensitive, which means that all tags of the same type must have the same case. In other words, if you start a node with* <Name> *and terminate it with* </name>, *you're asking for trouble!*

- *You can have only one root node.*

One more thing to note before you begin working with XML is that the clean XML structure shown in the address-book example above is not necessary. The carriage returns and tabs are there to make it easier for *us* to read. These tabs and carriage returns are called *white space,* and you can add or delete them without affecting the overall structure.

USING THE XML OBJECT

Nearly everything you do with XML in Flash involves the XML object and falls into one of the following categories:

- Formatting XML

- Parsing XML (extracting the information)

- Loading XML

- Sending XML

With the XML object you will be able to load XML from an external source such as a static file or a server-side script. Once this XML document is loaded, you can access its information using the methods and properties of the XML object. Also using the methods and properties of the XML object, you can create your own XML document. Once this document is created, you can use it in your Flash movie or send it out to a server-side script. All the ActionScript needed to do these things is covered in this section.

Formatting XML

The XML object in Flash has several methods, all of which you can use to create and format XML documents. Truth is, though, you're unlikely to employ them because they're difficult to use—and there's a better way! We'll show you how to create a string and then convert it into an XML object—a much easier (and more common) way of formatting XML objects.

To create an XML object in Flash, you must use its constructor. Here is how you create an empty XML object:

```
myXML = new XML();
```

To populate the object with XML-formatted data when it is created, you can pass (inside the parentheses of the constructor) the name of a variable that holds an XML-formatted string or another XML object.

If, in Flash, we wanted to create the following XML document:

```
<MyFriends>
    <Name Gender="female">Kelly Makar</Name>
    <Name Gender="male">Free Makar</Name>
</MyFriends>
```

we would do two things: create the document as a string, and convert the string to an XML object using the XML object constructor, new XML().

Here is an example:

```
myString = "<MyFriends><Name Gender=\"female\">Kelly
→ Makar</Name><Name Gender=\"male\">Free
→ Makar</Name></MyFriends>";
myXML = new XML(myString);
```

The above ActionScript creates the XML document as a string and then converts it to an actual XML object called myXML. This object can then be sent to the server using the send-related methods described later in this section.

Parsing XML

The word *parse* simply means to analyze something or break it down into its parts. Thus, when someone speaks of writing a script to parse an XML document, he or she is talking about writing a script that extracts information from that XML document. The XML object has many properties to help you do this. We'll use the XML object you created in the previous subsection, myXML, to illustrate the use of a few of the most common properties.

firstChild

This property points to the first node in the tree structure. For example, `myXML.firstChild.firstChild` returns the following:

```
<Name Gender="female">Kelly Makar</Name>
```

The first child node of the XML document is the root node (MyFriends), and the root node's first child is Name, as shown.

childNodes

This property returns an array of the child nodes at any given point in the tree structure. For instance:

```
myArray = new Array()
myArray = myXML.firstChild.childNodes
```

Here, myArray contains two elements whose values are the same as those of the two Name nodes.

nextSibling

This property points to the next node in the same level of the tree structure. For instance, `myXML.firstChild.firstChild.nextSibling` returns the following:

```
<Name Gender="male">Free Makar</Name>
```

attributes

This property returns an associative array of attribute names. Thus, `myXML.firstChild.firstChild.nextSibling.attributes.Gender` returns "male".

myXML.firstChild.firstChild.nextSibling.attributes.Gender

```
<MyFriends>
        <Name Gender="female">Kelly Makar</Name>
        <Name Gender="male">Free Makar</Name>
</MyFriends>
```

The list above includes the most commonly used properties of the XML object; others work in the same way, referencing different parts of the tree structure.

Loading XML

Typically, you'll only work with XML in Flash when you're loading it or sending it out. To load XML from a remote source, you do the following:

1. **Create an XML object.**

2. **Use the** load() **method of the XML object to load XML-formatted data from an external source.**

For example:

```
myXML = new XML();
myXML.load("http://somedomain.com/info.xml");
```

As the example shows, this URL does not need to point to a static XML file. It can point to an ASP (or another scripted page) whose result is an XML document.

It's easy to determine when the XML has finished loading into an object by using the onLoad event available to the XML object. You can define this event to call a function when the document is finished loading. Take a look at the following example:

```
function init () {
    //parse script here
}
myXML = new XML();
myXML.onLoad = init;
myXML.load("http://somedomain.com/info.xml");
```

As the next-to-last line shows, when the XML document is finished, loading the init function will be called.

Sending XML

The XML object allows you to send XML to a URL. It also lets you send XML *and* load the resulting document simultaneously.

To send XML to a URL, use the send() method and specify a destination URL. For instance:

```
myXML = new XML("<Message><Text>Hi!</Text></Message>");
myXML.send("http://somedomain.com/somedestination.asp");
```

To send XML and receive a response, all in one shot, use the sendAndLoad() method of the XML object. With this method, you must specify an XML object whose contents you wish to send, a URL in which to send the XML document, and an XML object in which to receive the response. As shown with the load() example in the previous section, you must define an onLoad event to handle the loaded XML. Here is an example:

```
URL = "http://www.electrotank.com/projects/tfts/using_xml/
→ UserLogin.asp";
function init () {
    trace(objToReceive);
}
xmlToSend = "<Login><UserName>Jobem</UserName><Password>hayes
→ </Password></Login>";
objToSend = new XML(xmlToSend);
objToReceive = new XML();
objToReceive.onLoad = init;
objToSend.sendAndLoad(URL, objToReceive);
```

objToSend

```
<Login>
        <UserName>Jobem</UserName>
        <Password>hayes</Password>
</Login>
```

objToSend.sendAndLoad(**URL**, **objToReceive**)

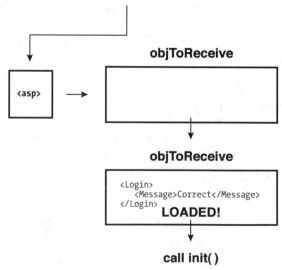

objToReceive

```
<asp>
```
→

objToReceive

objToReceive

```
<Login>
    <Message>Correct</Message>
</Login>
```
LOADED!

call init( )

The above ActionScript creates an XML object (objToSend) containing log-in information, and then sends that information to a URL where it waits for a response from the destination. When the response is fully loaded into the receiving XML object (objToReceive), the init function is called.

INTRODUCING SOCKET SERVERS

A *socket server* is an application that can accept "socket" connections. Socket connections are *persistent*, which means they let you remain connected to a server, rather than keeping a connection just long enough to download information. Unlike a scripted page, a socket server is an application that's always running. It can accept numerous simultaneous connections and exchange information between them. Thus, while connected to a socket server, you can send or receive information any time. Using socket connections to continually transfer data to and from the server is how most chats and multiplayer games are created in Flash.

A key thing about using socket connections with Flash is that you don't have to request information to get it—for example, in a chat a message can be *pushed* into Flash at any time without Flash asking for it.

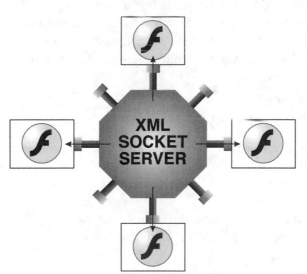

You cannot, however, just drop a socket server into the CGI bin of your Web site or place it in a normal Web-accessible directory. Usually written in Java, C, C++, or Visual Basic, socket servers require root-level access to the Web server—which usually means that you need to be running your own dedicated server. You can, however, set up a socket server on your own personal computer so that you can develop with it. For more information on that topic, see Appendix B, "Multiuser Servers."

Using the XML Socket Object

Before you can connect Flash to a socket server, you must create a new XMLSocket object. You can then use the methods of that object to connect to a server and exchange information. In this section, we'll show you how to create and use an XMLSocket object while also using the XML object methods and properties introduced earlier in this lesson.

To create a new XMLSocket object, you must use the constructor for XMLSocket. Here's an example:

```
server = new XMLSocket();
```

The above line of ActionScript creates a new XMLSocket object named server. To connect the XMLSocket object to a server, you simply employ the connect() method of the XMLSocket object using the following syntax:

```
server.connect(hostName,port)
```

The hostName parameter is the IP address on which the socket server resides—usually a numeric sequence (for example, 65.134.12.2). Since you'll be connecting to your own machine in this exercise, you can use either the sequence "127.0.0.1" or "localhost." Both 127.0.0.1 and localhost are valid references to your own computer. If you were to type http://localhost in your Web browser's address bar, the browser would try to connect to your computer as if it were a Web site. The port parameter refers to the port on which the server is listening. Flash can only connect to ports higher than 1024. For example,

```
server = new XMLSocket();
server.connect("localhost", 9999)
```

You can close a connection with a socket by using the close() method, which looks like the following:

```
server.close();
```

To send information via the socket connection, simply use the send() method and pass in the object you wish to send. For instance,

```
server.send("<Text>Hi</Text>");
```

The XMLSocket can respond to the following types of events:

onConnect

This event fires when the connection is accepted or when it fails.

onXML

This event fires when information arrives via the socket connection. This lets you know that new information has arrived.

onClose

This event fires when the connection with the socket is lost.

As we did with the onLoad event in the XML object, we have to define these event handlers with the XMLSocket we create.

For example,

```
function serverConnected (success) {
    trace(success);
}
server.onConnect = serverConnected;
```

The serverConnected() function is called when the onConnect event is fired. The success parameter, shown in the function definition, has a value of true if the connection was successful; false if it wasn't.

The onXML event is used as follows:

```
function xmlReceived (data) {
    trace(data);
}
scrver.onXMl = xmlReceived;
```

The xmlReceived() function is called each time information arrives via the socket. The data parameter contains the XML document pushed into Flash.

The onClose event handler can be defined and used as follows:

```
function socketClosed () {
        //notify the user
}
server.onClose = socketClosed;
```

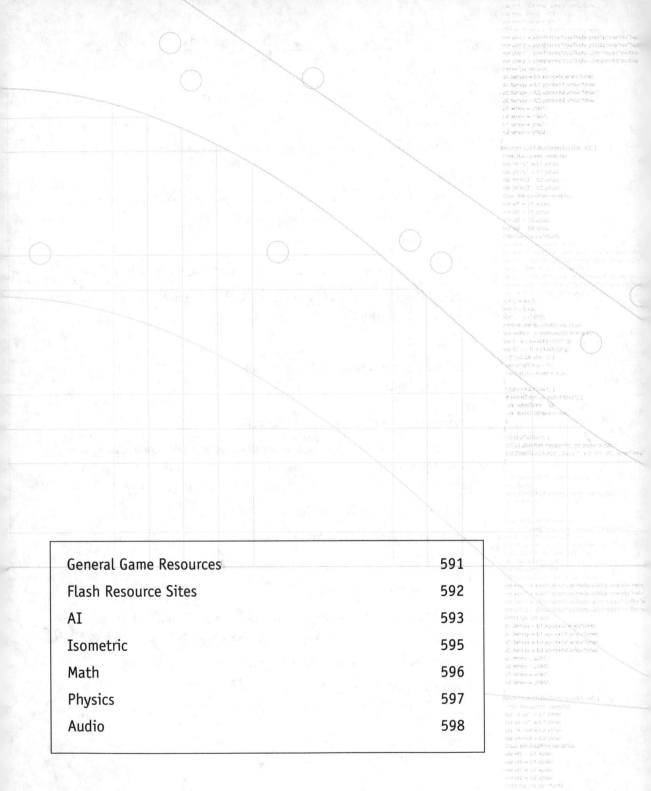

APPENDIX E

DEVELOPER RESOURCES

IN THIS APPENDIX YOU'LL FIND OUT WHERE YOU CAN GET MORE information about a variety of game-related topics, including online communities, books and Web sites on the elements of game design, and audio resources.

GENERAL GAME RESOURCES

On the Web

Gamasutra

www.gamasutra.com

This is the most popular game-development resource site in the world. It is focused on game development on all types of platforms. You will find some amazing articles on a variety of game-specific topics (some of these references are included later in this appendix).

GameDev.net

www.gamedev.net

After Gamasutra, GameDev.net is the most popular game-development resource site. It also contains many interesting articles and features, as well as user forums where you can discuss issues with other developers.

Books

Game Programming Gems 3
Edited by Dante Treglia
Charles River Media
ISBN: 1584502339; $69.95; www.charlesriver.com

This book contains numerous techniques developed by programmers in the game-design industry. While it is not Flash-specific, it does present many ideas and techniques that can be used in Flash games.

FLASH RESOURCE SITES

Flashkit
www.flashkit.com

Flashkit is the largest Flash resource site on the Internet. With thousands of source files and highly active user boards, Flash developers are sure to find help on just about anything. One of the drawbacks of Flashkit is that it may have too many source files, and no garbage control; there are many great files on the site, but there are also many not-so-great ones, so finding what you want may take a while.

We're Here
www.were-here.com

We're Here has hundreds of source files to offer, and is similar to Flashkit in its variety of support options, but most people use this Web site for the great boards. If you are looking for specific FLA examples, you may be better off looking elsewhere, but if written help is what you need, then this is the place to be.

Ultrashock
www.ultrashock.com

Ultrashock provides an advanced level of source files, forums, games and cartoons, tutorials, and more. What sets Ultrashock apart from other Flash resource sites is that it is geared toward the advanced programmer, and each source file is screened for quality and uniqueness before being offered to the public. If you are looking for help on advanced topics or just need a good example of an advanced FLA file, then this is the place to go. You won't have to spend hours sifting through garbage to find the treasures.

MotionCulture
www.motionculture.org

This resource site provides source files and user boards that cover many topics. MotionCulture is unique in that it provides resources and many non-Flash topics such as HTML, CGI, and Photoshop. If you need help in more than one area of Flash design, this can be a useful place.

Moock.org
www.moock.org/webdesign/flash/index.html

Here you will find brilliant tutorials and learn some of the best programming practices. This site is not a one-stop shop for all of your Flash needs, but it will certainly meet a few needs more than any of the other resource sites can. For instance, you will find the best Flash detection script on the Internet on this site!

AI

On the Web

"Smart Moves: Intelligent Pathfinding"
www.gamasutra.com/features/19970801/pathfinding.htm

This article gives a brief rundown of all the major pathfinding algorithms, and then discusses A* in detail. I learned A* from a variety of articles, but this one helped me the most. Check out the downloadable demo; it contains an amazing little program that lets you design maps and perform any of about ten pathfinding searches. You can build a map and try pathfinding with A*, tracing, and more. Also, you can slow down the search and watch *how* it searches to better understand the algorithms. (You need to join the site to access the article; membership is free.)

"Amit's Thoughts on Path-Finding"

http://theory.stanford.edu/~amitp/GameProgramming/

This is another A* article. It comes highly recommended and appears to be very thorough.

"A* Algorithm Tutorial"

www.geocities.com/jheyesjones/astar.html

Yet another A* article.

TIP

It definitely helps to read several different articles on a confusing topic so that you can fully understand it.

"Toward More Realistic Pathfinding"

www.gamasutra.com/features/20010314/pinter_01.htm

While A* always gives the path with the lowest score, it does not always look natural. This Gamasutra article provides a look into how you can make pathfinding paths look more realistic.

"The Game AI Page"

www.gameai.com

This Web site is dedicated to AI in games. You can find information on a lot of AI topics, including links to other useful Web sites.

"Scrabble—Source Code"

www.gtoal.com/wordgames/scrabble.html

Yes, there is actually a Web site dedicated to the AI involved in computerized games of Scrabble. Check it out.

Books

AI Game Programming Wisdom

Edited by Steve Rabin
Charles River Media
ISBN: 1584500778; $69.95; www.charlesmedia.com

This book has proved to be one of my most valuable purchases. It is a collection of articles from expert game programmers. You will find great ideas on handling AI for enemy behavior, pathfinding, racing games, and many more interesting topics.

ISOMETRIC

On the Web

"Introduction to Isometric Engines"
www.gamedev.net/reference/articles/article744.asp

This article provides a fairly in-depth introduction to isometric views. While it is the most popular online resource I could find on this topic, I don't think it is presented very well. However, if you first read Chapter 8, "The Isometric Worldview," in this book, you may find this article of some added help.

"Isometric Basics"
www.xaraxone.com/guest/guest05/index.htm

Graphic artists, this link's for you! This is an excellent article on how to create graphics for an isometric world.

"Tiled Terrain"
www.gamasutra.com/features/20011024/peasley_01.htm

This article shows how to graphically create tiles for a tile-based world in isometric and other kinds of games.

Books

Isometric Game Programming with DirectX 7.0
By Ernest Pazera, edited by Andre LaMothe
Premier Press, Inc.
ISBN: 0761530894; $59.99; www.premierpressbooks.com

This book comes highly recommended from some of my colleagues. It discusses many isometric-gaming topics that can be applied to games in Flash.

MATH

On the Web

"Eric Weisstein's World of Mathematics"
http://mathworld.wolfram.com/

This Web site is like a giant comprehensive math book—you can find information on just about any math topic here.

Books

CRC Standard Mathematical Tables and Formulae, 30th Edition
By Daniel Zwillinger
CRC Press
ISBN: 0849324793; $51.95; www.crcpress.com

A must-have for anyone who uses math frequently. It does not teach any math; it's just the most comprehensive math reference I have ever seen. It is a required book for many hard-science degree programs.

Schaum's Outline of Trigonometry
By Robert E. Moyer and Frank Ayres, Jr.
McGraw-Hill
ISBN: 0070068933; $15.95; www.mcgrawhill.com

The Schaum's Outline books are like Cliffs Notes for math and science. They are concise references in an easy-to-use format.

PHYSICS

On the Web

At this time I have not seen any physics resources on the Web that I think are worth recommending. If you find any, let me know!

Books

Physics for Scientists and Engineers with Modern Physics, 5th Edition

By Raymond A. Serway and Robert J. Beichner
International Thomson Publishing
ISBN: 0030317169; $142.95, www.thomson.com

This book is the best college-level introduction to physics. It presents the most fundamental physics concepts in a way that will be understandable even to those with a minimal math background. If you are interested in learning physics, this is the book to get. Once you have these concepts down, you can move on to the book mentioned above.

Physics for Game Developers

By David M. Bourg
O'Reilly & Associates
ISBN: 0596000065; $39.95; www.oreilly.com

The title tells it all: This book was written as a physics reference for game developers. You can find information on gravity, collision detection, and many more very advanced physics topics and how they can be applied in games. This book is intended for people with a basic college-level science background.

Audio

Sound Libraries

SoundEffects
Vilkki Studios
Both free and fee-based; www.stonewashed.net/sfx.html

Ultimate Sound and Music Archive
Advances.Com
Both free and by subscription; www.ultimatesoundarchive.com

Drum Machines

ReBirth
Propellerhead Software
$179; www.propellerheads.se

Our favorite beat-creation software.

Dream Station
Audio Simulation
$49; www.audio-simulation.de

Highly recommended. If you can't afford ReBirth, get this.

Fruityloops
Image-Line Software
$49–$139; www.fruityloops.com

Tough learning curve, but affordable and very powerful.

Voyetra eJay
Voyetra Turtle Beach
$9.95–$29.95; http://voyetra.com/site/products/ejay

Great for beginners, value priced.

HammerHead

ThreeChords.com
www.threechords.com/hammerhead

The simplest drum machine imaginable. Free!

Audio-editing software

Sound Forge

Sonic Foundry
$399.96 and $499.96; www.soundforge.com

Industry standard for professional audio; most powerful and simple.

WaveLab

Steinberg Media Technologies
$600; www.steinberg.net

Very similar to Sound Forge, with native VST support.

Cool Edit/Cool Edit Pro

Syntrillium Software
$69 and $249; www.syntrillium.com

Best value and price, most popular for both professionals and nonprofessionals.

Audacity

SourceForge.net
Free; http://audacity.sourceforge.net

Promising and cross-platform!

Also worth a look: **Using the ACID Chopper**.
Sonic Foundry; www.sonicfoundry.com/tutorials/English/
  ACIDChopperBasics/start.htm

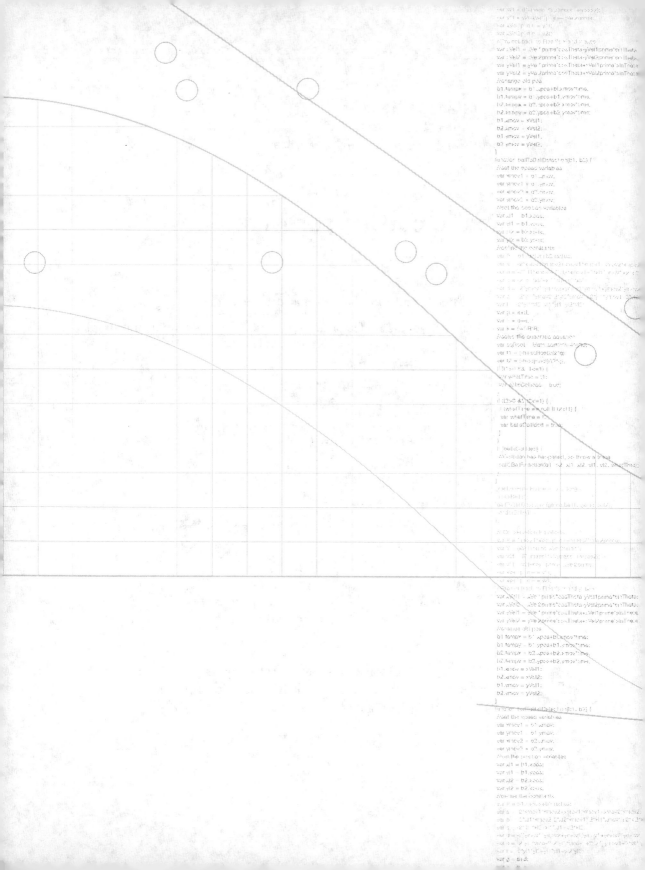

APPENDIX F

OTHER GAMES

As I worked through the material for this book, I created (or sometimes encountered) games and games-in-progress that didn't quite fit in, but that I think would be useful and informative as you get more adventurous in your game development—or if you just want to have fun. These games, partial games, and game-related files are all included in the OtherGames directory on the CD and are described briefly here. Enjoy!

3D_race.fla

I created this file to prove the concept that a real-time 3D racing game in Flash is possible. This file contains only the most basic level of the game—a limited 3D engine you can use to move through an environment. It is a good starting place for learning how to create 3D racing games.

asteroids

This directory contains files contributed by Aaron Silvers, who has created a very good clone of the commonly known game of Asteroids.

cards.fla

Jennifer Rosenthal created this deck of playing cards. Most decks in Flash games are imported as JPEGs or GIFs and have a total file size of a few hundred kilobytes. These vector cards weigh in at just under 8 KB!

foxandgeese.fla

I created this simple puzzle game with Flash 5. It is just waiting for someone to give it nice graphics. The rules are easy to understand and are included in the game.

fruit_smash.fla

This is the main engine for a game I've been working on called Fruit Smash. It is an addictive puzzle game similar to some you may have seen on the Internet. The hard part (the engine) has been done. Select any two horizontally or vertically adjacent pieces of fruit by clicking them; they swap positions. If swapping these positions results in a vertical or horizontal match of three pieces of fruit, they disappear and new ones come in.

invaders

This directory, contributed by Paul Neave (www.neave.com), contains a well-written clone of Space Invaders.

iso_maze.fla

This is one of my successful simple experiments. In Chapter 9, "Artificial Intelligence," we discuss random maze generation. In this file we use the random-maze-generation algorithm but display it as an isometric maze. You can move a ball around through the maze.

jigsaw.fla

This was one of my first game attempts with Flash MX while it was still in beta. It is a simple-looking jigsaw-puzzle game that uses dynamic masking to randomly generate the shape of each puzzle-piece mask and also mask a movie clip. The great thing about this jigsaw puzzle is that it can even cut up an animation! Unfortunately, I would consider this a failed test; all of the pieces are generated properly, but the dynamic masking proves to be a huge performance hit. As a result, when dragging pieces around, you experience much visual lag. However, this works perfectly for puzzles with small numbers of pieces (under 20).

matching.fla

This is a simple memory game I created with Flash 5. The goal is to flip two matching cards. If you flip two that are not matching, they flip back over.

pacman

Another great clone contributed by Paul Neave.

projectile_motion.fla

In Chapter 3, "Trigonometry 101," and Chapter 4, "Basic Physics," we covered all of the information needed to develop projectile motion in Flash. Here is a simple working example of how that is implemented.

raiseTheBlocks.fla

This game was created with Flash 5. It is an isometric grid of 25 blocks. The goal is to raise all of the blocks. When you click one block, the height of that block and its vertical and horizontal neighbors changes. If the blocks are raised, then they lower; if they are low, then they rise. The object is to raise them all. It's a very tough puzzle!

robust_tracing

This directory contains a very good AI pathfinding routine contributed by Klas Kroon (http://outsideofsociety.idz.net).

shared_object_highscore_list

This directory contains a well-documented example of a high score list that uses local shared objects. Its main use is for offline games.

ship.fla

You are probably familiar with top-down-view games like Asteroids, in which a spaceship can be controlled with the arrow keys. It rotates and you can shoot. This file contains the absolute basics needed to make something like that work.

shuffle_deck.fla

As a member of many Flash resource sites, I have seen the issue of shuffling a deck of cards come up frequently. In this file there are no graphics, just a function that handles taking a deck of cards in memory and randomly shuffling it in the fastest possible way.

tic_tac_toe_ai.fla

This is a nice file I created in Flash 5. It contains a simple AI computer opponent so you can play tic-tac-toe against the computer!

tile_boat

In this directory you'll find another great resource contributed by Klas Kroon. It is an example of the basics behind creating a top-down-view boat-racing game.

INDEX

Symbol

+= operator, 63

A

A* algorithm
  about, 229, 246–247
  additional resources on, 248
  basic terminology and functionality, 249–250
  handling terrains with, 254, 258
  implementing, 254–257
  pseudocode for, 251–253
  variations on, 247, 257–258
acceleration, 65–69
  applying with ActionScript, 67–68
  defined, 65–66
  Newton's Laws of Motion and, 71–73
  sounds of, 331–335
action games, 9
actions
  Don't Fall! actions not defined in functions, 510–511
  equal and opposite reaction to, 74
  Ice World actions not defined in functions, 420–423
  pinball actions not defined in functions, 441–443
Actions layer
  of highscore.fla, 268–269
  of Ice World, 415
  of position.fla file, 204–206
ActionScripts
  for accurate friction calculations, 77–79
  in Actions layer of position.fla file, 204–206
  adding character in character_in_grid.fla, 176–180
  adding obfuscator to, 528–530
  analyzing code-execution time in 9-ball, 495
  applying acceleration with, 67–68, 72–73
  arrays and two-dimensional arrays, 165
  attaching to sound object with, 327–335

baddyDetection() function in Ice World, 432–433
ball_floor.fla, 141–142
balloon example, 52
buildCharacter() function, 215–216, 513–514
buildFloor() function of depth.fla, 209–210
buildGrid() function, 168, 169–170, 184–185
buildMap() function in pinball, 445–451
buildWorld() function, 214, 511–513
calculateDepth() function of depth.fla, 209
calculating momentum of object in motion, 146
changeGroundTile() function in iso_world.fla, 217, 218
changeManyGroundTile() function in iso_world.fla, 217, 218
for chat, 359–369
chats created with ElectroServerAS object, 553–555
checkCollision() function in pinball, 454
checkForWin() function in tic-tac-toe, 470
checkTile() function in Don't Fall!, 519
choosing category in Word Search, 381–384
collectableDetect() function in Ice World, 433
collected in Actions layer of Ice World, 415
configuring for high score list, 268–269
controlling sound to reflect changing speeds of object, 330–331
createBoard() function in Word Search, 385, 390–392
createFlipper() function in pinball, 451
creating game object in grid.fla, 168, 169
defining relative mass, 150–151
detectDOT() function, 185
detectObjects() function in iso_world.fla, 221–222
determineFall() function in Don't Fall!, 517
developing collision-detection, 131
equation for kinetic energy in, 147